THE JOY OF
HANDWEAVING

THE JOY OF
HAND WEAVING

By
Osma Gallinger Tod

DOVER PUBLICATIONS, INC.

NEW YORK

Published in Canada by General Publishing Com-
pany, Ltd., 30 Lesmill Road, Don Mills, Toronto,
Ontario.
Published in the United Kingdom by Constable
and Company, Ltd., 10 Orange Street, London
WC2H 7EG.

This Dover edition, first published in 1977, is
a republication of the work first published by
Bonanza Books in 1964. The six color plates which
appeared in the original edition are omitted from
the present edition.

International Standard Book Number: 0-486-23458-4
Library of Congress Catalog Card Number: 76-42959

Manufactured in the United States of America
Dover Publications, Inc.
180 Varick Street
New York, N.Y. 10014

Dedication

This book is dedicated to hand weavers everywhere with the hope that through its use they and their friends may discover the joy of hand weaving in the unlimited beauty ready for hands to create through the use of the loom.

The author in her studio.

Preface

For over two decades it has been the author's privilege to teach weaving and to write directions for students interested in the making of cloth. During this time thousands of people, young and old, have become fabric-minded and cultured in an appreciation of home textiles and personal clothing. Weavers have been able to enhance their homes with tapestries, rugs, and draperies of their own making and far more suited to their moods and tastes than those they could buy, and at less cost. Moreover, they have found it possible to clothe themselves and their families in quality suiting and dress materials far lovelier and more suitable in coloring than any available in stores.

The processes of weaving give healthier physical well being, alertness, and a development of touch and manual dexterity to the participant. Weaving often provides additional income to individuals and groups. Underprivileged or handicapped persons, or those who have suffered injury or loss, have reached for a thread of hope in weaving which has turned into a cord of security. Many young people start out in weaving industries, men and women forced by fate to live alone find companionship and often a part-time income from their looms, and many build up their club life by active weaving. The craft's power to refresh both mind and body is unquestioned.

The author is happy to give the result of many years of devotion to hand weaving in this book, which is truly and aptly named THE JOY OF HAND WEAVING. Successful study of the book requires very little equipment. Many of the projects in Part One may be carried out by the use of weaving frames made of cardboard or small pieces of wood, and odds and ends of colored thread. The careful planning necessary while constructing each part demands and leads to a clearer knowledge of the working of the loom and its parts. More complete equipment should be added for the projects in Part Two in order to investigate further possibilities of pattern weaving with its unlimited field of variation in color, texture, and design. A practical use for the fabric being produced on the loom should be considered in the case of advanced projects, such as weaving upholstery for a chair, making and covering a footstool, designing a reception room or lounge of handwrought furniture and fabrics, and planning material for screens, sewing kits, wall panels, or tables in the home.

Italics and boldface type have been used throughout the book to designate names of important parts and processes. This is done to emphasize the point discussed. To derive the most benefit from this book, supplementary material for the development of a scrap book should be gathered and books on weaving topics should be collected.

The author wishes to express sincere gratitude to all who have provided inspiration and guidance in the writing of this book. Among these are the following leaders who have given generously of their talents and techniques to the National Conference of American Handweavers: Miss Helen Louise Allen, Mrs. Mary Meigs Atwater, Miss Florence E. House, Miss Berta Frey, Miss Evelyn DeGraw, Mrs. Clara McNulty, Mrs. Donnel B. Young, Mr. Rupert Peters, Mrs. H. P. Kessenich, Mrs. Dorothy Hulse, and Mrs. Dorothy McCloud. In addition there are many art supervisors and teachers who have made it possible for the author to observe methods of teaching in our schools and hospitals, and thus conveyed helpful ideas in the writing of this book.

Appreciation is also expressed to the many creative weavers in the United States, Canada, and other countries who by their lectures, original patterns, and writings have assisted in the expansion of the field of weaving. Thanks are extended to the editors of the *Handweaver and Craftsman*, *McCall's Decorative Quarterly*, and *Woman's Day* for permission to use partial reprints of articles by the author. Finally, sincere gratitude is expressed to Clay Aldridge, formerly Director of the Everhart Museum, Scranton, Pennsylvania, and the Joe and Emily Lowe Art Gallery, University of Miami, Coral Gables, Florida, for helpful assistance and the loan of photos from these museums.

The Second Edition of THE JOY OF HAND WEAVING has been brought up to date by the addition of descriptions of a large number of synthetic yarns recently fabricated, by the use of new and significant photographs, and by the inclusion of new techniques for a more extensive range of weaving.

OSMA GALLINGER TOD

319 Mendoza Avenue
Coral Gables, Florida

Contents

Appendix

Introduction

Hand weaving is one of the most productive and popular crafts of modern times. Individuals weave for many reasons —to create fabrics for their homes or personal attire, to sell in shops or use as gifts, as well as for the many accompanying pleasures of the craft itself, such as the fun of creating, the interest in weave structure, the history of fabrics, the exercise involved, and the spiritual satisfaction of completing something useful and beautiful.

For any craft there are three essentials, the equipment, the raw materials, and the ability or skill to use the raw material and equipment for creative purposes. The equipment of the weaver is his loom, and the raw material is his thread. With very little training he can develop the skill necessary to combine them creatively.

1. EQUIPMENT: THE LOOM AND ITS MEANING

The loom is one of the most important machines of all time. Rodier says, in his *Romance of French Weaving*, "Through all the ages the path of the weaver has been the path of true civilization . . . and there where a loom is waiting, the night of savagery is over." Whenever tribes settled down long enough between wars to use their hands for domestic purposes, culture took a step forward.

The loom is also one of the simplest devices ever invented. Even the large modern factory looms which turn out thousands of yards of cloth are operated by exactly the same principle as the hand looms of early times. It is significant that today's textile mills seek out the creative weaver to design on a hand loom fabrics which can be reproduced by machinery.

The looms of today are well balanced and easy to operate. They are simply and beautifully made of soft toned woods.

Home weaving is a simple and basic art. Its tools have not changed. Rather, weavers have learned its greater potentialities.

Acquaint yourself with the various kinds of looms before buying one. Looms are classified by their construction, as table or floor looms; by their technical action, as counterbalanced or jack looms; and by the complexity of the weaves they produce, as 2-, 4-, or 8-harness looms.

Floor Looms Versus Table Looms

With a floor loom the weaving action requires both hands and feet. The feet take over half the work, and the hands are free to manage the shuttle. Therefore one can weave faster on a floor loom than on a table loom. Floor looms are also larger and stronger, and they provide more stability and permit the use of a stronger "beat," which is what makes good, firm, and durable cloth.

Table looms accomplish the same results as floor looms, but are limited by their size and sturdiness and by the fact that their weaving action is slower. They are used for training purposes by schools whose space and funds are limited, by students who want an accessory loom, by those who wish to take a loom with them when traveling, by weavers who lack space in their homes, and by those who wish to make only a small investment until they become more familiar with the craft.

Counterbalanced Versus Jack Looms

With a counterbalanced loom the harnesses counterbalance one another when the shed is made. With a jack loom the harnesses are lifted apart by the treadle action when the shed is made. Counterbalanced looms are known to have an easy action, and will perform all types of weaves if the shed is a wide one. With jack looms the foot must carry the weight of the harnesses when lifted. For weaves in which one harness is treadled against three, the shed is easier to secure and maintain on a jack loom. Multi-harness looms are almost always jack looms.

Number of Harnesses

Two-harness looms produce plain weave and many variations wrought by texture, color, and warp handling (laces, laid-ins, tapestry, tufts, and so on). Four-harness looms offer more possibilities as to pattern and design in addition to all that can be woven on a two-harness loom. As the number of harnesses increases to six, eight, or more, the design possibilities increase by almost geometric proportions.

The following tabulation indicates the things you can make on the various types of looms.

A. 4″ to 8″ Two-Harness Table Looms

Articles: Belts; Hat Bands; Scarves; Purses; Neckties (woven lengthwise); Book Covers; Tie-Backs; Sandal Straps; Bell Pulls; Pin Cushions; Narrow Towels; Mantel Runners; Shelf Trim; and Boudoir Slippers.

Techniques: Plain Weave; Stripes; Plaids; Log Cabin; Tufting; Laces; Tapestry; Texture Stripes; Alternate Dark and Light; Laid-in Weaves; Pile Mats; Warp-Face and Weft-Face Designs.

B. 8″ to 18″ Two- or Four-Harness Table or Floor Looms

Articles: All articles in A, plus the following: Mats; Doilies; Napkins; Wall Panels; School Bags; Beach Bags; Knitting Bags; Purses; Small Pillows; Luncheon Sets; Dresser Scarves; Handkerchief Cases; Guest Towels; Kitchen Towels; Laundry Bags; Pouches; Chair-Back Sets; Mufflers; Men's Scarves; Neckties Woven in Two Diagonal Strips.

Techniques: All techniques in A, plus the following: Four-Harness Overshot Weaves; Two-Row Summer and Winter; Bronson; M's and O's; Huck; Twills; Waffle Weave; Patch Patterns.

C. 18″ to 24″ Two- or Four-Harness Table or Floor Looms

Articles: All foregoing plus the following: Narrow Dress Goods; Suitings; Blouses; Linens; Tunics; Smocks; Aprons; Sweaters; Narrow Drapes; Homespun; Large Pillows; Wool Scarves; Piano Scarves; Table Runners; Screen Panels; Wool Jackets; Bath Mats; Porch Pillows; Strips of Couch Throws; Radio and Chest Covers; Large Towels; Chair Seats; Footstool Coverings.

Techniques: Same as B.

D. 24″ to 36″ Two- or Four-Harness Looms

Articles: All foregoing plus the following: Wide Rugs; Half Strips of Afghans; Coverlets; Couch Throws; Blanket Strips; Portieres; Drapes; Upholstery; Dress and Suit Materials.

Techniques: Same as B.

E. 36″ to 52″ Two- or Four-Harness Looms

Articles: Same as foregoing plus the following: Stair Carpets; Upholstery, Suitings, and Neckties Complete in One Strip; Baby Blankets; Coverlets; Draperies.

Techniques: Same as B.

Multi-Harness Looms, with 6, 8, or More Harnesses

Articles: Any of the foregoing, choice of type of loom depending on kind of article.

Techniques: All foregoing plus the following: Multi-Harness Weaves; Summer and Winter with three or more rows; Advanced Weaves for from five to eight or more harnesses; Damask Weaves; Fancy Twills and Suiting; Double Weaves.

2. RAW MATERIAL: THE THREAD

The weaver may buy his yarns from weaving supply houses which carry every conceivable color and kind. Weaving threads are more reasonable than any other kind since they may be purchased by the pound or ounce. Threads for the weaver are often spooled to suit his purpose on small spools or tubes for warping and on large cones for weaving. This saves time in unwinding skeins.

Weaving yarns range from the finest of gossamer cottons and silks, waxey linens, and soft wools, to thick heavy blanket or rug yarns, jutes, and so on. In between, one finds threads of all sizes and kinds—mercerized or unmercerized, metallics, synthetics, soft twist, hard twist, thick and thin, smooth and nubby. Thread companies often send out packets of samples for weavers to choose from. Many department stores handle weavers' yarns.

There is a fascinating history in the origin of thread, the discovery of such natural fibers as wool, linen, cotton, and silk, and finally in the making of artificial threads, such as rayon and modern synthetics, from pulp. A world of adventure awaits the weaver as he lays out a rainbow of colors and textures and paints with threads.

3. SKILL: LEARNING TO USE THREADS ON A LOOM

People learn to weave easily. Weaving may be a gentle relaxing exercise or a rapid exhilarating one. The exertion depends on one's speed, which is optional. A weaving rhythm is soon established which carries one along and adds pleasure to the process. Weaving brings manual skill, creative ability, confidence, knowledge of colors and textures, and last but not least, lovely products to use or sell.

Weaving is not hard on the eyes. It depends on a foot or hand action to separate the warps so that a filler thread can be put through easily. The blind are often skillful weavers. It is true there are some weaves requiring greater eye concentration, but there are ways to simplify these for ease of workmanship.

It is not difficult to thread a loom. The eyes of the heddles, or loom "needles," are large. Some people enjoy threading as much as weaving. All the processes are simple and may be mastered by older people as well as the young. As in all things, a minimum of training gives one a better chance of making a success of the craft and enables him to obtain the best results from the investment in a loom.

Weaving instructions show how to handle threads, what kinds to use for what purposes, and how to make the loom serve efficiently. A good teacher can save the weaver endless expense and frustration. There are good weaving courses in schools as well as private studios, and colleges and universities are now offering excellent courses in the fabric crafts, both in design and technical training. Through weaving magazines one can locate weaving schools and studios, as well as correspondence courses for those who cannot avail themselves of personal instruction. Libraries carry a wide range of weaving textbooks for the benefit of the self-taught weaver. This very book is planned as a step-by-step course of instruction.

PART I

Simple
or Plain
Weaving

1—The Story of Thread

THREAD is a filament made by twist-ing fine fibers together. Man learned how to weave before he acquired the art of making thread. At first, his sole means of clothing himself had been animal furs and leaves of trees. Because this covering was ill-fitting and not fully serviceable, and because of his desire to better his means of living, he soon learned to weave grasses and split bark together for improved cov-ering. Such covering still was uncomfort-able. So, it was the advent of thread, and with it a fuller development of weaving, that helped man produce more satisfac-tory clothing. Today's comfortable, useful, and attractive clothing and accessories are results of perfection in use of thread and weaving during the last centuries.

For a full appreciation of the joy to be found in weaving, special attention must be paid to the basic material which makes the craft possible. At the close of this book there is a bibliography which details many sources for full information regarding par-ticular phases in the craft of weaving. However, it is well to include here a brief coverage of history and fundamentals in the production of various fibers from which thread is made.

Take a piece of thread, untwist it, and examine what you find. Note the minute bits of hair-like substance, called **Fibers.** Pull one out and see how weak it is. As a matter of fact, you probably will need a magnifying glass to see it clearly. But, weak as one fiber is, the twisting of many of them results in a strong thread which one can put to many uses. The heavy hawser used to bring a giant ocean liner to its dock is a perfect example of strong thread, being made up of many small parts twisted together. Then there is the tiny cord used for tatting, in which many fibers are twisted together to make a thread that is strong, yet dainty and at-tractive when knotted into lace.

Kinds of Thread

A further tracing of the phenomenon of thread will reveal not only that there are varied uses for it but also that there are many kinds, such as wool, silk, cotton, linen, asbestos, and glass. Both **Wool** and **Silk** come from animals, and hence are designated as "**Animal Fibers.**" Wool, which is sheared from the backs of sheep, is short, kinky, and soft. Silk is a long fiber taken from the mouth of the silkworm.

Cotton is a fiber found in the fluffy seed pods of the cotton plant; and **Linen** is made from tough flax fibers taken from the stem of the flax plant. These are clas-sified as "**Plant Fibers.**" Other plant fibers are those from ramie, pineapple, and jute plants and hemp, coir, and kapok.

Strange as it may seem, some fibers are taken right out of the earth. For example, fireproof **Asbestos** occurs naturally; and **Glass** is made by melting minerals to-gether. Accordingly, asbestos and glass are classed as "**Mineral Fibers.**"

As a result of man's ingenuity, there are still other textile fibers, which are made from a variety of materials and are termed "**Synthetic Fibers**" because synthetic means "**put together.**" Fibers in this class

1

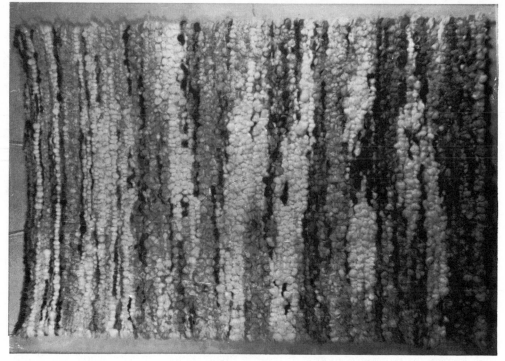

(*Courtesy Elsa Frielinghaus*)

Fig. 1—Rug, "White Caps" made of handspun wool on a linen and mohair warp.

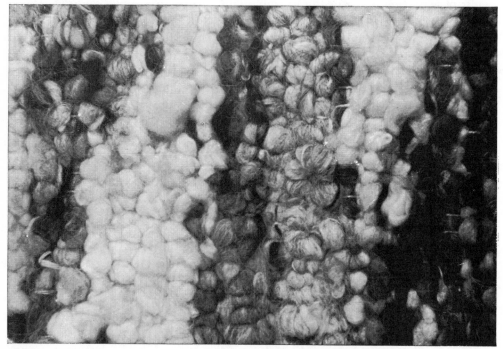

(*Courtesy Elsa Frielinghaus*)

Fig. 2—Detail of "White Caps."

Fig. 3—This baby blanket was woven of yarn from rabbit's hair on a small loom. Narrow pieces of weaving were sewed together to make the blanket. In the circle you can see the pretty weaving stitch and the soft fringe.

are scientifically made, and have quick-drying, non-flammable, pleat-retaining, and wrinkle-repellent properties. These new fibers are used alone or in combination with natural fibers to contribute some of their assets. The result is a great variety of new and reasonable fabrics, such as rayon, acetate, orlon, nylon, and dacron, described under **The New Man-Made Threads.**

The quality of the woven cloth depends on the kind of thread chosen, its size and structure, and the design of the weaver. One can add to the pleasure and skill of weaving by knowing important facts about the threads used.

Wool

Each year at springtime thousands of sheep raised in such countries as Australia, England, Argentina, and the United States have their wool sheared from their backs. The soft, kinky hair is sheared close to the skin, and is then sent in bags to market to be thoroughly washed and dried. It is then untangled by the "carding" process and lastly is made into thread or yarn through a procedure called "spinning."

The cleaned fibers of wool are very small, but each one has still smaller barbs or scales along its sides. When these fibers are twisted together to make yarn, the little hooks or scales of one fiber cling to the scales of the next. Dyeing the yarn may make it still firmer because the heat needed for producing many colored dyes causes the fibers to shrink.

Wool today is often blended with other fibers—with linen to add lustre, with silk to add resiliency, with cotton to give a more washable texture.

Wool is not only fleece from sheep or goats; it may include the following fibers.

Cashmere is a rare fiber, soft and silky, taken from the Cashmere goat of China and India. It is used most widely in blends with man-made fibers or with wool.

Fig. 4—Pulling flax with modern machinery on a flax farm in Oregon.

Vicuna is the very softest, finest, and rarest of the wools. It is a natural tan in color, and comes from wild llamas of the Andes.

There are two kinds of **camel's-hair wool** which come from the back of the camel. The first is the long, wiry hair that shows on the outside of the animal's skin. This is used for blankets and carpets. The other is the short, downy hair growing close to the camel's skin. This is the means of making a soft yarn, although it is expensive. It is either a pretty brown color or black, because it cannot be changed to lighter colors like some wools. Incidentally, **imitation camel's-hair wool** is made from sheep's wool and other suitable fibers.

Both the Angora goat from Asia and the Alpaca from Peru in South America have fine silky hair which can be spun like wool into yarn. The hair of the Angora goat is called **Mohair.** The cloth made from it is fine and fluffy and has a hairy surface. Although it is expensive, it is also very durable. **Imitation mohair** is made from wool and synthetic fibers.

The hair of the Angora rabbit may also be spun like wool into **rabbit's-hair yarn.** It makes fluffy warm articles. The wool is soft, elastic, and strong. In warm weather it absorbs moisture, and in cold weather it insulates the body.

The name **"worsted"** is given to articles made from yarns spun of long, parallel fibers. They are smooth, compact, and wear well. **"Woolens"** are made of yarns from shorter fibers which are not so carefully combed. They are soft, loosely spun, and textural.

Silk

Of all the natural fibers, silk is regarded by many persons as the most beautiful. It already is made up into a very fine thread when found in the cocoon of the silkworm, which lives on the leaves from the mulberry tree.

The silkworm changes the substances of the mulberry leaves into a gum that turns into thread as it comes out of the small animal's mouth. There are two tiny corkscrews, called **"spinnerets,"** on the worm's lower lip, and two lines of the silk gum pass over these organs. The lines are thus twisted together and made into thread which the worm wraps around and around about itself in a cocoon. The worm then goes to sleep inside the cocoon. When the silk is unwrapped from the cocoon, it comes off in a long strand which is so very fine that ten or more strands from as many cocoons are needed to make a silk thread strong enough for use.

Long ago, silk was raised only in China. It was discovered by a child empress, Si Ling Chi, known as the "silkworm goddess." For thousands of years, the Chinese zealously guarded this secret until a young princess left China to marry a prince in Persia. The story goes that she hid some silkworms in her hair so that she could start raising silk in her new home.

Silk is now popular around the world because of its many advantages. It has a glossy, lustrous texture, drapes well, and does not soil readily nor wrinkle easily.

Linen

The best flax for making linen is grown in Belgium, Russia, and Ireland, although a very good product is grown in the United States in Oregon, Michigan, Washington, Wisconsin, and Minnesota. The slender graceful flax plant with its blue flowers has strong, smooth, shiny fibers; and the linen cloth which is made from thread produced from these fibers is admired and used everywhere. Linen goods grow softer and more beautiful each time they are washed, and they last a long time. They become snowy white, are clean and cool looking, and are particularly serviceable for table linens as well as for cool summer clothes.

The fibers are taken from the stem of the flax plant but, as is so often the case, there are other parts of the stem that cannot be used. To separate the good fibers from the waste materials, the flax is first soaked in water for several weeks. The useless parts become soft and decay. These are combed away, and the fibers that are left are twisted into smooth, glossy linen thread. It is interesting to note that flax was among the first of the useful plants grown by the Pilgrim fathers.

Linen is a very durable fiber. It is pliable, drapes well, and has a soft lustre which improves with age and washing. Its absorbency makes it a cool fabric for warm climates.

Cotton

Cotton is called **"the crop that clothes the world"** because it provides more clothing than any other fiber. It is grown in China, Japan, India, Africa, many of the South Sea Islands, and in most of the Southern States in the United States. The

Fig. 5—A flower and several seed-pods of cotton.

plant grows from 2 to 6 feet high. It has spreading branches about 2 feet long around its lower part, and the branches gradually become shorter toward the top. The flowers look something like hollyhock blossoms, being white the first day and pink the second. Soon the flowers wither and drop off, and in their places come green bolls.

The boll is the seed pod of the cotton plant. It is small and almost round at first, and grows to become about the size of a walnut. In it are many dark seeds wrapped closely in a mass of cotton fibers which are fastened firmly to these seeds. When the bolls are full grown, they turn brown and then open slowly. The cotton fibers come out in the sunshine, making fluffy white puffs which look like snow-balls.

Because rain is likely to injure this new cotton, workers pick it as fast as it ripens in the fields. New methods have been invented for picking cotton by machinery, and less hand labor is now required.

The cotton gin was invented by Eli Whitney in 1793. The cotton is carried up into the gin through a huge sheet-iron tube. It first enters a machine which combs out the seeds, and is then passed to another machine where it is put into layers and compressed into bales, which are sold to the textile mills. Here the cotton is spun into threads which are wound on spools or into skeins ready to be used for weaving.

Cotton is an easy thread for the weaver to handle. It is strong, has life and elasticity, takes dye readily, and is easily washed. It also absorbs moisture and is therefore a cool fabric for summer wear. Mercerized cottons are polished to a lustre which enhances the beauty of their colors. Cotton yarns range from fine sheer threads to heavy rug fillers.

Ramie

Ramie is a tall plant whose fibers are perhaps longer than any other natural plant used for thread. While some plant fibers are hardly visible to the naked eye, a single ramie fiber is several feet long. (It is cut into shorter lengths for easier handling.) The soft fibers lie underneath an outer stem often bearing spikes or nettles. Ramie is grown in China, India, Japan, and the East Indies. It has also been grown successfully in Florida.

Fig. 6—Ramie grows very tall, taller than a man.

Ramie fibers are mixed with cotton and wool to add strength to the finished yarn, and ramie is also used alone as a linen substitute for luncheon sets, rugs, mats, carpets, and upholstery.

Pina Cloth

Pineapple leaves from the Far East and the Philippine Islands are split into very fine and shiny fibers to make thread for **Pina Cloth.** The natives of these areas dye the woven cloth in gay colors. Pina cloth makes filmy tablecloths and napkins so thin that the air can blow through them. The cloth appears to be starched and since it stands away from the body, is comfortable in hot weather.

Jute

Burlap bags and gunny sacks are made from fibers taken from the **Jute** plant, which grows as high as 15 feet in the swamps of India. Natives, standing waist-high in dirty water, prepare jute for thread by beating the bark away from the fibers. Jute is a cheap fiber used for bags and the backs of rugs and linoleum.

Hemp

Hemp, first discovered by the Chinese, has always been an important plant. Its fibers are used for cloth, its seed for food, its oil, flowers, and leaves for drugs, and

Fig. 8—Jute is a tall fibrous plant that grows in swamps.

Fig. 7—Pineapple leaves have very fine fibers, which are used in the Philippines for weaving sheer materials.

its stalks for fuel. It is used for the strongest ropes and cables, wrapping cord, stair carpets, boat sails, fishing lines, shoe-strings, heavy belting, packing materials, and even heavy clothing. While the best hemp grows in the Philippines, it also grows well in many states of the United States. It is good for the soil and destroys weeds. Hemp lasts longer and is stronger than jute.

Coir

The tough, stringy husks of the coconut fruit, which grows in the tropics, contain a fiber called **Coir.** This material is seen mostly in the familiar brown doormats. The fibers of coir are stiff and form sturdy bristles.

Kapok

Kapok, like cotton, is a soft, silky fiber which comes from the seed pods of the Ceiba tree. It is used to stuff pillows and mattresses and sometimes to make cloth. Kapok fiber usually is found in the tropics, much of it coming from West Africa.

Asbestos

Asbestos is found in the form of a solid fibrous rock. It is pulled apart into long delicate fibers of whitish, green-gray color, and twisted into thread for weaving cloth. The fibers are also pressed into flat, stiff asbestos pads which are placed under hot irons or behind hot stoves or pipes. Im-

Fig. 9—Hemp is grown in almost every country of the world.

portant because of its safety characteristics, asbestos padding is used in fireproof buildings. When it gets soiled, it is simply heated in a fire which burns off the dirt but does not damage the material. It is said that Charlemagne owned an asbestos tablecloth which he threw into the fireplace for cleaning after a meal—a novel and rapid means of laundering!

Glass Thread

The poet Dante said: "All things may be woven, even the sands of the sea." Sand is a component part in glass manufacture. It is now possible to draw out melted glass into a fine long thread, one-tenth the size of a human hair and as light in weight as eider down. Glass fibers are impervious to decay and moths. They are also fireproof and do not settle down in a flat mat as cotton does. The fine, light fibers make beautiful thread that can be used by the handweaver for gossamer stoles or draperies.

THE NEW MAN-MADE THREADS

Nothing is more exciting than man's discovery of how to make thread fibers by machinery, thus adding to those spun from the natural animal, plant, and mineral sources. This discovery has revolutionized the world of textiles, giving an unlimited range of synthetic yarns for the making of new cloth products, both commercially and by the handweaver.

About 200 years ago, a Frenchman named Chardonnet developed the process of making Rayon. Chardonnet copied the methods used by the silkworm, observing how silk was really only fine hardened gum made from the vegetable substance in mulberry leaves. He made gum out of the same kind of vegetable pulp, called Cellulose. It was run through tiny tubes

and came out as a filament much like silk in its softness and fineness. The thread was called rayon, which means "ray of light." The discovery has brought just this to people everywhere who can now enjoy soft garments of synthetic silk, wool, or even velvet, luxuries that were once prohibitive in price when made only of natural fibers.

Many kinds of thread are now made from cellulose which is found in wood pulp, plant life, and cotton linters. Rayon and acetate are two large groups of cellulose fibers. In fact, by changing the combinations of cellulose, protein, and chemicals, different thread variations occur.

Following the creation of rayon and acetate, chemists began to make thread by linking together molecules caused by chemical reactions, without a basis of pulp. This idea gave birth to an unlimited range of still newer fibers. These are the true synthetics. The filaments are either twisted together to form larger filament threads or cut up in pieces and spun into soft new yarns. Nylon was the first thread of this type to be made. Synthetic filaments are also combined with natural fibers, such as cotton, linen, silk, or wool, either to strengthen the resulting thread or to add beauty and interest. Below is a list of some new man-made fibers. Many of these are available to the handweaver for the creation of new textures.

PROTEIN FIBERS

Aralac: made from skimmed milk, combines with rayon.

Azlon: made from milk caseins, corn, and peanuts; has qualities similar to wool; combines with other fibers.

Vicara: soft, elastic, wrinkle resistant; is blended with other fibers.

Merinova: quite similar to wool; sometimes spun for weaving purposes.

CELLULOSE FIBERS

Rayons

Characteristics: an absorbent fiber, similar to cotton; takes color well, washes easily, irons at cotton-pressing temperature; appears in many forms, fine, heavy, firm, soft, dull or glossy; should be handled with care when wet; combines with natural fibers.

Uses: fabrics made to resemble wool, silk, linen; makes high fashion clothes, underwear, upholstery, carpets.

Varieties: Avril, similar to cotton; Avlin, feels like linen; Corval, soft and wooly, retains pleats; Topel, blends well with cottons, acetates, and nylons; Zantrel, good for wash-and-wear apparel; Viscose; Bemberg; Fortisan; Cordura; Colorspun; Coloray and Jetspun; Topel; Cupione; Cupramonium; and Avron.

Acetates

Characteristics: makes cloth of elegant feel that drapes well, can be pleat-set, is moth and mildew resistant, irons at low heat.

Uses: evening dresses and lingerie because it dries quickly.

Varieties: Celanese, Celaperm, Airsco, Estron, Cromspun, Arnel, and Triacetate.

TRUE SYNTHETICS MADE FROM CHEMICALS

Polyamide (Nylon is the chief example.)

Characteristics: strong, lustrous, and elastic; ranges in size from sheer to heavy;

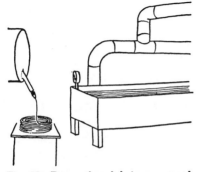

Fig. 10—Rayon thread being squeezed out of a fine tube from a pulpy mass of cellulose.

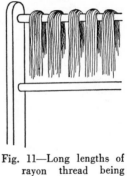

Fig. 11—Long lengths of rayon thread being dried over a frame.

washes and dries easily, sheds water, and holds pleats well; injured by too much sunlight; moth and mildew resistant.

Uses: clothes, drapes, upholstery, bathmats, sails.

Other Varieties: Caprolan, suitable for clothing and decoration; Antron, a lustrous fiber; and Nylenka.

Polyester

Characteristics: holds pleats well when heat-set; sheds water and resists wrinkles; dyes well; mildew and moth resistant; strong, elastic, and nonshrinking; can resemble wool or cotton; requires care in ironing.

Uses: wide range of strong lightweight fabrics for clothes, decorations, and commercial uses.

Varieties: Dacron; Teron or Fortrel; Vycron; Dacron, Type 42, similar to silk; Kodel, used for blends and to give woollike bulk.

Acrylic

Characteristics: a family of strong nonelastic-fibers; soft and fluffy; fills up well; warm and light; resistant to sunlight, moisture, and moths.

Uses: curtains, dresses, furlike fabrics, blankets.

Varieties:

Orlon: used for anything from sheer dresses and drapes to car tops; Orlon-Sayelle, which resembles wool; and many new types.

Acrilan: resembles Orlon, but holds color better; combines with wool to make soft blankets and suiting yarn.

Fig. 12—Remnants of hand-woven wool, raytone, and bouclé were used to make these use-
ful articles.
Upper left—Bureau tray covered with Bouclé
Upper right—Plaid pin cushion made on a circle of cardboard
Left center—Zipper purse in textured squares
Right center—Small round box covered with pattern weaving
Lower left—Jewelry box covered with plaid material
Lower right—Covered bureau tray
Directions for covering boxes with hand-woven materials are given in Lesson 41.

Creslan: holds warmth; can resemble fur; dyes well; does not fade or shrink; resists moths, mildew, and perspiration.

Zefran: accepts dye well; has good wearing qualities; special types blend with wool and cotton.

Modacrylic

Characteristics: durable; quick drying; retains shape; moth, mildew, and fire resistant; iron at low temperature.

Uses: in soft fluffy form makes pile carpets; blends with cotton; good for blankets and outer wear fabrics.

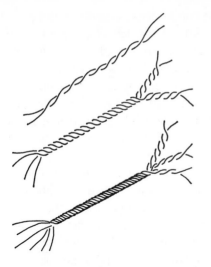

Fig. 13—Single useless fibers are twisted or spun on a spinning wheel into strong useful threads.

Varieties: Verel and Dynel.

Saran

Characteristics: tough and flexible; stain, chemical, moth, and fire resistant.

Uses: carpets, drapes, upholstery, seat covers.

Varieties: Rovana, Mills Plastic, Velon.

Vinal

Characteristics: strong; heat and mildew resistant; can look like wool, silk, cotton.

Uses: apparel, fish nets, surgical threads.

Olefin

Characteristics: similar to Dacron, but with a more waxey feel; dyes readily; iron with care.

Uses: car robes, seat covers.

Varieties: Polythylene, Polypropylene, Polybutylene.

Nytril

Characteristics: a luxury fiber with the feel of Cashmere; wrinkle repellent.

Uses: women's coats, blends with worsted for suiting, furlike fabrics.

Varieties: Darlan, Darvan.

Rubber

Characteristics: composed of natural or synthetic rubber wrapped with other fibers to make elastic thread.

Uses: swim suits, underwear, surgical products.

Metallic

Characteristics: composed of metal or plastic, or both; has glitter.

Uses: drapes, upholstery, purses, dresses.

Varieties: Lurex, Lamé, Metlon, Superfine.

Vinyon and Bristrand

Characteristics: durable, warm, quick drying; holds shape, fills well; moth, fire, and mildew resistant.

Uses: fish nets, filters.

Spandex

Characteristics: strong elastic fiber, very lightweight; resists body acids.

Uses: clothes, underwear.

Other fairly new synthetic fibers include Curon, an insulating fiber; Dynel, a durable soil-resistant fiber used in rugs; Flecton, a fiber which reflects lights in the dark; Super-L, a soil-resistant rayon carpet fiber; Tycora, applied to Dacron, processed for bulk; Urethane, used as a light foamy interlining; Verel, moisture absorbent; Clefin, very lightweight; Vinyon, used for fish nets.

Other names you may recognize are Avisco, Styrene, Phenolic, Urea, Melamine, Nyponge (made of nylon and rayon), Vinyon, Melo-Polo, Rhovyl-T (used in blends).

Among the weaving thread trade names are Rayon and Metallic, Cotton and Metalic, Rayon Spiral Nub, Rayon Ratine', Rayon Boucle', Wool and Rayon Twist, Guimpe, Jute-Tone, Alpaca, Wool and Mohair, Looped Mohair, and Twinklelite.

Fig. 14—Fibers are straightened out by being carded.

Natural Thread Is Spun from Fibers

You can make thread. Take some fuzzy cotton from a bundle of cotton batting and see how easy it is to pull out the fibers and twist them into a fine thread, as shown in Fig. 13. Pull them out further and further and keep twisting them in the same direction until you have a strong white thread. "Thread" is a long length of fibers twisted together.

Suppose you had to make thread by the yard in this way. It would require a long time, and even then the finished product might not be very smooth or perfect. But it was done this way before the benefits of machinery were realized. The spinning wheel was a very popular and necessary piece of equipment in the home. Enough cloth for an entire family was twisted, or "spun," by it. Not only was it necessary to spin the fibers into thread —a process which in itself required flying fingers—but the fibers also had to be washed and combed prior to the spinning process. There are several processes connected with the art of spinning fibers into thread.

Step 1: Washing the Fibers. When cotton is picked from the seed pods of

the cotton plant, some seeds and particles of dirt are still left. So, the cotton must be freed from its seeds and washed clean. When wool is sheared from the sheep's back in the barnyard, it contains a great deal of grease and dirt. And this is true of most fibers. Therefore, before anything else can be done, fibers must be washed clean and dried.

Step 2: Combing out the Fibers or Carding Them. When the fibers have been cleaned and dried, they are all matted together in bunches and must be straightened out. This is done by running them between two spiked boards or cards, the process being known as **Carding**. By running the fibers through the cards (Fig. 14), little waste pieces of stem or dirt are removed and the fibers may be spread out in smooth, even, fluffy layers or rolls. For especially fine yarns the fibers are combed on a cotton comb after carding.

Step 3: Twisting the Fibers Into Thread, or Spinning. In ancient days thread was made by letting a weight hang from the twisting fibers, something like a top spinning in mid-air. The spinning of the weight twisted the fibers together, making the thread. Our great-grand-mothers were faced with the task of twisting or spinning thread on a spinning wheel. The big wheel was attached to a pedal, and by pressing on the pedal the big wheel went round and round. This wheel in turn was attached to a smaller wheel, which went around whenever the big wheel did. The spinner held the fibers in her hand and, as they were twisted together by the wheel, she wound them on a little spool, called the **spindle**, which was controlled by the smaller wheel.

As the population grew and people needed more and more clothing, it was not possible to make enough thread by the slow process of spinning. So, a man

Fig. 16—On crude looms, primitive women the world over weave colorful belts and homespuns.

World discovered their secret. In Arabia, Syria, and Persia, there were fabrics woven of real gold metal, as well as thread colored with royal-purple dye extracted from a little purple snail called the **murex** and found in Tyre. In fact, in those days, fabrics were valued on a par with gold and were often used for barter in place of coin.

Although we have few examples of the weaving of ancient Greece, we know that this most artistic of all nations was versed in the art. The superb Grecian statuary shows that these peoples were masters in draping materials as well as weaving them. Tradition tells us that Helen of Troy kept a household of women busily weaving, and that she herself embroidered historical events in fabrics of her own creation.

The weavers of medieval England were the first laborers to form themselves into a guild. These guilds were the first trade unions established by laborers for their protection. Members of the weavers' guilds had self-imposed rules, one of them being that no one could weave by candlelight or between Christmas Day and Purification Day.

The American Indians were expert weavers. All of their products were simple lengths of cloth made complete and ready-to-wear on a loom. There was no waste by cutting; they used their woven blankets for dresses and coats, and made girdles, saddle girts, and smaller pieces in suitable widths. The Indian's chief thought was to work out in brilliant colors patterns symbolizing his worship of Nature.

To a land where the natives already knew how to spin the wool from their sheep, and weave it into rugs and clothing, came the early American colonists with no looms and only a memory of the weaving methods used in England. From

(Photograph from U. S. National Museum, Washington, D. C.)

Fig. 17—A typical two-harness Colonial loom used for weaving carpets and linen in Maine about 1810.

the hewn timbers of the forest they had to build their own weaving structures, huge and cumbersome loom-frames that we know today as the early American Colonial looms. A typical loom of this kind is shown in Fig. 17.

The Simple Loom Is a Necessity of Civilization

A **Loom** is the framework across which threads are stretched for the weaving of cloth. There are almost as many kinds of looms as there are countries, but the principle is the same in all of them. A loom provides a means of stretching taut the threads that go the long way of the cloth, in order that the weaver can interlace other threads across them. Some looms consist merely of bars with the threads held taut between two stationary ends, as in Fig. 16. Others are frames made of flat boards with the long threads wrapped around them, Fig. 37. Some looms, like the tapestry looms of the Eastern rug makers, are placed vertically in front of the worker. Others stand on the floor with the threads stretched horizontally between the beams, like the modern home and school looms of today (see page 99). There are table looms and

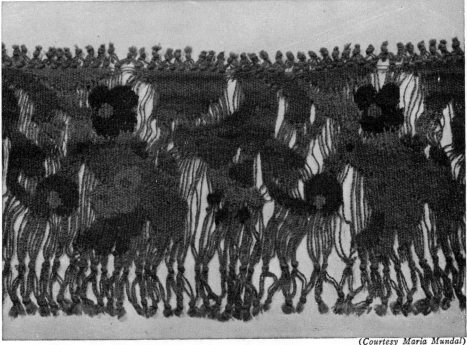

(Courtesy Maria Mundal)

Fig. 18—Traditional transparent tapestry in tones of red and brown wool with warp left partially unwoven. Original tapestries add distinction to the home.

cardboard looms; floor looms; looms of wood and of metal; simple looms and complex looms. But the principle of weaving never varies; one always weaves a continuous weft thread back and forth across long warp threads stretched taut on the loom, no matter what kind it may be.

For the American colonists weaving was a pure necessity. Building their own looms from timber in the forest, they made warm clothing, blankets, and rugs. Weaving was a family project with the men weaving and the women and children gathering wool and flax to spin into thread. They dyed their yarns with vegetable dyes and wound them into bobbins. The men devised new pattern contours and developed what we now know as **Colonial pattern weaving.**

In Scandinavia home weaving became a way of life, partly from necessity and

partly from an innate love for the beautiful. Here, there was a greater trend toward free design and color blending. On the Continent and the British Isles weaving was developed into intricate forms which were perfected by the guilds and the tapestry and rug factories.

Today home and commercial weavers the world over study weaving as an art from the point of view of creating new designs, new textures, and color harmonies in order to produce outstanding articles of apparel and home decoration. So successful has been the growth of creative weaving that today commercial enterprises are inclined to engage the original weaver to fabricate new textures for reproduction. We find in weaving not only a constructive home craft but an art medium for the expression of beauty with an opportunity for textile design.

Fig. 19—Luncheon set in the famous "Log-Cabin" or "Basket" Weave. Two alternating colors are used on a two-harness or four-harness loom to make this attractive texture. For the method, see Fig. 80, No. 3.

3—What It Means to Weave

~~~~~~

Interlacing of Threads

IF YOU LOOK in the dictionary to learn what it means to "weave," you will see that **"Weaving is the interlacing of threads to form a fabric or cloth."** So the purpose of making so many threads throughout the world must be to provide enough to weave into cloth for mankind. To see if cloth is really made in this way, take a piece from the mending scraps in the home work basket. Along one ragged edge study the way the threads cross or interlace at right angles to one another. Pull off a thread, marked **A** in Fig. 20. It is plain to see that it passes under and over many threads going in the opposite direction. Pull off one of the threads going in the opposite direction, marked **B**. This thread, too, passes under and over all the threads going in the first direction, or the threads beside **A**. So it must be true that **woven "Cloth" is made up of many threads that cross or "interlace" one another at right angles.**

We Should Know How Cloth Is Made

In school we learn that the three things most important to mankind are food, shelter and clothing. That is why we should know more about how clothing is made. This would help us to choose the warmest things to wear in the winter, the softest and best blankets to keep us warm at night, and the most comfortable clothes for any time of year. We should know, too, how to buy the best things for our own homes, things that will last a long time and look well.

There Are Many Kinds of Cloth

Have you ever thought how many hundreds of kinds of cloth there are in the world? In every home there are many different kinds: curtains, sheets, blankets, couch covers, table-cloths, and napkins, and even our American flag. Among the clothes of the family you will find more: father's thick suits, mother's silk evening gowns, and—prettiest of all—baby's thin dresses that seem almost too fine to be made of anything at all. In your neighbor's house there are still other kinds of cloth of different colors. Some are thick and some thin; some are put together tightly and some loosely. But in almost every single piece of cloth you will find that the threads pass under and over one another in various ways. Sometimes they have been matted so tightly together by machinery that you cannot find the separate threads. Sometimes you will discover that a thread will go under and over more than one thread. But each thread always comes up again and is held in place by a thread going in the opposite direction.

Cloth Is Strong and Useful

The wonderful part about cloth is that it is made up of single strands of mere thread passing back and forth across one another. Cloth made in this way can be a hundred times as strong as the threads

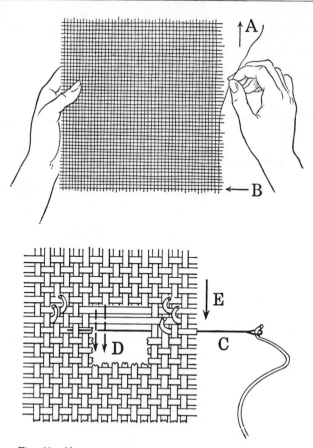

Fig. 20—Above, examining a piece of fabric. Below, repairing a hole in a plain-weave fabric.

themselves. You remember that something like this was true of thread, made up of finer fibers twisted together. It is true of many things in the world. The mighty seashore is made up of tiny grains of sand. A big wooden house is made up of smaller pieces of wood. The great bridges that span our rivers are held up by cable that are nothing more than big ropes of wire. These big wire ropes are made up of hundreds of lengths of narrow steel twisted together in the manner of thread. Any one thing alone seems to be quite useless, but when it is put with other things it becomes quite powerful.

4—First Weaving Lesson—
Learning Plain Weave

WEAVING can be done at home by hand, and almost anyone can actually make cloth by interlacing threads. You can perform this fascinating weaving process without a loom.

To get acquainted with cloth, find samples of many kinds, and then separate their threads, as shown in Fig. 20, to see how they combine. You will be surprised at the may ways the warps and wefts are interlaced to make the kinds of cloth woven today. Among these are Plain Weave, Basket Weave or Hopsacking, Gabardine, Tweed, Serge, and Double Cloth. The differences in their surface appearance is largely the result of the way the threads are laid together. For instance, in Plain Weave (Fig. 22,

(Courtesy Carolyn Lewis)

Fig. 21—A scarf and hat woven of black and white mohair on a two-harness loom in simple
in-and-out weave.

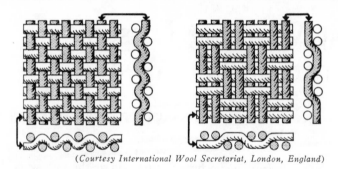

Fig. 22—The construction of Plain Weave and Basket Weave, also known as "Hopsacking." Left, single light wefts interlacing dark warps. Right, pairs of light wefts interlacing pairs of dark warps.

left side) the light horizontal threads go under and over the dark vertical threads; in Basket Weave or Hopsacking (Fig. 22, right side) pairs of light horizontal wefts go under and over pairs of dark vertical warps, and they alternate; in Twill Weave, shown at **E** in Fig. 107, single wefts go under and over single warps, but in each row they are staggered one thread to the right so that a diagonal design results.

Figure 110 shows four more effects: upper left, Step design; upper right, Dornick; lower left, Dogstooth; lower right, Herringbone with mixed colors. Still more variations are the result of using colors in stripes and plaids, as shown in Fig. 21.

It is possible to weave many of these on a loom. The simplest cloth is the Plain Weave which is given with many variations in Part One of this book. Pattern weaves and other fascinating weaving forms are given in Part Two.

There is no better way of getting acquainted with fabrics than to reconstruct their stitches in order to see how the warps and weft threads interlace. This process is known as **"Reweaving."** When skillfully practiced, it can result in a profitable home business.

Choose a coarse piece of cloth, such as burlap or basket weave, in which you can see the stitches with the naked eye. Cut a square hole in this plain weave fabric, as shown at **D** in Fig. 20. Sew in a scaffolding of horizontal threads, starting them back in the weaving, as shown at **C**. Now pass in and out with the vertical threads, shown at **E**. This is one of the ways a commercial reweaver repairs fabrics. Woolens, linens, and cottons woven with coarse yarns can have any damage replaced by an actual passing in and out of the warps and wefts. These are found by unraveling the seams of a garment so that the same material can be used. The reweaver is helped in his knowledge of cloth repair by first learning how to weave.

Another way to practice weaving is with a **"Weavit"** frame. Stretch stocking loops vertically across frame, and interlace these with loops crossing the other way.

(*Courtesy Josephine Del Deo*)

Tapestry, "The Orange Tree." The background is of natural raffia in coarse plain weave. The design is darned with green, orange, and rose raffia.

5—Preparing to Weave a Bookmark

REPAIRING a frabric showed us how to weave. If we weave in the very same way on a small board, we can make a useful **bookmark**, such as that shown in Fig. 23. To weave such a small object, stretch a number of warp threads taut on a suitable board and interlace them with slightly heavier weft threads, filling the spaces well. Fig. 24 shows a hand-woven bookmark in use.

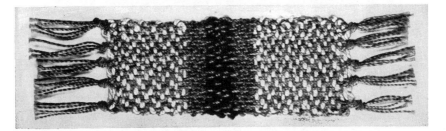

Fig. 23—A bookmark made on a board by a school pupil.

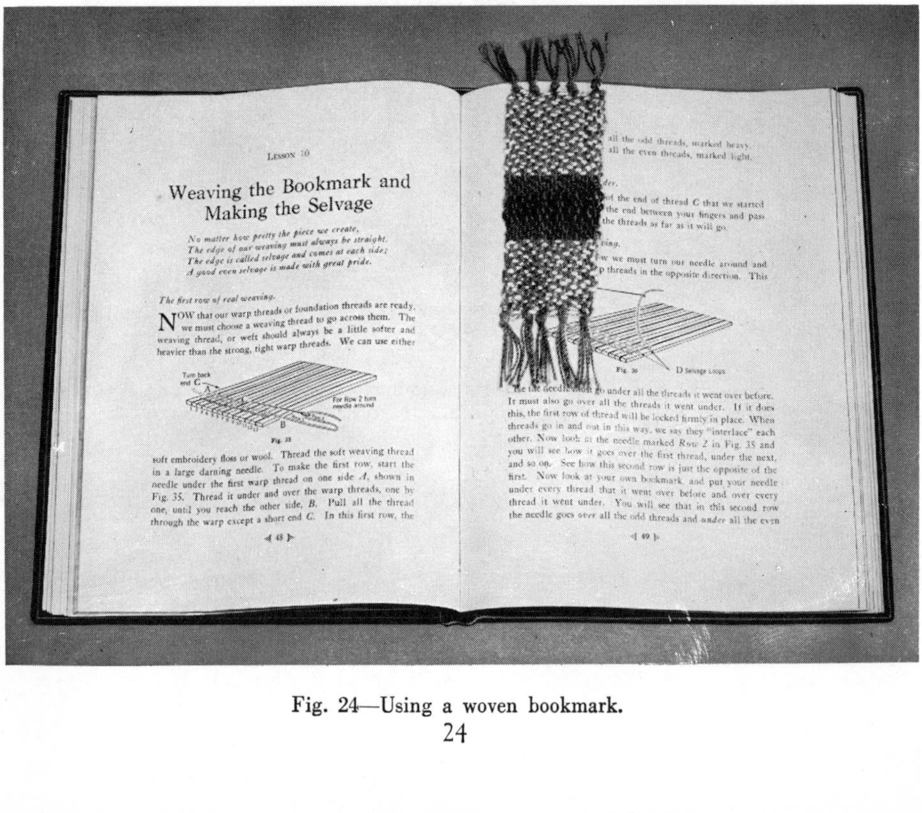

Fig. 24—Using a woven bookmark.

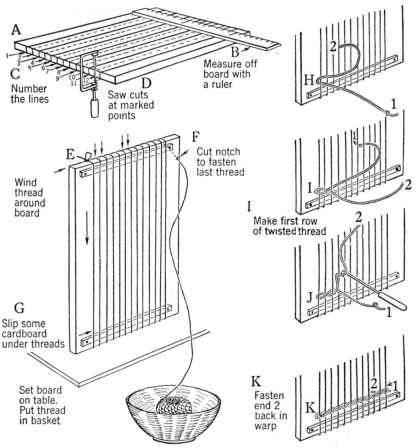

Fig. 25—Starting to weave a bookmark.

How to Plan the Bookmark

Step 1: Measuring the Board. To make the board on which to weave, we need a cigar-box lid, or some other thin piece of wood. Cut your board with a saw to measure 8 inches long and 4 inches wide. Sandpaper the edges smooth. The finished board is shown at **A** in Fig. 25.

Step 2: Marking off the Ends. We must mark the two ends of the board with pencil marks at even distances, to guide us in laying down our first threads side by side and parallel. To do this, lay a ruler along one end, as at **B** in Fig. 25, and mark off points ⅛ inch apart. Do the same at the other end. Then connect the points with straight lines. Count off the lines with numbers, 1, 2, 3, 4, 5, 6,

and so on, as you see in the picture at **C**. Write the numbers with pencil on your board. Now make all the lines with odd numbers—like 1, 3, 5, and 7—very heavy. Leave the lines with even numbers—like 2, 4, 6, and 8—very light or dotted. If you have a red pencil, draw red lines along the light or dotted lines. This will help you to see clearly which rows are odd and which are even. Nick the little pencil marks at each end with a knife or a saw, as you see being done at **D**.

Step 3: Laying down the Warp Threads. For thread we can use regular white grocery-store string or crochet cotton. We drop the ball of string in a basket or box beside the table, and begin winding the string around the board. The first

time around we tie a knot, as at **E.**
Then we go once around the board at
every pencil mark and nick, as shown
by the little arrows. The last time around,
we fasten the end by bringing the thread
through an extra notch, **F,** to hold it
tight. To be very sure that each row of
our thread is stretched the same, let us
go back to the first thread E, and tighten
all the threads across the board. The
straight threads side by side are called
the foundation of the weaving or the
warp threads. A board or frame around
which thread is wrapped at a tension to
provide warp for weaving is called a
"wrap around" loom. The same principle is used in the larger looms of Figs.
39 and 42.

To keep the warp threads from lying
too close to the board, we cut two pieces
of cardboard 1 inch wide and slip them
under the threads at each end, as in Fig.
25 at **G.** To hold the pieces of cardboard
in place, we tack them down.

**Step 4: Separating the Warp Threads
at Even Intervals.** To keep all the warp

threads in place and equal distances
apart, we fold a piece of string double,
as at **H,** calling the two ends 1 and 2.
Tie a knot on end 1 so as to see it better.
Now study the picture closely to see how
these two ends are twisted. Loop end
1 under the first warp thread at the left,
and end 2 under the second warp thread,
as at 1. Now cross end 1 over end 2, and
put end 1 under the third warp thread.
Next cross end 2 over end 1 and pass it
under the fourth warp thread, as at **J.**
Keep on crossing the threads over one
another in this way, and passing them
under the next warp thread, all the way
across the warp. This is the same process
as that described in Lesson 8 as "wattling." See Fig. 34.

A fast way of putting the threads
across is to hook each one up under the
next warp thread with a crochet hook.
When we have been all across the warp
with the strong twisted edge, we fasten
end 2 back into the weaving and cut off
end 1, as in Fig. 25 at **K.** The warp is now
ready for the weaving.

6—Weaving the Bookmark

The First Row of Real Weaving

NOW that our warp threads or foundation threads are ready, we must choose a weaving thread or "**weft thread**" to go across them. This weft should always be a little softer and heavier than the strong, tight warp threads. We can use either soft embroidery floss or wool. Thread the soft weaving thread in a large darning needle. To make the first row, start the needle under the first warp thread on one side, **A**, as shown in Fig. 26. Pass it under and over the warp threads, one by one, until you reach the other side, **B**. Pull all the thread through the warp except a short end **C**. In this first row, the needle has passed under all the odd-numbered threads, marked heavy, and over all the even-numbered threads, marked light.

Fastening in the End of the Thread

We must take care of the end **C** of the weft thread that we started with. To do this, take the end between your fingers and pass it around the last warp thread, and then back over and under the warp threads as far as it will go.

The Second Row of Weaving

For the second row of weaving we must turn our needle around and go back across the warp threads in the opposite direction. This time the needle must go under all the threads it went over before, and over all the threads it went under. If it does this, the first row of thread will be locked firmly in place. When threads go in and out in this way, we say they "interlace" one another. Now look at the thread in the row marked **Row 2** in Fig. 26, and you will see how the needle goes over the first warp thread, under the next, and so on. See how this second row is just the opposite of the first. Now look at your own bookmark, and put your needle under every thread that it went over before and over every thread it went under. You will see that in this second row the needle goes **over** all the odd-numbered threads and **under** all the even-numbered threads, just the opposite of the first row. Push this second row close against the first row with a comb.

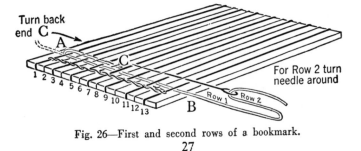

Fig. 26—First and second rows of a bookmark.

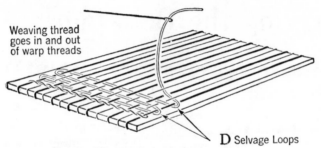

Fig. 27—Weaving the weft thread in and out.

Making the Edge of the Bookmark; the Selvage

When we come to the end of the second row, again we turn our needle around and go back across the warp threads, going under every thread that we went over in the last row. As we turn the needle to go back, a little loop of thread is formed at the edge. **A row of these loops makes the straight edge of the bookmark, called the Selvage or "self edge."** The arrows **D** in Fig. 27 point to two loops of the selvage. At **E** in Fig. 28 we see how the selvage loops make the edge of the cloth. Care must be taken to form a smooth selvage with even loops.

Laying in the Rows of Thread

Each time we carry the weaving thread across our warp threads, we must be careful not to pull the thread tight; or it will make the selvage pull in. We therefore fix the thread on a slight slant before we push it down against the last row, as shown in Fig. 29 at **F**. This gives the thread a little more length and keeps it from pulling in. It also makes a good even selvage. Pull the weft thread close to the last warp thread each time it reverses, and leave each new weft thread on a slant. Then push it tight against the last row with a comb. The selvage will remain smooth and even.

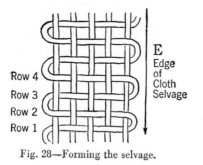

Fig. 28—Forming the selvage.

Fig. 29—Making a good selvage.

Fabrics of the author. Left to right: (on wall) flower panel in Dukagang; (under vase) runner in Crackle Weave; tablecloth with Laid-in design on Whig Rose threading; drapery in Perle and Bouclé; wool blanket in Twill blocks; Crackle Weave tablecloth in Perle 10 with orange border.

7—Finishing the Bookmark

Packing the Threads Tight

WHEN interlacing threads it is not necessary to pack the threads very tight, but in weaving our bookmark we want to have the threads close together in order that they will make a firm piece of real cloth. So we use a comb, as at **A** in Fig. 30, and push each row close against the row next to it. Ancient people who wove cloth packed the threads tight by using a piece of wood cut like a comb. Such a device is called a **Beater**, because it beats the threads together. Keep on weaving back and forth between the two sides, packing the weft threads tight. Always go under the warp threads you went over before, and go over those you went under before.

How to Put in a New Thread

If you come to an end of the thread, or if you wish to put in a pretty stripe of color, you must know how to piece the thread. Putting in the new thread beside the old one is called "**Piecing.**" To piece two threads together, take the old end of thread and cut it so that only 1 inch comes out beyond the weaving. Lay this short end back under and over sev- eral of the warp threads, as at **B** in Fig. 31. Now lay the new thread right beside the old end. The two threads must extend in opposite directions. When we pack this row down with our comb, the place where the piecing was done will hardly be noticed. If the new thread has a different color, we can lay it beside the first color. We can change back and forth between two colors in this way.

Tying the Fringe

When our bookmark is about 5 inches long, it is ready to be cut off the board. Turn the board over to the wrong side and cut the warp threads straight across the board. The cut should be right in the center of the space that has not been woven. You will need 2 inches for the fringe. Tie groups of two or three threads together, as at **C** in Fig. 31. The fringe will be in the color of the warp. Sometimes, when we have finished our first row of fringe, we tie a second row, taking part of the threads in each knot for a knot between them, as in Figs. 43 and 83. This is called a double fringe. Press the bookmark with a hot iron under a damp cloth.

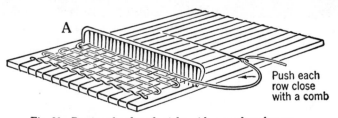

Fig. 30—Beating the threads tight with a comb or beater.

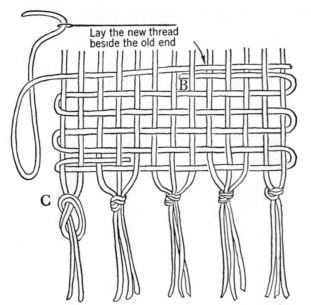

Fig. 31—Finishing the bookmark, piecing, and tying fringe.

Things to Make on a Board-Loom

By weaving back and forth on a small board-loom, as described for the bookmark, we can make many things, such as those shown in Figs. 32 and 33. Some of these things are:

1. Bookmarks.

2. Pads for hot plates at the table.

3. Doilies to put under flower vases.

4. Straps to hold books together.

5. An ornament for a pillow.

6. Hat trim, bows, bands, etc.

7. Several pieces to be sewed together end to end to make a belt.

8. Several pieces to be sewed together side by side to make a purse, a bag, a doily, or a book-cover.

9. Straps for sandals.

10. A necktie, which may be made if a long board is used.

11. Bell pulls or decorative wall hangings.

12. Colorful bands by which to hang pictures or panels.

13. Trim for shelves, boxes, desk sets, footstools, and lampshades.

14. Girdles and pouches.

15. Dress trim, collars and cuffs.

Descriptions for the articles shown in Fig. 33 follow:

1. This bag is 10 in. long and 6 in. deep. For the handles use a strip of hand-woven material, folded double lengthwise and stuffed with cotton to give body. Stiff belting may be used single. Add zipper, and line bag.

2. A stunning bookmark is made from a bit of striped belting that is fringed at ends.

3. A luncheon set is made by weaving strips in two colors. Sew the strips together as desired. Hand-stitch across the two ends, and fringe.

4. A doily with design running in opposite direction adds variety. Fringe either at sides or ends.

5. A knitting bag is made by joining several woven strips with rows of heavy crochet.

Fig. 32—Clothing accessories made of narrow strips of hand-woven material. Directions for belt at upper left are given in Lesson 30, Fig. 120.

6. This attractive container is made by sewing strips over an oatmeal carton. Alternate two kinds of striped belting.

7. For a pincushion, take the top of an ice-cream carton, turn it upside down, stuff it with fine sawdust or human hair, cover it with a piece of soft material, and run a strip of colorful belting around the edge. Human hair is an excellent filling for a home-made pincushion because the natural oil of the hair keeps pins and needles from rusting. Save and wash the combings from a brush for this purpose.

8. Straps for doilies or linens are made of firm belting that is pointed at one end and has snaps added.

9. A memo pad adds a gay touch when hung in place by this colorful narrow hand-woven strap.

10. Book-covers are made as shown here. Sew strips together and paste them down over the front and back of cardboard. Make an entire cover or use the strips to hold groups of pages together, as shown in the small sketch below 10.

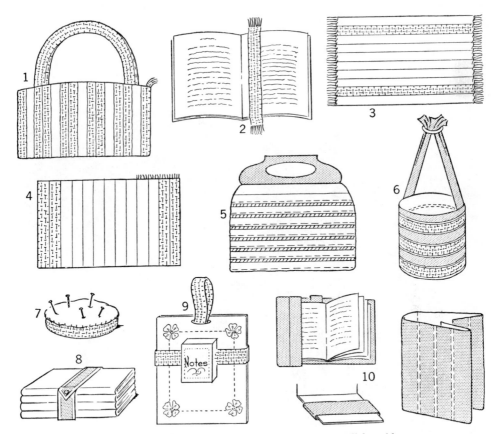

Fig. 33—Making gift articles from strips woven on small board-loom.

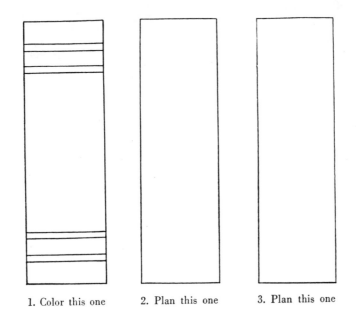

1. Color this one   2. Plan this one   3. Plan this one

A variety of patterns can be woven on the simple, inexpensive Inkle loom. Beautiful belts, bookmarks, sandal straps, curtain tie-backs, and bags can be woven quickly and easily by weavers of all ages. The Inkle is a valuable loom to start on because it is inexpensive to maintain, yet possesses the principles of larger, mechanical looms. It is said to come to us from England, where it was used to weave practical articles such as straps and suspenders.

8—Weaving a Rug on a Frame

How Weaving Developed

WEAVING first started as a development of basketry. It was the process of interweaving twigs that suggested the interlacing of fibers to make cloth. Many of the weaving stitches are similar to

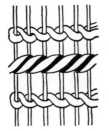

Fig. 34—Part of a mat with strands held together by "wattling."

those in basket work. The plain **"In-and-Out-Weave"** of cloth is the same process as the **"Simple Weave"** of basketry. The **"Pairing Weave"** was one of the first basket stitches. Men had to have some means of holding together the sticks that made up their shelters. They did this by interlacing the rigid sticks with pairs of softer fibers twisted about them. This process was known as **"wattling."** It is the same process that we know as **"pairing"** today. The twist was made between each two adjacent sticks, as shown in Fig. 34, just as we twist slender willow twigs between the spokes of a basket.

How Braid-Weaving Is Done

Recently the method of pairing with pliable material has been applied to the making of rugs, like those in Figs. 35 and 36. In this case, the worker has warp threads instead of sticks about which to twine his pairs of soft rags. The warp threads are stretched across a board-loom or frame. This method of making rugs is called **Braid-Weave Rug Weaving**; but it is quite different from the ordinary braid-

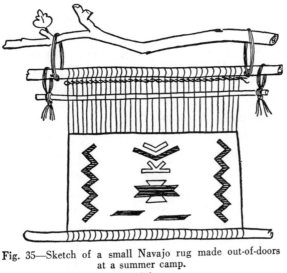

Fig. 35—Sketch of a small Navajo rug made out-of-doors at a summer camp.

35

Black   White   Grey   Red

Fig. 36—An Indian rug design.

ing of rugs. In Braid-Weave rugs, two rags are intertwined about the warp threads and are thus fixed permanently in place in the rug, instead of being first braided and then sewn together. The advantages of a Braid-Weave rug are that it is twice as thick as an ordinary woven rug, since it is made with two weft threads; and it is also the same on both sides and is therefore reversible. Making a Braid-Weave rug is an excellent problem for the beginner, as the process is performed entirely by hand; and the fascination of it lies in the weaving of one's own original patterns and designs.

The Indians Were Rug Makers

Before starting to make the rug, let us take a glimpse at the rug-making of the Indians. The rug-blankets of the Navajos were stretched between two long poles, and the upper one was fastened by ropes to a horizontal branch or bar (see Fig. 35). At each end the warp threads were wattled to the poles by special threads twisted about them, binding them in place and preventing them from slipping. At the foot of the blanket the Indian woman sat working, rolling up the finished weaving on the lower pole. In the next lesson we will learn more about

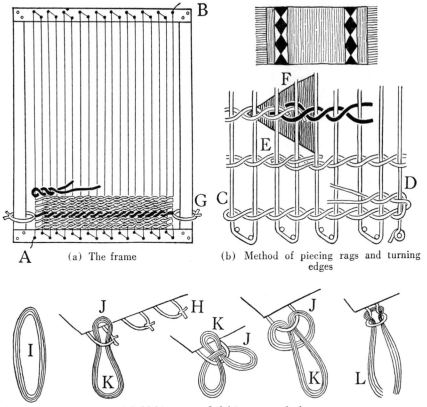

(a) The frame

(b) Method of piecing rags and turning edges

(c) Making a tasseled fringe on end of rug

Fig. 37—How to weave a rug at home on a board frame.

the Indian method of weaving. Making the Braid-Weave rug provides preparation for this future work.

Dimensions of the Rug Frame

In making a frame for a Braid-Weave rug, use side pieces, as well as end poles, to support the weaving in between. A typical frame is shown in Fig. 37.

Loom frame for large rug:
  Two end pieces: ¾″ × 2½″ × 24″
  Two side pieces: ¾″ × 2½″ × 36″
Loom frame for small rug:
  Two end pieces: ¾″ × 2″ × 19″
  Two side pieces: ¾″ × 2″ × 24″

Constructing the Frame

Lay the two end pieces on top of the two side pieces, as shown in Fig. 37, their

ends being even and the four pieces forming right angles at the corners. At each corner start two holes for screws, one at the very corner ⅜ in. away from the edge, and the other diagonally toward the inside. These holes are put in to prevent the boards from splitting when the screws are inserted. Drive the screws part way into the holes with a hammer, and then fasten them in place securely.

Sandpaper the frame. If you have an old large picture frame, you may use this for a board-frame by bracing the corners in the back with diagonal cross-pieces.

On each end of pieces **A** and **B** of the frame, drive a series of ¾-in. brads alternating in two rows. The first row should be ¾ in. from the outside edge, and the other row the same distance from the inside edge. Place the brads ½ in. apart, arranging them so that those in the inside row are half-way between those in the outside row. This arrangement is shown in Fig. 37. The heads of all the brads should stop at the same distance from the board. To obtain this result, lay a wooden strip about ¼ in. thick, like a yard stick, under each brad; and hammer the head until it just comes down upon the stick.

Stringing the Loom-Frame

Tie the end of a ball of strong warp thread or string to the outside brad at one corner of the loom-frame, as at the left end of piece **A** in Fig. 37. Pass it across the loom to the opposite brad on piece **B**; pass around this brad and the very next brad, which will be on the inside row; then pass across the loom to the opposite brad on piece **A**; and so on. Be careful to have the tension even as you stretch the thread between the brads. When you finish, tie the thread to the last brad, as at the right end of piece **B**. Now tighten all the rows of warp thread, starting at **A** and finishing at **B**. Tie the end securely.

Planning the Design

Plan the design on check paper; make the space proportions on the paper represent those of the rug. Bright colors on a soft dull background look well in a rug. Choose the desired colors. Tear the rags in similar widths and keep them in a box beside you to use as you go along.

The design given in Fig. 36 is of Navajo character. The original designs of the Navajos were very beautiful in coloring and symbolization. They dyed their own colors and carried their designs in their heads. Few weavers today have enough skill to do this, but we can copy the good old designs, plan them out on paper, and be guided in the choice of color. The color scheme of this rug is indicated on the pattern. Gray is the usual background color of the Navajos; the white may be dead white or cream, or even a light yellow may be used.

Weaving the Rug

When the warp is set up, the rug may be woven either by the In-and-Out Weave as described in Lesson 7 or by the Braid-Weave method which follows. Fold a strip of rag, 4 or 5 ft long, at a point two-thirds of its length from one end, and place the longer strand around the left-hand warp thread, as in Fig. 37 at **C**. Lay this strand across the first warp thread and the other strand, and carry it in back of the second warp thread. Also, bring the short strand in front of the second warp thread, lay it across the other strand and pass it behind the third warp thread. Thus, each strand crosses the other strand between the warp threads. This is the same principle as that called "pairing" or "wattling," Fig. 34. Weave in this way across the warp from left to right to the other side. Then, make an extra twist on the outside of the last warp thread, and reverse the direction of the weave, as at **D**, returning across the warp from right to left to the first side again. Continue weaving back and forth. As you add row to row, push down the work with a stick or a comb. The tighter you crowd the rags, the firmer and smoother your work will be.

Piecing the Rags

It is best to splice the rags while weaving instead of sewing them together beforehand as in ordinary rugs. Work with a short length, about 3 ft long. Taper the end with scissors for smoother piecing. Before you reach the end of a rag, lay another tapered rag parallel to it, as in Fig. 37 at **E**. Continue with both rags for 2 in.; then drop the old end and continue with the new. The ends may be tucked down into the weaving. The frequent renewing of rags makes it very easy to put in a design. As you come to the place where the color changes from light to dark, as indicated by the shaded portion at **F**, change rags, as shown at **E**, behind adjacent warp threads. In the same way change back to the original color.

Keeping a Straight Selvage

It is the tendency of amateur weavers to pull in the selvage, making the rug narrower as they proceed. To prevent this, when you have woven 6 inches or so, fasten the woven edges to the side pieces of the loom, as shown in Fig. 37 at **G**. Do this every 6 inches. Make an effort to weave a smooth straight selvage; crooked edges are unattractive and lessen the value of the woven rug.

How to Make a Tasseled Fringe

When the weaving has been completed up to the end board, push the woven rows together as closely as possible; then cut the warp threads at the middles of their loops, making both ends even. Tie each two adjacent warp threads together,

close to the finished weaving, as in Fig. 37 at **H**.

To make a tasseled fringe, wind some warp thread several times around a book 6 or more inches high, with a wooden block inserted. The block is added so that, when it is pushed out, the warp may be removed readily from around the book. Tie the two ends of thread together. Fold the loop of threads over on itself so that it will be twice as thick as when wound, forming a coil **I**. Insert this coil of threads into the loop like that at **H** made by two tied warp threads. Call the top of the coil **J**, and call the bottom **K**. Draw end **K** up through end **J**. Continue to pull on **K** until **J** is fastened right about the warp loop **H**, as shown at the finish. Cut **K** through the middle, **L**. Put a tassel into every warp loop. Comb out the tassels and trim off even.

The Efficient Use of the Loom-Frame

A Braid-Weave rug must not be made in a hurry. For this reason do the work at frequent intervals in margins of time. Set your loom against a wall or place it on a table or chair easy of access. If you have made a good strong loom-frame, it will produce many useful mats and rugs. Weaving Braid-Weave rugs is pleasant work for winter days and they make wel come Christmas presents.

9—How the Indian Weaves

Important Advance in Early Weaving

IN THE WEAVING of the Braid-Weave rug described in Lesson 8, there are two weft strands that twist around and cross each warp thread in succession. This is quite different from the making of the bookmark described in Lesson 6, where there is a single weft thread that passes under and over every other warp thread. This interlacing of warp and weft threads is the principle underlying the making of most cloth. In weaving a narrow piece of cloth, it is very easy to count out the warp threads and to lay the weft thread under and over them; but, if we need to make a wide piece of cloth like a skirt or a blanket, it takes too long to do this. Ancient weavers, who had to weave all their clothing and blankets, soon found this out. So they devised a method of lifting up all the alternate warp threads at the same time, thus forming an opening for the weft thread to pass through. The perfecting of this simpler and quicker way to make successive rows of weaving was one of the most important advances in early weaving. The Indians of our own country developed a very clever way of doing this. A real Indian rug woven thus is shown in Fig. 38.

The Indian Loom Device

The warp threads of the Indians were stretched between two poles, as in Fig. 39 at **A** and **B**. The weight of the lower pole held these warp threads tight. You will see that the method of winding warp thread around the two poles is much the same as that we used for wrapping our thread around the board to make the bookmark. The Indians knew how to keep their warp threads equal distances apart. They beat the weft threads tight by pounding the cloth with a sword or a flat stick.

Step 1: The First Opening. Fig. 39 shows how the Indians made the arrangement for half of the threads to come up at the same time, in order that they could weave under and over the threads quickly and easily. The weaver took a long flat stick and passed it under and over the threads all the way across the warp, as shown at **C**. If you look closely, you will see that the flat stick passes under all the odd-numbered threads, or those numbered 1, 3, 5, 7, and so on, and over all the even-numbered threads. To put a weaving thread through, he simply turned the flat stick on edge. The opening thus made was called a "**shed**," which means "to separate." Into this opening he laid the first row of soft weaving thread or weft. You will see this thread in the picture going from right to left, from **D** to **E**. When this thread was laid in, the weaver beat it down with a sword.

Step 2: The Second Opening. Now the weaving thread was ready to come back across the warp, for the second row. This row was just the opposite of the first row. The weaving thread had to pass under the even-numbered threads. These threads are numbered 2, 4, 6, 8, and so on in Fig. 40.

40

Fig. 38—A real Indian rug woven between two poles.

To make all the even-numbered threads come up at the same time, the weaver fastened them to a rod or pole, as indicated in Fig. 40 at **G.** The threads were fastened by looping a cord under every other thread and then attaching the cord to the rod with two half-hitches, as you see being done by the hand at the left in Fig. 40. By lifting the pole, all the threads that were tied to it could be brought up at the same time. The weft thread could thus be put through this second opening or shed very quickly to make the second row of weaving. You may see this row in

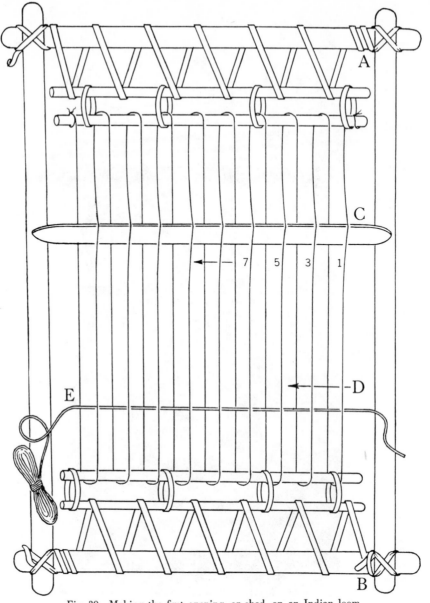

Fig. 39—Making the first opening, or shed, on an Indian loom.

the picture, going from **E** to **F**. To make the third row, like the first row, the weaver lifted up the odd threads, numbered 1, 3, 5, 7, and so on, by turning the flat stick on edge again. The loops of soft cord on the rod did not hinder the making of the first shed again. For the fourth row, which is like the second row, the weaver brought up the even-numbered threads, 2, 4, 6, 8, and so on, by lifting the pole and its attached loops. One could keep on weaving very easily and quickly in this way.

A frame on which to stretch warp threads for weaving is called a "Loom." The arrangement of the Indians, with warp threads stretched between two poles, was one of the first kinds of looms.

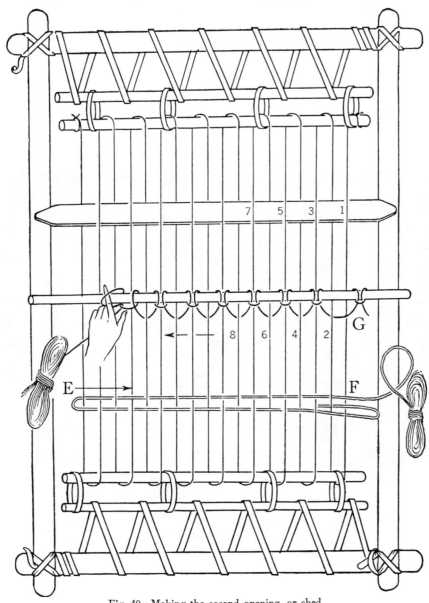

Fig. 40—Making the second opening, or shed.

The essential parts of a loom are (a) two rigid posts or beams between which threads can be stretched, (b) a means of separating these threads into openings called sheds, and (c) some devise or tool, such as a sword, comb, or beater, to press the woven threads close together to form cloth. With these, you can make short cloth, as in the Indian frame in Fig. 40 or the wrap-around loom in Fig. 42.

To weave a piece of cloth longer than the loom, use a warp roller on which to store thread and a ratchet to draw this forward for new warp after each woven section is finished. (This will be described in the following lessons.)

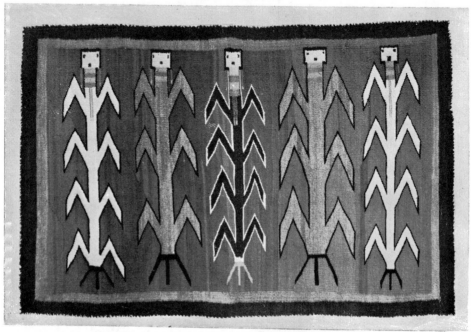

*(From the collection of C. Clay Aldridge, Director,
El Paso Museum of Art, El Paso, Texas)*

Fig. 41—The Indian ceremonial rug, known as a corn blanket, demonstrates the ability of South-western Indians to weave a colorful fabric in a tapestry technique. Vegetable dyes are used for the most part to create the handsome reds and yellows used in the composition. The figures are "rain gods," to whom the Indians appealed for good corn crops. The gods are represented as glorified stalks of corn.

10—The Shed and Its Variations

Importance of the Shed

A SHED is the angle made by the separation of the warp threads to form an opening for the weft threads to weave through to make a row of cloth. In all weaving there must be successive openings, or sheds, for the thread to go through. The handweaver lays in the threads, row after row, by hand, and then beats the rows close together. In factories, the openings are made rapidly by machinery. The rows of yarn are laid in and beat up into cloth so rapidly that the process is hard to follow with the naked eye. Texture is determined by the tightness of the rows.

The kind of opening made in the warp determines the resulting pattern as the thread is woven through. The cloth can also be altered by the choice of thread, its setting, or the manner of beating, but the shed controls the pattern effect.

In simple weaving described in the last lesson, alternate threads are raised and lowered for the successive rows of weft thread to make the simplest kind of cloth, or Plain Weave.

Changes in the Shed

Now it should be clear that if two successive warp threads were raised, the next two lowered, and so on, instead of one up and one down, we would have a far different result—pairs of warps being woven through, as in Fig. 22. In this manner a coarser cloth would be produced. Again, if the threads were to come up in uneven groups, or in groups carefully planned, a set pattern would result when a filling thread was inserted, as in Fig. 100. This gives an idea of how important the shed is and how it controls the results in weaving.

Color in the Shed

Primitive people did a great deal with color on Plain Weave sheds by planning bands of bright stripes in the warp. When they wove through these colors, vertical stripes resulted. On plain warps they designed bands of color to make horizontal stripes or borders of various sizes. When they combined both vertical and horizontal stripes, and wove across warp stripes with weft bands, the result was a cloth of plaid design.

Texture in the Shed

Many different effects can be obtained by beating the rows of weft snugly together to form firm cloth, or lightly to form a mesh. Among the closely woven fabrics are rugs, linens, napkins, and upholstery. The mesh effects are suitable for drapes, light wearing apparel, stoles, and so on.

Choice of Yarns

In recent years the weavers of America have done a great deal of creative work by using different textures of yarn through any one type of shed. The colors, textures, and kinds of yarn, both natural and man-made, are innumerable. Many yarn supply houses serve the handweaver and furnish a galaxy of fascinating threads.

45

The kind of yarn you use has an important effect on the finished product. Yarns can be dull or shiny, fine or coarse, bright or subdued, smooth or nubby, stiff or flexible.

Laying in Designs

In addition to the regular weft put through a plain shed, you can add a heavier yarn over certain spaces to make free or conventional designs. The colors and textures are chosen so that the design will stand out against the plain-weave background. This process is called "Laid-in Weaving." It is really embroidery on the loom. (See pages 135 to 141.)

Weaving Lace

There are also ways of twisting the warp threads together or passing around groups of warps with the weft thread to make lace on the loom. This is a fascinating kind of weaving and results in useful and beautiful table linens, sun curtains, and stoles. (See pages 133-135.) First learn to weave the lace in simple rows. Then leave some spaces without lace for background, and against this, weave sections of lace design. Very beautiful church cloths, with motifs of crosses, lecterns, and conventional forms, have been woven by the lace-weave method. Any cross-stitch motif may be followed to duplicate the same design in a lace texture.

Combinations of Effects

All these variations are possible on a plain shed. These variations are described in Part One of this book. They consist of stripes, plaids, color variations, laid-in designs, texture and lace weaves. In Part Two you will learn how to make patterns with more than two sheds and with shed openings planned in spaced formations. As the number of sheds which can be made on a loom increases, more and more combinations can be made. Begin by mastering each type of variation. Then learn to combine thread colors and textures, while at the same time arranging the shed in many interesting successions so that as the warps appear in different groups, the weft is set off in countless ways.

The best way to weave is to feel that you are painting with threads. Arrange a table of many kinds of thread and choose those that seem to show up best on the loom. Try as many variations as possible. With different effects laid out, a final texture is created.

11—Weaving a Table Mat or Rug on a Loom

Equipment Needed

LET US PLAN to weave a small Indian rug or mat. You can use this to put under the lamp on your table or, if folded double, to make a pouch or purse. The mat is also useful under a vase of flowers or as a desk or table covering.

Indian rugs are made of red, gray, white, and black wool. Sometimes a little blue or yellow is used. You will love the bright colors. To make the rug you will need some white string (the kind the grocer uses for small packages) and some red, white, black, and gray wool. You should also have a sharp pair of scissors. You should place your loom on a big table so as to have plenty of room on which to work. Make your rug 10 in. in length and 7 in. in width. You can weave it on a piece of board 12 in. long and 9 in. wide, or on a loom.

A "Loom" (Fig. 42) is a frame on which threads are stretched evenly and tightly for the weaving of cloth. It enables folks to weave useful and beautiful things with ease and pleasure. On a loom

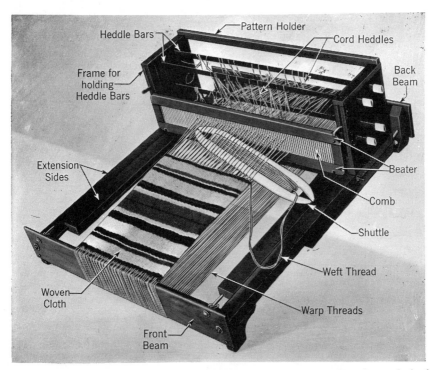

Fig. 42—Weaving on a loom. The parts of the loom are named. For the method of making a loom of similar type, see Figs. 44 and 45.

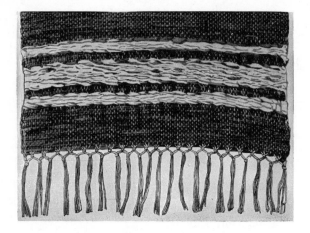

Fig. 43—A rug woven with rags. The border is in Braid-
Weave. Note the neatly tied double fringe. See Fig. 83, J.

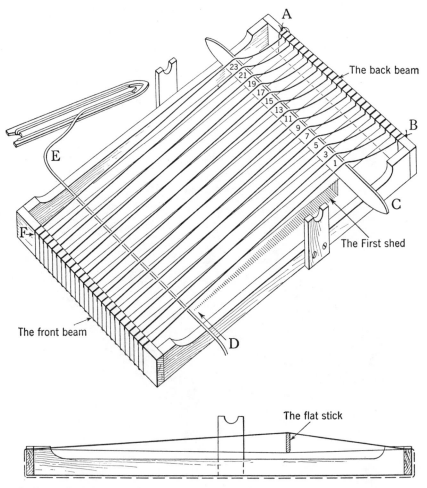

Fig. 44—Winding the warp thread around the loom. The first shed is made with a
shed-stick.

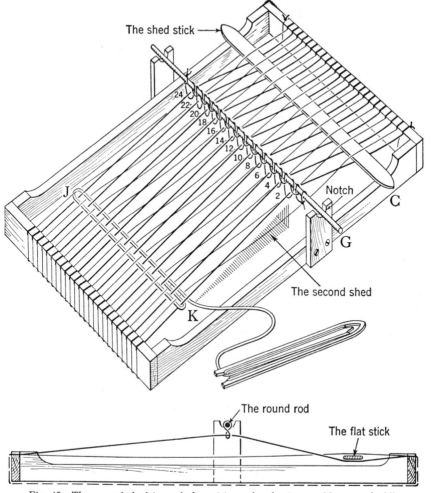

The shed stick →

24
22
20
18
16
14
12
10
8
6
4
2

J

Notch

C

G

The second shed

K

The round rod

The flat stick

Fig. 45—The second shed is made by raising a bar having cord-loops or heddles
attached to it.

there is always an arrangement for lifting the warp threads quickly and easily to make the shed opening. In the loom of Fig. 42, one can readily see the method used.

There are several lifting bars. The cords or loops attached to these lifting bars are now called "heddles." The bars or rods that hold these loops or heddles are the "heddle bars." A good loom is strong and the warp threads may be stretched tightly between its back beam and its front beam, also called "breast beam." One part of the loom, a comb-like device called the "reed", keeps the

warp threads spaced evenly. The "stick shuttles" are thin flat sticks with grooves at their ends on which the weft thread is wound lengthwise. They usually come with the loom.

A small box-loom built on the same principle as the loom in Fig. 42 is shown in Figs. 44 and 45. Plan to weave a mat or runner on this loom. It is similar to weaving a bookmark on the small board-loom in Lesson 6, but this box-loom is larger, making it possible to weave longer articles. The front part of the box is called the **Front-Beam**. The back part of the box is called the **Back-Beam**. We wind our warp threads around the loom, and they are stretched tight between the front and back beams. Such a loom is called a **Wrap-Around Loom.** The warp threads can be only as long as the distance around the loom. You can purchase looms very much like this one in a department store, but be sure to get one that is large enough to make something useful. Better still, learn to make a box-loom for yourself in the shop or at home. Diagrams for making a wrap-around loom are given in Figs. 44 and 45. The lovely things shown in Fig. 50 were all made on this loom.

Winding the Warp Thread Around the Loom

We tie the warp string to the back beam, as you will see in Fig. 44 at **A.** Then we wind this string round and round the loom. Each time the string or warp thread goes over the front-beam, it must pass through one of the dents or nicks, marked **F,** that look like little teeth on a comb. This keeps the threads evenly spaced and acts as a reed. When we have wound enough warp threads to make a warp 8 in. wide, we tie the string to the back of the loom, on the other side, as you see in the picture at **B.**

The First Shed

On our loom we can make an arrangement to form a good shed, just as the Indian did on his pole loom. First we pass the long shed-stick under the first thread, over the second, under the third, over the fourth, and so on, under all the odd-numbered threads, across the entire warp. The "shed-stick," shown at **C** in Figs. 44 and 45, is a thin, wide, flat stick with smooth pointed ends that comes with most table looms. It should be as long as the loom is wide. We call it a shed-stick because it aids the weaver in finding and keeping the shed-opening. After we have carried the shed-stick under and over all the warp threads, we turn it on edge to form the first shed. We now wind our shuttle with some of the pretty bright wool and lay in our first row of weaving, from **D** to **E.**

The Second Shed

After we have put in the first row, we shove the shed-stitch to the back of the loom. In the first shed we raised all the odd-numbered threads, 1, 3, 5, 7, etc.; and in the second shed we will raise all the even-numbered threads, 2, 4, 6, 8, etc. We can do this just as the Indian weaver did, as described for Fig. 40 in Lesson 9. Make loops as directed under all the even-numbered threads; and fasten the end of the cord to the rod. The loops are called **cord-heddles.**

We are now ready to make our second shed by lifting all these even-numbered threads at the same time, as indicated at **G** in Fig. 45. As we lift them, we place the rod in the little round supports at the sides of the loom. This holds the shed open while we use our hands to weave in the thread for the second row. You will find this row marked **J** to **K** in the picture. You can use a comb to push the second row close to the first.

We have now made our first row of weaving by putting a thread through the first shed, using the shed-stick to lift the odd threads. We have also made our second row of weaving by putting a thread through the second shed, using the rod with tied cord-heddles to lift the even threads. Now all we have to do to go on weaving is to keep on making a first shed with the stick, followed by a second shed with the rod and its loops. Each time we make a new shed, we lay a

(*Courtesy Lowe Galleries*)

Fig. 46—A very colorful Peruvian bag of fine wool, showing the
possibilities of weaving on a handloom. Intricate designs
are made by lifting cord heddles to make the shed.

row of weft thread through the opening.

For the very next row, which would be
the third row in Fig. 45, just lift the bar
off the side posts and lay it gently down
on the warp threads. Then slide the wide
shed-stick forward as far as you can, turn
it on edge, and make the first shed again
just the same as in Fig. 44. Put your

third row of thread through this shed.

For the fourth row, push the shed-stick
back and lift the rod on the posts. This
makes the second shed just as in Fig. 45.
Put your fourth row of thread through
this shed.

Keep on weaving through the first shed
and the second shed in this way.

12—The Colors for the Rug

Choosing Colors

THE INDIAN weavers delighted in the bright colors of wool with which they made their rugs and blankets. Most of the best Indian rugs are woven very tightly with heavy wools (see Fig. 38).

They still make rugs like this today. The possible variety of colors and designs is shown in the scarves and belt in Fig. 47.

In the scarves you see different colors worked out in stripe designs. When weaving your mat, plan stripes much like

Fig. 47—Three scarves and a belt woven on a real loom.

52

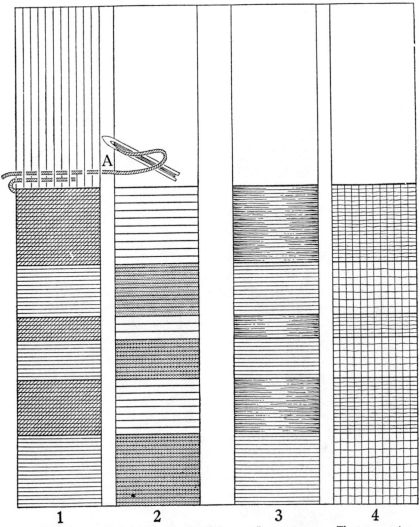

Fig. 48—Different kinds of threads give different effects in texture. The same stripes may be woven in dark colors against a light background, or in light colors against a dark background. For suggestions in stripe weaving, see Lessons 20 and 22 and Figs. 81, 85, and 88.

those in Figs. 47 and 48, but make them three or four times as large as these in the actual cloth on your loom. These strips add up to 3 to 5 inches of space in the pictures, but in your woven piece they might cover 10 to 12 inches or so. You will also enjoy making a design of your very own, first using crayons to make the stripes on paper, and then weaving these with thread into the cloth.

In Fig. 48 you can see different kinds of wool used for stripes. One of the nicest

things about weaving is that you can use the colors you like best and weave them together in any way. If you weave colors that look attractive to you, they are likely to blend well.

Changing Colors

When you change colors, just run the old end of wool through the threads in the shed as you see in Fig. 48 at **A**, and lay the new end right beside it. Then go on weaving with the new end.

(Fabric, Courtesy Martina Lindahl, Director, Hartland Area Crafts, Hartland, Mich. Decorative accessories, Everhart Museum Collection, Scranton, Pa.)

Through the use of color and simple design a striking modern drapery is easily created on the four-harness loom.

13—Color Combinations from Nature

AFTER we have learned how to weave, it is possible to make many things. In the department store we see scarves, school bags, belts, aprons, pouches, towels, curtains, mats, and pillows, all of which we can make on a loom.

So we start planning to make some useful things for ourselves and even some gifts for our friends. But what colors shall we use? There are hundreds and hundreds of colors of thread from which to choose. Which will look best together?

Of course an art teacher can tell us a great deal about color and we can also learn more in books, but it would be fun to learn about color from the beautiful things around us. And the most beautiful things in all the world are the flowers and birds and butterflies that we find out under the open skies in Nature's Kingdom.

Let us go out for a walk and just study the colors we find. Here is a beautiful orange, black, and yellow butterfly. How beautifully these colors go together. And here is a meadow lark, brown and rust and gray—such soft, pretty colors. And here is a sweet-pea flower, pink and deep rose and white. As you watch living things in the Spring, Summer, and Fall, you will find many beautiful colors that look just right together. And in the Winter, you can watch the sunset skies, and the dark blue and gray shadows on the pure white snow.

Fig. 49—Getting color from Nature.

Fig. 50—These attractive and colorful fabrics were woven on a small table loom. Top left: a mat to put under a vase of flowers. Top right: a rug sample in tufted or pile weave. Center left: a purse made with Twill weaving. Center right: a table doily in red, white and blue stripes. Bottom of page: a pillow made with imitation pattern weaving on a two-harness loom (see Fig. 95, No. 4).

After you have studied Nature, you will know what colors look well together. But before you weave the colors into a piece of cloth, you will want to plan your purse or scarf on paper. With a box of crayons or paints, put the colors together

as you see in Fig. 51 at A. Take three colors—a light one, a dark one, and a medium one. First try the darkest color next to the lightest, then the medium color next to the darkest, and so on. When you have put them all on your

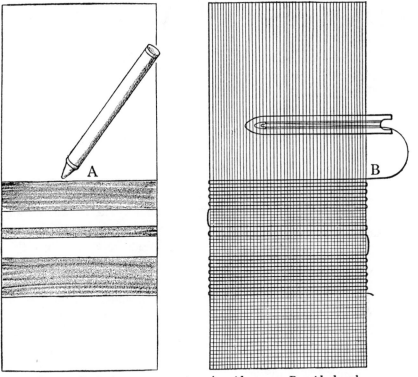

Fig. 51—Designing your own stripes. A—with crayon; B—with thread.

paper, you will see which combination is the prettiest. Then weave colors as nearly like those in your picture as you can. You will see that the shuttle at **B** looks very much like the crayon at **A**. In the one case we paint our colors on paper with the crayon. In the other case we weave the same colors on the loom with the shuttle. Notice the different designs in Fig. 48 and also in the many photographs of stripes and plaids in Lessons 20, 21, and 22.

14—The Process of Weaving on a Two-Harness Loom; Threading Plain Weave from a Draft

Plain Weave

"PLAIN WEAVE" consists in the regular interlacing of two sets of threads crossing each other at right angles, as shown in Fig. 52. Look at a plain hand-

Fig. 52—Plain Weave or Tabby.

kerchief or a piece of unbleached muslin through a magnifying glass to see this texture. We have learned how to interlace weft threads across warp threads to produce it. First, in Lesson 4 we learned the correct way to darn a stocking. Second, in Lessons 5, 6, and 7 we wove a bookmark on a small board. Third, in Lesson 9 we learned how the Indian weaves rugs in Plain Weave by lifting half of the warp threads at the same time to make an opening or shed for the weft; and how he makes the first shed with a flat stick, and the second shed with cord-loops attached to a rod. This process of lifting up alternate warp threads by means of some device is used in all weaving. When the first shed opening is

made, every other thread is thus raised and the alternate threads remain below; and, when the second harness is raised, the threads reverse. When the weaver lays successive weft threads through the alternate openings thus made, there results an in-and-out texture, shown in Fig. 52. It is called **Plain Weave, Tabby Weave, Gingham Weave, Linen Weave, Simple In-and-Out Weave,** and **Basket Weave.** The names generally used for this weave are Plain Weave and Tabby. Although the underlying character of this weave is always the same, with its interlacing of warp and weft threads, the effect may be varied greatly by changing the colors or textures of either warp or weft threads or both, in stripes or plaids like those shown in Fig. 53 and in many other ways.

Method of Making the Two Sheds in Plain Weave

We have shown the primitive method of making the two sheds in Figs. 39 and 40; and the method used for a simple table loom is shown in Fig. 54. Ancient weavers made their own looms and attached their own heddle-loops of cord to them, in the manner shown in Figs. 17, 44, and 45. Even in foreign countries today, many tribes that do beautiful weaving make their own looms by hand and weave in this way. It is easy to see how,

Fig. 53—Plaids and stripes of coarse materials. Above: Pillow top woven on a table loom
in different shades of carpet warp set at 16 threads per inch. Below: Stunning runner
woven with strands of raffia laid in hit-and-miss fashion. The warp is Perle 10, set at
20 threads per inch; and the fringe is double tied, as shown in Fig. 43.

as men became more skilled in making
their loom-frames, they added conven-
iences and improved their methods. One
of the improvements was to replace the
pick-up stick that made the first shed
with another rod with loops attached
like that used for the second shed in Fig.
45. Thus, weavers gradually came to use
two bars with heddle-loops attached, as
in Fig. 54 at **D**. Either of these could lie

down on the warp while the other was
lifted to make its shed, in the manner
shown in Fig. 54 at **A**, **B**. The shed-stick
A was sometimes inserted to widen the
opening thus made before weaving
through it. The bars were held in place
on a side support as at **C**. These two bars
with their **Cord-Heddles** are now called
"**Harnesses**," and the frame that holds
them is called a **Two-Harness Loom**.

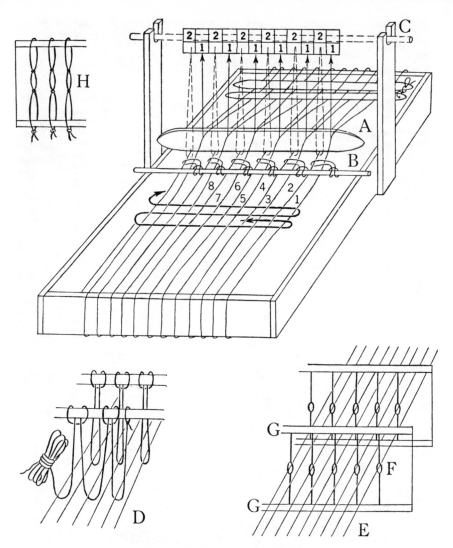

Fig. 54—Development of the heddle.
A, B, C. Making a shed by means of a bar and cord-heddles.
D. Making cord-loops or cord-heddles.
E, F, G. Modern harness frames with steel heddle-rods and steel heddles.
H. Cord-heddles made by hand.

Gradual Development of the Heddle

The cord heddle-loops gradually became known as "Heddles" or "Healds." Improvements were added to these step by step. Instead of the single loops hanging beneath a bar, as in Fig. 54 at **D**, a double Cord-Heddle was attached to bars at both top and bottom, with the opening for the thread midway between, as shown at **H**. The bars at top and bottom that held the heddles were called **Heddle-Bars** or **Heddle-Rods**.

This type of cord-heddle is still used today and can be made at home. To have all the cord-heddles the same length, with the opening coming exactly at the same point on each, make a frame for tying them, consisting of long nails hammered upward into a heavy board at the proper distances to make the cord-heddles the right size. To make it easier to thread a loom when using cord-heddles, choose cord of a different color for the heddles of each harness. The person threading will know in an instant which heddle to choose for each thread.

The principle of the cord-heddle with its central opening was later transferred to a **metal heddle**, which slips more easily along the heddle-rods. This type is shown in Fig. 54 at **E**. It is made of wire or steel and is used today in all power weaving mills as well as on a great many looms for hand-weaving. There are large factories busily engaged in producing steel heddles by the thousand for the looms that make the fabrics needed in the world. Heddles of stainless steel on a home loom glisten in the light as the harnesses are raised and lowered, forming a beautiful contrast to the softer wood tones of the loom frame.

Either cord-heddles or steel heddles for threading generally come with one's loom. Since they are attached at both top and bottom, the harnesses may be either raised or lowered to make the shed, instead of being just raised in the manner of the primitive heddle shown at **D**.

Plain Weave is easily woven on a two-harness loom. One can use either a two-harness table loom, like that shown in Fig. 58, or a two-harness floor loom, Fig. 18. The loom speeds up the process of weaving, and one can spend the extra time thus saved for choosing good colors, making pretty designs, and doing more perfect work. Weaving on a real loom is also much more enjoyable than weaving on a frame. A great French writer, Rodier, once said, "Nothing has ever been invented to take the place of the loom, or to rob it of its usefulness."

Laying the Foundation, or Stretching the Warp Threads

Before the frame or loom can be threaded and made ready for weaving cloth, the foundation or warp threads must be measured off and stretched across it. There are three essentials of a good foundation or warp for one's weaving:

1. The threads must be **stretched taut** on the loom-frame, all being at the same **tension**.
2. They must lie **in consecutive order and parallel** as they run from the front to the back of the loom.
3. They must be **spaced evenly** to produce a smooth even texture.

The **tension** on the warp threads depends on the weaver's care in stretching them taut and maintaining the same tension.

The **order** of the threads depends on keeping each thread in the same order when threading as when winding.

The **spacing** of the threads depends on threading them through a certain size dent or reed, or through spaces marked off by tacks or notches on the loom-frame. See Figs. 42, 44, and 58.

Warping "Wrap-Around" Looms

Warps stretched on wrap-around looms (Figs. 42 and 44) are made taut by the gradual winding round and round of the warp thread by hand, with each round pulled up to a certain tension. By laying the warp through successive dents in the front-beam, or reed, the threads stay in the same order as when wound.

Warping Looms Having Warp-Rollers

Looms having warp-rollers in the back, on which the warp thread is wound for future use, such as those in Figs. 58 and

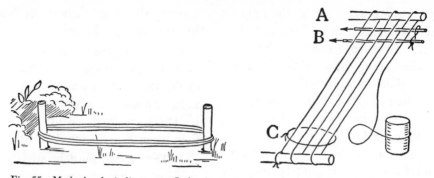

Fig. 55—Methods of winding warp. Left: Ancient weavers wound their warps between two upright posts sunk into the ground. Right: A short warp for a hand-loom of today may be wound between bars or bed-posts.

59, require a warp wound apart from the loom and then stretched on it, wound around its warp-roller, and threaded through the heddles of the harnesses and the dents of the reed.

Primitive weavers wound warps of this kind between two vertical stakes sunk into the ground, as in Fig. 55 at the left. Short warps of several yards may be wound between two bed posts or stationary bars, as in Fig. 55 at **A**, but during the winding the threads must be kept in order and side by side without overlapping. Before removing the warp from the bars, two flat rods or sticks must be inserted, as shown at **B**. These rods pass alternately under and over the successive threads, so that the threads are held permanently in the same order as when wound. The sticks should be tied together at both ends to maintain the alternation of the warp threads, which is called the "Cross" in weaving. The sticks are called "**Lease Rods**" because they maintain this cross. The ends of the thread are tied together with a cord, as at **C**, and the cord is drawn taut to keep them from slipping. When the warp threads are cut and removed from the posts or bars, they are ready for threading. Care must be taken never to let the threads slip off the cross on the lease

rods until the threading is finished. This cross is shown maintained on the loom in Fig. 57 at **A** and **B**.

Longer warps are stretched on a frame called a **Warping-Board**. The processes of winding these warps and arranging them on a loom are described in detail in Lesson 17.

How to Write the Threading Plan for Plain Weave

Our next step is to thread the warp on the loom. It is simple to represent the threading of the warp threads by a plan on cross-barred paper. Draw a frame around two rows of squares, as shown in Fig. 56, Method No. 1. Call the first row heddle-rod or harness No. 1; and call the second row heddle-rod or harness No. 2. Let each square represent a warp thread. Number the threads, as shown in the successive squares, starting at the right and working toward the left. The first square marked is No. 1 on the first row, and this number means to pick up or thread a warp thread through a loop or heddle on the first heddle-bar or harness. The next square marked is No. 2 on the second row, and this number means to pick up or thread a warp thread through a loop or heddle on the second bar or harness. Continue thus to form the re-

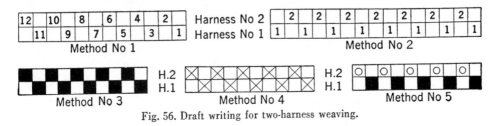

Fig. 56. Draft writing for two-harness weaving.

peated pattern all across the two rows of squares.

Method No. 2 in Fig. 56 shows a system of numbering the alternate squares 1, 2, 1, 2, and so on, for harnesses 1 and 2. This method is used in threading the loom in Fig. 54. Method No. 3 shows how the same draft may be represented by shaded squares. Method No. 4 shows a similar arrangement, using checks or crosses. Method No. 5 shows how a warp of two colors can be planned on squared paper. Each dark block on harness 1 means to use a dark-colored warp thread at this point; and each circle on harness 2 means to thread a light-colored warp thread in between the two adjacent dark threads.

There are still other short-cut methods of notation used by expert weavers, such as just dots or lines marked in the successive squares of two rows.

Reading Draft from Right to Left

A threading plan on paper is known as a "Threading Draft." All drafts for weaving are read like the Chinese language, that is, from right to left. So, in the drafts in Fig. 56, one starts reading the notation at the right-hand side with thread No. 1 and proceeds toward the left. In Method No. 1, all the odd-numbered threads come on harness 1, and all the even-numbered threads come on harness 2. This shows clearly that when harness 1 is raised all the odd-numbered threads will be raised for shed opening

No. 1; and when harness 2 is raised all the even-numbered threads will be raised for shed opening No. 2.

Threading the Loom by Following the Draft

Fig. 54 shows how the draft corresponds exactly to the threading of the loom. Here the first shed is being made by the shed-stick A. The arrows point upward to the draft directly above the threads, signifying that all the odd-numbered threads on harness 1 are being raised. The dotted lines show how the second shed will be made by the bar with its cord-loops. At present, for shed opening 1, the bar and its loops are lying down on the warp, as shown at B. For the next shed, the bar with the loops carrying all the even-numbered threads will be lifted to the tops of the side supports, as shown by the dotted loops and dotted bar at C.

The first shed, instead of being formed by a shed-stick, may also be made by means of loops on a second bar similar to the shed for harness 2, as shown in Fig. 54 at D. In this case, while each bar or harness is being raised, the other bar or harness will lie flat on the warp, as at B. This is the origin of the two alternating harnesses used on looms today, and is the improvement in weaving methods referred to earlier in this lesson. The loops, as F and H, through which the warp threads are threaded, are called Heddles. These are attached to rods G at both top and bottom of each harness, these rods being known as Heddle-Rods.

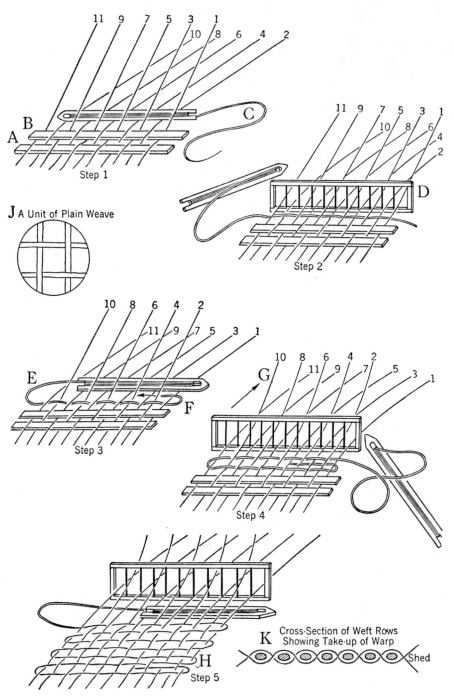

Fig. 57—The steps in weaving.

Making the Warp Threads Even

At the beginning of any new weaving it is a good idea to even up the warp threads by putting in two rows of heavy yarn, rags, or smooth narrow sticks, as in Fig. 57 at **A** and **B**. Raise the odd-numbered threads by lifting the first heddle-rod or harness, and lay in a smooth stick or heavy yarn, **A**. Raise the even-numbered threads by lifting the second heddle-rod or harness and lay in a second stick or heavy yarn, **B**. Press the second row tight against the first row with a comb or beater. You are now ready to make the Plain Weave with the regular weft thread, **C**.

Choosing the Weft Thread for Correct Texture

The weft thread must be of the right weight or size to fill in the spaces between the warp threads so as to make a smooth, firm, even texture. You will see that in a linen handkerchief the weft threads are the same size as the warp threads, and the material looks the same along its length as along its width. Your first weaving will be coarser than this, but its texture should be even, and the weft should be either the same weight as the warp or a little heavier. Then, if the warp and weft threads do not interlace evenly, the warp threads should be set either closer together or further apart, until each crossing of warp and weft forms a square like that shown in Fig. 57 at **J**. Such a square is called a "Unit of Plain Weave."

The Steps in Weaving

Fig. 57 shows the steps to follow in making Plain Weave.

Step 1: Raise the first harness to lift the odd-numbered threads up; weave through from right to left with a shuttle

of weft thread, as shown at **C**. This makes the first row of weaving.

Step 2: Bring beater **D** forward, and push the first row tight. On a homemade loom a coarse comb may be used for this purpose. Push the beater back into place.

Step 3: Raise the second harness to lift the even-numbered threads up; weave a weft thread **E** through from left to right to form a second row. Turn the end of the first row back into the second row, as indicated by arrow **F**.

Step 4: Again bring the beater forward and pack this row tight. Push the beater back into place, as indicated by arrow **G**.

Step 5: Continue raising the first and second harnesses one after the other, weaving rows of weft thread, and beating them tight. You are making cloth in Plain Weave, just as threads are put together to make a linen handkerchief. The finished cloth at **H** consists of a number of units like that at **J**.

A Cross-Section of Weaving, Showing Take-up of Warp

A cross-section of weaving is shown in Fig. 57 in the small sketch at **K** at the lower right. This view is taken along a section cut parallel to the selvage. The circles represent cross-sections of weft, and the curving lines are two alternating warp threads. The way in which the rows of weft cause the warp threads to curve up and down clearly shows that there is a definite "take-up" or loss of warp yardage all along its length. This must be considered in planning all warps; extra yardage must be allowed accordingly, with more for heavier yarns and less for finer ones. There is also a take-up in the weft, and the sketch at **K** may also represent a similar cross-section going the other way of the cloth.

A lace runner in black and white. This method of weaving lace rows and designs is known as Brooks Bouquet and requires only a two-harness loom. Note the lace fringe made by hem-stitching at the start of the fabric.

15—Making a Two-Harness Table Loom

Equipment for Plain Weave

ALTHOUGH Plain Weave may be done on any kind of a loom, a simple two-harness loom with cord-heddles and stick-shuttles is adequate for learning how to weave. Two-harness looms may be either table looms or floor looms; a two-harness table loom is shown in Fig. 58. The manner of weaving is the same for either type. When one harness is raised, alternate warp threads are lifted, making the first shed; and, when the second harness is raised, the other threads are lifted, making the second shed.

A two-harness table loom produces hot mats, bookmarks, purses, runners, small towels and doilies, bags, and belts. A two-harness floor loom may produce all of these, as well as wider articles, such as rugs, bath mats, blankets, textured dra-

Fig. 58—A reliable two-harness table loom. The material being woven is a plaid in colors of carpet warp. A similar plaid design is shown in Fig. 53.

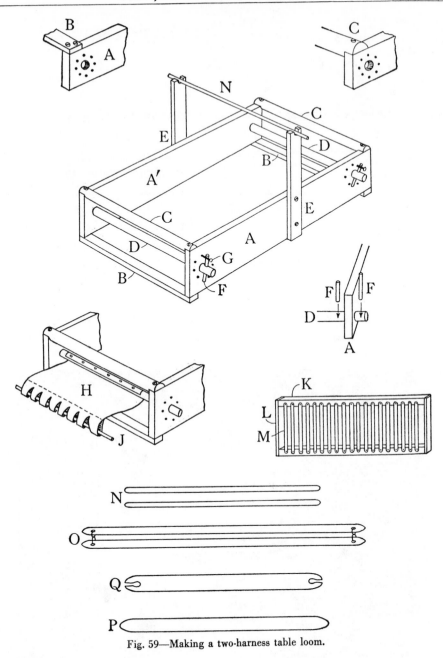

Fig. 59—Making a two-harness table loom.

pery or upholstery materials, table-cloths, doilies, napkins, aprons, and dress or suit goods.

Any loom produces articles as wide as the reed or beater used; and it produces articles that are fine or coarse, the texture depending on the sizes of the warp threads and weft threads and on the num-

ber of threads used in an inch of the reed.

A two-harness loom on which to learn the first principles of weaving is easy to make. The type shown in Figs. 54 and 59 is made from soft wood such as white pine or bass. Wood from boxes will do if the dimensions are adhered to. The tools needed are a hammer, a screw driver, a cross-cut saw, a brace and bit, and a coping saw. Screwing the parts together is preferable to nailing them.

Dimensions of Parts of Loom
(Fig. 59)

The parts of the loom, shown in Fig. 59, and their dimensions are given in the following list. The completed loom measures 14 in. wide, 22 in. long, and 3½ in. high. Unless otherwise stated, the material is soft wood.

Side-pieces, A and A′: Two pieces, ¾″ ×3½″×22″.

Front and back supports, B: Two pieces, ¾″×1½″×14″.

Front-beam and back-beam, C: Two beams 14″ long cut from broomsticks or dowels 1″ in diameter.

Warp-roller and cloth-roller, D: Two rollers 15″ long cut from the uniform parts of broomsticks or dowels 1″ in diameter.

Harness supports, E: Two pieces ¾″ ×1½″×8″.

Pegs to turn rollers, F: Two pegs 3″ long and two pegs 2″ long, all cut from ⅜″ doweling.

Nails to hold roller pegs, G: Two 6-penny, 8-penny, or 10-penny nails about 3″ long.

Screws: 16 screws 1¼″ long to put loom together.

Aprons, H: Two pieces of canvas or heavy unbleached muslin, 13″ wide and 14″ long.

Apron-rods, J: Two pieces of ⅜″ doweling, 12″ long.

Parts of reed:
Long bars, K: Two bars, ⅜″×⅝″×11″.
Side bars, L: Two bars, ⅜″×⅝″×4″.
Strips to make openings, M: Enough pieces, ⅛″×3⁄16″×3½″, made of thin cedar in cigar boxes, to go across reed.

Rods to lift up shed, N: Two rods 17″ long cut from ⅜″ doweling.

Lease-rods to separate threads, O: Two rods 12″ long cut from ⅜″ doweling.

Pick-up stick to find shed, P: One stick, ⅛″×1¾″×12″, made from a slat of a Venetian blind or from an orange crate.

Stick-shuttles for weaving, Q: Three pieces, ⅛″×1¾″×12″.

Directions for Making Loom
(Fig. 59)

In the right side-piece A, Fig. 59, bore two holes for the insertion of 1″ dowel pieces, D, 1¼ in. from each end and midway between the top and bottom of the board, as shown in the detail at the upper left. Also draw a circle 2¼ in. in diameter all around each hole, and bore 12 holes for ⅛″ dowels at uniform distances. The two 1″ holes provide for placing the cloth-roller and warp-roller, D; and the smaller holes around them are for inserting nails.

In the left side-piece A′, bore two 1″ holes at the same distance as those in the right piece, but bore them only halfway through the wood from the inside. These openings will hold the rollers but will leave the left side-piece smooth on the outside.

Screw the front and back supports B to the side pieces, putting two screws into each. Turn the sides upside down to do this, as shown in the detail at the upper left.

To add the front-beam and the back-beam C, saw down into both ends of the 14″ lengths of broomstick, making the saw-cuts as far as the center of the depth and ¾ in. in from the end, as in the detail at the upper right. Sandpaper the cut surfaces smooth; and screw these two beams on the tops of the sides with one screw at each end.

To add the cloth-roller and the warp-roller D, pass the 15″ lengths of broomstick through the 1″ holes, putting the rods in the holes at the right side and pushing them as far as possible into the half-holes at the left side. To provide for holding the rollers **D** in place, proceed as follows: Mark points on the rollers ¼ in. inside and outside of the right side-piece, as at the arrows in the detail at the right center; at these points, bore holes clear through the rollers for the ⅜″ dowel pegs **F**; insert the 2″ pegs in the holes to the left of piece **A** and the 3″ pegs in the holes at the right, and glue the pegs in place. The longer peg turns the roller **D** when it is desired to wind the warp or to change the tension. It also keeps the roller from slipping since it rests against a nail **G** placed in one of the holes to provide tension. The two pegs in one roller keep the roller in place but leave it free to turn.

In each harness support **E**, make a groove ¼ in. deep in the top. Screw these supports vertically in place on the sides of the loom, 12 in. from the front, using two screws in each.

The aprons **H**, which are placed at the front and back of the loom and to which the warp threads are tied, are made as follows: Cut two pieces of unbleached muslin 13 in. wide and 14 in. long, hem the sides, and form a 2-in. hem at one end of each apron, reducing the effective length to 12 in. Slit the hem of each apron into tabs 1 in. wide, as shown in the detail. Fold the other end of each apron under; and tack one apron across this fold to the cloth-roller at the front and tack the other apron to the warp-roller at the back.

Sandpaper the wood apron-rods **J**, and round off their ends, so that they will slip easily through the apron-loops.

To make the reed, first prepare the strips **M**, which are tacked to the long bars **K**. To keep the strips from splitting, make holes ¼ in. from the ends of each, using a fine awl. Tack the strips to the two long bars, allowing ¼ in. between the ends of strips and the outside edges of the bars. Draw a line on the bars as a guide, and bring the ends of the strips up to this line.

Taper the rods **N** slightly at the ends and sandpaper them smooth.

In the lease-rods **O** bore ⅛″ holes ½ in. from the ends; sandpaper the rods smooth; and tie them ½ in. apart with string.

Sandpaper the pick-up stick **P** smooth. This stick is used to find the new shed before attaching the cord-loops. It may also be used to pick up special threads to form a design. See Lessons 23 and 24.

Cut notches in the ends of the stick-shuttles **Q** with a coping saw, forming a half-circle 1 in. deep to make room for winding the threads. Sandpaper the sticks very smooth.

16—Making a Plan for Threading the Loom

Making a Plan for Setting up the Loom

NOW that we have made a real two-harness table loom with all parts complete, we understand better the purpose of each part. In Fig. 42 the parts of a table loom are pictured and named. The woolen jacket in Fig. 60, with its attractive pattern, was woven on a loom of this type, called a "wrap-around loom." The belt was woven in Plain Weave, and the tiny crosses were embroidered on it after the weaving was finished. Such simple designs as these may also be woven right into the fabric by the method described in Lesson 24.

We plan to thread the loom and put all its parts into action, while weaving many useful articles and developing beautiful effects of color and texture in hand-woven fabrics. Preparing the loom for action consists in winding the warp, beaming it, and threading it. These processes are called "Setting up the Loom" by some weavers and "Dressing the Loom" by others. Both terms are appropriate, for a loom that is properly threaded for use has attractive rows of warp threads stretched to an even tension, like so many violin strings. When these are arranged in perfect order, running parallel through the reed and glistening in their fibrous sheen, the loom is indeed "set up" or "dressed" for the occasion of starting to weave. And it is always a thrilling moment when the weaver starts his first article after a new threading of the loom.

Setting up a loom is not hard. The processes follow one another step by step, and there is pleasure in handling and arranging the threads carefully. The more perfect the warp, the better the weaving will be. A poor warp produces imperfect cloth throughout its entire length; bagginess is caused by alternate loose and tight sections, and many difficulties arise which result in loss of time while weaving. Dressing the loom takes time, but one's efforts are repaid by having the opportunity to create beauty during the untold hours of pleasure that follow. The dressing process may be regarded as a preparatory period full of anticipation for future work.

Ten Questions to Ask and Answer

Before dressing the loom, the weaver should consider the following ten questions:

(1) What is to be made—a dress scarf, a necktie, a purse, or a towel?

(2) Is the texture to be fine or coarse, and what colors are preferred?

(3) What kind of warp and weft will be used?

(4) How wide should the warp be?

(5) How close should the threads be set?

(6) How many warp threads will be needed?

(7) What length is desired for one article or for two or more articles?

(8) What is the total number of warp yards that will be necessary?

71

Fig. 60—Woolen jacket in Pattern Weaving, and belt in Plain Weave with embroidered
crosses.

(9) What is the total amount of weft that will be necessary? (This will be about the same as the amount of warp, for the weft covers the warp with about the same number of threads to an inch.)

(10) What will be the total cost of all the threads used to make one article?

The Warp Plan

Write down a list of the answers to the foregoing ten questions in a definite plan, as follows:

(1) Article: Scarf.

(2) Texture and color: Heavy; two shades of blue.

(3) Warp: Germantown yarn, dark blue. Weft: The same, light blue.

(4) Width in reed: 10 in.

(5) Threads per inch: 8 threads.

(6) Total number of threads: 80. (Multiply the number of inches of width in item 4 by the number of threads in 1 inch in item 5.)

(7) Length of warp for one scarf: 54 in. or 1½ yd (makes scarf 1¼ yd long after shrinking).

(8) Total number of warp yards necessary: 120 (80 threads 1½ yd long).

(9) Total number of weft yards necessary: 100 (less weft than warp is necessary since the material is not woven quite to the ends).

(10) Resulting cost of one scarf: 57 cents.

The cost of our scarf is computed as follows: The total yards necessary for warp and weft is 220 (120 warp yards plus 100 weft yards). The yardage in 1 pound

is 1500. Therefore, 220 yd is $\frac{220}{1500}$ lb or about 1/7 lb. Since Germantown costs approximately $4.00 per pound, we find that each scarf will cost about 1/7 × $4.00 or $.57.

Weaving Rules

The following rules will be found useful in weaving:

(1) To figure the number of threads across the warp, multiply the number in 1 inch by the width of the warp.

(2) To figure the total number of yards of warp necessary, multiply the number of warp threads (item 1) by the length of the warp.

(3) To figure the total number of yards of weft needed for 1 yard of woven material, multiply the distance across the warp by the number of threads needed to weave 1 inch; and multiply the result by 36 (the number of inches in a yard).

(4) To find the cost of your woven piece, add the total number of yards of warp and the number of yards of weft necessary to finish it. Divide this result by the total yardage in 1 pound of thread, and multiply the fraction thus obtained by the cost of a pound.

(5) To determine the best setting for your chosen thread, consult the thread chart in Lesson 35.

Threading and Weaving Plans

In addition to the warp plan, there must also be a threading plan and a weaving

Fig. 61—The MacArthur Plaid used for a bookmark. This beautiful green, black and gold plaid, the authentic Scotch Tartan of this family, is suitable for blankets, dress goods or scarves and neckties.

plan. For a two-harness loom these plans are simple to prepare, because the threading is simply an alternation between the two harnesses, and the weaving is usually a succession of the two sheds. However, if one has a striped warp (see Figs. 58 and 99), one must make a definite threading plan; and, if one wishes to weave stripes or different textures, one must think about choosing the colors and kinds of thread for the weft. Directions for making such plans will be presented in future lessons. A plaid bookmark made on a striped warp is shown in Fig. 61.

(Courtesy Mrs. Clay Aldridge)

Lace samplers. Left: Leno Lace with varying sizes of interlaced groups; threading similar to M's and O's. Right: Spanish Openwork, Leno Lace, Danish Medallion, Brooks Bouquet. (See Fig. 93 for directions.)

17—Preparing the Warp; Setting up the Loom

The Function of the Warping Board

TO WEAVE any great length of material on a loom, it is necessary to have longer warp threads than are required for a single small article. A short warp of 1 or 2 yards may be wound between posts, as shown in Fig. 55, but to measure off 3 or more yards, a **warping board** is used, as shown in Fig. 63. This is a square framework or cylindrical drum of wood with pegs arranged in such positions that a definite number of yards may

Fig. 62—This fabric is woven of Ribbon, Bouclé, Worsted, and Mohair.

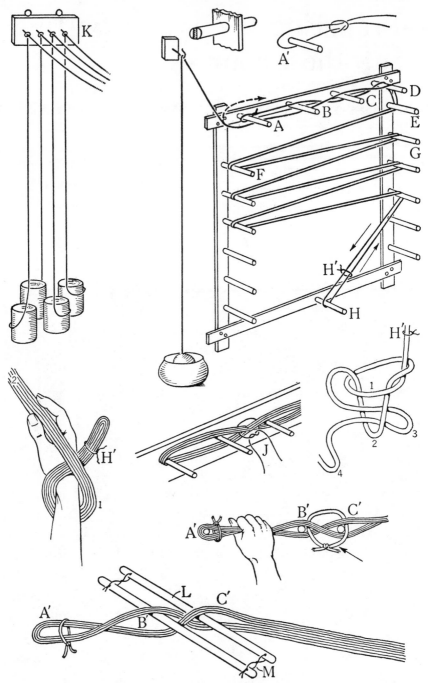

Fig. 63—Use of the warping board.

be measured off between them when winding the warp thread. The purpose of the warping board is to make it possible to lay in perfect order the required number of threads for the width of the cloth; to keep them in regular succession so that they will not tangle; and to make them the desired length. The method of warping is to find the length of one thread and then to make all the threads that length. The warping is accomplished on a framework by winding the yarn back and forth between the pegs arranged on the framework. If the warping device is a cylindrical drum, the threads are measured by wrapping them round and round the drum which measures a certain distance in circumference.

In an emergency a strong picture frame will serve as a base for a warping board; but it should have an extra layer of wood at least ½ in. thick screwed to the back on all four sides to give it enough body to hold the pegs. A strong new warping board may be made according to the following directions.

Materials for the Warping Board in Fig. 63

Sides of frame: Four boards ¾″ × 2½″ × 42″.

Pegs: Seventeen pegs, 1″ × 6″.

Bolts to fasten corners: Eight bolts, two at each corner.

Wedges to make pegs fast: Seventeen wedges, ⅛″ thick at back, 1″ wide, and 1½″ long.

How to Make the Warping Board (Fig. 63)

The warping board is a sturdy frame made of four bars of wood screwed together and braced at the four corners. These bars should be long enough to meet the weaver's requirements. They are bored with holes into which the warping pegs fit. The distance between the pegs from left to right is a definite length, such as 1 yard, to aid one in measuring the warp accurately. The pegs on the side bars are placed vertically from 5 to 7 in. apart, but the top one on the right at **E** is set 3 in. higher than the top one on the left at **F**, so that the warp threads run diagonally downward each time across.

Across the top there are four pegs, **A, B, C,** and **D**. The starting peg **A** is placed 10 in. to the left of peg **B**; pegs **B** and **C** are placed 9 in. apart at the center of the top bar; and peg **D** is 10 in. to the right of **C**. Pegs **B** and **C** form the most important part of the warping board, for between them a cross is made by which the threads are kept carefully in order for threading.

To make the frame, first cut and sandpaper the side bars; and bore holes for the pegs. Fasten the four bars together by inserting two bolts at each corner of the frame in the positions indicated. Put the pegs in the holes; place a wedge in a slit at the back of each peg, as shown in the detail at the lower left, and then drive the pegs firmly into their holes.

Stretching, or Measuring off, the Warp (Fig. 63)

Place the ball of warping thread in a basket beside the frame to keep it from rolling. Let the thread travel from the basket over a hook or through a screw-eye above the warping board at its left side, as shown in Fig. 63, which represents the conditions after a circuit has been completed. Tie the end of the thread to the peg **A**, using a slip knot, as indicated at **A′**. Carry the thread over **B**, under **C**, over **D** and **E**, across to and around **F**, and across to and around **G**; then proceed back and forth until you have as many yards of thread stretched as you wish, 5 yards or more usually being planned. Then carry the thread around the bottom peg **H** and reverse your direction until you reach **C**. Here pass **over C** where before you went **under**, and **under B** where before you went **over**. Pass under **A**, then over it. Repeat the first trip of the thread downward, going over **B**, under **C**, around **D** and **E**, etc. When you reach **H**, reverse. Make as many trips with your warp as you wish threads in the article you are making. Always go over **B** and under **C** on the trip down to **H**, and go over **C** and under **B** on the trip up from **H**. Try to keep the **tension** of the threads even. The tension is an important factor in stretching a warp. If all the threads are wound at the same tension, they will maintain similar lengths and will go on the warp roller easily and smoothly and without tangling. This is why it is found best for each person to finish his or her own warp, as different hands pull at different tensions.

Tying Warp Threads in Groups

When twenty threads have been measured off, keep them together as a group by tying a colored cord around them as shown in Fig. 63 at **J**. Slip the ends of the cord through the peg opening, and tie the ends together in a single overhand knot. Let the ends hang down in front of this first group until another twenty threads are ready; then bring the ends forward through openings made by these twenty threads at the pegs, and tie this second group with a single overhand knot. Continue warping groups of twenty threads and tying them together; it is easy to keep track of the count by means of these groups. The last group may have a few more or less threads to make the warp count come out right. When all are finished, fasten the last warp thread at either peg **A** or peg **H**.

Securing the Lease or Cross

The cross between pegs **B** and **C** is called a **portee-cross** or a **lease**. It keeps the threads in their proper order and prevents them from tangling. To keep this cross, proceed as follows: Before taking the warp from the frame, run a continuous heavy cord from the front through the opening at peg **B**, carry it around and out through the opening at peg **C**, and then tie its ends as shown in Fig. 63 at **B′** and **C′**. The smaller cords which tied the groups of twenty threads are no longer necessary; remove them carefully. Also tie cords around the warp threads at their reverse points, **A** and **H**, as shown in Fig. 63 at **A′** and **H′**.

Chaining off the Warp

To keep the warp from becoming tangled, wind it in a chain as it is removed from the pegs. This process is known as **chaining off the warp**. It is shown in the lower right of Fig. 63 at 1, 2, 3, and 4. The end of the warp as it is taken from the warping board is at **H′**. Loop the warp over your hand, as shown, and pull the long length marked 2 down through loop 1. Pull more warp, loop 3, through loop 2; then pull loop 4 through loop 3; and so on. This resembles making a crochet chain with a hook, but here the hand is used to make the chain loops. Chain all the warp off the board, removing the cross carefully with the hand, as shown at **A′**, **B′**, **C′**. Now slip the two flat lease-rods **L** through the openings at **B′** and **C′**, where the cross is maintained by the heavy cord; and fasten the rods together by tying the cords at their two ends. Use an extra knot to keep the rods ½ in. apart, as shown at **M**. These sticks are called **lease-rods** because they preserve the cross or lease. The warp is now ready to be put on the loom so as to provide thread for weaving. Some weavers tie the warp with cord at intervals along its length before chaining off, in order that the many threads will not tangle in case the chain slips off the pegs. This is a good precaution until you have become skilful in warping and chaining off.

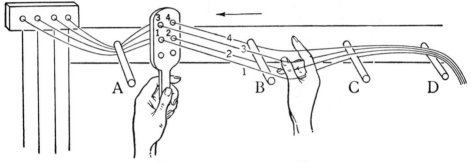

Fig. 64—Use of a warping-paddle.

Warping Several Threads Together

It is possible to **warp several threads at a time,** each group of four or six threads being treated as a single thread in the foregoing directions. To do this, place four to six spools at the base of the warping board, but have each thread first come through a separate screw-eye before being stretched on the board, as shown in Fig. 63 at **K.** This arrangement keeps them parallel and prevents their tangling. Measure off the groups of warp threads, chain off the warp as before described, and put the lease-rods through the cross. In threading into the reed, take the threads in the order in which they seem to lie, as in Fig. 65 at **G.**

The Use of a Warping-Paddle (Fig. 64)

Warping several threads at a time is not so satisfactory as warping them singly, unless one can keep the threads of a group in order by means of some device such as the **warping-paddle** shown in Fig. 64. Bring each thread through a hole of the paddle. Carry the paddle ahead of the new warp threads. In the illustration, the weaver is on the return trip upward. When arriving at pegs **B** and **C,** separate the threads with the fingers, as shown, placing the odd-numbered threads 1 and 3 over **B** and under **C** and placing the even-numbered threads 2 and 4 under **B**

and over **C.** On trips downward, turn the paddle and insert the fingers so that threads 1 and 3 again pass over **B** and under **C,** and threads 2 and 4 pass under **B** and over **C.** This arrangement gives the same alternation as that described for winding with a single thread. It is a good idea to number the threads at their respective holes in the paddle, as shown.

Threading and Beaming the Warp (Fig. 65)

Consult Figs. 65 and 66 for the following directions. Lay the lease-rods and the warp **A,** Fig. 65, on top of the front-beam **B** of the loom, with the ends of warp at **C** toward the reed. Cut the tying cord and spread out the threads. Then cut through the ends of the loops, thus making single ends of thread. Our next task is to thread the warp threads through the reed.

The Purpose of the Reed

The reed is a steel or wood device having separate openings or "dents" spaced at even distances, like the teeth of a comb, through which the successive warp threads are threaded. The warp threads are first taken through the reed **D,** Fig. 65, to spread them evenly apart. Later the reed is used to pack the weft threads tight, to make firm cloth. The reed is placed between the cloth beam and the heddle-bars or harnesses, as

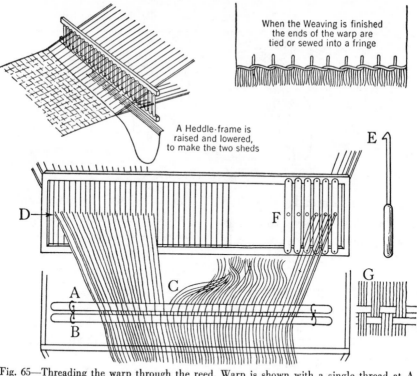

Fig. 65—Threading the warp through the reed. Warp is shown with a single thread at A and with groups at G. Section of a heddle-frame is shown at F, and a threading-hook is shown at E.

shown in Fig. 66. The warp threads are put through each opening of the reed in succession. The reed is sometimes called a **beater**; but in reality the reed is the comb-like device, while the beater is the frame that holds it and moves it forward and back to beat the cloth. The number of openings or dents that a reed has in 1 in. of its length gives the reed its name. Thus, a 10-dent reed has ten openings per inch; a 16-dent reed has sixteen openings per inch; and so on. **The number of dents controls the texture of the cloth.** If there are only a few dents per inch, the warp threads will be spread far apart and will weave up into a coarse texture; if there are more dents per inch, the texture will be closer and, therefore, finer.

Centering the Warp in the Reed

The weaver can make his cloth the full width of the reed or any width less than

this. The warp should always be threaded as near to the center of the reed as possible. To center the warp, count the total number of threads in your warp, such as 96 threads. Also count the number of dents per inch in your reed, such as 8 dents. Divide the total number, as 96, by the number per inch, as 8, to get the final width of your warp, or 12 in. If the reed is wider than this, such as 16 in., there will be 4 in. to spare; so leave 2 in. vacant at each side of the warp.

Threading the Warp Through the Reed; the Use of a Hook

This process is sometimes called "Drawing in." Start threading at one side. Put the first pair of warp threads as they come from the lease-rods in Fig. 65 at A through the dent at D where you have decided to start. Put the second pair of warp threads through the next dent. This

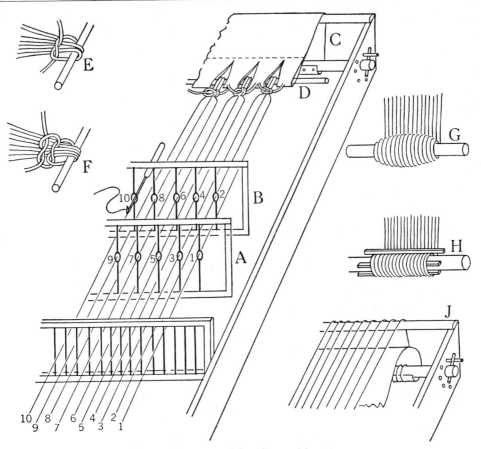

Fig. 66—Processes of threading and beaming.

A, B. Threading warp through harnesses.
C, D. Tying warp to warp-roller.
E, F. Square knot.
J. Winding warp.

G. Wrong way to wind, without sticks or paper.
H. Keeping tension even and roller smooth
   by use of warp-sticks or paper.

provides for double warp threads at the sides, making a stronger selvage. From now on, pass a single thread through each dent in succession until you come to the last two dents. Here, again, thread a pair of warp threads through to make this side like the first side. If warping fine threads for fine material, use single threads instead of pairs at the edges.

Two people sometimes work together, using a **threading-hook** like that shown in Fig. 65 at **E**. One person stands at the front of the reed and takes each thread in succession from the lease-rods—first a thread from over the first bar, then a thread from over the second bar, and so on. The second person stands in back of the loom and reed, and puts the threading-hook through the reed dent to receive the warp thread; then, as the first person places the thread over the hook, the second person draws it through to the rear. This makes the threading easier and saves time.

Threading the Warp Threads Through the Harnesses (Fig. 66)

After all the warp threads have been threaded through the dents of the reed, their ends lie in back of the reed but in front of the heddle-bars or harnesses. The next step is to thread them through the loops of the harnesses in the proper order. Take each thread in succession through loops on alternate harnesses. Put the first thread, No. 1 in Fig. 66, through the first loop on the first harness **A**. Put the second thread, No. 2, through the first loop on the second harness **B**. Continue thus, threading all the odd-numbered threads through the first harness, and threading all the even-numbered threads through the second harness. The threading-hook may be used for drawing the warp threads through the eyes or loops of the heddles, as shown in Fig. 66 for thread No. 10.

Tying Down, or Tying the Warp Threads to the Warp-Roller

The next step is to attach the warp threads to the warp-roller at the back of the loom, so that they can be wound around this for future use. Pull the threads through from the back of the harnesses to the back-beam **C**, Fig. 66, of the loom. Leave them hanging while you tie them in groups to the rod **D** that passes through the muslin loops on the warp-roller. Divide the warp into as many parts as there are loops to the muslin strip, and use a square knot to tie each group of threads to the rod at points between loops, as shown at **E** and **F**. Be careful to even up the ends of the threads before tying them. Then tie the first part of each knot, as at **E**, all across the warp; and finish the second part of the knot all across, as at **F**.

Now, from the front of the loom run the warp through your fingers or a comb until any tangles in the first 2 feet have been pulled through the warp and toward you. Then start turning the warp-roller and wind up this much of the warp, as indicated at **J**. Use the dowel or tension holder of the loom to prevent the roller from slipping. Continue to pull out any

tangles in the warp at the front of the loom. The chain will undo itself as you work.

After winding the warp thread once around, lay a heavy paper or stick over the row of tied knots and between them and the second round, so as to true up the warp and prevent an uneven start. See Fig. 66, **H** and **J**. The secret of good warping is to keep the warp firm, taut, and even.

Efficient Method of Working

Two people should work together. One person stands at the back of the loom, holds it in place, and winds the warp around the warp-roller when ready. The other person stands at the front of the loom, pulls out the tangles of the warp, and holds it taut while it is being wound. If there is no second person available, clamp the loom to a sturdy table.

Untangling the Warp

To free the warp of tangles, pull the warp out at the front of the loom while your partner holds the loom firm at the back. Untangle 2 or 3 feet at a time. Take half of the body of threads in each hand. Run the fingers or a coarse comb through the tangles of the first 3 feet, letting the warp slide between the thumb and the other fingers. Keep pulling and combing until the warp is smooth and free from tangles. Shaking the warp vigorously also helps.

Beaming the Warp, or Winding on Roller

Hold the warp with both hands, pulling it very taut while your partner winds up all the warp you have untangled on the warp-roller. This process is called **beaming**. When new tangles reach the reed, step out in front of the loom an-

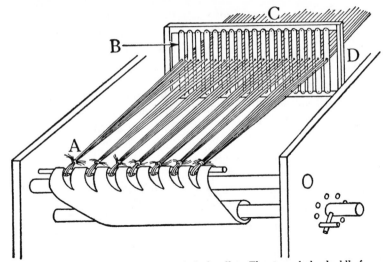

Fig. 67—Tying warp down to apron of cloth-roller. The use of the heddle-frame is shown.

other 3 feet, divide the warp between the hands, and proceed as before. In winding, always hold the warp tight with all the threads at the same tension.

Keeping the Warp-Roller Smooth

After a few rounds on the roller, the new warp is apt to cut down into former rounds, thus shortening some of the threads and causing lumps across the width of the warp or a curved warp like that shown in Fig. 66 at **G**. To avoid this, cut heavy wrapping paper the width of the roller, and wind this under each new round, as at **J**. Place more paper whenever necessary. Sticks measuring ⅛ in. thick and not less than ½ in. wide are also successfully used, as at **H**. These are called **warp-sticks**. Their purpose is to keep all the threads level and at the same length. When weaving on a bowed warp such as that shown at **G**, the shortened threads at the edges form tight selvages and ruin the finished product.

Tying Down to Front Roller or Cloth-Roller (Fig. 67)

Keep on pulling out warp and winding it up on the warp-roller until only 2 feet

of ends are left in front of the reed. Now separate these ends into as many groups as there are loops on the front muslin strip, pull out the remaining tangles, and tie the groups to the rod of the cloth-roller, as shown in Fig. 67 at **A**. This is called **tying down** the warp.

Try to pull each group to the same tension. Use the square knot, shown in detail in Fig. 66 at **E** and **F**, in tying the warp threads to both the warp-roller and the cloth-roller. It is easily untied so as to loosen or tighten any warp threads that are not at the same tension as the others. Tie the first part of the knot all across the warp; test the tension; tighten any loose sections; then finish with the second part of the knot. The loom completely threaded and beamed and ready for work should look like the diagram in Fig. 67.

The Use of a Heddle-Frame or Combination Reed and Harnesses (Fig. 67)

An ancient device, used in place of two harnesses, is known as a "Heddle-Frame." This consists of a frame with lengthwise openings, called **slots**, alternating with holes made at the centers of the heddle-strips, as shown in Fig. 67 at **B**. The odd-numbered warp threads are threaded through the holes, and the even-numbered ones are passed through the slots. When the frame is raised, the odd-numbered warp threads in the holes are lifted, forming shed No. 1. When the frame is lowered, the odd-numbered threads are also lowered while the even-numbered warp threads in the slots are left raised above the others, forming shed No. 2. A heddle-frame is sometimes called a **slot-and-hole heddle**.

Making a heddle-frame is a clever way of providing for the two sheds used in two-harness weaving; and, if its construction is strong, it may also be used as a beater. It is especially useful if one is constructing one's own loom, for this single device takes the place of three items on a regular two-harness loom, i.e., the first and second harnesses and the reed.

Threading the warp through a heddle-frame is shown in Fig. 65 at **F**, and a complete heddle-frame is shown in Fig. 67. A heddle-frame is quite a wonderful little contrivance, really being a loom in itself. One can use it as a loom in belt-making by just threading a few warp threads alternately through the slots and holes and stretching the warp between two firm posts. The weaving is done merely by lifting and lowering the heddle and weaving weft threads through the successive shed openings.

Making a Heddle-Frame (Fig. 67)

In a wooden heddle-frame, the heddles are narrow strips of wood, as shown in Fig. 67 at **B**, fastened with brads to two horizontal bars **C** and connected at the ends by two vertical side-pieces **D**. The best kind of wood for making the heddle-frame is soft wood, as pine, basswood, or cedar. It is possible to obtain pine from boxes for the bars, and cedar from cigar boxes makes excellent heddle-strips.

Dimensions of Heddle-Frame

Heddle-Frame for the Large Table Loom, 14 in. Wide, Shown in Fig. 59:
Make two long bars $3/8'' \times 5/8'' \times 11''$. Connect them with two side bars $3/8'' \times 5/8'' \times 4''$.

Heddle-Frame for a Small Table Loom, 8 in. Wide:
Make two long bars $3/8'' \times 5/8'' \times 6''$. Connect them with two side bars $3/8'' \times 5/8'' \times 4''$.

Heddles or Strips:
The strips are the same size for both looms, and measure $1/8'' \times 3/16'' \times 3 1/2''$. Make as many as needed, one strip for each two warp threads.

Method of Making Heddle-Frame

Bore holes 1/4 in. from the ends of each strip **B**, Fig. 67, to prepare for nailing with brads. This prevents the wood from splitting when the brad is inserted. At the middle of each strip make a hole $1/16$ to $1/8$ in. in diameter with an awl, a red-hot nail, or a small bit. Make a 1/8-in. hole, if possible to do so without splitting the wood, as this will give more room for the play of your warp threads. These threads should be well twisted and strong so that the wood will not cause them to fray in passing back and forth over them. Sandpaper all the heddle-strips before tacking them to the bars.

Draw a line in the middle of each bar **C**; and, in nailing on the heddles, let the ends come just to this line. If the long bars **C** tend to split when nailing on the heddles, plan to divide the brads into two rows, as was done for the rug frame in Fig. 37. There should be a good $1/16$ in. of space between each two heddles to form the slot. When all the heddles are in place, brace the ends of the long bars with the side bars **D**. Sandpaper the heddle-frame thoroughly; there must be no roughnesses.

Threading the Warp Through the Heddle-Frame

Thread the warp threads alternately through each hole and slot of the heddle-frame, as shown in Figs. 65 and 67. If desired, thread double threads through at the sides. It is thought by some weavers that this insures a stronger edge. Take the first pair of threads and thread them through a hole, as in Fig. 65 at **F**. Take the next pair of threads and thread them through the following slot between two heddle-strips. Thread the next single thread through the next hole, the next one through the next slot, and so on, alternating between holes and slots all across the warp. Thread pairs of warp threads through the last slot as well as through the last hole. The threads come in regular succession from the lease-rods, as at **C**, and they are taken in regular order—first a thread from over the first lease-rod, then from over the second, and so on. Do not change this succession; otherwise, the warp threads will cross and tangle as they come forward, causing trouble in weaving. If you have wound your warp with groups of threads, take each thread as it seems to come, **G**.

When all the warp threads have been threaded through the heddle-frame, they are ready to be tied in groups to the apron-rod on the warp-roller at the back of the loom. Follow the same directions as previously given for tying down and winding the warp threads around the warp-roller, as shown in Fig. 66, and for tying them to the apron-rod of the cloth-roller at the front of the loom, Fig. 67.

Weaving with the Heddle-Frame

First lift the heddle, raising every other thread. Then pass a thread through this opening to make a row of weaving. Next lower the heddle-frame to make the alternate warps rise, and then bring the heddle-frame forward. This locks the weaving row already there, and another row of weaving can be made in the new opening.

To weave, simply lift the heddle, weave in a row, lower the heddle, weave in another row, and continue. After each row, press the heddle-frame forward to make firm cloth.

Heddle-Frame Versus Reed

Today steel reeds replace the wood heddle-frame of the first weavers. This both distributes the warp threads and beats up the finished rows of cloth. The way the warp threads are distributed in the reed determines the texture of the cloth.

Plain Weave Texture: Warp-Face, Weft-Face

If the warp and weft are well balanced with about as many weft rows per inch as there are warps to the inch, the cloth will be very even, and a Plain Weave, like burlap and linen, will be the result.

If the warps are set so close that the weft or filler is entirely or nearly covered, the texture is called "Warp-Face." (see page 110).

If the warps are set so far apart that the filler sinks down between them and covers the warp, the texture is known as "Weft-Face." Tapestries are woven in this manner (see Figs. 90 and 92).

18—Preparing the Weft

THE PREPARATION of the warp thread for the loom was described in Lesson 17. It is equally important to know **how to prepare the weft thread** for the weaving process. Moreover, the quality of the fabric woven depends as much on one's choice of thread to weave with and its relation to the warp as on one's preparation of a firm, smooth warp.

Comparative Sizes of Warp and Weft Threads

1. The Tabby Weft. In general the Tabby Weft, used for Plain Weave and for binding in pattern threads, should be of the same weight as the warp, or very little heavier.

2. The Pattern Weft. The Pattern-Weft threads, woven in addition to the Tabby, should be fairly soft in texture and heavier than the warp threads or the Tabby. They thus serve their purpose of filling in the pattern spaces and making a design that shows up well against the background Tabby.

How Threads Are Wound (Figs. 68 to 71)

1. Warp Threads. Threads for warping come wound on spools, tubes, or cones of various sizes containing anywhere from 1 ounce to several pounds of thread. Some types of spools and cones are shown in Fig. 68. If warping by the chain method, the weaver uses from one to eight large spools, drawing off as much thread as he needs. If warping by the sectional method, he requires more spools of smaller size. In the **sectional method of warping**, used for more extensive weaving, the warp-roller is divided into sections, and each section is wound with thread directly from a rack or "creel." On the creel there are arranged as many spools of thread as

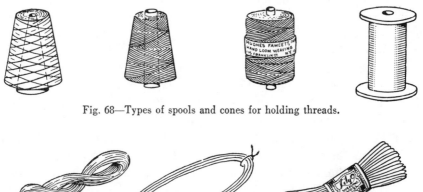

Fig. 68—Types of spools and cones for holding threads.

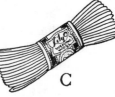

A   B   C

Fig. 69—Skein winding.

86

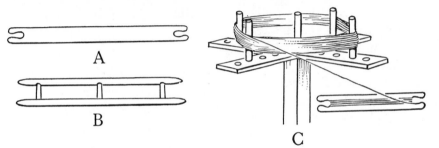

Fig. 70—Winding thread on stick-shuttle.

are required for each 2-in. section of warp. This method is shown in Figs. 103 and 104.

2. Weft Threads. Threads for the weft may be taken from large spools like those in Fig. 68; from smaller 2-oz or 4-oz spools; from balls; or from **skeins** like that in Fig. 69 at **A**. The skein, unwound and tied at several points to keep it from tangling, is shown at **B**. A commercial skein is shown at **C**. From the skein or cone or ball of thread, the weft thread is wound on a **stick-shuttle**, shown in Fig. 70 at **A** or **B**, or on a **cop** or **bobbin**,

shown in Fig. 71 at **A**, **B**, or **C** and used in a **throw-shuttle D**. If winding from a skein, place the skein around an adjustable **skein-winder** shown in Fig. 70 at **C**; cut the fastenings and draw the thread directly from the rotating skein to the shuttle or cop.

Types of Shuttles Used for Weft

There are three types of shuttles used for holding weft thread.

1. Simple Stick-Shuttle. The stick-shuttle shown in Fig. 70 at **A** is made of a bar of wood from ⅛ to ¼ in. thick, with

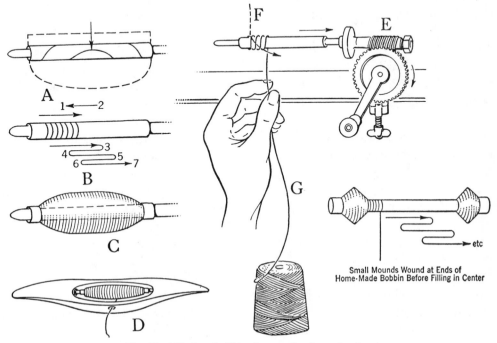

Small Mounds Wound at Ends of
Home-Made Bobbin Before Filling in Center

Fig. 71—Winding bobbin for use in throw-shuttle.

openings at the ends. Wind the thread back and forth between the ends. Stick-shuttles are of many lengths and widths.

2. Rug-Shuttle. The rug-shuttle, shown in Fig. 70 at **B**, is used for large amounts of heavy weft. Rug-shuttles look like two enlarged stick-shuttles joined by cross bars. They measure from 1 ft to 3 ft in length. Tie the end of the weft thread with a slip knot to an end bar of the shuttle. Wind the thread around the end bars to fill the inside of the shuttle.

3. Throw-Shuttle. The throw-shuttle, shown in Fig. 71 at **D**, is a boat-shaped device containing a bobbin for holding thread placed on a steel pin or heavy steel wire inserted in the shuttle opening. From the bobbin, the thread comes through an opening at the front of the shuttle (the side with the outward curve); and, as it is used, it unreels gradually. Weaving with a throw-shuttle is by far the quickest method, and one who weaves a good deal should be equipped with several of them. The bobbin or container of thread is also called a **cop** or **quill.**

The Use of a Bobbin-Winder

To wind the small spools, cops, or bobbins just described, it is necessary to use a **bobbin-winder**, shown in Fig. 71 at **E.** The tube-like cops or bobbins are placed on the steel rod of the winder. This rod is tapered, being thickest at the right near the arrow. By shoving the cop toward the heavier end in the direction of the arrow, it is held tightly in place during its winding.

A bobbin-winder may be made by having a steel rod soldered into the end of a rotating sander or some such device. The steel rod may also be attached to the bobbin-winder of a sewing machine; or may be inserted into an electric cake mixer or an electric fan.

Making Cops or Bobbins

Wooden bobbins are available at some weaving supply houses. However, bobbins can be made at home out of wrapping paper. As indicated in Fig. 71 at **A** by the dotted lines, cut the paper in half-moon shape, with the straight edge of the half-circle measuring 1 in. less than the length of the opening in the throw-shuttle. Roll the half-circle tightly around the rod of the bobbin-winder, with the left side of the paper about ½ in. from the small end of the rod, and paste down the end of the paper, as shown at the arrow at **A.**

Winding Bobbins or Cops for Use in Shuttles

To wind a bobbin or cop, place it on the rod of the winder, as shown in Fig. 71 at **E,** and shove it toward the thicker end so that it is held firmly in place. Carry the thread to be wound upward from its spool. Bring its end up in back of the cop at the left side, as indicated by the dotted line at **F.** Turn this short end down over the front of the cop and wind the long end around it several times to secure it firmly in place. Now start winding the cop by turning the handle of the bobbin-winder clockwise.

Before filling a home-made paper cop or bobbin, when beginning to wind, build up a small mound or pyramid of thread ½ in. away from the left end and from ¼ in. to ⅜ in. high. Now carry the thread rapidly over to the right end and build up a similar pyramid. These two mounds at the ends take the place of the raised parts at the ends of a wooden cop.

In filling either a wooden cop or a home-made one with built-up ends, the course of the thread on the bobbin should be guided gradually at first from left to right but with back and forth progres-

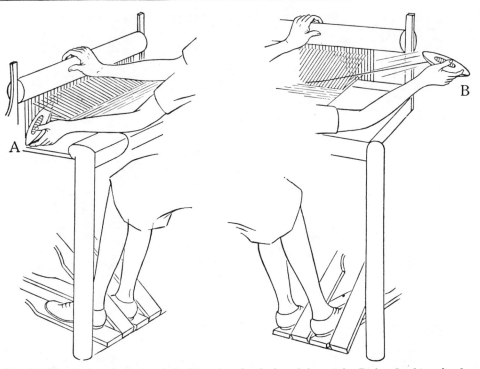

Fig. 72—The rhythm of weaving. Left: Throwing shuttle from left to right. Right: Catching shuttle in right hand and beating cloth with left hand.

sion, as shown in Fig. 71 at **B**, much as a sewing-machine bobbin is wound. Go forward ½ in. to point 1, then back ¼ in. to point 2, then forward ½ in. to 3, back ¼ in. to 4, and so on, until the right end of the cop is reached at 7. Reverse at least ¼ in. from that end of the cop. Then repeat the process to the left—forward ½ in., back ¼ in., etc. As the bobbin starts to fill, do not wind out to the ends, but make the bobbin taper off, as at **C**. In winding a bobbin, hold the thread in the left hand between the thumb and the forefinger and fairly close to the cop, as at **G**. Maintain a slight tension when winding, for the bobbin should be fairly firm and tight when finished. A finished bobbin is shown at **C**.

To Insert Bobbin in Shuttle

The easiest way to insert a wound bobbin in a shuttle is as follows: Take out the

steel pin of the shuttle. Set the bobbin in the opening with the thread coming toward you from **under** the bobbin, as shown in Fig. 71 at **D**. Thread its end through the hole on the rounded front side of the shuttle.

Now insert the steel pin in place, passing it through the center of the cop and into holes at the ends of the wooden cavity; shove it first into the end having the spring, and then adjust it into position at the other end.

How to Use a Shuttle

The use of a stick-shuttle is shown in Fig. 65. One simply inserts the stick-shuttle through the open shed, unwinding enough material for each row to give sufficient length for this row.

In the use of a stick-shuttle there is a bit of delay in unwinding the weft. In using the throw-shuttle, however, one can

Fig. 73—Use of loom bench.

throw and catch it rhythmically without stopping, for the thread unreels itself from the bobbin smoothly as one weaves.

To weave with a throw-shuttle, hold the shuttle in the cup of the left hand, as shown in Fig. 72 at A, while the right hand pushes the beater back after having beaten down the last row. Give a slight push to the shuttle by moving the wrist of the left hand, and send it through the opening to the other side. Catch the shuttle in the cup of the right hand, as at B, drawing it up until the weft thread comes against the left selvage. Leaving the thread on a slant, bring the beater forward with the other hand; then change the shed. Reverse the process, throwing with the right hand and catching with the left.

If desiring a more closely packed fabric, give a second beat after changing the shed and before putting in the next row; thus, throw, catch, beat, change the feet, and then beat again.

Weaving to a Rhythm

Both the stick-shuttle and the throw-shuttle may be used on either a table loom or a floor loom. However, weaving with a throw-shuttle on a floor loom is the most efficient method of all, for the feet change the shed while the shuttle is transferred rapidly from hand to hand without interruption. The repeated throwing and catching of the shuttle row after row, with the recurring thump of the beater, produces a rhythm in the weaving. To acquire this rhythm is a delightful experience. It causes a feeling of health and well-being, for it increases bodily activity; and it also improves the quality and speed of the weaving. Some weavers sing at the loom, their songs keeping time to the beat. Others chant a little rime, like the following:

> Throw and catch, firmly beat,
> Hold the beater, change the feet.

The Fell of the Cloth

The fell of cloth is the horizontal line formed by the last weft thread between the finished cloth and the unwoven warp.

If the beater is not hung so as to lie parallel to the front-beam, the fell will be on a slant. To keep your beater true, always grasp it at the center.

Position at the Loom

One should use a loom bench or comfortable chair while weaving. Such a bench is shown in Fig. 73. The height from which to weave depends on the weaver's choice, but in general the arms should slant slightly downward from the elbows, so that one can throw and catch the shuttle with ease; and the knees should be a little below the level of the thighs.

The loom bench shown in Fig. 73 was made in the carpentry shop. It is adjustable; the pegs holding the lower shelf are nearer to the ends of the sides than are those holding the upper shelf. Therefore, by turning it over, one can increase the height. Also, the seat has an opening on the inside which serves as a storage box for weaving supplies. The enterprising weaver shown here has woven her own blouse and apron and helped in the weaving of the draperies for her home.

19—The Handling of Threads

THE KNOTS USED IN WEAVING

Purposes of Knots

AN IMPORTANT consideration in the use of thread, cord, or twine is the tying of knots. There are many kinds of knots used for different purposes. In general, they may be divided into two main groups: (1) **knots meant to hold** and not to pull out even when subjected to strain; (2) **knots which are tied temporarily** with the intention of undoing them, and which will pull out easily if given just the right twist. In weaving we use knots to fasten single threads or groups of threads together. We need them in warping, in counting off, in attaching short lengths of weft, in mending broken warp ends, in tying treadles to the loom, and for other purposes. The weaver should learn the most useful knots, and should practice making them until he can do so quickly and easily. Various types of knots are shown in Fig. 74.

The Square Knot

The **square knot**, shown in Fig. 74, No. I, is a knot which becomes tighter and tighter if pulled on in a certain way, but which may also loosen if treated otherwise. It is, therefore, very useful in attaching threads temporarily, but should never be relied upon for safe tying. It may be used to fasten any two threads together to make a longer thread. It is especially useful in attaching weft threads in winding; for the knots may later be loosened when necessary to splice the threads. It should never be used to fasten two warp threads together, for the rubbing of the reed against the knot tends to loosen it.

To make a square knot, proceed as shown in Fig. 74, No. I, at **A** and **B**.

Step 1: Working from right to left, turn one end **A** first over, then under, and again over the other end **B**, as indicated by the arrow.

Step 2: Reverse end **A** and bring it back in the opposite direction. This end is now labeled **A′** and is now brought under, over, and then under the other end **B′**, as shown.

To **tighten** this knot, pull on the ends **A′** and **B′** at the same time, as indicated by the two arrows in the sketch for Step 2.

Step 3: To **loosen** this knot, pull on ends **B** and **B′** together or on ends **A** and **A′** together; i.e., pull on the two ends of the same thread. In doing this, hold one end in each hand and pull the thread taut. The knot will straighten out, as shown in Step 3 at **B** and **B′**; and one thread, as **A**, may be shoved off the other thread, as **B**.

The fact that the knot separates in this way is what makes it unsafe for use in mending warps. This is the knot used by stage performers in shaking handkerchiefs apart that seemed to be tightly tied together. Practice making this knot, first with two coarse threads of contrasting color and then with two threads of the same color. Practice tightening and loosening it.

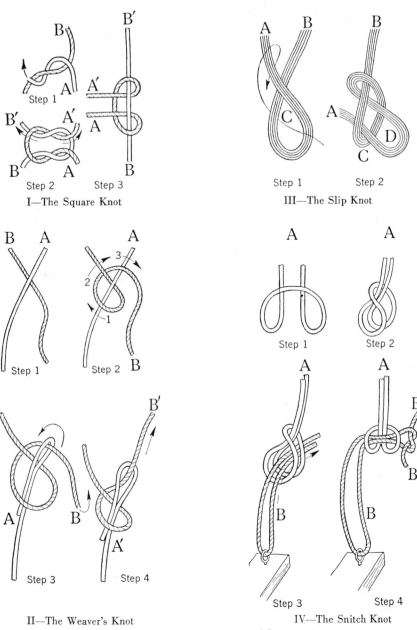

I—The Square Knot

III—The Slip Knot

II—The Weaver's Knot

IV—The Snitch Knot

Fig. 74—The knots found most useful in weaving.

The Weaver's Knot

The **weaver's knot**, shown in Fig. 74, No. II, is sometimes said to be the smallest and tightest knot that it is possible to make. It is known in knotting as "a bowline on a bight." It is used for fastening broken warp threads together on thou-sands of looms throughout the world, both in factories and in homes. It cannot be untied easily, once it has been tightened.

Step 1: Place the short end **A** of the strand to be mended from left to right across the short end of the new strand **B**. Hold these two ends at their intersection between the thumb and forefinger of the left hand.

Step 2: With the right hand turn the long end of **B** from right to left over the long end of **A** (arrow 1), under its own short end (arrow 2), and over the short end of **A** (arrow 3).

Step 3: With the right hand turn the short end of **A** down over both parts of **B** and into the opening, as shown. The short end of **A** now lies against its own long end.

Step 4: Hold the two parts of **A** together with the left hand, as at **A'**. Pull upward on the long end of **B** with the right hand, as at **B'**. Do not touch any other parts of the knot. This knot will tighten firmly.

The Slip Knot

The **slip knot**, shown in Fig. 74, No. III, is correctly named for, while it holds temporarily, it may be pulled apart in an instant. We learned in Fig. 63 how to start winding a warp by fastening the end of one or more warp threads to the first peg with a slip knot. This knot may also be used in starting belts, in fastening threads to stationary posts, or in attaching any thread end to a peg or bar.

The slip knot is also used to tie groups of warp threads together to prevent them from slipping back through the reed or harness after threading. For this purpose tie the knot as shown in Fig. 74, No. III.

Step 1: Loop the short end or ends **A**, to be kept from slipping, back over the long end or ends **B**, forming a loop **C**.

Step 2: Insert the right hand upward through loop **C**, grasping **A** midway between its end and loop **C** (see the arrow). Bring **A** down through loop **C** but do not pull it completely through. Instead form a second loop, **D**.

To open the knot quickly so as to free the ends for threading, just pull on the ends at **A**; the knot will then come out.

The Snitch Knot

The **snitch knot**, shown in Fig. 74, No. IV, is used to tie treadles to harnesses. It is made with two looped strands of strong cord, preferably Jacquard Twine. The value of the knot lies in the fact that, by adjusting the two ends of the lower cord, the distance between treadles and harnesses may be shortened or lengthened in an instant.

Step 1: Make a loop of one cord **A** at its center. Attach its two ends to the lower part of a harness or to a **lam** so that the loop hangs downward.

Step 2: Turn the loop back upon itself, bringing the two parts together like two half-hitches, as shown.

Step 3: Slip the other cord **B** through the screw-eye of the treadle. Bring its two ends up through the turned loop of the first cord, as shown by the arrow.

Step 4: Turn the two ends of cord **B** around each other in an overhand knot, as shown at **B'**.

To lessen the distance from harness to treadle, pull up on the two ends **B'**. To increase the distance, loosen ends **B'** and pull back on the lower loop of **B** to make it longer. Then tighten ends **B'** again.

PIECING OR SPLICING WEFT THREADS; HANDLING COLOR CHANGES

Do not worry about the mending of broken warp threads or the splicing of weft threads. There are neat ways of doing both. Simply practice each method until you become proficient and enjoy the process. Time is saved and the weaving

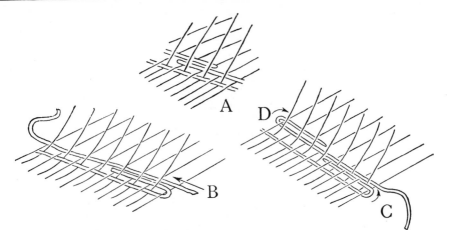

Fig. 75—Piecing weft threads.

is improved by watching one's threads closely and piecing or splicing them as soon as necessary.

Piecing Weft Threads

There are in general three instances in which the weaver needs to splice weft threads together. These are shown in Fig. 75.

1. When an old end gives out while weaving, one must add a new end to it.

2. When a knot occurs in the weft because two ends were joined by a square knot when winding, the ends must be taken apart and spliced together through the shed.

3. When it is necessary to change weft colors, one must know how to make the transition smoothly.

Regular Splicing of Weft Ends Through the Warp Shed

A regular overlapping of old and new weft ends at any point across the warp was shown in Fig. 31. This same method may be used, as shown in Fig. 75 at **A**, for any soft weft where the overlapping of the two ends will not cause a lump or unevenness, or where this unevenness does not mar the desired texture. It is all

right for linen thread, where there are apt to be nubby places, and this extra raised portion is in character. It is all right for soft wool yarn, but one should tear the ends of wool, instead of cutting them, so that they taper down gradually. It is not so good for cotton, silk, or synthetic threads, where the extra thickness at the splice is apt to stand out noticeably against the smooth texture.

Piecing Ends at Selvages

The best point at which to piece threads or to change colors is at the selvage. Bring the old end into the new shed for about an inch. Add the new thread beside it, this thread to proceed in the same direction through the same shed, as indicated in Fig. 75 at **B** by the arrow. Leave ½ in. to 1 in. of the new end projecting beyond the selvage. After several rows, trim off this end; it is not necessary to turn it in, since it already overlaps the old end which is turned in and covers the selvage at this point.

Piecing Heavy Wefts

If weaving with heavy weft yarn, such as rug yarn, cut or tear off half of the thickness of the old end for an inch or

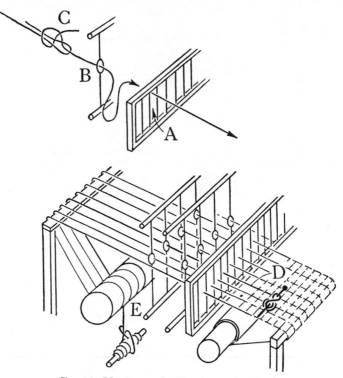

Fig. 76—Mending and adding warp threads.

so. Do the same with the new; then lap the half thicknesses. The piecing will thus be made without adding unattractive bulk to the texture. See Fig. 83 **F, G.**

Changing Colors or Textures

When it is necessary to finish one color before starting another color or kind of thread, the weaver tries to make a clean cut line between them. To do this, keep the last shed of the old color open, while bringing the old thread end around the last warp and back into the same shed, as shown in Fig. 75 at **C.** Change the shed. Start the new color in the new shed but at the opposite selvage. Carry its end around the last warp thread and back in the same shed, as at **D.** Change the shed again and proceed with the new color in regular weaving.

In this method of starting a new thread at the opposite selvage, one is obliged to reverse the direction of the weaving. For instance, if one has been weaving from right to left on the first shed, one now finds one's self weaving left to right on this same shed. However, this makes no difference in the cloth and the weaver can remember the new direction until the color changes once again and the old direction is established.

HANDLING WARP DIFFICULTIES; MENDING BROKEN WARP ENDS

Mending Broken Warp Threads

If a warp thread breaks, mend it by inserting a new warp thread at this point. This must also be done if a knot comes forward in the warp. Simply cut out the knot and add a new smooth thread at this point. Follow the method now to be described.

Replacing a Broken Warp Strand

Be sure to find the right place to insert the mending thread; otherwise, it will cross the other warps, interfere with the shed, and keep breaking. Find the opening A, Fig. 76, where the dent of the reed is empty. Spread out the threads on each side to locate the empty heddle B. Put a length of new warp through this heddle and tie it to the broken end of the warp at the back of the loom with a weaver's knot, as at C. This knot is small and may come through the reed later on without further trouble. If not, you can again add a new thread as the knot comes forward and thus push it further back and out of the way. Thread the new end through the empty heddle-eye and the proper dent of the reed.

Tying Down the New Warp End

If the old end is still extending from the cloth at the front, loop it around the new end and insert both ends into a row of weaving—one end to the right side and the other to the left side. If the old end is gone, bring the new end forward on the cloth as in Fig. 76 at D and pin it down, wrapping the end around the pin several times, as shown. After taking the material from the loom, thread the new end into the material with a needle.

Inserting an Additional Warp Thread

If the warp has a missing thread end, or if you wish to add a strand of a different color or texture to a warp, wind a new thread on a bobbin, as in Fig. 76 at E, wrap it twice around the warp-roller, bring the end forward at the desired point, thread it through the heddle and reed, and pin it down as at D. Weave as far as desired over the added thread; re-move it when necessary. When the added strand is a color thread or texture thread, add it at the same point as a base thread and through the same heddle and eye. This basic warp thread remains when the added thread is removed.

TAKING FINISHED MATERIAL FROM THE LOOM

As the weaving progresses, the finished material may be either cut from the loom or wound around the cloth-roller. It is not necessary to cut off each piece. Tying the cut warp threads down again for the next piece of weaving takes a good bit of time and also wastes one's thread. Furthermore, it is difficult to get the tension just right without considerable effort. The best plan is to cut off only when necessary and then to conserve as much thread as possible. There are several methods to use.

Method No. 1: Cutting off Finished Goods as Far as Woven

How to Cut off the Material. Before cutting, loosen the tension of the loom. Also bring plenty of extra warp thread forward to prevent the warp from slipping back through the reed. Use a sharp pair of scissors and plan to cut straight across the cloth between the last row of the weft and the next to the last row, to get a perfectly straight line.

If leaving fringe, to provide for even fringe ends lay the finished cloth 3 or more inches beyond the front-beam of the loom and cut square along the straight edge of the beam.

Cut only about 1 inch of warp first. Then tie this inch of cut warp into a slip knot in front of the reed. This is done to prevent the warp from slipping back through the reed.

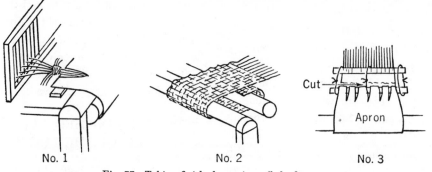

No. 1   No. 2   No. 3

Fig. 77—Taking finished weaving off the loom.

Now cut entirely across the warp, but at the other selvage again grasp the last group of warp threads in the hand to prevent them from slipping, and tie them into a slip knot. Next tie all the warp threads into groups, using the slip knot.

How to Tie Down the Cut Warp Ends. In tying down, be sure that all threads are at the same tension and use the square knot and the method shown in Figs. 66 and 67; this method is also shown in Fig. 77, No. 1. Test the threads carefully for tension. Retie any group that is not taut enough. In starting to weave again, bring the warp threads together by weaving several rows with coarse yarn or thin smooth sticks. In this method one loses considerable warp thread.

Method No. 2: Weaving Extra Yardage to Leave on Loom

Weave extra material on the warp in advance of what you need, as shown in Fig. 77, No. 2. Then cut below this extra length, tuck the cut cloth under the end of the apron, and wrap it with the apron around the cloth-roller. This extra length

then acts as an additional apron to hold future material. Be sure to lay the cut piece around the roller so that its edge lies straight along the roller and is parallel to the front-beam. Then wind the material smoothly without wrinkles.

In order to be able to cut accurately on a straight line between two pieces, weave two rows of colored thread between them to guide the eye. Cut between the two rows. In this method one loses no warp thread whatsoever.

Method No. 3: Using a Stick to Aid in Tying Down

Instead of weaving a full yard of extra material, weave an extra full inch of fabric, and then weave in a stick and follow this with two more rows of weft only. Now release the tension on the warp. Cut cloth off in a straight line between the added inch and the finished goods, as at the arrow in Fig. 77, No. 3. Then tie the stick down to the apron-rod with strong cords, as shown in Fig. 77, No. 3. In this method one loses only an inch or so of warp.

(Courtesy of Creative Crafts, East Berlin, Pa.)

A weaver maintains correct position and rhythm of movement while weaving a plaid necktie on a striped warp tied down at perfect tension.

20—Two-Harness Design Methods

STRIPES AND PLAIDS

MANY variations are possible on a two-harness loom, using Plain Weave or Tabby as a basic texture. One can warp the loom with any succession of colors, forming beautiful **stripes in the warp;** one can weave stripes across plain warp, thus forming **stripes in the weft;** one can weave stripes across a striped warp, thus forming **plaids.** One can use heavy threads between fine threads in both warping and weaving, thus forming **texture lines.** One can also weave designs in color on the background of Plain Weave by laying additional design threads in between the regular rows of Tabby. This is called **"Laid-in Weaving."** A number of variations of Plain Weave are shown in Figs. 78, 79, 80, 81 and 82. One can do so many interesting things with Plain Weave that it would take a large book to describe them all.

Directions for some of the most useful variations are given in this book. Later, the reader can learn others, such as leaving spaces in the warp to form mesh work, twisting the warp to form laces, making loops of the weft, and sewing embroidery stitches over the warp.

In Fig. 78 are shown striped mats for the summer luncheon table or breakfast room, made of carpet warp, raffia, and paper. At the top and bottom are raffia mats made with stripes in both warp and weft. The warp is set at 10 threads per inch or, for a heavier texture, at 8 pairs per inch. The mats with their stripe designs may be woven with raffia in bright colors, or tufting cotton, or carpet warp used double. The doily at the center was made with a weft of Dennison's rolled crepe paper, packed tight and shellacked after finishing to make it durable. All these mats may be washed by brushing with soap suds and water.

In Fig. 79 are shown useful articles made of "thrift" materials. At the top left is a bag with handles carved from cigar boxes. The bag is woven with two alternate colors of rags cut from stockings (see Fig. 80, No. 2). At the top right is a pot holder made of remnants of yarn in the Monk's Belt Pattern (see Lesson 30). In the center are circular pot holders made of alternate colors in the weft (see Fig. 80, No. 2). At the bottom left is an interesting runner in which the warp was made from cuttings of many colors of carpet warp set at 16 threads per inch and the weft used was carpet warp, all the same color except for the two bands at the ends. To make the duster at the lower right, remnants of carpet warp were used, cut from the end of a finished warp. These were fastened to a clothes-pin; the head of the clothes-pin was wrapped with carpet warp, and a tassel was attached. The clump of threads was put on the base of the clothes-pin with glue which was allowed to dry, and then the threads were turned over and fastened down by wrapping around them with the carpet warp, thus making the collar of the duster. The top of the duster may also be made in the form of a doll's head.

Fig. 78—Mats in stripes and plaids for the summer luncheon table or breakfast room.

WARP STRIPES

Achieving Interest by Attractive Warp Stripes

The very simplest way to get beautiful color effects in one's weaving is to plan a striped warp of different colors. This can be done on paper. In Fig. 56, for example, it was shown how to make a pattern in two rows, on a piece of squared paper; and it was also shown how to read the pattern from right to left when threading it on the loom. To plan such a pattern with stripes, all we need to do is to use a crayon to color the alternating squares to suit our fancy. For instance, in the little pattern in Fig. 80, No. 1, we can plan equal stripes: four threads of

Fig. 79—Useful articles made of thrift material.

dark blue (represented by the crosses); then four threads of gray (represented by the circles); then four of blue and again four of gray; and so on. This will make equal columns of color when woven, as shown just below the threading plan.

Striped Bands of Equal Size

Design No. 1 in Fig. 80 is formed by the alternation of two even bands of color. Two contrasting colors may be chosen, or two shades of the same color may be used. The bands may be of any width, containing any selected number of warp threads. Stripes 1 to 2 inches wide, or even as wide as 6 inches, look well in light and dark alternation. Again very narrow stripes give unusual effects. Even one or two light threads and one or two dark threads arranged in regular alternation are most effective.

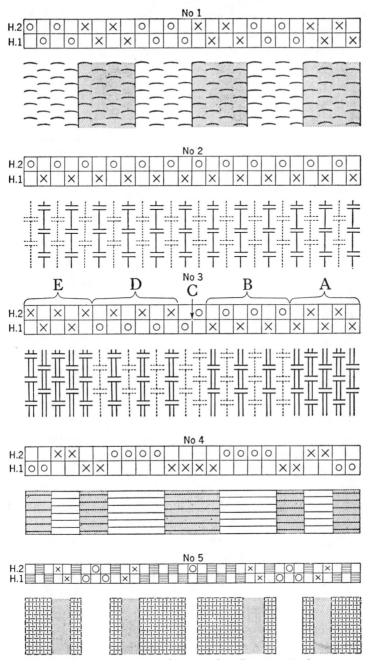

Fig. 80—Some interesting two-harness color effects in striped warps.

Equally interesting, if not more so, are stripes having widths in the proportion of 2 to 1 or 3 to 1. Such a design may consist of 2 inches of the first color and 1 inch of the second color, or 3 inches of the first and 1 inch of the second, the two colors occurring in regular alternation.

Warping and Threading Stripe Designs. To warp the threads for a striped-warp design, such as that in Fig. 80, Design No. 1, first wind four threads of one color. Then change to the second color, tying the end of the new thread to the cut end of the first thread. Wind four threads of the contrasting color; change to the first color and wind four more; and continue to alternate the colors. Chain the threads off the warping board in the usual manner, as shown in Fig. 63, and arrange them on the lease-rods. They will lie in the same order as when wound, ready for threading; i.e., the first four will be of one color, the second four of the contrasting color, etc.

In threading, take the threads as they come, first on one harness and then on the other. For instance, thread No. 1 (blue) will go on the first harness; thread No. 2 (blue) on the second harness; No. 3 (blue) on the first harness; No. 4 (blue) on the second harness; No. 5 (gray) on the first harness; No. 6 (gray) on the second harness, etc.

Weaving Across Striped-Warp Designs. To weave across a striped warp, one can use a single continuous weft of unchanging color. The entire length of the material will then appear in a vertical design of the warp stripes planned. Since the weaver does not have to stop to change weft colors, the weaving goes rapidly—first through one shed, then back through the other shed. The color of the weft should blend in with the color of the outside warp stripe, so that it will not show too much at the selvages, where it forms loops in reversing.

Alternating Two Contrasting Colors

One can alternate two colors in the warp, forming a mottled texture, as in Fig. 80, Design No. 2. Here a cross in a square on the paper plan means to thread a dark color on harness 1; and a circle means to follow this dark thread with a thread of light color on harness 2.

One can weave this kind of warp with a weft that is all of one color; or one can use alternately two shuttles containing different colors to form first a row of one color and then a row of the second color. This will bring out the pebbly effect still more. This pebbly effect is shown in the small flat bag in Fig. 79 at the upper left.

Shifting Colors Between Harnesses to Form Columns and Blocks of Design; "Log-Cabin Weave"

Design No. 3 in Fig. 80 shows the same pebbly effect as No. 2, but here the effect is arranged in columns obtained by shifting colors at intervals between harnesses. Again a cross means to use a thread of a dark color, and a circle means to use a thread of a light color. Two distinct effects are secured by weaving this warp design in different ways: first, an effect of vertical columns; second, an effect of blocks of color, generally known as "Log-Cabin Weave" but sometimes called "Basket Weave."

Planning the Warp. Use a succession of two alternating colors, like that shown in Design No. 2, for a space; then interrupt the succession by adding one extra thread of the same color as the preceding thread, as in Design No. 3 at C. The warp starts at the right side with five dark threads in column A. Next there are three pairs of alternating colors in column B, with the dark threads on harness 1 and the light threads on harness 2. At C the succession is interrupted by using an extra light thread on harness 1. This throws the next dark thread on harness 2, so that in the section D of three pairs of alternating threads, the dark threads are on harness 2 and the light ones are on harness 1.

The pattern may be extended to make a wider warp by omitting section E, which is the left border, and repeating sections B, C, and D in sequence. Add

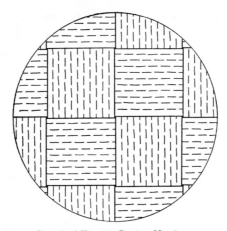

Detail of Fig. 80, Design No. 3.

section **E** after the last repeat to form the left border. Also the blocks may be made larger by threading more than three pairs of threads in each section before adding the extra thread.

Effect No. 1: Weaving Vertical Columns. It is easy to see what happens in the weaving of vertical columns. Weave with one weft only. The first shed is made with harness 1 lowered and harness 2 raised. The colors on harness 2 show as far as they extend. When the interruption occurs, the other color shows. Glance across row 2, and observe the threads which will be raised when the first shed is made. Read from right to left. Dark colors show on harness 2 at **A** for two threads; then light colors show at **B** for three threads; then there is an interruption of light at **C** to make the outlining stripe; then there are three dark threads at **D** and more dark threads at the end border **E**.

When the second shed is made, the light color shows where the dark showed before, but the shifts of color occur at the same points as the shifts in the former row. Successive weaving therefore produces columns, with a very slight change of texture between adjacent columns.

Effect No. 2: Weaving Blocks. The procedure in weaving blocks is as follows:

A. First Block:
  On shed No. 1, use color No. 1.
  On shed No. 2, use color No. 2.

Be careful to interlock the two separate weft threads at the selvage **A.** Repeat these two alternating weft rows for a section of weft equal to the width of a column; i.e., if column **B** is 1 in. wide, weave 1 inch of weft as just described. Then after weaving on shed No. 2 with color No. 2, add an extra weft row, using color No. 2 again on shed No. 1. This shifts the weft colors so that they change harnesses and we are ready for the second block.

B. Second Block:
  On shed No. 2, use color No. 1.
  On shed No. 1, use color No. 2.

Repeat these two alternating rows for a block the same size as the first block. Then, after weaving on shed No. 1 with color No. 2, add an extra weft row, using color No. 2 again on shed No. 2.

Repeat blocks **A** and **B** throughout the entire pattern. This results in the popular Log-Cabin Weave shown in the detail for Fig. 80, design No. 3. This design may be woven on a two-harness loom or a four-harness loom with the same color plan.

The Log-Cabin Weave, Fig. 80, Design No. 3. The Log-Cabin Weave, also called Basket Weave, although threaded as Tabby on a two-harness or four-harness loom, has the effect of small squares of design. It makes a quaint pattern for rugs, runners, draperies, and table linen, as well as for neckties and dress materials. In the threading in Fig. 80, design No. 3, two contrasting warp colors alternate regularly for a space to form one design block; then they change places to form the second design block.

It is a fascinating weave, appearing much more intricate than its simple construction. By combining two unusual shades, one may produce a most effective balance of blocks with each color predominating at intervals. A dark square forms when the dark colors are up, and a light square forms when the light colors are up. The weft threads carry out the same alternation. The effect is similar to a checkerboard, as shown in the accompanying detail. The spaces of design may also be oblong as well as square. One simply continues the same alternation a longer time before changing. This applies to warping as well as weaving.

A Pattern for Neckties or Scarves in the Log-Cabin Weave.

Warp Plan:

Warp: Fine 2-ply yarn set at 24 per inch. Two alternating colors.

Weft: The same.

Width: Any desired width.

Threading on a Two-Harness Loom: Choose two colors, light and dark. The blocks are about 1 inch square.

Block A. Thread light warps on harness 1, dark on harness 2. Repeat 12 times, using 24 threads. Add one dark thread on harness 1.

Block B. Thread light warps on harness 2, dark on harness 1. Repeat 12 times, using 24 threads. Add one dark thread on harness 2.

Repeat blocks A and B for the desired distance. Finish with Block A.

Threading on a Four-Harness Loom: Use a draft with a tabby shed, as twill.

Block A. Thread light on harness 1, dark on harness 2, light on harness 3, dark on harness 4. Repeat 4 times, using 24 threads. Add one dark thread on harness 1.

Block B. Thread light on harness 2, dark on harness 3, light on harness 4, dark on harness 1. Repeat 6 times, using 24 threads. Add one dark thread on harness 2.

Continue threading: Light on harness 3, dark on harness 4, light on harness 1, dark on harness 2. Repeat 6 times. Add one dark thread on harness 3. (Same effect as Block A.)

Continue threading: Light on harness 4, dark on harness 1, light on harness 2, dark on harness 3. Repeat 6 times. Add one dark thread on harness 4. (Same effect as Block B.)

Repeat all as desired. Finish with Block A.

This same threading may be used for rugs or drapes with heavier thread for the warp. Always use two contrasting tones or textures.

Weaving the Log Cabin. Use two weft colors, a light and a dark.

A. First Block:
Weave light weft on the first shed and dark on the second shed. Repeat 12 times, making 24 rows. Add dark weft on the first shed.

B. Second Block:
Weave light weft on the second shed and dark on the first shed. Repeat 12 times, making 24 rows. Add dark weft on the second shed.

Repeat all as desired.

Imitation of Four-Harness Pattern

Design No. 4 in Fig. 80 does not follow the rule for using alternate warp threads on alternate harnesses, but adopts a trick used in two-harness weaving to

example is shown in the finished necktie at the center in Fig. 88. The weaver can plan any combination, but it is a good idea first to weave a plaid in the authentic way, with warp and weft proportions the same, and then to create variations later. For other plaid designs in this book, see Figs. 53, 58, 85, 86, and 87.

Textured drapes. Left, heavy wefts alternating with very fine wefts. Right, fine Bouclé weft in Plain Weave, woven in half-inch bands with single rows of heavy wool yarn, woven intermittently on a pattern shed.

21–The Weaving of Rag Rugs in Plain Weave

Three Textures of Plain Weave

THE TEXTURE of Plain Weave depends on the way the warp is set in the reed. Three kinds of surfaces can be made in Plain Weave: balanced warp and weft, warp-face cloth, and weft-face cloth.

1. Balanced Warp and Weft. In the texture made by balanced warp and weft, there are the same number of weft threads in an inch of woven material as there are warp threads set to the inch. This kind of cloth is sometimes called "fifty-fifty fabric," with warp and weft evenly balanced. It is like the perfect linen in a handkerchief. For instance, a certain size warp, if set at 20 threads per inch, is spaced at just the right setting to cause the weft to beat down to 20 rows per inch. The knowledge of how to set certain size threads for this result comes from experience or from the careful use of a thread chart, such as that shown in Lesson 35.

2. Warp-Face Cloth. The second kind of fabric has the warp threads set so closely together that the weft is entirely covered and does not show at all, except at the selvages where it reverses to make each next row. This is known as "warp-surface," or "warp-face," fabric. It was probably the first kind of weaving known, and was developed at a time when there were no reeds to keep the warp threads apart. In this kind of Plain Weave one plans an attractive series of stripes in the warp, and the weft may be anything at all

since it does not show. Old sheets torn up or drab uninteresting material may be used, as long as it is fairly strong and forms the bulk necessary to bring out the colors in the warp. The same weft may be used throughout the piece. The design is in the warp, running lengthwise, and the warp is planned to provide all the beauty of color and interest. The material when woven is very strong and durable. It was used in ancient days for belts and wide girdles and straps. Today it also proves practical and useful for belts and bands, footstool coverings, sturdy pillows, mats, and purses. See the example in Fig. 79 at the lower left. The resulting texture of warp-face fabric has ridges running across the width of the material, or from selvage to selvage. It therefore is sometimes known as "weft-rep."

3. Weft-Face Cloth. The third kind of Plain Weave is known as "weft-surface," or "weft-face," fabric because in this only the weft shows and the warp is set so far apart that the weft packs down between the warp threads. The warp can be plain and uninteresting, since it does not show, but it should be strong. The weft must be of such a character as to pack down well over the warp; either soft wools or perle cottons are best. A design should be planned in a series of interesting horizontal weft stripes. Vertical stripes may be formed by using first a weft of one color and then a weft of a second color, these being alternated regularly. Weft-surface cloth is used for decorative mats, panels, striped wall hangings, and rugs. It is the kind of texture made by the Navajo Indians in their tapestry rugs. See examples in Fig. 38, Fig. 49 at the top left, and Figs. 90 and 92. The resulting texture of weft-face fabric has ridges running lengthwise of the material or along the length of the warp. It therefore is sometimes known as "warp-rep."

In between the mean (or balanced texture) and the extremes (or warp-face and weft-face textures), one may use any preferred setting of threads for certain desired results.

Rugs in Plain Weave

It is a practical plan to start one's weaving by making rugs, for they are made of fairly inexpensive materials that weave up quickly and provide a widely used and salable item. Very beautiful striped or plaid rugs are woven with the commercially spun cotton known as "Rug Yarn" or "Rugro." Choice wool rug yarns are also on the market, and braided wool filler is excellent for rugs of durable yet soft texture. Cotton chenille makes a popular texture for use in either bedroom or bathroom. Rags, either old or new, may be cut in wide strips to form heavy rugs; or may be cut finer to make gay market bags, knitting or school bags, small table mats, and chair seats.

Rag-Rug Weaving in the United States

In our own country the craft of weaving rag rugs was developed to considerable perfection in Colonial days. These rugs were of fairly durable weight and were used almost entirely to cover the floors of the homes of that day. Long strips were used for stair carpets; attractive lengths in "hit-or-miss" design were sewed together to make wide rugs for room coverings. Short lengths made "scatter rugs." Often the warp was striped and a plaid effect was obtained by using similar stripes across the weft.

Foreign countries took advantage of the popularity of rag rugs in the United States, and organized large industries to manufacture them on a large scale. In one year alone, before World War II, 13,000,000 square yards of rag rugs were imported from Japan. There is ample opportunity at present for the American rug weaver to make and sell rag rugs of recognized quality and beauty. We have also developed into a most popular and useful article the Colonial Overshot Pattern Rug, like that shown in Fig. 105. This type of rug requires two wefts, the Pattern weft and a binder or Tabby. For the former, one has a wide choice of beautifully dyed cotton or wool rug yarns; and, for the binder, one uses the same weight of thread as the warp, natural or colored. The infinite variety of many beautiful patterns to develop into attractive rug designs, often framed by stunning borders, makes rug weaving a delightful and ever-changing experience, while its products are a welcome addition to any home and give back their just reward for the effort of making.

Canadian Thrift Weaving

In Canada, there is a profitable trade in the making of articles from so-called thrift materials, either inexpensive new rags or discarded old rags. The rags are carefully colored, cut in narrow strips, and sewed together so that the finished weaving strands look like heavy yarn.

Fig. 82—Two handsome rag rugs.

Out of these are woven couch throws, seat mats, pillows, bags, chair backs, and upholstery materials. These products are very charming with their bright strips of color accented against neutral backgrounds or with series of gay bands in endless variety on plain or striped warps. Practical home or studio furniture, such as benches and porch chairs, are made in woodworking shops and upholstered with these sturdy rag hand-woven products, known commercially as **Catalognes.**

The Rugs of Mexico

The rug products of our other adjacent country, Mexico, as well as those of the American Indian, are often of more elaborate design, being woven with woolen weft yarns that cover the warp with stripes or tapestry techniques, as described in a later lesson. These are typical weft-face rugs. Each country develops its own characteristic type of hand-woven article, which is often the result of the availability of certain materials. It is a fascinating study to learn these types and thus to add variety to one's own hand-weavings. Each type is suited to a different kind of home decoration.

Typical Rag Rugs

In Fig. 82 are shown two handsome rag rugs. The American Colonial rag rug in the background was woven out of fine rags from discarded dresses on warp set at 12 threads per inch.

The rug in vertical strips was made out of rags torn from one complete old sheet. The four strips were woven white, but two of the finished strips were dyed a dark blue, and the other two were dyed a light blue. The strips were sewed together after weaving. This shows how to use a narrow loom for wide articles.

Dimensions:
Size of finished rug: 32"×48".
Size of each strip: 8"×48".

Warp Plan:
Warp: 8/4 carpet warp.
Weft: Rags cut 1 in. wide.
Threads per inch: 12.
Width of warp per strip: 9 in. (Shrinks to 8 in.)
Total threads per strip: 108.
Length of warp for four strips: **7 yd.**

Weaving Plan for Each Strip:
Leave 4 inches of fringe unwoven.
Tabby at beginning: ½ inch woven with carpet warp.
Main part of rug: 50 inches woven with plain white rags.
Tabby at end: ½ inch woven with carpet warp.
Fringe: 4 inches unwoven.

Making Rug:
Sew strips together with in-and-out stitching (Fig. 83 at **K**).
Tie ends of warp into fringe (Fig. 31 and Fig. 83 at **H**).

General Hints for Weaving Rugs in Plain Weave

1. Start rags for winding on the shuttle with a slip-knot, as in Fig. 83 at **A**.

2. Use the same kind of rags for any one piece and cut them the same width. Any variation is in the color or design, not in the material. For instance, the weft of a rug should be all cotton, all wool, all silk jersey, etc. The warp may be cotton, wool, or linen, but should never be a mixture (except of colors).

3. Always cut rags lengthwise of the goods, except with jersey materials which are cut round and round. Some material can be torn lengthwise; but, if it frays or puckers, it should be cut with sharp scissors.

4. If silk stockings are used, the best method is to cut the stockings into loops, as in Fig. 83 at **B** and **C**. Lay the loops together, as at **B**; and pull one loop through the other, as at **C**. Stockings may also be cut in a long spiral, round and round, from the top of the leg to the heel. Jersey cotton or silk underwear is best cut round and round or across the width.

5. In weaving with silk stockings or jersey material, always leave weft on a good slant or angle in the shed, and do not pull the weft tight when beating. This allows plenty of room for take-up; all jersey cloth is elastic and tends to shrink after weaving.

6. Sew cotton or wool rags together with a double fold, as in Fig. 83 at **D**; or with a single lapping, as at **E**. The former method holds heavy material in a flatter fold. Stitch diagonally across the overlapping distance of from 1½ to 2 in., as shown by the dotted lines.

7. When changing color, finish up the old color at the selvage. Cut the end of

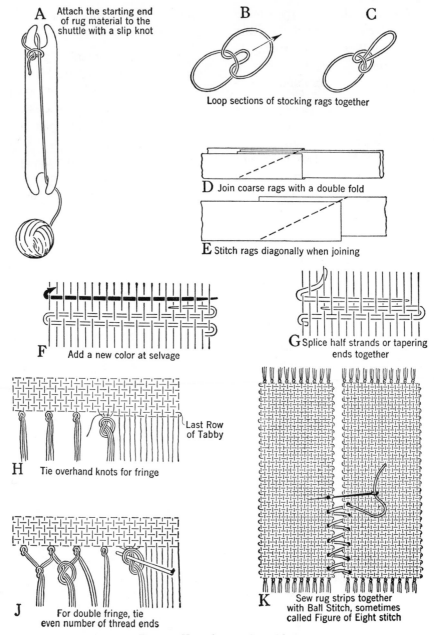

A Attach the starting end of rug material to the shuttle with a slip knot

B

C

Loop sections of stocking rags together

D Join coarse rags with a double fold

E Stitch rags diagonally when joining

F Add a new color at selvage

G Splice half strands or tapering ends together

H Tie overhand knots for fringe

Last Row of Tabby

J For double fringe, tie even number of thread ends

K Sew rug strips together with Ball Stitch, sometimes called Figure of Eight stitch

Fig. 83—Hints for weaving with rags.

the old strand so as to taper it off gradually and turn the end in on the next shed. Start the new end beside the old one, tapering this off slightly also. Do not turn in the new end, but cut it off flush with the edge. See Fig. 83 at **F.**

8. Splice the ends of old and new strands of the same color anywhere along the weft, but cut both ends until they taper, so that, when overlapped for a distance of from 1½ to 2 in., their combined thickness will be the same as that of a single strand, as at **G.**

9. For a rug with a fringe, leave 4 inches of warp unwoven at the start. Then weave ½ in. of Plain Weave with

carpet warp, to act as a narrow heading. From here continue with the rags for the central section. At the other end, weave the heading and leave the fringe. Tie the fringe as shown in Fig. 83 at **H** and **J**.

When planning the fringe, always remember to leave plenty of unwoven warp, at least 4 in. of thread being needed to tie the fringe easily; and always weave ½ in. or more of Plain Weave or Tabby to tie the fringe against, as at **H**. Let the last row of Tabby act as a safety or reserve thread to prevent the rows just above from fraying out. Keep the safety thread in until ready to tie each knot, and then pull it out for a limited distance only. Choose the number of threads needed for a knot of desired size, such as 4, 5, or 6 threads, and keep this number uniform for all the knots. Use the overhand knot as shown at **H**; keep the knot loose until ready to push it close against the Tabby, and then tighten it. A crochet hook or large needle may be inserted into the knot opening to shove it up to the heading, as shown in Fig. 83 at **J**.

10. If planning a double fringe, which is somewhat more decorative, allow 1 inch more of unwoven warp. Plan an even number of threads for each knot, such as 4 or 6 ends. Tie the first row of knots all across the warp. Then split the knots in half, and for each new knot take half of the threads from one knot and combine them with half of the threads from the next knot. In starting and finishing this second row, take all the threads from the end knot of the previous row and half of the threads from the next knot, as shown in Fig. 83 at **J**. If tying three rows, however, leave half of the threads of the end knot hanging until ready to tie the third row. Examples of double fringes are shown in the belt of Fig. 23 and the rug of Fig. 43.

11. For rugs hemmed at the ends, without fringe, weave 1 to 2 inches of Plain Weave at the ends, using carpet warp for the weft. If there is 1 inch of Tabby, roll it into a tight hem; if there is 2 inches, make the hem from ½ to ¾ in. wide. Always allow a bit extra for fraying.

12. When strips of rugs are to be sewed together, weave the separate strips exactly the same length, match them together carefully, and attach them to one another by means of the under-and-over "Ball Stitch," also called the "Figure-of-Eight Stitch" (see Fig. 83 at **K**). Use a strong linen twine in sewing, or a well twisted cotton strand doubled and waxed.

Rug Weights

Rags are used for weaving heavy rugs and runners, as well as lighter weight pillows, mats, and upholstery. Their weight and the use to which they may be put depends on the kind of cloth selected and its width in cutting. In Fig. 92 is shown a pair of door hangings woven of finely cut rags dyed rust and beige.

Heavy Weight: Use heavy rags or medium-weight rags cut wide for all-over carpets, runners, stair carpets, and rugs. Cut the rags wide enough so that, when twisted tight in the hand, there bulk will equal a diameter of ⅜ in. to ½ in.

Medium Weight: Use medium-weight rags of moderate width for lighter-weight rugs and bath-mats. Cut the rags so that, when twisted, their bulk will equal a diameter of between ¼ in. and ⅜ in. A conveneint rule to go by is to cut the rags of such a width that one strip, when twisted very tight, will equal the thickness of a lead pencil.

Fine Weight: Use narrow light-weight rags for upholstery, couch throws, pil-

Fig. 84—A handweaver's cozy corner. The maple chair is covered with rust colored handwoven upholstery, with matching lampshade and head rest. The scatter rug is beige with rust borders of finely cut rags in the same pattern as the chair.

lows, mats, and runners. Cut the rags so that, when twisted, their bulk will equal a diameter of ⅛ to ¼ in.

Rugs of Balanced Warp and Weft

Rag rugs woven in Plain Weave, with the warp and weft both showing, are possibly the type most usually made commercially. They are practical and cheap, being woven at the rate of from 1 to 2 ft per hour, and they are always salable. They may have a warp of one color, in which case one may use colored rags to give variety to the weft; or may have a striped warp of several colors, in which case the weft may be plain because the warp stripes will lend color and life to the rug. Borders may be added as desired. Instructions for different settings follow.

1. **Setting for Heavy-Weight Rags for Making Thick Rugs:** For the warp, use pairs of carpet warp set at 6 to 8 pairs per inch. Put the threads in pairs through the heddles and dents of the reed. For the weft, use thick rags.

2. **Setting for Medium-Weight Rags for Making Scatter Rugs:** For the warp, use 8/4 cotton, regular carpet warp, set at 10 or 12 threads per inch. For the weft, use rags cut so as to form a diameter of ¼ to ⅜ in. when twisted tight.

3. **Setting for Light-Weight Rags for Making Couch Throws, Upholstery, Chair Seats, etc.:** For the warp, use 16/3 or 10/3 cotton, or bedspread or crochet cotton set at 16 to 20 per inch. For the weft, use rags cut fine, from ¼ to ½ in. wide, which will form a diameter of about ⅛ in. when twisted tight.

Good Designs for Rugs of Balanced Warp and Weft

Good designs for rugs of balanced warp and weft may be obtained as follows:

1. Warp All One Color, Either Light or Dark: See the designs in Fig. 81 at the right and Fig. 82.

(a) With plain dark or light warps, use a background color for the main weft. Add borders at the ends, or a section of stripes at the center, using a weft of a contrasting color; or make the borders of rags cut from flowered or figured material.

(b) If using figured rags for the main background weft, make borders at the ends or plan a central stripe with plain materials. Borders may also run at intervals throughout the entire length.

(c) For pleasing two-color effects, use two shuttles of different colored rags and alternate them, as shown in the bag in Fig. 79 at the upper left, so as to make a closely striped texture. The entire rug may have a background texture of this two-shuttle weaving, or the background may be plain with interesting sections made in the two-shuttle effect.

2. Warp of Two or More Colors, in Even or Uneven Stripes: See the designs in Fig. 80 and in Fig. 81 at the left.

(a) Use up odds and ends of warp by mixing many left-over colors or remnants together with no plan whatever. The colors blend together and make an interesting effect when woven with a plain weft. See the attractive mat in Fig. 79 at the lower left.

(b) Make even lengthwise stripes by warping first an inch of a light color and then an inch of a dark color. See Fig. 80, No. 1.

(c) Make stripes in even alternations by making a design repeat on checked paper and repeating the series all across the warp. See the two plans in Fig. 81 at the upper left.

(d) Weave plaid rugs by setting up a striped warp and then crossing it with bands of weft in various proportions and colors. See the design in Fig. 81 at the center right. Plaids are good for all-over carpets. These are made by joining strips of weaving. A good size for the plaid design is a repeat of 6 to 9 in.

(e) Weave mottled squares by threading and weaving as described for Fig. 80, No. 3.

Warp-Face Rugs With Warp Only Showing

Fabrics woven in the warp-surface texture with the warp only showing are very durable, and are used for mats, bags, upholstery, and rugs. The same principle applies to all. The warp threads are set so close together that the weft shows little, if at all, between the adjacent warp threads. Any interest of color is given by planning the warp in stripes, and any interest of design is made by threading the warp in groups of various widths, as in Fig. 81 at the lower left.

The procedure in setting is as follows: The warp must be a good grade of carpet warp, heavy linen, or closely spun wool, and should be set at from 20 to 30 threads per inch. The weft may be of colorless rags or waste material; it shows only at the selvages. For this reason, the warp threads at the selvages are often made the same color as the weft, so that the latter will blend in and not show as an unexpected accent.

Good designs may be produced in the following manner:

1. Use alternate colors in the warp, a single thread of a dark color being followed by a single light thread.

2. Use any of the stripe effects given in Fig. 81.

3. Add a color accent at intervals in the warp by placing one, two, or three very bright threads at the center of a dark field, or placing several dark threads at the center of a light field.

4. Use color blends between a band of dark and light by making a section in which both colors are used alternately.

Weft-Face Rugs With Weft Only Showing

A great many beautiful rugs, mats, and hangings are made in the weft-surface texture. This is also the way in which most tapestries are woven. The warp threads are strong, but are set far enough apart to permit the soft weft yarns to slip down between them and completely cover them. The rows of weft must be closely packed with the beater. Two settings follow:

1. Very Heavy Rugs: The warp is either 8/4 carpet warp or a heavy linen set at 6 pairs per inch. Thread the warp in pairs or clumps. The weft is rug wool.

2. Medium-Weight Fabrics: For the warp, use strong carpet warp set at 8 to 10 threads per inch. For the weft, use heavy weight wool, such as Germantown double; or use a group of as many strands as necessary to make the desired weight.

Pleasing designs may be obtained as follows:

1. For pleasing soft toned effects in the weft, use blending hues of the same color.

2. For gay all-over stripe repeats, use weft colors of contrasting tones or bright colors in harmony.

3. Plan designs in figures as described in Lesson 23. See Figs. 90 and 92.

Since the warp is concealed, it may be perfectly plain and of any uninteresting color; but this fact also makes it possible to plan a warp that will use up odds and ends of the same kind of thread. If desiring colorful fringe, plan an attractive colored warp—either plain or striped.

22—Useful Articles Woven With Striped Warps and Wefts

Proportion and Color in Stripes

MANY beautiful hand-woven articles other than rugs depend for their appeal upon the use of good proportion and color in stripes, either in the warp or in the weft, or in plaids that have stripes going both ways. This lesson is devoted to an explanation of how to weave some attractive articles in stripes and plaids, how to count off the colors for the warps, and how to weave them to obtain different color effects.

Blue and White Striped Curtains

In Fig. 85 are shown cottage curtains in vertical stripes with plaid borders. The thread used is an inexpensive blue and white cotton thread, size 12/2. For the warp, it is set at 24 threads per inch, and the same thread is used for the weft. The design of this fabric is a type of Pennsylvania plaid used in the early days for table linens. It is shown being woven on the loom in Fig. 99. Above the curtains in Fig. 85 is given a draft for threading the warp in two colors.

These curtains are easy to plan and make. Weave them in Plain Weave, Tabby texture. The warp design is in stripes, according to the threading plan given in the following instructions and in the draft in Fig. 85. Repeat the plan eight times for a curtain 22 in. wide. The base of each curtain is woven as a plaid, in blue and white; then all of the upper part of the curtain is woven in one tone, white. The stripes of the warp show through to make vertical stripes. For each pair of curtains weave two pieces 22″×42″. Each piece or curtain panel shrinks down to a width of 20 in. and a length of 40 in. With a 2-in. hem, the curtains will be 36 in. long.

Warp Plan:

Warp: Cotton in a color and white; choice of sizes 20/3, 14/2, 12/2, and 10/2.

Weft: The same.

Width of warp on loom: 22 in.

Number of threads per inch: 24.

Total number of threads: 528.

Length: For each curtain 36 in. long, warp 42 in. of warp; and add ½ yd at each end of the entire warp for waste.

Threading Plan: Repeat the pattern draft shown in Fig. 85 from right to left 8 times. This draft reads as follows: 17 blue, 8 white, 5 blue, 6 white, 5 blue, 8 white, 17 blue (total 66 threads). Repeat all across the warp. The 17 blue threads at the beginning of a repeat and those at the end of the preceding one will come together, forming wider bands throughout the center, in accordance with the plan. At the right and left selvages this blue band will be half-width.

Weaving Plan: Border at base of curtains: First 5 in. blue (2½ in. of this for hem); then 8 white threads, 5 blue, 6

119

Fig. 85—Cottage curtains in vertical stripes with plaid borders.

white, 5 blue, 8 white, 36 blue; repeat from the first 8 white threads once again; this finishes the border. For the upper part of the curtain weave 32 in. of white. The total length of each curtain is 42 in.

In Fig. 86 are shown a purse and a case of an authentic Scotch plaid. This purse and case were made from hand-woven plaid cloth. There are two motifs which alternate to form the design.

Motif 1: 16 green, 2 red, 4 white, 2 red, 4 white, 2 red, 16 green.

Motif 2: 8 red, 2 blue, 4 red, 2 white, 4 red, 2 blue, 8 red.

Fig. 86—Purse and case of an authentic Scotch plaid.

Alternate these two motifs both in the threading count and when weaving. Weave in Plain Weave, securing the design by color change only.

To make the purse, proceed as follows: First make the inner case of stiff buckram lining. Cover this on the inside with silk. Baste the zipper on the outside of the lining case. Make an envelope of your woven material, this being a bit larger all around than the lining. Sew up the sides. Turn it inside out and press it. Insert the covered lining case into the out-side envelope. Attach it to the envelope with blind stitching, going all around the top edges.

Plaid Luncheon Sets, Mats, and Runners

In Fig. 87 are shown plaid designs for household linens. Plaids in colors to match the dining-room dishes, or in tones to form a harmonious background for them, make very successful table linens. Mats or runners combining the colors of

Fig. 87—Plaid designs for household linens. Top left: A textured doily. Top right: Scotch-plaid doily. Bottom left: Stunning table doily for "fiesta ware," woven on table loom in Fig. 42. Center: Doily or napkin with simple border. Bottom right: Blue and white breakfast set.

the living room add charm to the whole effect. All the designs in Fig. 87 are woven as true plaids, which means that the colors and proportions used in the warp are carried out in the weft and the material appears the same when looked at from all sides. These same designs may be used for doilies and napkins, mats, and runners, or for larger bridge-table covers or table cloths. Directions for weaving the five practical doilies shown in Fig. 87 follow.

1. Textured Doily.

The stunning doily for a luncheon set, shown in Fig. 87 at the upper left, is woven of gray linen with texture plaid in a heavy white mercerized thread.

Warp Plan: Two colors, gray and white.
Warp: Gray, size 30/2 or 14/1 linen.
Texture rows: White, size 3/2 mercerized or crochet cotton used double.
Threads per inch: 24.
Width in reed: 12¾ in.
Total threads: 308.
Weft: Same as warp; or linen slightly heavier, such as 12/1.
Size finished: 12″×18″ plus fringe.

Threading Plan:

	No. of Threads
36 Threads of gray linen, size 30/2 (covers 1½ in.)	36
*1 Heavy texture white thread..	1
12 Threads of gray linen (½ in.)	12
1 Heavy white thread	1
60 Threads of gray linen (2½ in.)*	60
Total	74

Repeat between asterisks (74 threads)
3 times 222

Then finish the other side as follows:

1 Heavy texture white thread..	1	
12 Threads of gray linen, 30/2..	12	
1 Heavy white thread	1	
36 Threads of gray linen, 30/2.	36	
Total	50	50
Total warp threads		308

Weaving Plan: Weave in Plain Weave in two colors, gray linen, size 30/2, and white mercerized, size 3/2.

1½ in. of gray; *1 heavy white thread, ½ in. of gray, 1 heavy white thread, and 2½ in. of gray.*
Repeat between asterisks as desired.
Finish with 1 heavy white thread, ½ in. of gray, 1 heavy white thread, and 1½ in. of gray. Overcast the edges with gray linen on the loom at the beginning and end of the work.

2. Scotch Plaid Doily.

The type of doily shown in Fig. 87 at the upper right can be made in colors to match one's china. The plaid shown here is in gold and black with accenting bars of red. Use any two suitable colors with a third color for accent.

Warp Plan: Three colors—one background and two accenting tones.
Warp: 20/2 cotton, colored.
Threads per inch: 30.
Width in reed: 12⅔ in.
Total threads: 380.
Weft: Same as warp.
Size finished: 12″×18″ plus fringe.

Threading Plan: Warp and thread the stripes in the following order:

	No. of Threads
Right side: 2 red, 12 gold	14
Main part: *8 black, 2 gold, 8 black, 2 gold, 8 black, 12 gold, 2 red, 12 gold.*	
Repeat between asterisks (54 threads) a total of 6 times	324
Add: 8 black, 2 gold, 8 black, 2 gold, 8 black	28
Left side: 12 gold, 2 red	14
Total warp threads	380

Weaving Plan: Weave in Plain Weave. Use three colors, the lightest one being for background. Carry out the same series of colors as in the threading plan.

3. Stunning Table Doily.

The table doily shown in Fig. 87 at the lower left is made of natural carpet warp and tufting cotton, with borders in bright colors to match peasant china.

Warp Plan: Four colors—a natural or neutral color and three bright colors.

Warp: Carpet warp used double.

Threads per inch: 8 pairs.

Width in reed: 13¼ in.

Total threads: 106 pairs (212 threads).

Weft: Tufting cotton.

Size finished: 12"×18" plus fringe.

Threading Plan:

Right side and border:	Pairs of Threads
10 pairs of natural carpet warp (20 threads)	10
7 pairs of blue warp	7
5 pairs of red warp	5
7 pairs of green warp	7
Center: 48 pairs of natural warp	48
Left side and border:	
7 pairs of green warp	7
5 pairs of red warp	5
7 pairs of blue warp	7
10 pairs of natural warp	10
Total pairs of warp threads	106

Weaving Plan: Weave in Plain Weave. Use four colors—one a neutral background and any three others. Weave the first end like the right side and border, following the same succession of threads as in the threading plan. Continue with the center, using natural color and any length. At the second end, reverse the color succession of the first end. Overcast the ends of the doily on the loom to make the hand-finished fringe.

4. A Simple Design for a Doily, Napkin, or Mat.

At the center in Fig. 87 is shown a simple design for doily, napkin, or mat.

Warp Plan: Two colors—white and a dark accent.

Warp: Main texture, white cotton; choice of sizes 10/2, 14/2, and 20/3. Colored lines, crochet cotton or perle 5.

Threads per inch: 24.

Width in reed: 13⅙ in.

Total threads: 316.

Weft: Same as warp; or white linen thread about same size.

Size finished: 12"×18"; or desired length.

Threading Plan:

Border:	No. of Threads
36 white threads (1½ in.)	36
1 colored thread (perle 5 or 10/3)	1
12 white threads (½ in.)	12
1 colored thread	1
Center:	
216 white threads (9 in.)	216
Border:	
1 colored thread	1
12 white threads	12
1 colored thread	1
36 white threads	36
Total warp threads	316

Weaving Plan: Weave in Plain Weave. Use white cotton or linen for the main part, and a dark color for accenting lines. Follow the same count and succession as in the threading plan, but make the plain center any desired length.

5. Blue and White Breakfast Set.

The breakfast or luncheon set shown in Fig. 87 at the lower right is very reasonable to make and has a simple but effective design. The cross-bar plaid of both the doily and the napkin were inspired by a napkin found in the museum at Mt. Vernon, bearing in one corner the family signature of Washington, written "W*n"; a tiny cross-stitched star is placed between the "W" and the "n." This napkin was actually used by George and Martha Washington in Colonial days.

Two colors were used—one a background color for the main part, and the other an accenting color in a thread a bit heavier than the background. Both the doily and the napkin may be light with dark stripes, or dark with light stripes; or the doily may be dark with light stripes while the napkin is the reverse, having a light background and dark stripes. The plaid lines may be any color suitable for

Fig. 88—Necktie and scarf materials in stripes and plaids.

one's china—delft blue, cottage green, rose, tomato red, henna, orange, cream or ivory, or even black.

Both the doily and the napkin have the same number of threads in the warp, but the two have different texture lines. After finishing the napkins, add extra texture threads for the doily along the side of the regular white threads and through the same heddles and dents of the reed. See Fig. 76 for the method of adding such temporary warp threads.

NAPKIN

Warp Plan: Make the warp plan the same as that for the doily just described in No. 4, using white and a color, with a total of 316 threads.

Size finished: 12 in. square (if desired to make greater width, such as 16 in., add more warp threads at center).

Threading Plan:

Right border: No. of
                                           Threads

  30 white threads 30

  1 colored perle 5 1

  4 white threads 4

  1 colored thread 1

Center:

  244 white threads 244

Left border:

  1 colored thread 1

  4 white threads 4

  1 colored thread 1

  30 white threads 30

  Total warp threads 316

Weaving Plan: Weave in Plain Weave. Use white and a color with the same succession as in the threading plan. Allow 2 inches extra in the plain center for shrinkage.

Doily

Warp Plan: Like that for No. 4, with a total of 316 threads.

Threading Plan:

Right border: No. of
                                           Threads

  30 white threads, 1 colored, 2 white, 1 colored, 2 white, 1 colored, 2 white, 1 colored (40 threads) 40

Center:

  236 white threads 236

Left border:

  1 colored thread, 2 white, 1 colored, 2 white, 1 colored, 2 white, 1 colored, 30 white (40 threads) 40

  Total warp threads 316

Weaving Plan: Weave in Plain Weave. Use the same count and succession as in the threading plan, but make the plain center of the desired length.

Other Woven Articles

In Fig. 88 are shown necktie materials in stripes and plaids. The texture threads are of silk bouclé. For the warp, use fine 2-ply woolen yarn of long staple and with sufficient twist to prevent it from breaking or clinging to adjacent warp threads. Set the warp at 20 to 24 threads per inch, and weave with the same weight. One can work out the same proportions in his own necktie fabrics by enlarging the stripes or plaids of these designs. Use a magnifying glass for actual thread counts. Also, design some original stripe effects.

In Fig. 89 is shown a smart outfit, the design for which was an authentic Scotch plaid. This outfit was woven and made by a college girl. Both warp and weft were of cotton, size 20/6, used as a substitute for wool. The warp was set at 24 threads per inch and threaded and woven as Twill. If planning a similar material with warp and weft of wool, use a tightly spun 2-ply wool warp and set it at 24 threads per inch.

Fig. 89—This smart outfit with an authentic
Scotch tartan plaid design was planned and
woven in a high school class as a weaving
project, then sewed into a skirt and jacket as
a sewing project.

23—Tapestry Technique. Weaving Designs Into the Cloth

Explanation and History of Tapestry Weaving

WE HAVE LEARNED how stripes may be made a part of the warp or weft, or both, thus producing vertical or horizontal columns of design, as well as plaids. It is also possible to interweave designs of any form and color into the cloth, as a very part of its texture. This is called "Tapestry Weaving." Weavers of the past, in Europe and Asia, developed great skill in this technique, weaving large impressive tapestries and rugs in gorgeous colors and designs to adorn the walls of their castles. In our own land, a very simple and practical form of tapestry weaving is done by the Navajo Indians. They developed the famous Navajo rugs by interweaving their tribal motifs into a woolen texture, usually limiting the colors to red, white, gray, and black, but sometimes introducing a bright accent of yellow, purple, green, or blue. In learning Tapestry Weaving it is a good idea to imitate the simple Navajo method of making tapestry in wools as given in this lesson. By starting with coarse yarns it is easy to learn the method of joining, and later one can apply this to the making of finer tapestry cloth.

In Fig. 90 are shown two beautiful runners made of dyed strips of silk stockings; diagonal designs were used as described in this lesson. For the warp, perle 10 was set at 16 threads per inch. The weft consisted of finely cut silk stockings

dyed bright colors. A fine strong warp was chosen so as not to conceal the attractive silky weft. In the lower runner, two shades of warp give a subtle stripe effect to the woven piece.

Typical Indian designs used for tapestry rugs or blankets have horizontal stripes across the warp at intervals, and these are generally in bright colors against a background of soft gray, white, or cream. Between the stripes appear tribal motifs which are in square or angular contour and are woven in dark or bright colors accented against the softer background. Bands of color are often woven vertically at the side edges of the rugs. For your first project, make a table mat measuring about 12 in. wide and 18 in. long. See Figs. 45, 46, 47, and 48 for typical designs.

Materials to Use

Warp: For the warp, use 8 pairs of carpet warp per inch. Later learn to use a wool warp of tightly twisted homespun yarn set at 8 threads per inch. The warp is set far apart to provide for packing the weft tightly down between rows, thus completely covering the warp. Such a texture is known as a "weft-surface" texture, since only the weft shows. See Lesson 21.

Weft: For the weft use a soft homespun yarn or Germantown yarn. A finer wool may be woven double or triple.

Fig. 90—Two beautiful runners made of dyed strips of silk stockings.

METHODS USED IN TAPESTRY WEAVING

Tapestry Weaving in Vertical Lines; Reversing Wefts Around Same Warps

To weave vertical outlines at the sides of a rug or blanket, or square or oblong motifs of any kind, plan the design on squared paper and let each warp thread represent one square. One method of procedure is shown in Fig. 91, diagram 1. Count the number of warp threads over which each part of the design passes. Then choose a separate weft for each part, as shown at **A**, **B**, and **C**. Start each thread going in the same direction as shown. In the illustration the thread colors that are adjacent reverse around the same warp thread, and this makes a slightly uneven effect at the joinings; however, the unevenness is scarcely notice-

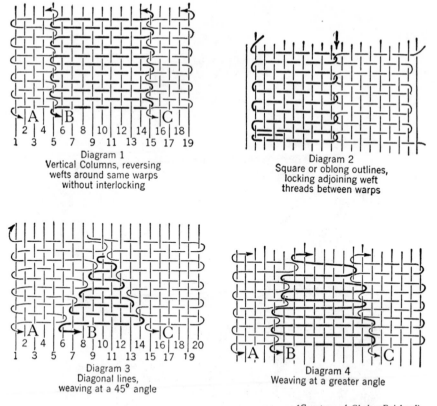

Diagram 1
Vertical Columns, reversing
wefts around same warps
without interlocking

Diagram 2
Square or oblong outlines,
locking adjoining weft
threads between warps

Diagram 3
Diagonal lines,
weaving at a 45° angle

Diagram 4
Weaving at a greater angle

(Courtesy of Gladys Reichard)

Fig. 91—Methods of interlocking weft threads in Tapestry Weaving.

able in the finished article. A narrow sample only is planned here. To make a larger piece, double or triple the counts; or greatly enlarge the center section.

Row 1: Make the first shed with all the odd-numbered threads—1, 3, 5, etc.—raised. Weave all threads from left to right. Weave **A** across 5 threads. Start **B** at the right of the 5th thread, and weave **B** across a certain number, such as 10 more threads, i.e., just beyond the 15th thread. Start **C** at the right of the 15th thread, and weave **C** to the selvage, i.e., around the 19th thread.

Row 2: Make the second shed with the even-numbered threads—2, 4, 6, etc.—raised. Thread the starting threads back in, as indicated by the arrows. Weave all threads from right to left, taking **A**, then

B, then **C**. Reverse **A** around the 5th thread, and weave back to the 1st thread. Reverse **B** around the 15th thread, and weave back to the 5th thread. Reverse **C** around the 19th thread, and weave back to the 15th thread.

Row 3: Make the first shed again. Weave from left to right, but now weave first with **C**, then with **B**, then with **A**. Reverse **C** around the 15th thread, and weave back to the 19th thread. Reverse **B** around the 5th thread, and weave back to the 15th thread. Reverse **A** around the 1st thread, and weave back to the 5th thread.

From now on, repeat rows 2 and 3 in succession until this part of the design is finished.

Locking the Adjoining Weft Threads Between Warps

Another method used in weaving vertical columns in tapestry is to lock the adjoining threads, as shown in Fig. 91, diagram 2. Here, instead of reversing around the same warp thread, two colors that lie next to each other reverse around adjacent warp threads and pass around each other when reversing. The interlocking occurs between the two adjacent warp threads, as shown at the arrow.

Tapestry Weaving at an Angle of 40° to 45°

To make designs of diagonal outline, such as triangles or slanting figures, reverse any two colors that lie next to each other around adjacent warp threads, as shown in Fig. 91, diagram 3. However, in each row, stop one of the colors short by one warp thread and include this warp thread in the row of the other color. What one color drops, the other picks up—an even exchange. We show here how one warp thread is exchanged in each successive row, but it is also possible to exchange two or more warp threads at a time and thus make the angle come in much more rapidly. To produce a **straight diagonal line**, it is necessary to drop and exchange the same number of warp threads in each row. The weaver can see, too, how it is possible to make a **curving line**; for instance, one may start at a steep angle by dropping one thread at a time, and may then pull the line down to a lesser slant by dropping two or more threads.

Row 1: Make the first shed in Fig. 91, diagram 3, with the odd-numbered threads—1, 3, 5, etc.—raised. Weave from left to right. Weave **A** across 5 threads. Start **B** around the 6th thread,

and weave **B** from the right of the 6th thread across the 14th thread. Start **C** around the 15th thread, and weave **C** from the right of the 15th thread across the 20th thread, or to the edge.

Row 2: Make the second shed with the even-numbered threads—2, 4, 6, etc.—raised. Fasten in the starting ends on this shed, as at the arrows. Weave from right to left, taking **A**, then **B**, then **C**. Reverse **A** around the 6th thread, and weave back to the edge. Reverse **B** around the 14th thread, and weave back; but stop short by one thread at the right of its starting end, i.e., now at thread 7. Reverse **C** around the 20th thread or at the edge, and weave back; but add one warp thread, now passing entirely around thread 14.

Row 3: Make the first shed again. Weave from left to right, but now weave first with **C**, then with **B**, then with **A**. Reverse **C**, and weave from left to right as far as the edge. Reverse **B**, and weave from left to right; but stop short by one warp thread, now passing only over thread 13. Reverse **A**, and weave from left to right; but add one more warp thread than it passed over in the previous row, now including thread 7.

From now on, repeat rows 2 and 3 in succession until this triangular motif is finished. The threads around which the weft reverses change at each row.

After completing a triangle, you can start in again with a point and enlarge the motif to a similar triangle upside down.

Tapestry Weaving at an Angle of 52° or More

To weave **abrupt angles** with outlines more nearly vertical than that in Fig. 91, diagram 3, cover the same number of

Fig. 92—A pair of portieres woven on a Colonial home loom out
of silk stockings by the use of the Tapestry Technique.

warp threads with two successive weft rows of the same color, as shown in Fig. 91, diagram 4. Thus, use **A** for weaving two rows over a certain number of warp threads; and use **B** and **C** in a similar manner. Then, in the next row change colors at the adjacent warp threads, and weave another two rows without changing.

Side Drapes of Narrow Rags

The panels in Fig. 92 are in Tapestry Weave made from finely cut silk stocking strips. Side pieces are 13 inches by 6½ feet; drop is 13 inches by 1 foot. Rags were dyed rust, leaves natural, lotus flowers coral. Worn sheets, dyed and finely cut, make good weaving material. Use natural carpet warp at 12 per inch.

24—Design Weaves

LACE WEAVES

LACE weaves are created right on the loom. They provide exquisite allover textures, and are used for table linens, draperies, stoles, altar cloths, and sheer dress materials. Handwrought laces of free design require only a two-harness loom. They are in direct contrast to lace weaves like Bronson (page 243) which are threaded to a set design on four or more harnesses and produce planned lace patterns at certain points.

Free lace weaves are used for weaving designs covering any space and in any form. While they take longer to weave than threaded laces, they also provide infinitely more variety. Two basic free lace techniques, **Leno** and **Brooks Bouquet,** are described below.

LENO OR LACE WEAVE (FIG. 93, NO. 1)

Leno lace is possibly the simplest of the lace weaves. It consists of making a lace shed with the fingers (Fig. 93, No. 1) and passing a shuttle of weft through the opening. Plain Weave, shown at **A,** acts as a base; the filled in selvages form a border at the sides, shown at **B;** and the lace itself forms single or successive rows, as shown at **C** to **C'.** You can make lace of single crossed warps, D-1; with pairs, D-2; or with groups of three, D-3.

Warp and weft should be planned so that there is an even distribution of each. Good textures are, **Heavy:** Cotton 10/3 or Linen 20/2 set at 20 per in. **Medium:**

Cotton 10/2 or 16/3 or Linen 40/3 at 24. **Fine:** Cotton 20/2 or Linen 40/2 at 30.

Forming the Lace (Fig. 93)

Weave a background, as shown at **A.** Start with shed in which outside thread at right edge is in upper level. Weave across a desired margin to **C,** back to **B,** and then to **C** again. Lift shuttle out. This fill-in brings sides up to level of lace. Go back and forth from **B** to **C** once more if necessary for fill-in. Lace can also be made all across warp with no margin, if desired.

To make a row, place left fingers within shed, pull upper warps to left in order to see lower warps. With a pick-up stick in right hand, draw off three warps from lower level, pulling off three warps from upper level in first cross. Keep this cross on the stick. From now on, pick up three warps from below, cross with three from above, for about six inches. Turn stick on edge, weave through to this point; continue to left, pulling three warps from below, pushing three down from above, and weaving through as far as you have made shed with fingers. After last cross, fill in margin with six rows, as shown at **C'.** Change shed, weave Tabby to right selvage, and add three rows across margin for proper level, as at **C''.** Use more fill-in if necessary. Weave three rows Tabby before a second lace row.

E shows a lace runner making use of the fill-in method at sides for laid-in designs. After the regular fill-in at each sel-

1. LENO LACE WEAVE

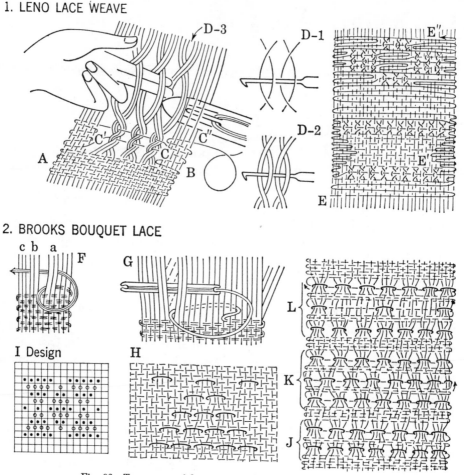

2. BROOKS BOUQUET LACE

Fig. 93—Two types of lace weaves, Leno and Brooks Bouquet.

vage of the lace row itself, an extra texture yarn is introduced at right, **E'**. At both sides the texture yarns make a diamond figure, each row followed by Tabby until time for next lace row. At **E''**, fill-in portions form lace designs within lace rows.

BROOKS BOUQUET
(FIG. 93, NO. 2)

Brooks Bouquet is an easy, attractive lace stitch. An entire row of lace is completed on one shed with little foot effort. It is faster than Spanish Openwork, which requires three shed changes per lace unit. The stitch consists of weaving nubs or back stitches at chosen intervals in a weft row. The nubs may be continuous, as at **F** (**a, b, c**), with spaces between nubs **G**; or with several nubs in succession followed by a space, as shown at **H**. Sections of nubs against Plain Weave form lovely lace designs. You design your own lace or follow a cross-stitch pattern.

Basic Stitch, F

Weave a section of Plain Weave, ending on the right side. Determine size of lace nubs or groups, usually three or four threads counted off on upper level. Make left shed and keep open. Weave to left under a group, bring thread out at **a**, backstitch around this group, carrying shuttle right to left in same shed under this group **a** and another group, **b**. Backstitch around **b**, go to left under **b** and another group, **c**. Continue, back over one group, forward under two groups.

You can pass under any number of warps between groups (see **G**). Establish a rhythm, such as back over one group, forward under four groups. After finishing a row of lace at left side, do not beat, but change shed and weave to right; a second row forms. Bring beater forward gently so as not to close up this second half of lace row. Weave two or four rows of Tabby before continuing.

Variations, H-L

Borders can be delightfully varied. **H** shows rows tightly beaten; **J** shows basic rows kept more open for lacier effects (each row followed by three rows of tabby); **K** shows latticework. For this variation, weave a basic row, four threads in upper shed per group, and follow with three or five rows Tabby. Start next row under a group of six warps, bringing nub to *center* of nub in first row. From now on, go back over four warps and forward under eight warps, making nubs come to center of former nubs. Third row is like first, fourth row like second, and so on. **L** shows a basic row, then three or five rows Tabby, a row of spaced nubs, Tabby, then third row like first.

In the design at **H**, worked out from a section of design **I**, start basic row one inch from selvage. Beat rows tight to make edge firm. Weave a basic row, leaving one inch of margin plain. Do not fill in margins, but weave five Tabby rows between lace rows, and beat all firmly. For the second lace row, start first nub two threads from beginning of nubs in last row, or half a nub to the left. From here on, make basic nubs, following second row of pattern in diagram **I**, lower right triangle. The open circles refer to alternate rows starting at half nubs. In free designs nubs occur unevenly.

LAID-IN WEAVING

Methods of Laid-in Weaving

ONE of the most interesting projects for the weaver is the making of designs with colored threads on a plain background fabric. This is called "Laid-in Weaving." It is really painting with threads, and the loom becomes an easel with pictures worked out in color. Two methods of making Laid-in Weaving are shown in this lesson: (1) Laying-in through picked-up groups of warp threads; (2) Laying-in through the regular Tabby shed, under single warp threads. Method No. 1 is like that used so effectively in Europe by the Scandinavians. It is called **Dukagang**, which means "the path of the cloth." Method No. 2 is a bit more detailed in the fineness of its texture, for the design thread goes through the regular Tabby shed. It is called **Straight Laid-in Weaving**, and sometimes **Simple Laid-in Weaving** or **American Laid-in Weaving**, since it is the method brought to such perfection in the hand-weaving of our own southern highlanders. In Fig. 94 are shown several laid-in motifs which add touches of bright color to useful fabrics. Laid-in Weaving may be done on either a two-harness loom or a four-harness loom. Still other types of Laid-in weaves are frequently used in foreign lands.

DUKAGANG

Dukagang on Two-Harness Loom

On a two-harness loom one lays-in the design for Dukagang by weaving with a heavy design thread under and over groups of warp threads, in between the regular Tabby rows, as shown in Fig. 95. One can count off the groups of warp threads for each row in front of the reed with a pick-up stick, but this takes time and is tedious. It is a better idea to count off the threads, when starting to weave, on a wide shed-stick at the back of the loom, behind both the reed and the harnesses. This new picked-up shed is kept throughout the weaving but is brought forward and used only when the design is desired between the rows of background Tabby. However, if the shed is to show up plainly to simplify the laying-in process, there must be wide heddle-eyes on the other two harnesses, so that the threads in the new picked-up shed can separate well. It is, therefore, a good idea to use cord heddles made at home, with eyes or openings ¾ to 1 in. wide, as shown in Fig. 54 at **H.**

Step 1—Planning the Design: Plan the design on paper that is squared off on both sides, as in Fig. 95 at **A**, for the design is worked with the **wrong side uppermost** on the weaving. First draw the design right side up. To get the reverse of this design, place the paper against a window pane so that the design will show through clearly and you can trace it on the back of the paper. This reverse pattern becomes a guide from which to count off the units of the pattern to transfer to the woven material.

Step 2—Counting out Groups of Warp Threads: Count off the threads of the warp—so many threads to equal a square—as in Fig. 95 at **B.** Do this by running a smooth flat shuttle or pick-up stick under three threads, over one, under three, over one, and so on, all the way across the warp at the back of the loom, as at **C.** Each group of three threads, as at **D**, corresponds to the distance across a check. The single threads, as those marked **E**, in between the groups of three, correspond to the lines on the squared paper. The height **F** of a square corresponds to three or four woven threads.

If the warp is fine and is put in with two threads per dent, it is best to thread the pick-up stick through as follows: under four threads, over two, and so on, as at **G**, being sure that the two threads passed over are a pair going through the same dent. In this case the four threads make the square and the two threads correspond to the line in between.

Step 3—Laying-in First Row of Design: For the first design choose a very simple figure, such .as a row of squares or a straight-line initial, as shown in Fig. 95 at **A**, where the initial "E" has been put on squared paper and then reversed.

Before starting the laid-in design, weave a section of Plain Weave or Tabby. For this the weft thread used should be either exactly like the warp or of the same size, but may be another color. The design thread **H** must be heavier than the warp and weft threads that make up the Plain Weave or Tabby of the background.

When starting the first row of the design, make the shed neutral; that is, let all the threads lie perfectly level without any shed, as at **J**. Now bring the pick-up stick forward to make the groups show up distinctly, as at **K**. These groups correspond to the squares of the squared-paper pattern. The first row of the design, which in this case is the monogram "E," has four squares. Therefore, run the first

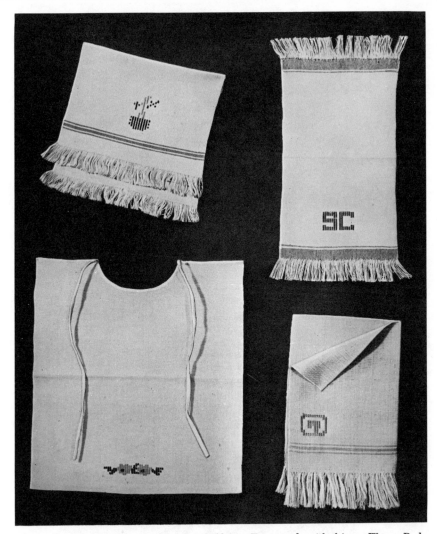

Fig. 94—Laid-in motifs for useful fabrics. Above: Two towels with fringe. Warp: Perle 10/2 cotton, set at 24 threads per inch; weft: the same. Lower left: Bib with warp of fine 24/3 cotton, set at 30 threads per inch and woven with fine linen. Lower right: Doily. Warp: Perle 10/2 cotton, set at 24 threads per inch; weft: 12/1 or 14/1 linen.

design thread under four groups of warp thread, as at **L**.

The simple steps to follow in laying-in each design thread are:

(a) Make threads all level without any shed.

(b) Bring the pick-up stick forward.

(c) Lay-in a row of the design.

(d) Push the stick to the back of the loom.

Step 4—Binding-in the Design Thread: After pushing the pick-up stick back, make the shed that would have followed your last row of Plain Weave, and put in the next Tabby thread, as in Fig. 95 at **M**.

Step 5—Filling up the First Row of Squares: It takes several rows of the heavy design thread to make each woven square as long as it is wide, **i.e.**, to make distance **F** equal to distance **D**. Therefore, put in two or three rows like the first row to

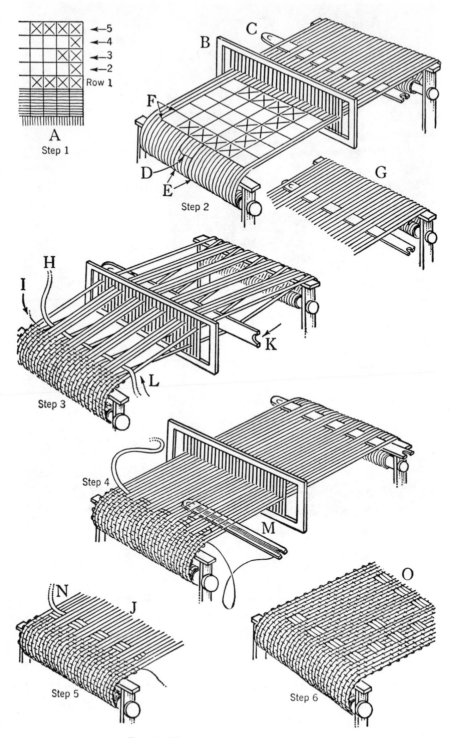

Fig. 95—Weaving designs in "Dukagang."

Fig. 96—Floral motifs woven in Dukagang Laid-in Technique on a background of Plain Weave.

complete the first row of squares on the paper pattern, as at **N**. A row of Tabby follows each row of design thread.

Step 6—Other Rows of Squares: Bring the pick-up stick forward and copy the next row of squares on the pattern, as row 2 of the design in Fig. 95 at **A**. In this particular design, there is only one square or group of warp threads in the second row of the squared-paper pattern. Use three design threads for this row, each being followed by a row of Tabby. Continue weaving the consecutive rows until the design on the cloth is complete.

Then continue with Plain Weave. The finished letter is shown woven at **O**.

Good Designs to Use

Simple designs are the best, like those in which the outline is not too broken. One can of course lay-in different colors for parts of the design. Some designs are shown in Fig. 96 and also in the diagrams in Fig. 98. Any cross-stitch design may be used. Hand-woven fabric pictures like those shown in Fig. 96 may be framed and used as small wall ornaments or as coasters on the table.

PART II

Pattern Weaving

(*Courtesy Dorothy V. Koolish*)

Living room with rug handwoven in four strips in a short Overshot Pattern. Color changes in the filler form square blocks of flame, apricot, lavender, and burnt orange. The corner window shows a transparent tapestry treatment with colorful design to go with the rug, but of such a texture as to let the light stream through.

25–How to Warp and Thread a Four-Harness Loom

Comparison of Types of Weaves

IN PLAIN WEAVING we learned how to make an even-textured cloth by interlacing threads of the same size at right angles. We learned how designs can be made in Plain Weave by changing the colors of warp or weft, or both, to form stripes and plaids.

In **Tapestry Weaving** we learned how to make more varied designs by joining adjacent weft threads of different colors together instead of weaving just the stripes and plaids of Plain Weave. We learned how one color interlocks and changes places with another, and how one color becomes a background while the other stands out in contrast to form a design. We observed that the design threads themselves are woven in as separate rows of Plain Weave, and there is no additional Tabby or binding thread.

In **Laid-in Weaving** we learned another way of painting pictures with threads. We learned how a heavy design thread is added and laid-in between rows of Plain Weave or Tabby; how it may start or stop where the weaver pleases, making it possible to weave quite interesting designs into the cloth. However, Laid-in Weaving takes quite a bit of time, for the warp threads must be carefully picked up and counted off while the design threads are laid in with the fingers. Hence, this kind of weaving is sometimes called Finger Weaving. The principles of Laid-in, or Finger, Weaving

prepare one for Pattern Weaving, which is explained in this lesson.

In **Pattern Weaving**, one plans to weave regular repeats of a set pattern all across the warp, instead of planning certain free designs on a field of Tabby, as in Laid-in on Plain Weave. The finished fabric thus becomes a **continuous** all-over pattern. In Laid-in Weaving any one of the repeated motifs can be a design unit, but to lay in all the figures of an all-over pattern would take too long and be too hard on the eyes. So the ingenuity of the weaver has come to the rescue, and he threads the loom in such a way that all the pattern threads may be picked up on an extra harness or bar at the same time. With this extra harness he can make a shed to lift **groups** of pattern threads above other groups, instead of lifting just **single** threads as in Plain Weave. The design thread shows plainly across the spaces, thus forming the motifs of the pattern. The extra shed is called a **Pattern Shed**, and this weaving is called **Pattern Weaving.**

To weave patterns by Pattern Weaving, one must have at least one extra harness in addition to the two harnesses that make the Tabby; and usually one employs four or more harnesses for the kinds of Pattern Weaving popular today. In advanced weaving and in the making of commercial goods, many more harnesses are added to make complicated and beautiful patterns, such as brocades

145

Fig. 99—Four-harness floor loom.

or table damask. The number of harnesses used gives the name to the loom. Thus, we have two-harness table or floor looms, four-harness table or floor looms, six-harness looms, eight-harness looms, etc. In Fig. 99 is shown a four-harness floor loom suitable for both Plain and Pattern Weaving. The plaid material being woven is the curtain fabric in Fig. 85.

Difference Between Design and Pattern

Design is a term applied to any changes in Plain Weave brought about by vari-ations in the character or color of the threads used; by the laying-in of extra threads between the rows of Tabby; or by the manipulation of the Tabby threads themselves. The word **design** then refers to any of the following: a **change in the color or texture** of the warp or weft threads, as when weaving stripes or plaids; an **added laid-in motif**, such as a Duka-gang design; or a **change of cloth structure** due to handling the warp or weft threads in various ways, such as inter-lacing the warp threads to form lace de-signs or mesh weaves. The word **pattern**

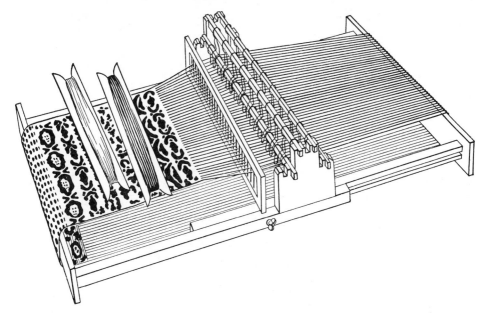

Fig. 100—Four-harness table loom suitable for weaving small articles in all-over Pattern Weaving.

applies to any changes in weaving brought about by the threading of the warp threads in definite groups to form set patterns.

Since the threads for any **design** are counted out by hand in contrast to those of a **pattern** incorporated in the threading of the loom, the designs it is possible to produce on a two-harness loom may follow any chosen plan of either regular or irregular motifs. Examples are conventional units or natural scenes and objects such as flowers, trees, and birds. Looms with only two harnesses therefore provide many possibilities of free design. These same simple design techniques may of course be wrought on looms with more than two harnesses when these are used for Plain Weave.

Looms with four or more harnesses, however, provide not only for Plain Weave and the many forms of Design Weaves, but also for the threading of an infinite number of Pattern Weaves. In these the entire surface of the cloth that is being woven has an all-over pattern effect, the configuration of which may be changed at will by threading the loom to different patterns. In Pattern Weave fine threads of Plain Weave are usually woven in after every pattern row, but these are used merely as binding threads to hold the pattern threads firmly in place and to act as a background for them.

In Fig. 100 is shown a four-harness table loom suitable for weaving small articles in all-over Pattern Weaving. In the case of this loom, the pattern is picked up by means of heddle-cords on the four successive heddle-bars or sticks. The warp is first wrapped around the loom frame, with the warp passing through successive dents of the reed at each round. The reed lies open without its top piece during this process. Then the tension of the warp threads is made perfect by drawing the thread taut round after round. A photograph of this type of loom is shown in Fig. 42.

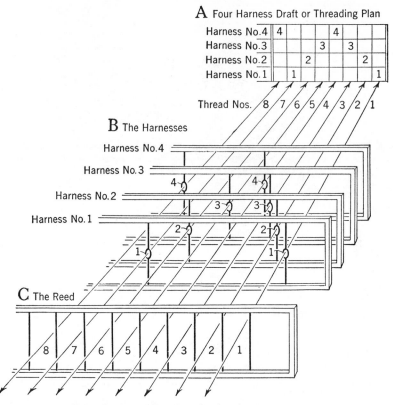

Fig. 101—Threading plan of a four-harness pattern.

To thread the loom, the warp threads are picked up for each harness in succession, the heddle-cord loops being passed under the chosen threads. This procedure corresponds to the threading of the warp threads through the heddle-eyes of four separate harnesses. When the heddle-bars are raised, the threads "picked up" on these harness bars are raised, and the desired shed is formed. Note that in this loom the chosen warp threads are raised to make the pattern shed. When threading a loom from a draft, follow the squares on the draft from right to left.

For the Rosepath Pattern in Fig. 101, pick up the warp threads as follows:

First harness or bar: Pick up one warp (harness 1); skip five warps (harnesses 2, 3, 4, 3, 2); pick up one (H. 1); skip one (H. 4). Repeat this succession all across the warp, picking up all the threads on harness 1 and skipping all the others.

Second harness or bar: Skip one (H. 1); *pick up one (H. 2); skip three (H. 3, 4, 3); pick up one (H. 2); skip three (H. 1, 4, 1); repeat from * all across the warp.

Third harness or bar: Skip two (H. 1, 2); *pick up one (H. 3); skip one (H. 4); pick up one (H. 3); skip five (H. 2, 1, 4, 1, 2); repeat from * all across the warp.

Fourth harness or bar: Skip three (H. 1, 2, 3); pick up one (H. 4); skip three (H. 3, 2, 1); pick up one (H. 4); repeat all across the warp.

Overshot Pattern Weaving

The extra harness or harnesses added for Pattern Weaving make it easier to weave the pattern thread across longer spaces than in Plain Weaving, thus forming small squares or "blocks" of color. The word **block** is used to designate a spot or area of color or texture where one or more pattern threads show through the gap formed by the raising or lowering of the warp threads. Any shed that brings up groups of warp threads in this way is called a **pattern shed**, in contrast to the plain shed of Tabby Weave. In Colonial days the rows of Pattern Weaving that passed over these groups of warp threads formed by the pattern shed were sometimes called "shots." Hence, this type of weaving—forming blocks of pattern squares—is called **Colonial Overshot Pattern Weaving** because the weft thread makes an **overshot** of pattern across each gap in the shed between the groups of warp threads. On the pattern draft, such blocks as those just described are usually written on adjacent harnesses, such as harnesses 1, 2, 1, 2; H. 2, 3, 2, 3; H. 3, 4, 3, 4; or H. 4, 1, 4, 1.

Principle of Threading or Dressing the Loom

To thread a loom, the heddle-bars or harnesses are hung near the center of the loom. They are much like the heddle-bars or harnesses shown in Fig. 66 at **A** and **B**. The heddle-bars hold cord or steel heddles similar to those in Fig. 54 at **G** and **H**. These heddles have openings like large needle-eyes at their centers. The warp threads pass through these eyes one by one in the order planned. If, for instance, several adjacent warp threads pass through successive heddle-eyes on the first heddle-bar or harness, raising or lowering this harness leaves a gap across the warp for the distance covered by this group of warp threads. The heavy pattern thread passes through this gap and shows up just as described in Lesson 24, Fig. 95,

where we counted across the warp threads one by one and then laid-in the design thread by hand. If we put all the warp threads in planned groups through the heddle-eyes of the various harnesses, we find that when weaving we can make pattern spaces all across the warp very quickly. This is known as **threading the loom to a pattern.** It takes a little time to **thread** the loom; but, when the threading is completely and properly finished, the loom provides an endless series of colorful effects, the detailed pattern variations depending on the ingenuity of the weaver. "Dressing the Loom" is the term applied to the consecutive processes of warping, beaming, and threading the loom. The high structure at the center of the loom, equipped with the harnesses and their heddle-rods and heddles, is called the harness apparatus, and sometimes the "Castle" of the loom.

Threading from a Plan

The threading plan of a four-harness pattern consists of small squares, representing threads, which are arranged from right to left—according to a set plan—on four horizontal bars or rows, as in Fig. 101 at **A**. Rows 1, 2, 3, and 4 correspond to harnesses of the same numbers. Each marked square represents a thread at that point. It means that a thread passes through a heddle of the harness marked with the same number. In the threading plan in the upper right-hand corner of Fig. 101, the number 1 means that the warp thread passes through a heddle on harness 1; the number 2 means that the next warp thread passes through a heddle on harness 2; and so on. The successive numbers of the warp threads themselves are shown just below the four-harness draft from thread No. 1 through thread No. 8.

Threading Through the Heddles of the Harnesses

Each harness **B**, Fig. 101, is provided with heddles having small openings, or heddle-eyes, through which the threads are threaded. Count off the threads from right to left on the draft, and thread from right to left on the loom. On the "Rose-path" Pattern in Fig. 101, the threads take their places on the successive harnesses, as shown in the draft. Thus, reading from right to left, the harness numbers are 1, 2, 3, 4, 3, 2, 1, 4. The first thread (No. 1) is on row 1 and is therefore to be threaded through a heddle on harness 1 (you can trace this thread from the draft through its heddle). Continue with each thread in succession to the left. The next thread (No. 2) is on row 2 and goes through a heddle on harness 2; the next thread (No. 3) is on row 3 and goes through a heddle on harness 3; the next thread (No. 4) is on row 4 and goes through a heddle on harness 4; No. 5 goes through harness 3; No. 6 goes through harness 2; No. 7, through harness 1; and No. 8, through harness 4. This completes one repeat of the pattern. Start again with thread No. 9 on harness 1 and keep repeating the same succession of threads, going from right to left until all the warp threads have been threaded through the heddles of the designated harnesses.

Threading Through the Reed

The warp threads are threaded through the reed or comb **C**, Fig. 101, in the same succession in which they are threaded through the harnesses, again starting at the right and working toward the left. Thread carefully and do not cross the warp threads as they come forward to go through the reed. In the four-harness plan shown in Fig. 101, thread No. 1 (on harness No. 1) is threaded through the first dent of the reed, which is marked 1; thread No. 2 (on harness No. 2) is threaded through the next dent to the left, which is marked 2; thread No. 3 (on harness 3) is threaded through the next dent, marked 3; and so on. Continue threading the warp threads in succession through successive dents of the reed, **C**, working form right to left. The process of taking the warp threads through the dents of the reed is sometimes called "sleying" or "reeding-in."

There are several methods of beaming and threading the warp threads of a loom after they have first been measured off on a warping frame, as was described in Lesson 17. The weaver may make his own choice of the methods described in this lesson, and the preference depends on which method works better on his loom for the particular kind of warp he is setting up.

Terms Used for Methods of Warping and Threading

In general there are two types of warping threads on a loom. In one type, known as the **Chain Method**, the warp threads, usually on large spools, are first measured off on a warping-board or frame where their cross is secured; and from here they are "chained off" by hand and transferred to the loom for beaming and threading. This method is shown in Fig. 63. In the other type, known as the **Sectional Method**, the threads come directly from many separate smaller spools arranged on a "creel," where their cross is secured and from which they are wound directly around the warp-roller of the loom. This eliminates their first being wound on the warping frame by hand and is considered a rapid, as well as efficient, method of warping. It is shown in Fig. 103.

When warping by the "chain method," there are again two methods of procedure to choose from. In the first method, the warp threads are first threaded through the reed and heddles; and are then wound on the warp-roller or "beamed." In the second method, the warp threads are first evenly distributed through a temporary reed or spreading device, wound on the warp-roller, and then threaded through the heddles and reed.

Method No. 1: The Chain Method and Its Procedures

A. Threading First, Then Beaming: This method is shown in Lesson 17, in Figs. 65 and 66. It is used for simple weaving and is possibly the quickest method when two people can work together. It may be used for either two-harness or four-harness looms. After measuring off and chaining, the warp threads, which are separated by the cross of the lease-rods, are placed at the front of the loom. The threads are now taken in succession from the lease-rods and are threaded or "sleyed" one by one through the dents of the reed. They are then threaded in the same succession through the eyes of the heddles of the harnesses. From the harnesses they pass to the back beam of the loom, where they are tied to the apron and wound around the warp-roller or "beamed." When this process is finished and all threads are smoothly rolled up at an even tension, the front ends of the warp threads are tied down in groups to the apron-rod or bar of the cloth-roller at the front of the loom.

The succession of processes used in Chain Method **A** is:

1. Insert the warp threads in succession through the dents of the reed.

2. Thread them in the same succession through the eyes of the heddles on the harnesses.
3. Tie them down to the apron-rod of the warp-roller at the back of the loom.
4. Wind them around the warp-roller in the process of beaming.
5. Stretch them taut and tie them down to the apron-rod of the cloth-roller at the front of the loom.

B. Beaming First, Then Threading: This method is shown in Fig. 102. The object is to wind, or **beam**, all the threads on the warp-roller first, and then to thread them through the heddles of the harnesses and the reed while sitting comfortably facing the loom. One person can thread alone by this method, although he may need help in beaming. This method has been successfully used for many years by weavers in both north and south, and is simpler than it sounds.

After winding the warp threads on the warping frame and chaining, the threads on the lease-rods are placed across the loom. The threads are then spaced in small groups through a **spreader, raddle,** or coarse reed, **A** or **A'**, with their end loops left uncut and slipped over a stick **B**. They are drawn through the center of the loom to the rear without threading, and are transferred in groups to the apron-rod of the warp-roller, as shown at **C**. To make room to spread the warp through the harnesses, the heddles are moved to the right and left and are tied to the sides **D** of the harness frame; or they are removed entirely by taking them out on their heddle-bars and laying them aside on a table. The lease-rods with the cross are slipped through the center of the loom to the front, **F**, and the threads are then wound, or beamed, around the warp-roller at a tension, as at **E**, warp-sticks or stiff papers being used to keep them even, as was shown in Fig. 66. One

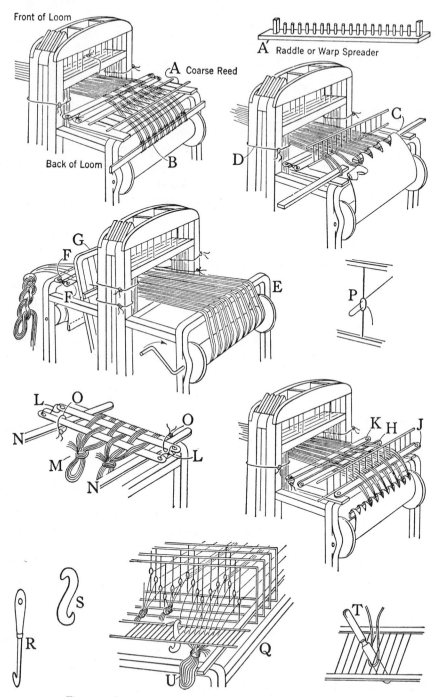

Front of Loom

A' Raddle or Warp Spreader

A Coarse Reed

Back of Loom   B

Fig. 102—Steps in beaming the warp and then threading.

person winds the warp at the back of the loom while a second person stretches it taut at the front. The lease, or cross, is still maintained at the front of the reed at **F**. During the winding, the raddle is clamped firmly to the loom in front; or, if a reed is used, this is inserted in its proper place in the beater-frame, as at **G**, where it may be braced against the harnesses during winding.

When the warp threads have been smoothly wound, they are ready for threading. However, before this can be done, the lease-rods must be transferred to the back of the reed, from their present position at the front at **F**. To change the lease-rods to their proper position on the loom, i.e., between the harnesses and the warp-roller, raise the lease-rod that is closest to the warp-roller on its side, as at **H**, thus making the first shed. Slip a temporary rod into this shed but on the other side of the reed, as at **J**, and draw out the corresponding rod **H** from this same shed at the front. Now turn the other lease-rod **K** on its side, making the second shed; slip a temporary rod into this shed, on the other side of the reed, i.e., between the reed and the first rod **J**, and draw out the corresponding rod **K** from this same shed at the front. Then put the true lease-rods into the two sheds held by the temporary rods at the rear. Tie the lease-rods together again at their ends, as at **L**.

Take the warp threads out of the coarse reed or raddle and remove this entirely. Tie the threads together in small groups, as at **M**, using the slip knot to prevent their slipping out of place on the rods. They now hang down in groups from the lease-rods at the back of the loom ready for threading.

Suspend the lease-rods at a convenient height back of the harnesses, and lay them across two long bars **N**, going from front to back of the loom and lying across the front and back beams. Attach the lease-rods to these bars, as at **O**, or to the harnesses at the center of the loom so that they will not slip off, for if this happens the warp threads might come off the rods and the cross would be lost.

To thread the loom, sit at the front and draw each thread in succession through its respective harness, as designated by the pattern draft and as described previously under "Threading Through the Heddles of the Harnesses." When each pattern repeat has been threaded, tie its warp threads in a group, as shown at **Q**; and, likewise, when each group has been taken through the reed, tie the warp threads under the reed as shown, to prevent their slipping out of place. Finally, tie the groups of warps to the apron rod at the front of the loom. See Fig. 67 at **A**.

The succession of processes used in Chain Method **B** is:

1. Space the warp threads in groups through the spaces of a raddle, or through skipped dents of a coarse reed.
2. Draw them to the back of the loom; tie them down to the apron-rod of the warp-roller.
3. Wind them around the warp-roller at a tension.
4. Thread them through the heddles of the harnesses.
5. Insert them through the dents of the reed.
6. Stretch them taut and tie them down to the apron-rod of the cloth-roller.

Arranging Warp at Center of Reed

Count the number of threads in your warp and the number of dents, or openings, in the reed, or comb. Subtract the number of threads from the number of dents, to find out how many dents will be left empty. Divide this by 2 to get the

number of dents to be left at each side
so as to place your warp at the center.
Leave this number of dents empty, start
on the right side with thread No. 1, and
thread the threads in succession through
successive dents of the reed, as shown in
Fig. 101.

Ways to Handle the Warp in Threading and "Sleying"

The method used in taking the warp
threads through the heddles and the reed
is optional. Some weavers use a threading hook (see Fig. 102 at **R** and Figs. 65
and 66). In this case it is best to have a
helper stand at the back of the loom and
lay each thread in succession across the
hook as this is inserted through its proper heddle-eye by the person threading
at the front of the loom. After all the
threads have been threaded through the
harnesses, the reed is placed upright in
the beater-frame, and again the helper at
the rear of the loom lays the threads in
succession over the hook as the person at
the front inserts it through successive
dents of the reed in the process of "sleying" or "reeding-in."

Other weavers prefer to thread alone.
With the left hand the weaver grasps the
next heddle to be threaded, and with the
right he picks up the next warp thread
in order from the lease-rods. Forming a
little loop near the end of the thread, he
inserts this through the eye of the heddle,
as at **P** in Fig. 102; then he slides the
threaded heddle to the right to make way
for the next empty one. When all the
threads have been threaded, the weaver
ties them into small groups with slip
knots, and then prepares to "sley" the
threads, or to take them through the
dents or openings in the reed. This is
placed flat across the two bars **N** at the
front of the loom, as at **Q**. The threads

are taken through the reed dents with
the threading hook **R**, a Swedish S-hook
S, or a kitchen knife **T**, which is excellent
to use because the band at its hilt keeps it
from slipping through the dents. After
each group of warp threads has been
sleyed, its threads are tied in a similar
group beneath the reed, as at **U**, to prevent their slipping out of place.

When all the warp threads have been
sleyed through the reed, the warp threads
are tied down in even groups to the
apron, or to the bar of the cloth-roller at
the front of the loom, with all the groups
pulled to the same tension. The warp is
now ready for weaving.

Method No. 2: The Sectional Method of Warping

This method is shown in Figs. 103 and
104. The warp threads are drawn directly
from separate spools arranged on a warping-creel or spool-rack to the warp beam
of the loom, instead of being measured
off on a warping frame, length by length,
from large spools. The object of this
method is to provide a quicker means of
beaming the warp threads at an exact
tension on the warp-roller than can be
done by the older hand method of warping and chaining off. It is an attempt by
the home weaver to make use of the effi-
ciency developed in the textile mills to
save time in the warping process, for it is
well known that a perfect warp saves time
in weaving, saves time in repair, and produces a better fabric. By this method one
person working alone can put on a 50-yd
warp 30 in. wide in 2 hours and with a
helper can finish it in 1 hour. With a
little practice one can learn to warp 100
yd of thread at a time. This is therefore
the best method of warping for the commercial weaver and for any organization
interested in developing an extensive

(Courtesy Creative Crafts, East Berlin, Pa.)

Fig. 103—Warping on eight-harness loom by use of sectional warp-roller and creel.

weaving program. While there is an initial investment for the creel, the sectional warp-roller, and a sufficient number of spools of thread, more is saved in the end by the conservation of strength and time. People who weave as a hobby after working hours, lacking sufficient time to warp by other methods, resort to this system, and use the time thus saved for greater enjoyment in the weaving process itself. Sectional warping may be used on all kinds of looms, with two, four, eight, or more harnesses, provided the loom is equipped with a sectional warp-roller. This is a large cylindrical drum provided with pegs at intervals. For the chain method of warping, a smooth warp-roller of smaller diameter is used.

Description of Warp-Roller and Creel

The **warp-roller**, shown in Fig. 103 at the rear of the loom, is divided into 2-in. sections by means of small pegs or steel wires; and narrow cloth tapes or loops are tacked to each section, as shown in Fig. 104 at **A**.

The **warping-creel**, shown in Fig. 103 at the right, holds a number of spools of thread equal to the number of warp threads planned for each 2 inches of weaving. For example, if one plans to make rugs, with 12 warp threads per inch, one purchases 24 spools of coarse warp thread to place on the pegs of the creel, thus providing 24 ends for each 2-in. section of the warp roller. If one plans to make towels, with 30 warp threads per inch, one purchases 60 spools of fine warp thread, thus providing 60 ends for each 2-in. section. These small spools are purchased by the home weaver from a thread company, and may be had in from 2-oz to 8-oz spools that turn easily around the pegs of the creel. In the absence of a creel, a spool-rack may be used, as shown in Fig. 104 at **B**; but in this case the weaver should also purchase a warp-tensioner, or some device to keep all the threads at the same tension.

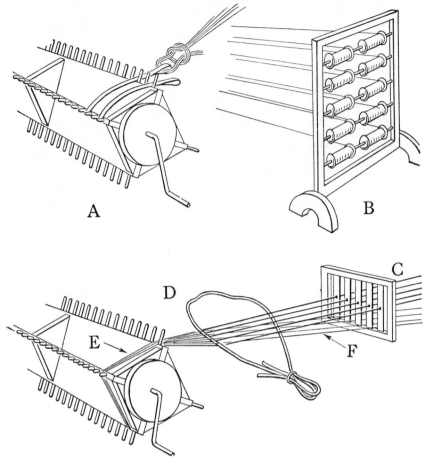

Fig. 104—Details of warping by the sectional method.

The threads, after leaving the pegs of the creel, pass through a distributor at the top of the creel, which keep them apart and in parallel order. From here they are drawn through a "lease-reed" which furnishes a "cross" for threading, as in Fig. 104 at **C**.

Description of the Lease-Reed

From the distributor, the threads are taken, one by one and in order, through a slot-and-hole heddle, known as the **lease-reed**, shown in Fig. 104 at **C**. This is generally made of steel, according to the principle shown in Fig. 65 at **F**. The purpose of the lease-reed is two-fold; it not only keeps the threads in perfect order side by side, but provides for the making of a shed to aid one in efficient threading. With the lease-reed one can secure the two sheds of the cross rapidly and easily. This cross is later transferred to the lease-rods for the threading process.

The number of dents in the lease-reed should be the same as the number of threads planned for each 2 inches of warp. Thus, if one is warping rugs to be set at 12 threads per inch, the lease-reed should have 12 dents per inch and should measure 2 in. across, with a total of 24 dents arranged alternately as slots and holes. The lease-reed may be held by a helper between the creel and the warp-roller while one winds the warp; or it may be inserted in a groove on the back-beam of the loom. The lease-reed shown is greatly enlarged for clarity and allows for only a few warp threads. Most lease-reeds are of steel and are more closely set.

Centering the Warp

From the lease-reed the thread ends are taken in a group and tied to a cloth tab of the warp-roller with a slip knot, as in Fig. 104 at **A**. One can easily center one's warp and know at which tab to begin by counting off the number of 2-in. sections required for the width of warp planned and figuring how many sections to leave vacant at each side. Start at one side of the warp and move straight across, section by section.

Winding the Warp on the Roller

The amount of warp to wind on each section may be accurately determined, for the warp-roller measures a certain distance around, such as 1 yd, and the weaver turns the crank around as many times as he wishes yards. Thus, if he plans a 25-yd warp, he winds each section of warp thread for 25 rounds. He must count carefully so as to have exactly the same number of yards on each section. It is also necessary to make sure when winding that the warp threads do not pile up across the 2 inches of any one section, but form a flat and level surface. One therefore stops occasionally when winding, at every tenth round or so, to survey previous rounds; and, if the thread has piled up somewhat, one moves the lease-reed from side to side to fill up any gaps which have occurred and to make the distribution more even.

When he has finished winding the 25 yards of the first section, the weaver raises and lowers the lease-reed to secure the two sheds, as in Fig. 104 at **C**, preserving

them with a colored cord **D**. He now takes another half-revolution of the warp-roller to bring the cross over the threads already wound on the roller, at some point like **E**. He then measures 1 ft back of the cross and cuts the warp at point **F**, being sure that 12 or more inches of the threads are left between **F** and **C**, so that they will not slip out of the lease-reed. The cut ends of the section just wound are secured to the nearest peg of the roller; and the freshly cut ends of unused warp are tied to the tape of the next section, where the warper prepares to wind another 25 yards. One must be sure to repeat all operations exactly the same for each section—cut at the same distances, fasten to pegs at the same level, etc. When through all the sections, the warper unfastens the ends of thread from each and slips the lease-rods through the shed openings made by the colored cords **D** until all sections are placed across the lease-rods. The warp is now ready for threading in the manner shown in Fig. 102, **L** to **Q**, but with a one-and-one shed.

For coarse warps sectional warping may be done without a lease-reed, in which case the threads come directly from the distributor of the creel and are wound around each section of the warp-roller. When finished with each section and while all threads are lying flat, one pastes gummed paper across them, thus keeping them in perfect order until ready for the threading; one then takes the threads one by one from the gummed tape and inserts them through the heddles.

The succession of processes used in the Sectional Method is:

1. Thread the creel with a number of spools of thread equal to the number of warp threads planned for each 2 inches of warp.

2. Provide some means of obtaining even tension for all warp threads.

3. Draw threads in perfect order through the distributor of the creel.

4. Draw threads in the same order through the slots and holes of a lease-reed, or a slot-and-hole heddle.

5. Tie the thread ends in a group to the tab of the first section of the roller on which the thread is to be wound.

6. Measure the warp-roller once around and determine the number of revolutions to wind in each section to secure the desired number of yards.

7. Wind each section, securing the cross of each shed by means of the lease-reed

after finishing it. Allow plenty of leeway between this cross and the lease-reed, grasp the group of warp threads in the hands to prevent their slipping, and cut across them.

8. If no lease-reed is used, maintain the order of the warp threads by pasting gummed paper across them.

9. After all sections are wound, transfer the cross from each section to regular lease-rods. If no lease-reed has been used, dispense with lease-rods and take the threads directly from the gummed tape.

10. Thread the loom by the regular threading process from the lease-rods or from the gummed tape.

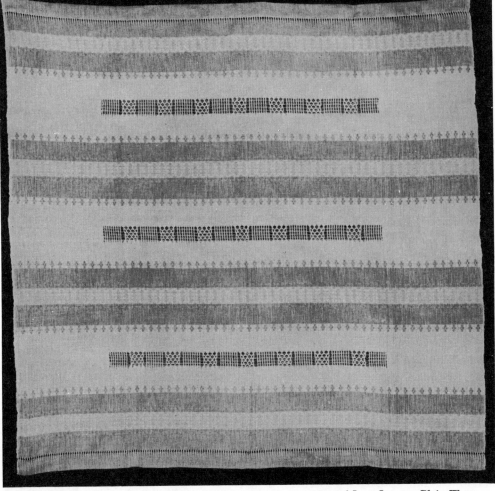

Lace tablecloth in white and tan linen showing intermittent sections of Leno Lace on Plain Weave background. Borders in pattern weave.

26—Weaving Both Plain and Pattern Weave on a Four-Harness Loom

Method of Weaving the Pattern

THE WEAVING of any pattern on a four-harness loom requires that each harness be tied to a lever or treadle and be raised or lowered when the hand or foot presses on the lever or treadle. When a harness rises or sinks, it brings with it all the threads on it, making a shed with openings at just the points where these threads occur. If a heavy pattern thread is woven across the warp, it shows as a spot of color wherever there is such an opening. As the harnesses are "treadled" one by one and colorful weft threads are woven through the openings, the pattern formed looks very much like the pattern plan, for of course the thread openings occur at the very same places as do the draft markings. In some looms the harnesses rise when one treadles to form the pattern openings, and in others they sink. The results are the same, although the weaver uses a different notation. However, for purposes of simplicity in this book, we will speak of the harnesses as being lowered during treadling, unless otherwise specified; and these directions can easily be changed for the other type of loom, as described on page 164. In Fig. 105 is shown a typical four-harness overshot pattern, the Wheel of Fortune, or Cup-and-Saucer, woven in such a way that the successive spots of color or "blocks" make concentric circles.

Variety of Overshot Patterns

Since in this kind of Pattern Weaving the weft passes over the warp openings, it is also further defined as **Overshot Pattern Weaving**, described in Lesson 25. There are many other types of Pattern Weaving, but in this book we will deal mostly with the many possibilities of **overshot pattern weaves**, developed by threading warp threads in certain groupings, and treadling or weaving them in various ways.

In Colonial days, weavers in different sections of the country exchanged successful drafts or pattern combinations, much as home makers exchange choice recipes today. Often all the members of the family worked over a pattern to bring out its beauty or to make some desirable change. When the altered draft was woven, it resulted in a prettier diamond, a more perfect circle, or a more gradual curve. Today we can enjoy the results of this work of our ancestors in the many clever pattern drafts that are our heritage. There are many types of patterns, having various motifs and outlines, such as Circles, Squares, Tables or fields of color, Diamonds, Crosses, Wheels, and Stars and Roses; as well as patterns formed in unique ways, such as bow knots or patterns radiating from centers. Often, several of these motifs are combined in a single beautiful pattern.

Fig. 105—Rug and pillow top in typical Colonial Overshot Pattern, called "Wheel of Fortune" or "Cup and Saucer."

Harness Combinations

In four-harness Pattern Weaving it is customary to bring down one, two, or three harnesses at a time. However, with two harnesses up and two down, there is a more even division of threads on the right and wrong sides of the material. The six combinations most frequently used employ two harnesses at a time: namely, harnesses 1 and 2; 2 and 3; 3 and 4; 4 and 1; 1 and 3; and 2 and 4. The first four combinations when woven produce certain pattern groupings in the resulting cloth pattern; the last two make Plain Weave. It is possible also to weave Hs. 1, 2, 3, together; Hs. 2, 3, 4; Hs. 3, 4, 1;

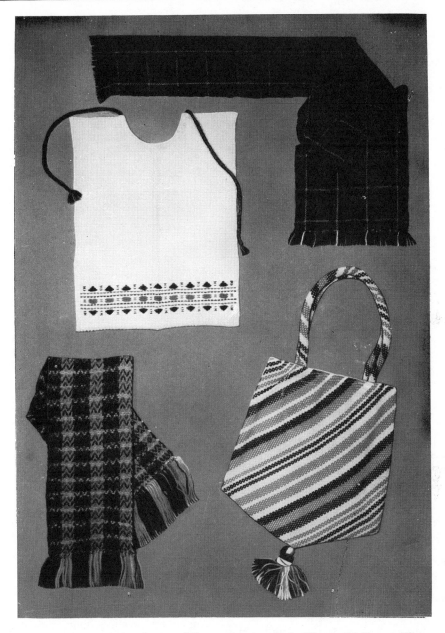

Fig. 106—Woven articles showing difference between Plain Weave and Pattern Weave.

Hs. 4, 1, 2; H. 1 alone; H. 2 alone; H. 3 alone; and H. 4 alone.

Methods of weaving both Plain Weave and Pattern Weave on four-harness looms are indicated in Figs. 106 and 107. Just how the effect of Plain Weave is secured on a four-harness loom is shown in the simple Twill pattern draft in Fig. 107 at C, where harness combinations 1 and 3 and 2 and 4 are woven alternately. In fact, we can take any one of the familiar pattern drafts for four-harness Overshot Weaving and show how Plain Weave can be developed from it by repeating alternately harnesses 1 and 3 and harnesses 2 and 4.

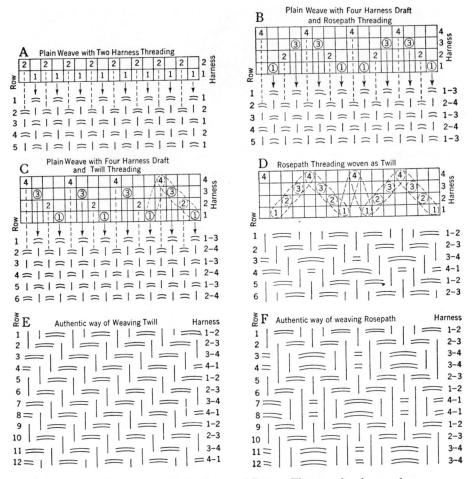

Fig. 107—Weaving both Plain Weave and Pattern Weave on four-harness looms.

Differences Between Plain Weaving and Pattern Weaving

The woven articles pictured in Fig. 106 show the difference between Plain Weaving and Pattern Weaving. The bag at the lower right and the man's plaid scarf at the top are in Plain Weave or Tabby. In both articles, the texture is an in-and-out interlacing of warp and weft, and only the colors change. The scarf at the lower left shows Pattern Weave as an all-over surface texture.

In the bib, the threading used is the Rosepath. This is developed into a section of Plain Weave, which occupies the entire width of the warp when used

alone; and this is followed by a pattern border woven as Rosepath with Pattern Weave used as a band all across the warp. The same threading is thus used to weave both the plain part of the bib and the pattern border. The desired result is obtained by pressing down different combinations of the treadles, as just described under **Harness Combinations**.

How to Weave Plain Weave or Tabby on a Four-Harness Threading

It is possible to represent any pattern on checked paper by imitating the weaving of the cloth rows, as in Fig. 107. To demonstrate Plain Weave or Tabby Weave on a four-harness loom in this way, use a simple threading such as the Rosepath at **B**. Thread in succession from right to left on harnesses 1, 2, 3, 4, 3, 2, 1, 4; and repeat. Since every other thread must be lowered to make a shed for Plain Weave, let us put a circle around every other thread in the plan. We note that every one of these circles comes on either harness 1 or harness 3. Therefore, if we lower harnesses 1 and 3 together, every other thread goes down, making shed No. 1. The weft shows as a row of Plain Weave exactly like that in shed No. 1 of the two-harness weaving in Fig. 107 at **A**, row 1. (Note the arrows indicating the lowering of the odd-numbered threads, 1, 3, 5, etc.) The effect is the same on the four-harness loom. (Note the arrows indicating the lowering of harnesses 1 and 3 with their odd-numbered threads in Fig. 107 at **B**, row 1.)

Now we see that all the even-numbered threads, 2, 4, 6, etc., are threaded on harnesses 2 and 4. Therefore, if we lower harnesses 2 and 4 together, the alternate threads go down, making the second shed, or shed No. 2. Thus, we get the second row of Plain Weave exactly as we did in the two-harness weaving of Fig. 107 at **A**, row 2. (Note the dotted lines to row 2 of the weft on the two-harness loom, indicating the lowering of the even-numbered threads, 2, 4, 6, etc.; and compare these lines with the dotted lines to row 2 of the weft on the four-harness loom at **B**.)

The Twill threading in Fig. 107 at **C** produces exactly the same effect as the Rosepath threading at **B**, if woven in the same way.

Rule to Follow: To make Plain Weave, or Tabby, from a four-harness Overshot Pattern, simply lower alternately the harness combinations 1 and 3 and 2 and 4. The final effect of this alternation of harnesses is shown very clearly on paper in Fig. 107 at **B**, with the horizontal markings indicating the successive weft rows 1, 2, 3, 4, etc.

Rule for Writing Drafts to Weave Tabby on Alternate Harnesses

We have just described how Plain Weave can be woven on a four-harness pattern threading. However, there is one rule to note: In writing a pattern draft that will produce the desired effect, such as that in Fig. 107 at **B** or **C**, the **even** harnesses must always be followed by the **odd** ones, and the **odd** ones must always be followed by the **even** ones. This rule can be stated more explicitly by the following conditions:

A thread on harness 1 must always be followed by a thread on harness 2 or harness 4, but never by one on 1 or 3.
A thread on harness 2 must always be followed by a thread on harness 1 or harness 3, but never by one on 2 or 4.
A thread on harness 3 must always be followed by a thread on harness 2 or harness 4, but never by one on 1 or 3.
A thread on harness 4 must always be followed by a thread on harness 1 or harness 3, but never by one on 2 or 4.

If the draft breaks this rule, the alternation of harnesses 1 and 3 and harnesses 2 and 4 will not make perfect Tabby.

Difference Between Rising and Sinking Sheds

You will note that we refer to the **raising** or **lowering** of the harnesses to form the shed. In each case the harnesses "separate," forming an opening to weave through, and the result is the same. The explanation of this is as follows: On some looms, known as **jack looms,** we have what we call a **rising shed,** whereby the harnesses are raised by jacks when pressing on the treadles. On other looms, known as **counterbalanced** or **roller-type looms,** we have what we call a **sinking shed,** whereby the harnesses are lowered when pressing on the treadles. In the explanations which follow, we will speak of making the shed opening by bringing down, or **lowering,** the harnesses of a counterbalanced loom. If your loom is a jack loom, simply regard the shed as being made by **lifting** the harnesses. The treadling then applies to exactly the opposite harnesses from those designated on the counterbalanced loom. The following comparisons should be kept in mind.

Guide for Transposing the Treadling of a Counterbalanced Loom to a Jack Loom, or Vice Versa

The following guide may be used to transpose the treadling from either type to the other type of loom.

Treadlings for Counterbalanced Looms	Corresponding Treadlings for Jack Looms
Harnesses 1 and 2	Harnesses 3 and 4
Harnesses 2 and 3	Harnesses 4 and 1
Harnesses 3 and 4	Harnesses 1 and 2
Harnesses 4 and 1	Harnesses 2 and 3

The directions for Pattern Weaving in this book are for the counterbalanced type of loom. If your loom is a jack loom, simply read the treadling in the guide directly opposite that given for the counterbalanced loom. The Tabby treadlings are the same on both types of loom; i.e., harnesses 1 and 3 are alternated with harnesses 2 and 4.

Warp Levels or Proper Balance of Counterbalanced and Jack Looms

For each of these types of Looms there is a correct level or position of the warp threads, which if adhered to produces a better shed. When no shed is being made, the harnesses are said to be "neutral" or "at rest."

On a counterbalanced loom, when the harnesses are at rest, the correct position of the warp is on a perfectly horizontal plane coming directly from the back-beam to the front-beam and lying just below the center of the reed.

On a jack loom, when the harnesses are at rest, the correct position of the warp is a slight inclination or dipping of the warp threads from both the front-beam and the back-beam toward the heddles. The warp must also lie flush against the bottom of the reed and the shuttle race, if there is one. Thus, the warp comes from the back-beam downward toward the eyes of the heddles and then upward toward the front-beam, lying close to the base of the reed in passing.

Starting to Weave a Background of Plain Weave

Use a tabby thread of the same size as the warp threads. Begin by lowering harnesses 1 and 3 together to secure shed No. 1, either by placing the hands on levers or the feet on treadles tied to harnesses 1 and 3, as shown in Fig. 72. Lay the fine tabby weft thread through the shed opening from left to right; bring the beater forward and push the weft thread into the V of the shed. Now change to harnesses 2 and 4; this brings alternate warp threads down over the filler, fastening it in place. Lay the second row of filler through this opening, from right to left; beat it tight. Continue treadling, first with harnesses 1 and 3 from left to right, and then with harnesses 2 and 4 from right to left. Weave 2 inches with the tabby threads, leaving each row of weft thread on a diagonal slant before beating it to keep from drawing the fabric in at the selvages.

Memorizing the Direction of the Tabby

It is customary to memorize the direction of each row of Plain Weave, so that the weaver can tell in an instant which row is to come next. This avoids writing down the harness combinations for Plain Weave, which alternate regularly and are therefore self-evident. It does not matter which direction the weaver chooses for each shed, so long as he consistently keeps to the same direction at all times. If you prefer to weave from left to right on harnesses 1 and 3, always carry out this plan; or you may find it more convenient on your loom to throw your shuttle from right to left on harnesses 1 and 3, and from left to right on harnesses 2 and 4. The same result is attained in either case; but never change after once establishing your direction. Also splice the ends of the threads so that the new thread continues in the same direction as the old, whenever possible.

Weaving Pattern Combinations

After weaving a background of Plain Weave on a four-harness loom, one can at any time put in a colorful pattern, using any or all of the other four harness combinations—harnesses 1 and 2, 2 and 3, 3 and 4, or 4 and 1—as shown in the border of the bib in Fig. 106. The shed openings made by these combinations bring the warp threads into attractive groupings. The pattern thread shows through these openings. To make the pattern rows secure, we usually follow each row of Pattern Weave by a row of Plain Weave, or Tabby.

Relative Sizes of Pattern and Tabby Threads

If the pattern thread is to show effectively through the warp spaces, it must be quite a bit heavier than the warp and tabby thread. Likewise, to make well-balanced Plain Weave fine enough to form a suitable background for the pattern texture, the tabby thread should be of the same kind as the warp, or of the same size. Variations from this rule are made in accordance with the weaver's choice, usually for texture effects only.

Following Each Row of Pattern with Tabby

When weaving patterns in the usual way—first a row of pattern, then a row of Tabby—use two shuttles, one filled with heavy colored pattern thread and the other with fine tabby thread. There is an accepted order in which to put down the treadle combinations to form the authentic development of the pattern; but the weaver is also free to choose any order in which to treadle his pattern for any desired effect. Usually each row of Pattern Weave is consistently followed by a row of Plain Weave, or Tabby. This acts as a binder and makes a firm pattern texture. There are ways of weaving Pattern without Tabby, but this is a matter of later experimentation.

Laying out the Pattern

It is a good idea to make one or two rows of each combination at the beginning of the weaving. Then the weaver can see what the possibilities are of combining the rows. See Fig. 107 at **D** for the possibilities of our sample pattern, the Rosepath. Taking each combination in succession (see the figures in the right column), this pattern is as follows:

Pattern row 1: Treadle harnesses 1 and **2,** and weave the pattern thread through. For the first row of Plain Weave to follow this, treadle harnesses 1 and 3, and weave this row with fine thread, thus binding in the pattern thread.

Pattern row 2: Treadle harnesses 2 and 3, in accordance with the pattern; weave with pattern thread. Then treadle harnesses 2 and 4; weave Plain Weave with fine thread.

Pattern row 3: Treadle harnesses 3 and **4,** and weave with the heavy pattern thread. Then treadle harnesses 1 and 3, and use fine thread for the Plain Weave.

Pattern row 4: Treadle harnesses 4 and 1, and weave the pattern with heavy thread. Then treadle harnesses 2 and 4, and make the Plain Weave with fine thread.

We have now woven each of the four pattern combinations, and can see what kind of pattern figurations may be made. By studying the results, we can plan any succession in which we should like to weave the combinations. Mark them down in the preferred order on paper, and then proceed to weave, following each row of pattern thread with a row of Plain Weave. A particular combination may be repeated any number of times, and the combinations may follow one another in any succession whatever.

We emphasize the fact that the Plain Weave need not be written down, for the weaver should know this, always weaving to the right on harnesses 1 and 3 and to the left on harnesses 2 and 4 (or in the other succession if that has been chosen).

The pattern will grow into attractive form as you weave.

To make each combination show up more, repeat it two or more times, as follows:

> Combination 1: Pattern, harnesses 1 and 2; and Tabby, harnesses 1 and 3. Pattern, harnesses 1 and 2 again; and Tabby, harnesses 2 and 4.
>
> Combination 2: Pattern, harnesses 2 and 3; and Tabby, harnesses 1 and 3. Pattern, harnesses 2 and 3 again; and Tabby, harnesses 2 and 4.

One may repeat each combination any number of times until the pattern spaces form little blocks or squares.

The Authentic Succession of Treadles

One way to weave a pattern is according to the way it is threaded. This is known as the authentic development of the pattern, or **weaving as threaded** or **as-drawn-in**, and also as **weaving on the diagonal.** One should weave a section in this way first; then create other desired effects by changing the order of the treadling.

It is easy to work out the authentic way of weaving a pattern from the succession of the harnesses on the paper plan of the pattern draft to be used. How to read a draft in the authentic way is shown in Fig. 107 at **D.** Starting at the right side of the draft, each successive combination of harnesses is enclosed in a dotted oval. Simply weave the various combinations of two harnesses in the order indicated. Follow each Pattern row with a row of Tabby. The result of weaving the harnesses by this authentic succession is shown in the texture in Fig. 107 at **F.** Reading from right to left in the draft at **D,** we have harnesses 1 and 2 together

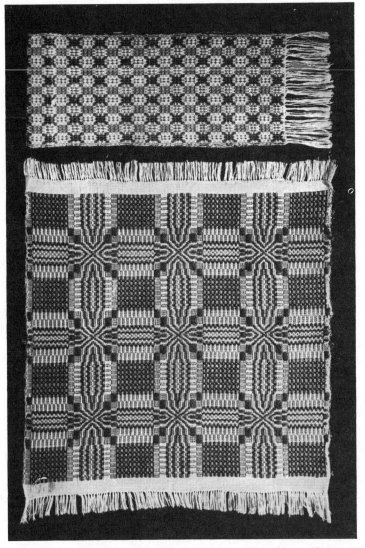

Fig. 108—Two Overshot patterns woven with two colors. Above, Christmas runner with dark block of deep green and light blocks of red. Below, Cross of Tennessee pillow top with large blocks of cross in deep red and all other blocks of alternating navy and deep red pattern thread.

(note the oval line around them). Weave these as Pattern; and follow by Tabby. The next combination is 2 and 3 (note the oval); the next is 3 and 4; and the next is 4 and 3. Since this last is the same as 3 and 4, the row with harnesses 3 and 4 is to be woven twice. The next combination is 2 and 3, the next 1 and 2, then 4 and 1, and then 1 and 4 (making 4 and 1 twice).

Notice that we always start each new group with the last number of the previous group. For instance, harnesses 1 and 2 form the first group. The second group starts with harness 2 and adds the next harness, or 3. The third group starts with harness 3 and adds the next harness, or 4; and so on. The complete weaving directions for the attractive Rosepath pattern shown in Fig. 107 at **F** will, therefore, be:

Harnesses 1 and 2 once (follow each
row by its proper Tabby)
Harnesses 2 and 3 once
Harnesses 3 and 4 twice
Harnesses 2 and 3 once
Harnesses 1 and 2 once
Harnesses 4 and 1 twice
Repeat

Any four-harness pattern draft should
first be woven according to the succession
of its threaded groups in this way, to get
its authentic weaving plan. Weaving it
any other way produces an entirely different fabric pattern. Note the effect of
weaving the Rosepath according to the
Twill succession of harnesses directly beneath its draft in Fig. 107 at **D**, i.e., harnesses 1 and 2, 2 and 3, 3 and 4, and 4
and 1; and repeat. This treadling forms
repeated zig-zag lines instead of the small
diamonds at **F**.

The simple Twill threading in Fig. 107
at **C** is woven as Plain Weave directly
beneath its draft, but at **E** it is woven in
the authentic way, forming diagonal lines.
Other patterns in this book shown woven
in the authentic way are: Figs. 113, 116,
118, 123, 129, and 130. The authentic
manner of weaving, or "weaving as drawn
in," acts as a standard guide in which one
may see future possibilities of creating
new textures by changing the succession
of harnesses and the number of their repeats. An example of the creative adaptation of a pattern is shown in Fig. 108,
where two colors are used for Overshot
Patterns woven "**as draw in.**" Wisely
chosen colors help to set off the pattern
figures.

Obtaining Variations by Different Harness Successions

Variations or departures from the authentic pattern development can be any
succession whatever, with Tabby usually
inserted after each row of Pattern. For instance, try the following for the Rosepath draft shown in Fig. 107 at **D**:

Variation No. 1

PATTERN THREAD	TABBY THREAD
Harnesses 2 and 3 once;	Harnesses 1 and 3
Harnesses 3 and 4 once;	Harnesses 2 and 4
Harnesses 2 and 3 once;	Harnesses 1 and 3
Harnesses 1 and 2 once;	Harnesses 2 and 4
Harnesses 4 and 1 once;	Harnesses 1 and 3
Harnesses 1 and 2 once;	Harnesses 2 and 4
Repeat	

Variation No. 2

Pattern: Harnesses 2 and 3 twice (follow
each row by a row of Tabby)
4 rows of white Tabby between this and
the border following.

Center Border of the Pattern:
Harnesses 1 and 2 once (follow by Tabby)
Harnesses 4 and 1 four times (follow each
row by Tabby)
Harnesses 1 and 2 once (follow by Tabby)
4 rows of white Tabby

Pattern: Harnesses 2 and 3 twice (follow
each row by Tabby)

The "Tie-up" of the Loom for Treadling. The Use of Lams

In the weaving directions given in this
lesson we have written each harness combination out in full. An example follows:

COMBINATION	HARNESSES
1	1 and 2
2	2 and 3
3	3 and 4
4	4 and 1
5	1 and 3 (Tabby shed 1)
6	2 and 4 (Tabby shed 2)

On looms in which the harnesses are
connected directly to the treadles, the
directions must be written as in the right-
hand column, and it is convenient to use
both feet in treadling (on a table loom,
a double handling of the levers is necessary). However, on some looms it is possible to depress two harnesses at a time

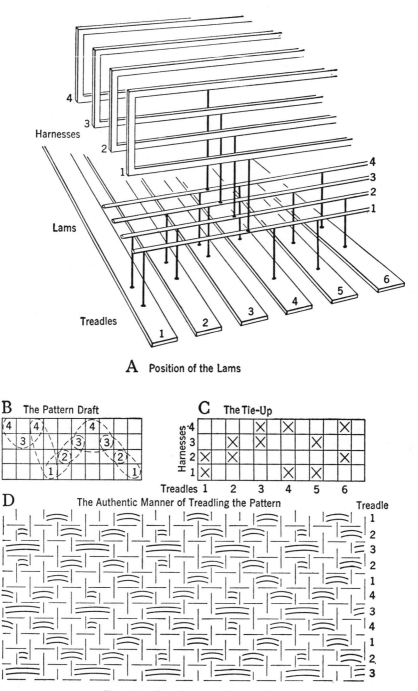

A   Position of the Lams

B   The Pattern Draft

C   The Tie-Up

D   The Authentic Manner of Treadling the Pattern

Fig. 109—Use of a tie-up for treadling.

by using one foot only (or a single hand action). On these looms there is an extra set of bars, called "lams," which are hung midway between the harnesses and the treadles, as shown in Fig. 109 at **A**. Each harness is attached to the lam directly beneath it, and one or more lams may be attached to each treadle, as shown in Fig. 109, where lams 1 and 2 are attached to treadle 1, lams 2 and 3 to treadle 2, lams 3 and 4 to treadle 3, lams 4 and 1 to treadle 4, lams 1 and 3 to treadle 5, and lams 2 and 4 to treadle 6. During the weaving a single treadle brings down the attached lams, which in turn bring down the harnesses directly above them and numbered like them.

If your loom has this construction, you can use what is known as a **"tie-up"** to designate which harnesses are to be connected, through their intermediary lams, to the treadles. In Fig. 109 a typical draft is shown at **B** and its tie-up is shown at **C**. The treadles are marked below the tie-up by the numbers 1, 2, 3, 4, 5, and 6. The harnesses are marked as usual, with a number beside each harness. The vertical row above any treadle number contains crosses designating the lams which are tied to this particular treadle and which will be drawn down when this treadle is depressed, bringing with them their corresponding harnesses.

The extensive use of the standard tie-up given in Fig. 109 was promoted by Mary Meigs Atwater, a pioneer of better weaving methods who helped restore the weaving of Colonial days for modern weavers. Hence, it is sometimes known as the "Atwater tie-up."

In weaving a pattern from its tie-up, the directions can thus be considerably shortened. For instance, reading the first combination of the draft in Fig. 109 at **B** in the detailed method, we write down:

Harnesses 1 and 2. By this new arrangement, however, we can write simply Combination 1 or Treadle 1 (abbreviated to Tr. 1); since, in our tie-up at **C**, harnesses 1 and 2 are connected to this treadle. To weave harnesses 2 and 3, simply write Tr. 2; for harnesses 3 and 4, Tr. 3; for harnesses 4 and 1, Tr. 4. Note that the two Tabby combinations (harnesses 1 and 3 and 2 and 4) are attached to treadles 5 and 6, respectively; so, to weave Tabby, we simply write Tr. 5 and then Tr. 6. One may tie up one's loom in other ways, numbering the combinations in the manner found most convenient. For instance, Treadles 3 and 4 are sometimes tied up as Tabby because they come at the center of the six treadles and it is easy to weave them frequently.

To treadle the pattern draft given in Fig. 109 in the authentic way, going from right to left and reading the combinations enclosed in the dotted ovals, we have: Harnesses 1 and 2 (Tr. 1); harnesses 2 and 3 (Tr. 2); harnesses 3 and 4 (Tr. 3); harnesses 2 and 3 (Tr. 2); and so on. This succession is given in the row of figures at the right of diagram **D** below the tie-up, where the effect of the authentic weaving is shown on paper. Read down the column, as follows: Tr. 1, 2, 3, 2, 1, 4, 3, 4, 1, 2, 3, etc. The weaver inserts the proper Tabby after each pattern row, depressing first Tr. 5 and then Tr. 6 in regular alternation for this purpose.

Note that in the pattern draft in Fig. 109 at **B**, for absolute correctness, the harness combination 3 and 4, or Treadle 3, should be woven twice in succession since it occurs twice in succession on the draft. This was shown in the drawing of Fig. 107 at **F**. However, this particular type of pattern is often woven with only one row of weaving at the point, as shown here. It weaves into a Diamond.

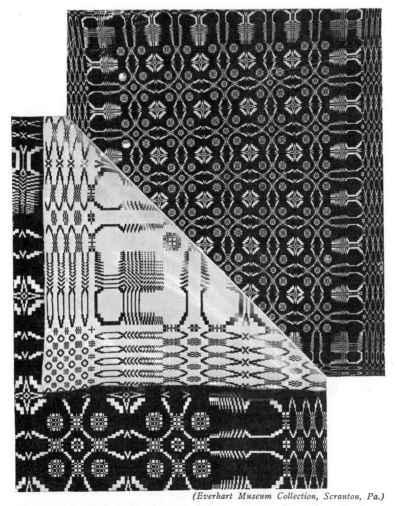

(Everhart Museum Collection, Scranton, Pa.)

The early American home always included a variety of coverlets. Handsome double cloth fabrics like the one shown are now collector's items. The blue and white textile is made of a handsome warp and weft and shows a Whig Rose type center motif with a Pine Tree border. The obverse and reverse sides are shown here.

27—The Twill Family of Weaves. Herringbone Variations

Why the Twill Weave Is so Popular

EVERYONE knows and likes the **Twill Weave**. It has a pleasing texture, with the weft showing along diagonal lines and forming long slanting rows of color and design. The standard Twill Weave and some of the effects produced by its weaving are shown in Fig. 111. It is really an all-over surface pattern, but is made so easily and with such a subtle blending of lights and shadows that it stands alone as a type of fabric, quite different from many of the materials woven on four-harness looms with large pattern figures. Cloth made in the Twill Weave is not only attractive but very durable, and this fact makes it an indispensable textile for both our clothes and our homes. Woolen cloth woven as Twill is known to us as **Serge**.

Most of the clothes we wear are woven with either Plain Weave or Twill, and the latter provides fully as many interesting possibilities as the former. There are many variations of the Twill. Thus, there are the **Herringbone Patterns** that have lines running zig-zag across the material like the V-bone of the herring, if you vision this as being repeated in its design; and there is the **Goose-Eye Pattern**, which is a Herringbone woven with a reverse so that the V's are closed and form little diamonds, with centers like small eyes. You have seen these patterns many times in suit materials. Two of the cloth samples in Fig. 110 are in the Herring-

bone pattern. At the upper right is shown men's suiting in a Herringbone pattern woven with nubby yarns. At the lower right is shown overcoat material in a repeated Herringbone pattern woven with three colors. At the upper left is material in the regular Twill threading woven with a reverse so as to produce zig-zag lines having a vertical trend. At the lower left is shown shepherds'-check fabric for ladies' dress or suit materials.

The Twill has so many variations that we can speak of the **Twill family of weaves**. They are all equally useful for both men's and women's suits and overcoats; for boys' and girls' jackets, tams, slacks, and trousers; for soldiers' and sailors' uniforms; for gay Scotch Tartan costumes; for scarves and neckties, belts, and purses. The very same qualities of durability and beauty, which make Twills so popular for clothes, prove their value for household usage, as in towels, table linens, draperies, upholstery, and twill blankets which are the last word in softness and comfort.

Technical Importance of the Twill Weave

Twill is the weave to study after one has mastered Plain Weave, for like the latter it requires only one shuttle for weaving and is the very simplest of the four-harness patterns to follow.

All weavers should become thoroughly conversant with the Twill Weave and its

Fig. 110—Suit and coat materials in the Twill Weave and
its variations.

principles and variations, for it lies at the basis of Pattern Weaving. Our effective patterns and their units are simply enlarged groups of Twill successions, and the many connections, reverses, and variations which occur to form different pattern plans and motifs refer directly back to the same variations of the Twill in its basic form.

Threading and Weaving the Twill Weave

The threading for the Twill consists in repetition of the four notes, harnesses 1, 2, 3, 4. Instead of weaving alternately on harnesses 1 and 3 and on harnesses 2 and 4, as in Tabby, one weaves adjacent harness notes together. Thus, one uses harnesses 1 and 2, 2 and 3, 3 and 4, and 4 and 1 in succession. Because the weft goes over such short spaces while weaving Twill (it goes over only two or three warp threads at a time) and progresses a single thread to right or left at each row, only one weft thread is necessary, as in the Tabby Weave.

The Twill Weave has its own construction and resulting character and texture. When weaving a piece of cloth as Twill, in the foregoing succession of harnesses,

Four Harness Twill Threading

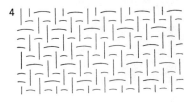

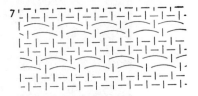

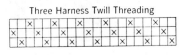

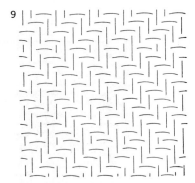

Three Harness Twill Threading

Fig. 111—Variations in Twill Weave by changing succession of harnesses.

one often starts and ends the piece with a section of Tabby which serves as a hem, the rest of the piece being woven with the same thread but with the Twill texture.

In the Twill Weave, it is possible to beat the successive weft rows more tightly together than in weaving Tabby; for there is an overlapping of threads in any two adjacent weft rows. One follows the combination of harnesses 1 and 2 with harnesses 2 and 3, thus causing harness 2 to carry its threads to the same level for two successive rows. Then harnesses 2 and 3 are followed by 3 and 4, and so on. The warp threads are always thus carried under and over two rows of weft. Likewise, the weft passes under and over groups of two threads and progresses in each row one thread at a time to a new pair. This overlapping of both warp and weft over two threads at a time gives more room for the beating of their respective threads together, in contrast to Plain Weave where both warp and weft pass under and over one thread at a time, making a close interlocking in which a thread held above in one row cannot move past the thread of opposite tendency in the next row.

History of the Twill Weave

History confirms our wisdom in using the Twill Weave in so many ways. This weave was used for linens in Biblical times. The name serge was given to woolen cloth woven in the Twill Pattern by the Romans nearly 2,000 years ago. The word serge comes from the old Roman word sarge, which was a square shawl worn by the Roman soldiers on the march. It served many purposes— as a cloak in the rain, as a blanket at night, and in peacetime as a bag slung from the shoulders to carry grain to sow in the fields. During wartime the Romans kept their slaves, the Gallic weavers, busily at work weaving sarges for them by the tens of thousands. In modern times we still find serge, or Twill cloth, one of the most durable and useful of our fabrics.

Characteristics of the Twill: Its Beauty, Simplicity, and Durability

The weaving of the Twill or its variations produces a very short overshot, with the weft passing over only two or three warp threads at a time; therefore, no Tabby thread is necessary to bind in the woven rows. When the Twill is woven as written, i.e., in the authentic way, the result is diagonal lines running across the material, as shown in Fig. 107 at E. The thread used for the weft should be of the same size as the warp or a little heavier. The resulting texture is an all-over surface design of fine figuration. Such all-over patterns as these, with their small figures, short weft skips, and no binding Tabby, are known as one-thread weaves. They are usually based on the Twill or its variations. In Figs. 111, 112, and 113 are given some patterns and weaving methods for variations of the Twill Weave. A sample of upholstery material in Herringbone is shown in Fig. 135 and a girl's Scotch-Plaid outfit woven as Twill is shown in Fig. 89. When an authentic Scotch-Plaid design is woven as Twill with homespun wool, it is known as a true "Tartan."

The following characteristics of the Twill family of weaves have made them popular and useful since early weaving days.

1. **Beauty:** The Twill Weaves produce very beautiful and interesting all-over

surface effects composed of repeated small-pattern figures.

2. Simplicity: The Twill Weave, itself, consists of the simplest succession of harnesses it is possible to thread on a four-harness loom. When woven, its texture lines are simple straight rows of color or texture running diagonally across the fabric. Yet this very simplicity is pleasing and provides a good background texture to utilize for many delightful weaving changes. The variations of the Twill have equally simple and beautiful texture lines, which are somewhat more broken but form pleasing figurations.

3. Durability: The Twill Weaves produce a durable texture when woven, the warp and weft threads overlapping to make a firm fabric, and usually being packed close together. In the Twill itself the weft usually passes over only two warp threads at a time; and in the variations, such as Herringbone and Rosepath, it never passes over more than three warp threads at a time.

4. Speed of Weaving: Because they require only one weft for weaving, Twills can be woven very rapidly. Yet they have the advantage of producing patterns which are often as attractive as those requiring two shuttles, i.e., a pattern weft and a tabby weft.

Rules to Observe When Weaving Twill

When weaving Twill, the following rules should be observed:

1. The Threading: This is the same as that for Tabby or Plain Weave on four harnesses, i.e., harnesses 1, 2, 3, and 4, and repeat; or harness 4, 3, 2, and 1, and repeat. Either succession may be used.

2. Numbers of Warp and Weft Threads: If you are using the same

thread for both a Tabby and a Twill Weave, and you wish to get about the same weight of cloth, hold back slightly on the beating of the Twill section, for the weft thread tends to pack down more closely in the Twill than in the Tabby. Likewise, for a Twill fabric one usually sets the warp a bit closer than he would if using the same warp for weaving a Tabby texture. The close warp setting prevents the weft from piling up too closely.

3. Sizes of Warp and Weft Threads: The warp and weft threads should be of about the same weight, or the weft should be very little heavier than the warp.

4. Perfectly Balanced Twill Fabric: One should weave so that there is exactly the same number of weft threads per inch as there are warp threads per inch. This too, as in Tabby, is sometimes called a "50-50 fabric." For instance, if the warp is set at 20 threads per inch, the best texture results from weaving 20 threads per inch in the weft. Choose warp and weft threads of such weights as to achieve this result. The number of weft rows per inch is also controlled by the firmness of the beat when weaving. One can be guided in the proper setting of the various sizes of warp threads by consulting the Thread Chart in Lesson 35.

Good Color Combinations

All of the Twills and their variations make attractive material; but in all of them the prettiest effects are obtained by using warp of one color and weft thread of the same size but of a different color, or a different shade of the same color. This suggestion applies to the Twill proper and to the Dornick, Herringbone, Rosepath, and Goose-Eye Patterns. Suggested pairs of color are:

Colors For Light Texture Effects

Warp	Weft
Beige	Bittersweet
White	Ecru
Gray	White
Tan	Gooseberry
Cream	Light brown
Gray	Dull rose
Gray	Blue
White	Sea-green
White	Yellow

Colors For Dark Texture Effects

Warp	Weft
Dark brown	Tan
Dark green	Light green
Navy	Gray
Old rose	Mahogany
Gray or blue	Black
Brown	Red
Green	Dark gray or black
Henna	Blue
Red	Black

Also use two shades of blue, green, rose, gray, tan, rust, etc.

Creating Variations in Twill Textures

Although the threading of Twill is so simple, it may be woven in so many different ways that it becomes a most resourceful pattern. This simple **threading**, as well as its **weaving**, may also be varied to obtain a wide range of patterns of the same character, which in general are known as Herringbone patterns. We will consider first the variations in the weaving of the regular Twill; and then variations in its threading, or the formation of the Herringbone patterns.

A. Varations in Weaving: Different effects in the woven texture of the Twill Weave are obtained as follows (see Figs. 110 and 111):

1. By changing the order of the treadling, thus forming subtle differences in the surface texture; or reversing the order, thus producing zig-zag lines having a vertical trend (see the suiting fabric in Fig. 110 at the upper left).

2. By adding stripes in the warp or weft or both, thus making columns of design or checks and plaids. Wherever there are color changes, the threads appear in different lights and shadows (see the fabric in Fig. 110 at the lower left).

B. Varations in Threading: The weaver may create a wide range of patterns which belong to the Twill family of weaves by altering the simple succession of the four harnesses that make up the regular Twill threading, i.e., harnesses 1, 2, 3, and 4, and repeat. Some of these variations are shown in Figs. 112 and 113. This changing of the threading results in texture variations or the altering of the Twill diagonals to form Herringbone angles, Diamond figures, etc.

A. WAYS TO CHANGE THE WEAVING OF THE TWILL

Method of Weaving Twill-Fashion

In the diagrams of Fig. 107, the draft or threading plan for each pattern is given above a sketch of its woven texture. The harness numbers 4, 3, 2, and 1 are placed at the right of each draft. One reads the draft from right to left, starting to thread at the right side of the loom. The weaving plan is given in the long vertical right-hand column of figures. For instance, in the pattern at **E**, one weaves by first putting harnesses 1 and 2 down together; then lowering harnesses 2 and 3, 3 and 4, and 4 and 1 in succession; and repeating. When this particular succession of harness combinations is used, we speak of the pattern as being woven **"Twill-Fashion."** This is the method of weaving given in Fig. 111, diagram No. 1. The many other effects shown in Fig. 111 are the results of changing this simple succession of harnesses.

Popular Weaving Variations of the Twill

The effects shown in Fig. 111 are obtained by varying the succession of the harnesses in the following manner.

No. 1. Simplest Twill Weave: To produce the effect in diagram No. 1, Fig. 111, two harnesses are lowered at a time, according to the succession indicated in Fig. 107 at E. This pattern is called **Two-and-Two Twill** (2 and 2 Twill) because for each row of weaving two of the harnesses are lowered while the other two are raised. The result is an equally balanced fabric, which appears the same on both the right and wrong sides. The diagonal texture is shown in diagram No. 1, Fig. 111. The best effect is obtained by making both the warp and the weft of about the same weight of yarn but in different colors. This arrangement sets off the small texture units, and brings out the attractive diagonals.

No. 2. The One-and-Three Twill and the Three-and-One Twill: For a fabric showing more warp on one side, and more weft on the opposite side, weave single harnesses at a time. On a counterbalanced loom, use harness 1 alone, 2 alone, 3 alone, and 4 alone; and repeat. When each single harness is lowered, the other three are raised, and more warp shows on the upper surface. This effect is called the **One-and-Three Twill** (1 and 3 Twill). For the same effect on a jack loom, first treadle harnesses 1, 2, and 3 together; then treadle harnesses 2, 3, and 4, harnesses 3, 4, and 1, and harnesses 4, 1, and 2; and repeat.

To obtain the opposite effect with more weft showing on the upper surface, weave the **Three-and-One Twill** (3 and 1 Twill) by depressing three harnesses at a time. Thus, on a counterbalanced loom, first weave harnesses 1, 2, and 3 together; then weave harnesses 2, 3, and 4, harnesses 3, 4, and 1, and harnesses 4, 1, and 2; and repeat. For the same effect on a jack loom, treadle harness 1 alone, harness 2 alone, harness 3 alone, and harness 4 alone; and repeat.

The One-and-Three Twill and the Three-and-One Twill are really the same. One treadling results in a weft predominance on the upper side of the cloth and a warp predominance on the under side; while the other treadling gives the opposite result. They are therefore quite interchangeable. On a counterbalanced loom the weaver will find it easier to weave the Three-and-One Twill, i.e., harnesses 1, 2, 3; 2, 3, 4; etc. On a jack loom he will enjoy weaving the One-and-Three Twill or treadling of single harnesses 1, 2, 3, 4, etc.

For either the One-and-Three Twill or the Three-and-One Twill, the best effects are obtained by using warp of one color and weft of another. Then, one side of the fabric will be predominantly of one of the colors, while the other side is of the second color. Heavy overcoat materials are sometimes woven this way. The fabric looks as if there were a separate colored lining, whereas this effect is only the result of weaving the Twill just described, with more warp on one side than on the other.

No. 3. Broken Twill: To produce the mottled effect shown, weave harnesses 1 and 2, 2 and 3, 4 and 1, and 3 and 4; and repeat. Here the succession of harnesses 3 and 4 and harnesses 4 and 1 is simply reversed

No. 4. Twill Weave Interrupted by Tabby: The rows of any Twill may alternate with rows of Tabby, shown by dots in diagram No. 4. The weave is as follows, the Tabby being given in parentheses: Harnesses 1 and 2, (1 and 3), 2 and 3, (2 and 4), 3 and 4, (1 and 3), 4 and 1, (2 and 4); and repeat. The thread in the Tabby rows may be the same as that in the Twill rows or different.

No. 5. Pebbly Effect: This is obtained by using alternating colors, and treadling as for No. 1: Harnesses 1 and 2, dark; 2 and 3, light; 3 and 4, dark; 4 and 1, light; and repeat.

No. 6. Twill on Opposites: To produce this effect, weave as follows with Tabby between rows: Harnesses 1 and 2, dark; (2 and 4, light); 3 and 4, dark; (1 and 3, light); and repeat.

No. 7. Smart Dress Texture: This is woven as follows: First, two rows of Tabby with 1 and 3, and 2 and 4; then two Twill rows with harnesses 1, 2, and 3, and harnesses 1, 2, and 4; then two more Tabby rows with 1 and 3, and 2 and 4; and two more Twill rows with harnesses 1, 3, and 4, and harnesses 2, 3, and 4. Repeat this pattern.

On a jack loom, you may weave this design with one treadle down instead of three, as follows: Harnesses 1 and 3, and 2 and 4; then harness 4 alone and harness 3 alone; harnesses 1 and 3, and 2 and 4; harness 2 alone and harness 1 alone.

No. 8. Reverse Treadling: By repeating the four rows given in diagram No. 1, the result is a fabric with its diagonal weave going all one way. By reversing the treadling, the diagonal lines show in the opposite direction, producing a zig-zag effect. To weave the short reverse in diagram No. 8, proceed as follows: Harnesses 1 and 2, 2 and 3, 3 and 4, and 4 and 1; then reverse to harnesses 3 and 4, and 2 and 3; and repeat all. This is the way the suiting material in Fig. 110 at the upper left was woven.

No. 9. Large Zig-Zag Pattern; This effect is obtained by repeating the regular treadling in diagram No. 1, Fig. 111, several times, and then repeating its reverse several times: Weave harnesses 1 and 2, 2 and 3, 3 and 4, and 4 and 1; repeat this sequence twice more; reverse to harnesses 3 and 4, 2 and 3, and 1 and 2; then weave harnesses 4 and 1, 3 and 4, and 2 and 3; and repeat all. The result is a fabric with longer diagonal lines traveling in repeated zig-zags.

No. 10. Three-Harness Twill: The three-harness Twill requires a special threading as shown. Its effect when woven is similar to the four-harness Twill but it has a closer texture. It was the first Twill used in weaving in olden days. It is woven by using harnesses 1 and 2, 2 and 3, and 3 and 1; and repeating. It cannot be woven as Tabby.

No. 11. Traditional Jeans Twill: This pattern has the three-harness threading shown in diagram No. 10, and is a combination of two textures made by first weaving two harnesses at a time, then one. It might be called a combined weaving, first of a Two-and-One and then of a One-and-Two Twill, as follows: First weave harnesses 1 and 2, 2 and 3, and 3 and 1, and repeat two or three times; then weave harness 1 alone, harness 2 alone, and harness 3 alone, and repeat two or three times; repeat all. The diagram at No. 11 shows first the One-and-Three Twill effect, then the Two-and-One effect. Since they alternate, it does not matter which comes first.

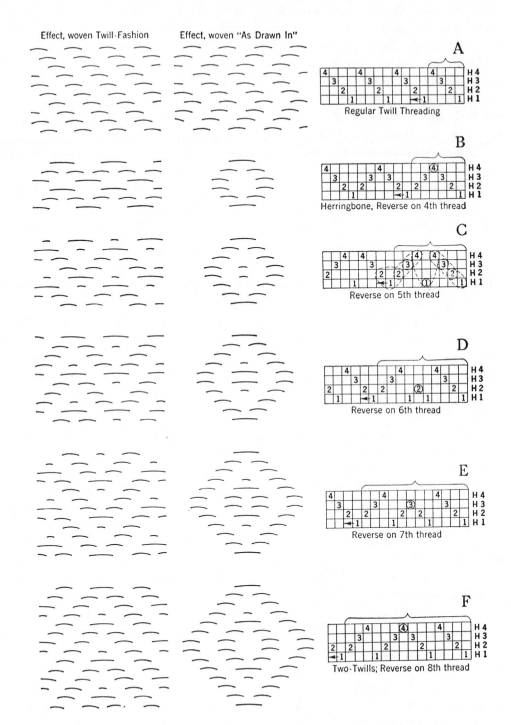

Effect, woven Twill-Fashion   Effect, woven "As Drawn In"

A
Regular Twill Threading

B
Herringbone, Reverse on 4th thread

C
Reverse on 5th thread

D
Reverse on 6th thread

E
Reverse on 7th thread

F
Two-Twills; Reverse on 8th thread

Fig. 112—Variations in Herringbone Pattern by reversing the threading at different points.

B. VARIATIONS IN THREADING THE TWILL

Effect of Reversing

We have just learned how various effects in Twill textures are obtained by changing the succession of the harness combinations in its weaving. As shown in Fig. 111, different textures appear as interrupted diagonals, as mottled patterns, as vertical zig-zag effects, etc. We will now learn how to produce horizontal zig-zag effects, as shown in Fig. 112, by reversing the threading at points. In Fig. 112 at **A** is a regular Twill. At **B**, there is a reverse on the 4th thread, or after one repeat. At **C**, there is a reverse on the 5th thread, i.e., on harness 1. At **D**, there is a reverse on the 6th thread, i.e., on harness 2. At **E**, there is a reverse on the 7th thread, i.e., on harness 3. In other words, we see how the threading of Twill patterns can reverse on any harness. After a reverse, or point, use the harness numbers in reverse order until you come to the starting harness again, i.e., harness No. 1. Here start repeating the complete pattern once more. In each of the drafts given in Fig. 112, one complete repeat of the pattern is marked by a bracket, the reverse point is enclosed in a circle, and the beginning of the next repeat of the pattern is marked by an arrow.

In Fig. 112 at **F**, we see the next reverse, i.e., on the 8th thread. This is really two complete repeats of the Twill and a reverse. The effect of weaving this pattern twill-fashion is shown in Fig. 113 from **A** to **C**, and at **D** in the texture sketch below the draft. The pattern formed by these two complete repeats of the Twill and its reverse is called a **Two-Twill Pattern**. In Fig. 113 from **E** to **G**, we have three complete Twill re-

peats and a reverse, or a **Three-Twill Pattern**. It is clear that we can have any number of Twill repeats and then their reverse. There are many more combinations. The Rosepath in Fig. 107 at **D** is a Twill variation with a reverse on the fourth thread and an interruption after the seventh thread made by adding a note on harness 4 before repeating the entire pattern. It may also be written: Hs. 1, 2, 3, 4, (1), 4, 3, and 2, and repeat, in which case it is simply a reverse on the fifth thread.

Herringbone Patterns

A Twill draft in which the succession of harnesses zig-zags consistently as the draft progresses from right to left, as described for Figs. 112 and 113, results in a pattern formation called a Herringbone. The simplest Herringbone consists of one Twill and its reverse, as shown in Fig. 112 at **B**. From here the Herringbones range from a reverse on the fifth thread to a reverse on the eighth thread, as shown in Fig. 112, **C** to **F**. For simplicity the weaver generally threads Herringbone to the complete Twill repeats and their reverses, such as the One-Twill and its reverse in Fig. 112 at **B**; the Two-Twill and its reverse in Fig. 112 at **F** and in Fig. 113 at **B**; and the Three-Twill and its reverse in Fig. 113 at **F**. There can be any number of repetitions of the Twill before a reverse point comes, such as four Twills and a reverse, a Five-Twill pattern, or a Ten-Twill pattern. One can also reverse on any thread whatever of the Twill, either in the middle of a repeat or at the end of a complete repeat. Herringbone patterns having a long series of Twill repeats before they reverse are used for very effective blanket textures and for fine table cloths.

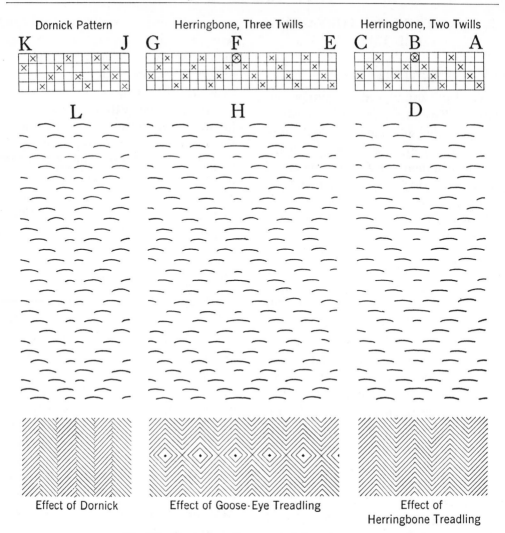

Fig. 113—Herringbone Patterns used for suit weaves.

Weaving Herringbone, or Twill Patterns Having Reverse Points in Their Drafts

Twill patterns may be woven in two ways, namely, **twill-fashion** and **as-drawn-in.**

1. In weaving **twill-fashion**, repeat the following regular succession of the four harnesses: 1 and 2, 2 and 3, 3 and 4, and 4 and 1. The result is the Herringbone effect shown in Fig. 113 at **D** in the texture sketch below the part of the draft from **A** to **C.**

2. In weaving **as-drawn-in**, use the harness combinations in the order in which they appear on the draft from right to left. This causes a reverse in the Twill weaving or treadling at the same point at which there is a reverse on the threading draft. For instance, by this method, the pattern draft shown in Fig. 112 at **C** is woven as follows: Reading the groupings in the dotted ovals from right to left and following the numbers, weave harnesses 1 and 2, 2 and 3, 3 and 4, and 4 and 1; reverse at this point to harnesses 4 and 1

again, 3 and 4, 2 and 3, and 1 and 2; repeat all.

There may be one, two, three, or more
repeats of the regular Twill succession
before reversing, this number of repeats
being given in the draft. The pattern
from **A to C** in Fig. 113 is woven with
two Twill successions of four rows each,
and there is then a reverse with the same
number. The pattern from **E to G** in
Fig. 113 is woven with three Twill successions followed by a reverse. Weaving
these patterns as drawn in results in the
enclosed diamond or lozenge effect
known as Goose-Eye, as shown at **H** in
the texture sketch below the part of the
draft from **E to G**. The weaving procedure may be described as follows:

To weave any Twill draft that has a
reverse point, i.e., any Herringbone, in
such a way as to bring out a diamond
effect, follow the harness numbers in
groups of two as they come in the draft,
reading from right to left. For example,
to weave the Herringbone draft shown in
Fig. 112 at **E**, use harnesses 1 and 2, 2
and 3, 3 and 4, 4 and 1, 1 and 2, and 2
and 3; reverse at this point (where you
find harness 3 enclosed in a circle), weave
harnesses 2 and 3 again, and then follow
with 1 and 2, 4 and 1, 3 and 4, 2 and 3,
and 1 and 2; and repeat all.

The effect of weaving the Herringbone
drafts of Fig. 112 twill-fashion is shown
in the column at the extreme left; and
the effect of weaving them as-drawn-in
is shown in the series of diamonds of different sizes in the center column.

Method of Reversing

The correct way of reversing when
weaving a Herringbone is to use the harness combination at the reverse point
twice, as just described. However, many
weavers follow the draft with only one
row throughout for each harness combination. Thus, for the draft in Fig. 113
from **A to C**, the weaving plan can be:
harnesses 1 and 2, 2 and 3, 3 and 4, 4 and
1, 1 and 2, 2 and 3, (3 and 4 once only),
2 and 3, 1 and 2, 4 and 1, 3 and 4, and 2
and 3; and repeat all.

The correct way of weaving this same
pattern as-drawn-in is: First, use harnesses
1 and 2, *2 and 3, 3 and 4, 4 and 1, 1
and 2, 2 and 3, (3 and 4 twice), 2 and 3,
1 and 2, 4 and 1, 3 and 4, 2 and 3, and (1
and 2 twice).* Then, repeat between the
asterisks.

When weaving two successive rows
with the same harness combination in
any one-thread weave, where there is no
Tabby to separate them, carry the weft
thread around the last warp thread before
weaving back on the second row. For instance, in the reverse on harnesses 3 and
4 just given, weave 3 and 4 the first time,
pass the weft around the last warp thread,
and then weave 3 and 4 the second time.
This prevents the weft thread from pulling out. The two rows of weft at the
reverse point add an accent of color and
texture which serves to bring out the
pattern.

The Dornick Weave

The **Dornick Weave**, shown in Fig.
113 from **J to K**, has a threading very
much like the Herringbone, but there is
a short break in it. It resembles the Two-
Twill Herringbone draft, shown from **A**
to **C**, but the seventh thread skips harness 3 and goes to harness 4, reversing
from here; while the seventh thread in
the reverse part skips harness 2 and goes
on to the next full repeat starting on harness 1. The pattern is written as follows:
harnesses 1, 2, 3, 4, 1, 2; 4, 3, 2, 1, 4, 3;

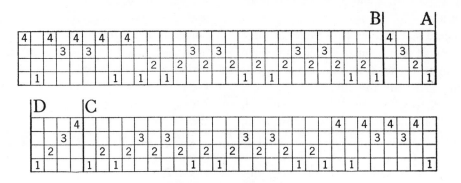

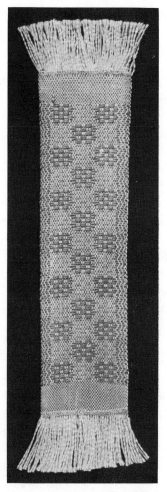

(*Courtesy of Elva Slider*)

Fig. 114—Miniature Dog-Tracks
Pattern with Twill border,
planned for a book-mark.

and repeat. Weave the Dornick pattern in any of the following ways:

(1) Twill-fashion, by using harnesses 1 and 2, 2 and 3, 3 and 4, and 4 and 1, and repeating.

(2) With a reverse, as in the Two-Twill Herringbone, by using harnesses 1 and 2, 2 and 3, 3 and 4, 4 and 1, 1 and 2, 2 and 3, (3 and 4), 2 and 3, 1 and 2, 4 and 1, 3 and 4, and 2 and 3, and repeating all.

(3) The pattern may be woven as-drawn-in for interesting texture effects. Weave harnesses 1 and 2, 2 and 3, 3 and 4, 4 and 1, 1 and 2, (2 and 4), 3 and 4, 2 and 3, 1 and 2, 4 and 1, 3 and 4, and (1 and 3), and repeat all. Or omit the Tabby combinations in parentheses, and otherwise follow the same succession.

The effect of the Dornick woven twill-fashion is shown in the texture sketch below the draft in Fig. 113 at **L**. The texture lines do not come to an exact point at the reverses, and this arrangement given an interesting variety to the weave. It is very popular for suits and overcoats.

Weaving Twill and Herringbone Threadings With Tabby After Each Row

While the accepted way of weaving Twill and Herringbone is to use one thread only for the Twill texture and to omit the Tabby, any pattern in this family may also be woven by following each Twill row by a Tabby row, either with the same thread or with a second thread that is finer. This gives variety to the textures possible.

In all these patterns, Tabby or Plain Weave may be woven at any time by alternating harnesses 1 and 3 and harnesses 2 and 4. On such weaves as the Dornick, this will not give a perfect Tabby, be-

cause of the skips in the pattern, but the texture will be interesting.

The Twill Threading Used for Borders

The simple Twill threading obtained by the regular succession of harnesses 1, 2, 3, and 4 is used to form a selvage or fine-textured border for a great many patterns. It is simple and effective in character, and may be repeated as desired. It is an easy border to plan and thread. Its variations, such as Herringbone and Rosepath, are also used for borders of similar texture but still greater interest in design. See Fig. 132.

In Fig. 114 is shown a bookmark made in the Miniature Dog-Tracks pattern, with a very effective Twill border, which is given in the draft from **A** to **B** and from **C** to **D** and is repeated four times at each selvage. The details of threading and weaving are as follows:

Warp Plan:
  Warp: Perle 20/2.
  Weft: Pattern—Perle 10/2.
  Tabby—20/2 cotton.
  Threads per inch: 60 (4 per dent in a 15-dent reed).
  Width of warp: 1½ in.
  Total number of threads: 87.

Threading Plan: Threads
  Right selvage: **A** to **B** four times..   16
  Pattern: **B** to **C** once..........   55
  Left selvage: **C** to **D** four times..   16
      Total   87

Weaving Plan: Follow each row of Pattern with a row of Tabby.
  First Star: Harnesses 1 and 2 twice; 2 and 3 twice; 1 and 2 twice; 2 and 3 twice; 1 and 2 twice.
  Second Star: Harnesses 4 and 1 twice; 3 and 4 twice; 4 and 1 twice; 3 and 4 twice; 4 and 1 twice.

Alternate the first star and the second star. For a Twill border at each end, weave harnesses 1 and 2 once, 2 and 3 once, 3 and 4 once, and 4 and 1 once; repeat as often as desired. Set off the pattern by weaving a short distance at each end with Tabby. For larger roses weave each combination four times.

TEXTURE WEAVES DERIVED FROM THE TWILL

The Waffle Weave

The Waffle Weave provides the creative weaver with the loveliest of textured surfaces, composed of small pockets of Plain Weave imbedded within raised ridges, formed by heavy warp and weft threads coming up above the regular Tabby surface, in the form of small squares. The weave looks exactly like the texture of a waffle; and if, as many weavers say, "they would rather weave than eat," they are served a popular dish when they decide to "weave a waffle." If the warp and weft are soft and thick, like bedspread cotton, Perle 5, or carpet warp, and if the setting is 12 to 16 threads per inch, the woven cloth is soft and absorbent—splendid for wash cloths and towels to match. With a closer setting, such as cotton 16/3 or linen 30/3 set at 20 to 24 per inch, and textured threads placed at the ridge points in the warp (see harnesses in parenthesis in the following instructions) and woven along the ridges of the weft, the resulting cloth is excellent for upholstery, drapes, pillows, and chairback sets. If warp and weft are of heavy cordy silks, linens, or raytones, the weave makes most unusual evening purses and bags.

Threading: The Waffle Weave is easily understood and threaded, being a variation of the reverse Twill in its simplest form. For a small waffle, thread as follows: Harnesses (1), 2, 3, (4), 3, 2 and repeat. For a larger waffle repeat the harnesses at one or both reverse points, threading harnesses 2, 1, 2, 1, 2, (3, 4, 3), or harnesses 2, 1, 2, 1, 2 (3, 4, 3, 4, 3), or harnesses 2, 1, 2, 1, 2, 1, 2, (3, 4, 3); or using some other similar succession.

Weaving: Use only one weft thread, of the same weight as the warp or a trifle heavier.

Tabby: One usually starts a towel or washcloth with the Tabby. For this, use harnesses 1 and 3 alternately with harnesses 2 and 4. Sections of Tabby may also be woven in between sections of Waffles in the same or different colors to give colored bands or borders. Try a section of Waffle (ridge, waffle, and ridge), then 1 inch of Tabby, and then another section of Waffle.

The Ridge: Weave harness 3 alone; then 4 alone, then 3 alone.

The Waffle: Weave harnesses 2 and 4; 1, 3, and 4 together; 2, 3, and 4; 1, 3, and (4); (*) then harnesses 2 and 4. If more rows are desired to make the waffle pockets square, add more repeats of harnesses 2, 3, 4, and 1, 3, 4 at the point marked (*).

Alternate ridges and waffles for the desired distance. Finish with a ridge before adding Tabby.

The Raindrops Pattern

Everyone loves the Raindrops Pattern, which is just as simple and soft in texture as the raindrops of Spring. It is nothing more than the Twill Reverse called the Herringbone Pattern woven in a way that is different. The woven cloth suggests small repeated drops of texture resembling tiny diamonds, and weavers love it for nubby towels and textured luncheon sets or draperies, as well as for dress goods that are different. The best results come with warp and weft of perles, flosses, or linens. If wool is used, one achieves a satisfying surface for blankets, couch throws, and scarves; and for baby blankets soft wool with silk flecks may be used and the weave is just right—a dainty and simple texture.

Threading: Thread harnesses 2, 1, 2, 3, 4, 3. This is just the same as the Herringbone (harnesses 1, 2, 3, 4, 3, 2), but it starts at a different point. The threading may also be written 1, 2, 1, 4, 3, 4, for this too gives the same results.

Weaving: Tabby may be produced by alternating harnesses 1 and 3 with harnesses 2 and 4.

Weaving Method 1: Use one weft thread only, slightly heavier than the warp. Weave harnesses 4 and 1; 1 and 2; 4 and 1; 3 and 4. Repeat all.

Weaving Method 2: Use a heavy pattern thread and a tabby thread of the same weight as the warp. Weave Tabby after each Pattern row, using for the pattern the following succession of harnesses; 3 and 4, two times; 4 and 1, once; 1 and 2, two times; 4 and 1, once. Repeat all.

Huck Toweling Pattern

This weave is splendid for towels, luncheon sets, or drapes, for summer dress goods in white perle or linen, and for textured bags and pillows. It is a speckled fabric with just enough texture for simple effective materials. This little weave also comes directly from the versatile Twill Reverse or Herringbone.

Threading A (for a small figure): Harnesses 1, 2, 3, 4, 3, 2 and repeat.

Threading B (for a large figure): Harnesses 2, 1, 2, 1, 2, 3, 4, 3, 4, 3 and repeat.

Note that this is the same as one of the Waffle weaves.

Weaving: Use only one weft thread, of the same weight as the warp or slightly heavier.

Weave A: Harnesses 1 and 3; 1 and 2; 1 and 3; 2 and 4; 3 and 4; and 2 and 4.

Weave B: Harnesses 1 and 3; 2 and 4; 1 and 3; 2 and 4; 1, 3, and 4 together; 2 and 4; 1 and 3; 2 and 4; 1 and 3; 1, 2, and 4 together. Repeat all.

Canvas Weave, or Monk's Cloth

The texture of this popular material has a coarse granular quality and is suitable for towels, drapes, luncheon sets, runners, purses, mats, etc. It is very much like the Huck, but has two successive threads on harnesses 1 and 4. This breaks the rule for writing drafts when we wish to weave Tabby from them; but we sometimes break the rule on purpose to achieve textural effects.

Threading: Harnesses 1, 1, 2, 3, 4, 4, 3, 2 and repeat.

Weaving: Use only one weft thread, of the same weight as the warp or a bit heavier. Weave harnesses 1 and 3; 1 and 2; 1 and 3; 2 and 4; 3 and 4; 2 and 4.

Basket Weave

One can make pairs of warp and weft threads interlock with each other to form a basket-like mesh. This fabric is splendid to use for outdoor table mats, heavy drapes, pillows, textured runners, sturdy bags, etc., as well as for blankets if woven with wool.

Threading: Again we use the harnesses twice in succession. Thread harnesses 1, 1, 2, 2, 3, 3, 4, 4, and repeat.

Weaving: When using only one weft thread, it should be of the same weight as the warp or slightly heavier. Weave harnesses 1 and 3, two times. When weaving two rows of weft through the same shed, pass these threads around the last warp thread to prevent them from being pulled out; or weave harnesses 1 and 3 only once, using a double-strand weft and flattening out the strands after they are run through. Next, weave harnesses 2 and 4 two times, passing the weft around the last warp thread in the same way as you have previously done for harnesses 1 and 3; or again weave harnesses 2 and 4 only once with a double-strand weft. Alternate harnesses 1 and 3 with harnesses 2 and 4 thus.

Indian Saddle Blanket Weave

If the Twill weave or any of its variations is threaded so that the warp threads are quite far apart, and the weft packs down closely enough to cover them, a thick blanket weave results. If this pattern is woven in changing colors, there results the very lovely Indian Saddle Blanket Weave used in the west for saddle blankets. This durable weave is useful to the hand weaver for bed blankets, couch throws, heavy pillows, and mats, as well as for knitting bags, men's belts, pouches, sandals, and purses.

Threading: For Twill effect, harnesses 1, 2, 3, 4 and repeat; for Herringbone, harnesses 1, 2, 3, 4, 3, 2; for repeats of the Twill and Reverses, such as Three Twills, harnesses 1, 2, 3, 4, 1, 2, 3, 4, 1, 2, 3, 4, 3, 2, 1, 4, 3, 2, 1, 4, 3, 2. Repeat.

Setting: Set a heavy warp, such as carpet warp, at 8 or 10 threads per inch, or a wool warp of Homespun at 8 or 10 threads per inch. Choose a weft that will cover the warp when beat closely.

Weaving: Use three separate wefts, all of the same kind of heavy cotton or wool, but of three different colors, such as red, white, and blue, for patriotic colors, or contrasting tones of the same color. Keep colors in the same order, as in the following schedule:

Row	Harness	Color
1	1 and 2	Red (a)
2	2 and 3	White(b)
3	3 and 4	Blue (c)
4	4 and 1	Red
5	1 and 2	White
6	2 and 3	Blue
7	3 and 4	Red
8	4 and 1	White
9	1 and 2	Blue
10	2 and 3	Red
11	3 and 4	White
12	4 and 1	Blue

Keep repeating all 12 rows.

Two-Color Twill, Also Called "Syncopated Weave"

In this weave two series of Twill successions are alternated with each other, each being threaded to a different color. We will write one series of harness notes with simple numbers, this series having threads of the first color; and will write the other series of harness notes with numbers in parentheses, this series having threads of the second color.

Threading: Thread from right to left on the draft as follows: harnesses 1, (3), 2, (4), 3, (1), 4, (2), 3, (1), 2, (4), and repeat. Note that each harness in parenthesis is the alternate of the harness preceding it that has no parenthesis. Any Twill or Reverse Twill weave can be written on a draft, with spaces left between successive notes; and these can be filled in with the alternates in a different color in this way. This method will always result in this unusual Syncopated Weave or Two-Color Twill.

Setting: For soft blanket textures set Germantown in two colors at 10 threads per inch; or set medium weight Homespun at 15 threads per inch. Weave with material of the same weight.

For sturdy mottled upholstery, set carpet warp or linen 10/2 at 15 or 16 threads per inch. Weave with carpet warp, linen 10/2, cotton 10/3, or Perle 3.

Weaving: Different effects are possible by weaving in three ways:

1. Use only one color weft. Weave as Twill or as Twill and its Reverse.

2. Use two alternating weft colors. Weave as Twill or Twill and its Reverse, with every other row of one color and alternate rows of the other color.

3. Use three or more colors. Weave as Twill or Twill and its Reverse, using the colors right along in the same succession. The effect will be somewhat similar to the Indian Saddle Blanket Weave but there will be more varied color effects.

Twills on Six and Eight Harnesses

On looms having more than four harnesses the Twill is written with harness notes in regular succession covering all the harnesses. Thus, a Six-Harness Twill is written as follows: harnesses 1, 2, 3, 4, 5, 6 and repeat; or, for a Herringbone, reverse to harnesses 5, 4, 3, 2, and repeat all. The Eight-Harness Twill is written in the following manner: harnesses 1, 2, 3, 4, 5, 6, 7, 8, repeat; or, for a Herringbone, reverse to harnesses 7, 6, 5, 4, 3, 2, and repeat all. Other eight-harness patterns are simply enlargements or developments of the Twill.

Weaving: Tabby on the Eight-Harness Twill threading is woven as follows: harnesses 1, 3, 5, 7 together; then harnesses 2, 4, 6, 8 together, and repeat.

Twill is woven in several ways, to produce various effects. In some the weft predominates on one side of the fabric with the warp hardly showing, and the opposite effect is produced on the reverse side. Again, the harnesses may be grouped in different ways to produce a more even balance between the amounts of warp and weft showing. Lastly the combinations may be such as to produce a damask weave or an effect of two alternating blocks.

1. A Long Weft Overshot Showing on One Side: Weave harnesses 1, 2, 3, 4, 5, 6, 7, 8, and repeat; or, for the reverse to form a zig-zag, weave harnesses 1, 2, 3, 4, 5, 6, 7, 8, 7, 6, 5, 4, 3, 2, and repeat. For slightly less weft showing, weave harnesses 1 and 2, 2 and 3, 3 and 4, 4 and 5, 5 and 6, 6 and 7, 7 and 8, 8 and 1, and repeat or reverse, etc.

2. Equal Balance Between Warp and Weft: Weave harnesses 1, 2, 5, 6 together; then harnesses 2, 3, 6, 7, harnesses 3, 4, 7, 8, and harnesses 4, 1, 8, 5; and repeat or reverse.

3. Damask Effect: Weave harnesses 1, 5, 7, 8 together; then harnesses 2, 5, 6, 8, harnesses 3, 5, 6, 7, harnesses 4, 6, 7, 8, harnesses 1, 3, 4, 5, harnesses 1, 2, 4, 6, harnesses 1, 2, 3, 7, and harnesses 2, 3, 4, 8; and repeat all.

There are endless ways in which to combine the harnesses of multi-harness looms for different effects. To weave them, however, there must be a tie-up of the harnesses to the lams so that several harnesses may be raised or lowered at a time. The system is much more complicated than that of four-harness weaving, which provides such countless variations that the weaver need not consider undertaking the more complicated types unless he enjoys experimenting. Many weavers find that two-harness and four-harness weaving provide enough creative pleasure to last a lifetime.

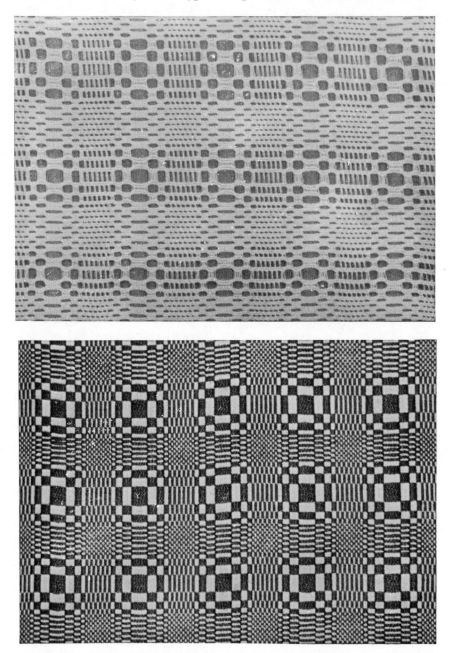

Two interpretations of the same pattern, called Optical Illusions, created by Helen Daniels Young. Above, woven as Honeycomb; below, woven as Overshot.

28—The Principles of Overshot Pattern Weaving

Use of Blocks of Design

WE HAVE LEARNED how in the threading of the Twill there is a succession of the harnesses in regular order, such as harnesses 1, 2, 3, and 4, and repeat; and how in the Herringbone threading this succession is carried on for a certain number of repeats and then reversed, such as harnesses 1, 2, 3, (4), 3, and 2, and repeat.

In this lesson we will learn how to enlarge the short groupings of threads that make up the Twill threading, such as harnesses 1 and 2, 2 and 3, 3 and 4, and 4 and 1, so as to form larger blocks of repeat. In this way we can plan patterns where the weft thread passes over more warp threads at a time than the two or three threads which form the short Twill overshot. The pattern spaces of the Diamond and other patterns presented here thus form more prominent blocks of design.

Overshot Pattern Weaving consists in weaving from that type of pattern draft in which the threadings of the harnesses form enlarged groups or blocks. When these harnesses are raised or lowered in groups, design spaces are formed through which the weft thread shows in set pattern formations.

Enlarging the Twill Threading

For instance, in the diagram given in the regular Twill Pattern (see the dotted ovals in Fig. 107 at **C**), our succession of small blocks is: harnesses 1 and 2, 2 and 3, 3 and 4, and 4 and 1. For the enlarged draft having this same succession of harnesses, i.e., the Stepladder pattern in Figs. 115 and 116, enlarge each group of two harnesses to four, as indicated by the dotted ovals in Fig. 116. We then have: harnesses 1, 2, 1, 2; harnesses 2, 3, 2, 3; harnesses 3, 4, 3, 4; and harnesses 4, 1, 4, 1. These blocks form the units of the Overshot Pattern Weaving.

Adjacent Blocks; the Thread in Common

In Fig. 116 note the overlapping of the same harnesses shared by adjacent groups. For instance, in the first four-thread block, which is composed of harnesses 1, 2, 1, 2, the last thread on harness 2 is a part of two blocks, namely, 1, (2), 1, (2) and (2), 3, (2), 3. In other words, there is a **thread in common** between these two adjacent blocks. The block (1, 2, 1, 2) continues until there is no further notation of the first note of this combination, i.e., harness 1, but the draft progresses instead to a new note, harness 3. Draw a circle or oval around all the (1 and 2) notes, but close this before adding **the** next note on harness 3.

The next block is now composed of the last note of the old block, harness 2, and a new note, harness 3, making the block (2, 3, 2, 3). This block continues until there is no further recurrence of harness 2, but the draft progresses to the new

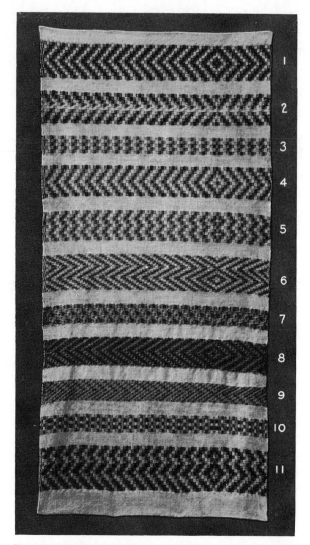

Fig. 115—Hand-woven sampler showing many possible variations of weave on the simple Stepladder Pattern.

thread on harness 4. Draw a circle around all the (2 and 3) notes, but close this just before the addition of the new note, harness 4. Continue thus, enlarging the draft and surrounding the blocks with circles, until the draft looks like the completed Stepladder pattern in Fig. 116.

The thread in common between the adjacent blocks adds to the beauty of this type of pattern when woven, for the transition between the blocks is more gradual than if each were cut off sharply before starting the new one.

Weaving the Draft as Threaded, or as Drawn in

In weaving the Stepladder pattern as written, i.e., according to the succession of blocks that occurs in the draft, the result is a series of blocks arranged in diagonal lines, similar to those of the

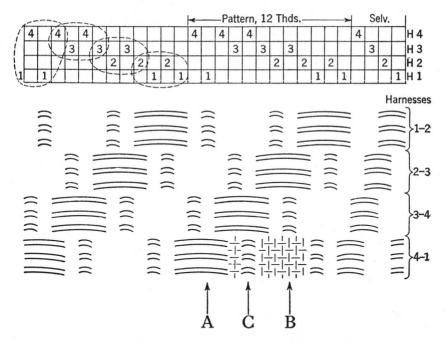

Fig. 116—Stepladder—a pattern of enlarged Twill blocks.

Twill but more prominent. The order of weaving the blocks therefore, becomes: harnesses 1 and 2, 2 and 3, 3 and 4, and 4 and 1, and repeat.

Number of Times to Weave the Blocks

It is the custom to weave each block with enough weft rows to make it appear square. For instance, to weave block (1, 2, 1, 2) of four warp threads so that it will appear square, there should be about this same number of weft rows. However, since the pattern weft thread is heavier than the warp, it takes up more room. Moreover, there is a row of Tabby thread after each Pattern row, and these Tabby rows also take up some space. So we usually find that the number of Pattern weft rows required to make the block square is one less than the number of warp threads in the block being woven. Thus, to weave the first block (1, 2, 1, 2) of the draft in Fig. 116 into a square,

treadle harnesses 1 and 2 together three times, each row being followed by a Tabby row. Follow this with the second block (2, 3, 2, 3), which is woven square by treadling harnesses 2 and 3 together three times and adding Tabby after each row. Then weave harnesses 3 and 4 three times, adding Tabby; and weave harnesses 4 and 1 three times, adding Tabby. Keep repeating for the stepped effect shown below the draft in Fig. 116.

If a very heavy pattern weft thread is used, the blocks will build up more quickly and fewer repeats will be required. The weaver should see to it that his pattern blocks become square, adjusting the number of repeats he makes for each combination to the weight of thread he is using.

The principle of squaring up the blocks in order results in the formation of a diagonal of square blocks running across the pattern at about a 45-degree angle and having a trend downward toward the left. This line is clearly shown in Fig. 116 and also in Fig. 118, in the row of blocks starting at the upper right corner and progressing toward the lower left through Y. If the pattern weft thread is too heavy or too fine to achieve this true 45-degree diagonal, the weaver is at liberty to weave the blocks fewer or more times; he should use the number of times which will make each block square as it is woven in order. The same block, such as the 1 and 2, may occur elsewhere in the draft with fewer or more threads, but you are concerned only with the number of threads it contains in the particular block you are weaving at the time along the diagonal. Later on, as you weave each block in order, you will reach the point where the same block, such as the 1 and 2 block, may have five or ten threads, in which case the number of times you will weave this combination will be one less than the number of warp threads the block contains at the point in question. When weaving each block, glance downward directly below it to the next place along the diagonal being woven, as this is the point at which you should square up the block—not somewhere else along the draft. When finished weaving this block, take the next group of harnesses to the left in the draft, glance downward to the next point along the diagonal line, and weave this combination until the woven block is square at this point.

Omitting the Tabby Notation

In the foregoing directions for the succession of blocks when weaving, and in the following weaving plans, the row of Tabby after each Pattern row is not given. It is taken for granted that the weaver will alternate the Pattern rows and the Tabby rows regularly.

Weaving the Pattern Twill-Fashion

In the Stepladder draft in Fig. 116, the pattern is started with four selvage threads. The pattern proper, of twelve threads, is then repeated as far as desired. The selvage is added after the last repeat, which ends on harness 4. The blocks occur in regular succession, there being four threads in each block.

The woven pattern results in a series of squares arranged along diagonal lines, there being a woven square for each block, as shown in the sketch in Fig. 116 below the draft. Since the blocks in the draft occur in the same order as the harness combinations of the Twill, and they are woven in the same order, we say that this pattern is threaded and woven twill-fashion. Thus, the sequence is as follows:

Harnesses 1, 2, 1, 2; Weave 1 and 2 three times

Harnesses 2, 3, 2, 3; Weave 2 and 3 three times

Harnesses 3, 4, 3, 4; Weave 3 and 4 three times

Harnesses 4, 1, 4, 1; Weave 4 and 1 three times

All patterns are not written with this particular succession of blocks. For instance, the succession of blocks in the Monk's Belt pattern, Fig. 120, is: block (1, 2, 1, 2) and then block (3, 4, 3, 4). But, no matter what the succession of blocks in the draft may be, any four-harness Overshot Pattern may be either woven **twill-fashion** (with blocks 1 and 2, 2 and 3, 3 and 4, and 4 and 1) or **woven as drawn in**, according to the succession of blocks in the draft.

Variations in the Weaving of the Stepladder Pattern

Interesting variations of the Stepladder Pattern are shown in the sampler in Fig.

115. One may even reverse the order of the blocks in the draft and produce a Diamond at this point, as shown at the right side of the first border. The several borders are described in order from the top downward.

1. The first border is woven as drawn in for about 2 inches; then the order of the blocks is reversed for another 2 inches, and an arrow design is thus formed at the reverse point.

2. In the second border the point of the arrow is accented by using a weft of another color at this point.

3. For the third border, one chooses any two adjacent blocks, such as the 1 and 2 and the 2 and 3, and weaves them alternately.

4. The fourth border is like the first with a dark-colored weft thread used for the first and last blocks to accent the outside edges.

5. In the fifth border one creates a zig-zag design of vertical trend by first weaving three blocks twill-fashion, then reversing their order, and alternating the two directions, each Pattern row being followed by a row of Tabby. The weaving sequence is as follows:

Harnesses 1 and 2, 3 times
Harnesses 2 and 3, 3 times
Harnesses 3 and 4, 3 times
Reverse to:
Harnesses 2 and 3, 3 times
Repeat all.

In the picture of this border in Fig. 115, you will see that only three blocks are woven before the reverse. There could be four or more, if it were desired to make longer zig-zag lines.

6. In the sixth border, one finds eight consecutive blocks woven twill-fashion before the reverse, there being long effective zig-zag lines. The weaving sequence follows: harnesses 1 and 2, 3

times; 2 and 3, 3 times; 3 and 4, 3 times; 4 and 1, 3 times; 1 and 2, 3 times; 2 and 3, 3 times; 3 and 4, 3 times; 4 and 1, 3 times; reverse to 3 and 4, 3 times; 2 and 3, 3 times; 1 and 2, 3 times; 4 and 1, 3 times; 3 and 4, 3 times; and 2 and 3, 3 times. Then repeat all.

7. The seventh border is woven twill-fashion, but with successive blocks in different colors, as follows:

Harnesses 1 and 2, 3 times, dark color;
Harnesses 2 and 3, 3 times, light color;
Harnesses 3 and 4, 3 times, dark color;
Harnesses 4 and 1, 3 times, light color;
Repeat all.

8. The eighth border is woven on what we call "opposites." Instead of using a row of Tabby to bind in each row, one uses the two harnesses that were not used in the regular Pattern row, and weaves these instead of the Tabby, using a thread of the same size as the regular pattern thread but of another color to set it off. The weaving sequence, using two alternating pattern weft threads of two different colors, is as follows:

Harnesses 1 and 2, dark; harnesses 3 and 4, light; repeat these two rows.
Harnesses 2 and 3, dark; harnesses 4 and 1, light; repeat these two rows.
Harnesses 3 and 4, dark; harnesses 1 and 2, light; repeat these two rows.
Harnesses 4 and 1, dark; harnesses 2 and 3, light; repeat these two rows.
Repeat all. Reverse the succession of harnesses when desired.

9. Weave the ninth border in the same way as the eighth, but use two colors of closer values, start the succession of harnesses in the reverse direction, and change later to the Twill direction.

10. The tenth border is woven with two contrasting colors, opposite harnesses being used for each color. The harnesses opposite to harnesses 1 and 2 are 3 and

4; the opposites to 2 and 3 are 4 and 1.
Weave as follows:

Harnesses 1 and 2, dark color; repeat 3
   times, each row followed by Tabby.
Harnesses 3 and 4, light color; repeat 3
   times, each row followed by Tabby.
Repeat all.

If desired, you can make a similar
border by alternating 2 and 3; and 4
and 1.

11. For the last or bottom border,
combine two colors in various ways, and
weave twill-fashion or Twill and reverse
for the distances desired.

The Three Textures Formed in Overshot Pattern Weaving

There are three distinct surface textures formed in Overshot Pattern Weaving: (1) the main Pattern texture; (2) the
background or Tabby texture; (3) the
Half-Tones, made up of part Tabby and
part Pattern.

1. The Main Pattern Texture: All
Overshot Patterns produce blocks of
color when woven, and these are arranged
according to the particular set threading
of each pattern. These blocks are distributed in certain ways to form what is
known as the cloth **Pattern** or **Texture.**
Each block consists of a square of color

formed by a heavy pattern thread that
shows above the main texture of the
cloth when woven across groups of warp
threads. See Fig. 116 at **A.**

In addition to the bright spots of color
that form the main part of each Overshot
Pattern, there are two underlying surface
textures which act as a background to the
pattern, i.e., the Tabby texture and the
Half-Tones.

2. The Tabby Texture: This refers to
the Plain Weave made wherever the
tabby thread or binder crosses the warp.
It consists of the interlacing of the fine
binding weft threads with the warp
threads. See Fig. 116 at **B.**

3. The Half-Tones: The half-tones
are those small areas found on either side
of adjacent blocks, where the pattern
thread passes over only one warp thread
at a time. The pattern thread shows up
very little, and its color is modified by
the surrounding background tone of the
Tabby. The resulting texture is therefore called **Half-Tone.** See Fig. 116 at **C.**

In Fig. 116, **A** designates a block of
Pattern; **B**, a section of Tabby; and **C**, a
Half-Tone. Find similar textures both in
the photographs of Overshot Weavings
in this book and in the developments of
specific drafts, such as the Diamond in
Fig. 117.

29—The Diamond or Cross Family

The Formation of the Diamond

WE HAVE just learned that, if the Twill is enlarged, we get a repeated step pattern of larger blocks. It is also possible to enlarge the small blocks of the Herringbone drafts shown in Fig. 112 so as to make large Diamond figures. We double the small blocks of the Herringbone pattern in the same way as was described in Lesson 28 for the Twill, threading and weaving the blocks in the order in which they occur on the draft, which is read from right to left.

Take, for instance, the draft in Fig. 112 at **C**. The small two-thread blocks occur in the following order: harnesses 1-2, harnesses 2-3, harnesses 3-4, (harnesses 4-1-4, the reverse block), harnesses 4-3, harnesses 3-2, and repeat with (harnesses 2-1-2, the reverse block). By enlarging these, we get the true Diamond draft in Fig. 118 with the following succession of blocks (indicated by the dotted oval lines which are shown on the second repeat only): harnesses 1, 2, 1, 2; 2, 3, 2, 3; 3, 4, 3, 4; (4, 1, 4, 1, 4, the reverse block); then harnesses 4, 3, 4, 3; 3, 2, 3, 2; and back to the starting block again or (2, 1, 2, 1, 2, the reverse block when repeating). Note that the block on harnesses 4 and 1 consists of five threads. The extra thread on harness 4 is added to provide for the reverse, bringing the draft back to a point where the next block (harnesses 4 and 3) starts. Likewise, when the pattern starts again with the 1 and 2 block, between **C** and **D**, the last thread 2 of the 3 and 2 block

is combined with the four threads of the 1 and 2 block to make a five-thread block 2, 1, 2, 1, 2.

In Fig. 117 are shown variations of the Diamond pattern used for footstool tops, purses, hot mats, and runners. These articles were woven by school girls. The footstool cover at the top shows the correct way of weaving the Diamond draft in Fig. 118. The purse at the center is woven in two colors, tufting cotton being used for the pattern weft on a warp of crochet cotton set at 16 threads per inch. It is lined with sateen and has a zipper across the top. The stand cover at the lower left is woven by reversing the treadling of the Diamond. The hot mat at the lower right is similar to the purse in pattern and texture, but is made in one color.

Weaving the Diamond as Threaded or as Drawn in

One of the most usable little patterns for both home and school purposes is the small Diamond Pattern shown in Fig. 118. When woven, it forms the smart over-all effect shown in the sketches. When used for rugs, it may be woven with either rug yarn or rags. When threaded on a fine warp, the pattern is excellent for an all-over upholstery texture.

To weave the Diamond as threaded or as drawn in, follow the principle that was described for the weaving of the Stepladder Pattern in Fig. 116. Simply

Fig. 117—Variations of the Diamond Pattern used for footstool tops, purses, hot mats, and runners.

weave the blocks in succession, reading from right to left on the draft of Fig. 118, as indicated by the dotted ovals in the repeat of the pattern. The sequence is as follows: Blocks (1, 2, 1, 2); *(2, 3, 2, 3); (3, 4, 3, 4); (4, 1, 4, 1, 4); (4, 3, 4, 3); (3, 2, 3, 2); (2, 1, 2, 1, 2); and repeat from the asterisk.

Number of Times to Weave the Blocks

To find the number of times to weave each block, again refer back to the directions given for the weaving of the Stepladder Pattern. The object is to square up each block in order, so that adjacent

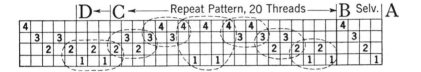

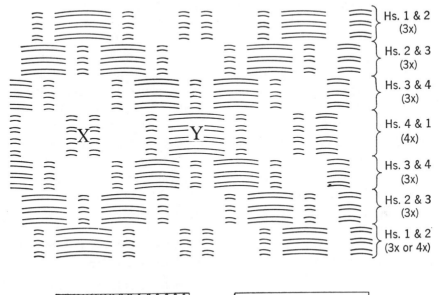

	Hs. 1 & 2 (3x)
	Hs. 2 & 3 (3x)
	Hs. 3 & 4 (3x)
	Hs. 4 & 1 (4x)
	Hs. 3 & 4 (3x)
	Hs. 2 & 3 (3x)
	Hs. 1 & 2 (3x or 4x)

Fig. 118—Diamond Pattern for rugs, bath mats, upholstery, and draperies.

blocks when woven will form a diagonal row of pattern squares. This is clearly shown in the development of the draft in Fig. 118. The number of Pattern weft rows necessary to make each block square depends on the number of threads in the block at this point and on the thickness of the thread used; so one must be guided by the actual building up of each block as one weaves the blocks in order, while progressing from right to left along the pattern draft. However, the following rule may be applied in general, and the

weaver may make his own adjustment to his particular material.

Make the number of Pattern weft rows one less than the number of warp threads included in the block. Thus, the first block (1, 2 ,1, 2), which consists of four threads (see the dotted oval in Fig. 118), should be woven three times; the next block in order (2, 3, 2, 3), three times; and the next (3, 4, 3, 4), three times. Then, the next (4, 1, 4, 1, 4), which consists of five threads, should be woven four times; the next (4, 3, 4, 3), three times;

and the next (3, 2, 3, 2), three times. When the draft starts its next repeat, the block (1 and 2) which occurs first must have an extra harness note on harness 2 to provide for the reverse to the next block (2 and 3) again. This extra note forms a five-thread block (2, 1, 2, 1, 2), which is to be woven four times. At the very end of the pattern, however, when weaving the last diamond, weave this 1 and 2 block three times only, since no further reverse occurs and the pattern should end with four threads.

In Fig. 118 note the brackets placed vertically at the right of the draft and the notations designating the harness combinations and the number of times each is woven. For instance, "Hs. 1 and 2, (3×)" means weave harnesses 1 and 2 three times, each row of course being followed by a row of Tabby.

The Diagonal Trend of the Blocks

If a pattern is woven as drawn in by following the succession of blocks from right to left on the draft, and if each block is "squared" as one weaves by using the number of Pattern weft rows necessary to obtain this result, the design on the cloth shows squares of color arranged along a diagonal line inclined at an angle of about 45 degrees. This same effect is shown by developing the draft on paper, as in Fig. 118.

However, if one should interrupt the succession by skipping a block or losing one's place on the draft, the diagonal line will at once show a break. This fact can guide the weaver; for, by glancing along the diagonal line formed by the squared-up blocks, he can at once detect any error in their succession. Also, if the diagonal line flattens out or lengthens, he can true it up by weaving each block

with a greater or smaller number of Pattern weft rows.

Colonial Overshot Patterns produce a diagonal when woven properly in blocks, but one cannot start just anywhere to get this effect. One must start at the right side of the draft, progress block by block toward the left, weave each block in order, and make that particular block form a square right next to the square last woven along the diagonal line and succeeding it diagonally downward to the left. When one has woven completely through all the blocks of the draft, one has a beautiful square of weaving, with diagonal lines crossing both from right to left and from left to right. See Figs. 105, 118, 129, and 130.

The Two Reverse Points or Centers of Diamond Patterns

Diamond patterns have two **centers** or **reverse points**. In weaving the pattern in Fig. 118 as threaded, we have found these points on blocks (1 and 2) and (4 and 1). Each of these blocks acts as a center: one is the center of a **Diamond**, as at **X**; the other is the center of a **Cross**, as at **Y**. Every Diamond Pattern can thus be visioned as an alternation of Crosses and Diamonds. Most of our Colonial Overshot Patterns consist of two alternating motifs, and likewise two reverse points or centers.

Weaving Diamond Patterns Twill-Fashion

Diamond Patterns may also be woven according to the regular succession of blocks in the simple Twill, without reversing their order, i.e., in the manner described for the Stepladder Pattern in Fig. 116. Simply weave the blocks as follows: harnesses 1 and 2, three times; harnesses 2 and 3, three times; harnesses 3 and 4, three times; harnesses 4 and 1, three times. Then repeat the entire succession. The resulting pattern on the cloth consists of a large Herringbone formation of blocks, with zig-zag lines crossing the cloth horizontally, there being no closed diamond. The effect of a Diamond Pattern woven in this way resembles the Herringbone Patterns woven twill-fashion, as shown in Fig. 112, left column; but, as shown in the case of the larger Diamond drafts, the blocks resulting from their weaving are much larger than the Herringbone figures.

Enlarging Any Herringbone Pattern to Form a Diamond

It is possible to enlarge any of the Herringbone Patterns in Fig. 112 in the manner just described, by doubling the number of harnesses in each block and writing the draft with the same succession of blocks. Thus, for each enlarged pattern, the reverse point will come on a different harness and an extra note will be added on the draft to provide for the reverse. Moreover, in each case the Diamond figure will be of a different size, just as it was for the Herringbone drafts shown in Fig. 112 with their small diamond-like figures at the left of each draft.

Diamond Pattern for Bath Mats and Upholstery

The draft in Fig. 118 may be used for weaving a bath mat or upholstery in accordance with the following directions:

Warp Plan

BATH MAT

Warp: Carpet warp
Weft: Pattern—Rug yarn or rags
  Tabby—Same as warp
Width in reed: 22 in.
Threads per inch: 15
Total number of threads: 331

UPHOLSTERY

Warp: 20/2 ply
Weft: Pattern—Crochet cotton, or wool
  Tabby—Same as warp or 24/3 ply
Width in reed: 30½ in.
Threads per inch: 32 (see note)
Total number of threads: 979

Threading Plan

BATH MAT

	Threads
Selvage (A-B)	4
Pattern (B-C), 20 threads, 16 times	320
After 16 repeats, add (C-D) to complete pattern	3
Selvage (B-A), harnesses 4, 3, 2, 1	4
Total	331

UPHOLSTERY

	Threads
Selvage (A-B), two times	8
Pattern (B-C), 20 threads, 48 times	960
After 48 repeats, add (C-D) to complete pattern	3
Selvage (B-A), harnesses 4, 3, 2, 1, two times	8
Total	979

Note: For upholstery with a 30-dent reed (a warp of 30 threads per inch), the width in the reed is 32 in., the pattern is repeated only 47 times, and 959 threads are used.

Weaving Plan

(Follow each Pattern row with Tabby)

BATH MAT

*Treadle: Harnesses 1 and 2, three times
  Harnesses 2 and 3, twice
  Harnesses 3 and 4, twice
  Harnesses 4 and 1, three times
  Harnesses 3 and 4, twice
  Harnesses 2 and 3, twice
  Repeat all.

UPHOLSTERY

**Treadle: Harnesses 1 and 2, four times
  Harnesses 2 and 3, three times
  Harnesses 3 and 4, three times
  Harnesses 4 and 1, four times
  Harnesses 3 and 4, three times
  Harnesses 2 and 3, three times
  Repeat all.

* When using heavy rug yarn for pattern weft, weave fewer rows for each block.
** Weave upholstery texture as drawn in.

For a small all-over Diamond Pattern for either bath mats or upholstery, repeat the foregoing treadlings. For a larger pattern, use the same repeat but take each group of harnesses more times, i.e., use harnesses 1 and 2 four to six times, harnesses 2 and 3 three to five times, harnesses 3 and 4 three to five times, harnesses 4 and 1 four to six times, and so on for the other harnesses.

(Everhart Museum Collection, Scranton, Pa.)

A corner of an early Jacquard coverlet. The introduction of the Jacquard loom in the nineteenth century produced a new taste in coverlet design. The old patterns were soon lost in attics in favor of the elaborate designs created on this new device. The American Eagle took first place among many patriotic motifs employed.

30—The Monk's Belt Pattern and Its Uses

Comparison of Monk's Belt and Honeysuckle Patterns

TWO PATTERNS that give attractive results when woven are the Monk's Belt Pattern and the Honeysuckle Pattern. The Monk's Belt produces small conventional blocks in tailored effect; the Honeysuckle weaves into borders or an all-over surface texture with graceful curving lines. These two patterns are simple and short, easy to thread, and very popular and useful. In this lesson and the next, we will give the plan for each of the patterns with several adaptations.

Characteristics of the Monk's Belt Pattern Written on Opposites

The Monk's Belt is one of the oldest and simplest of pattern threadings; it was known far back in olden times and has been preserved for us in the weaving of northern Europe. Its name is very suitable for, when the pattern is repeated, it makes long rows of square motifs that

Fig. 119—Similar border designs worked out in different ways. The top shows an excellent design for Monk's Belt, with only one block woven (see Fig. 121, M). The second mat has a heavy white Bouclé background with the border in repeated columns of looped pick-up. The long runner is of Dukagang in black cotton on a gold tabby background.

203

fit into a belt width. In Fig. 119 is shown a table mat woven in the Monk's Belt Pattern. The origin of this pattern may be connected with religious history, for it is made up of motifs resembling small crosses set between woven squares. The arrangement of these crosses may be altered at will. It is believed that this pattern was used for the girdles of the monks in European monasteries, the position of the crosses and the number of blocks between them designating the religious rank or attainment of the monk who made and wore the woven belt.

In modern days the Monk's Belt is popular because of its simple, clean-cut character and the ease with which it may be threaded and woven. It is a popular border pattern for drapes and hangings, runners, and towels, as well as for bright touches of color on aprons or smocks. It belongs to the family of **Patch Patterns** which are composed of contrasting motifs of square blocks said to be "on opposites." Other good patterns in this family are: Window Sash, Four O'Clock, The Waterfall, Youth, and Beauty.* The patterns of this group are more adaptable to modern decoration than to Colonial furnishings. The contrasting squares in the Monk's Belt and similar patterns result from the way the pattern is constructed. As indicated in Fig. 120, the blocks are written "on opposites." In the type of pattern known as "on opposites," a block on harnesses 1 and 2 is followed by a block on the opposite harnesses, 3 and 4; the 2 and 3 block is followed by the 4 and 1 block; the 3 and 4 block is followed by the 1 and 2 block; and the 4 and 1 block is followed by the 2 and 3 block. In the Monk's Belt Pattern given in Fig. 120, only blocks 1 and 2 and

* See *Shuttlecraft Book of American Hand Weaving*, by Atwater, p. 195-197.

blocks 3 and 4 are used. In some other patterns on opposites, one finds blocks 2 and 3 and blocks 4 and 1 as well. Note that there are no adjacent harness notes between the blocks; but, when each block, such as (1, 2, 1, 2), is finished, the draft goes directly to two new harness notes, as block (3, 4, 3, 4), instead of adding one new note only. If an adjacent pattern were being written at this point, the next block after block (1, 2, 1, 2) would add new harness 3 only and would retain harness 2; it would thus become block (2, 3, 2, 3).

Weaving on Opposites

In the method of weaving known as **Weaving on Opposites**, any two opposite pairs of harnesses may be used in alternation. Thus, harnesses 1 and 2 may be followed by harnesses 3 and 4; harnesses 2 and 3 may be followed by harnesses 4 and 1; harnesses 3 and 4 may be followed by harnesses 1 and 2; and harnesses 4 and 1 may be followed by harnesses 2 and 3. One may also weave any one harness alone and follow this with the other three harnesses woven together; thus, harness 1 alone may be followed by harnesses 2, 3, and 4, or vice versa, and so on. One may follow each Pattern row by a row of Tabby; or one may omit the Tabby altogether, for the two opposite treadlings of themselves hold the alternate rows firmly in place. This method of weaving on opposites without Tabby is sometimes used very successfully for rugs or mats. An example of textured drapery material woven in this way is shown in Fig. 47, fabric second from left.

One must be sure, in the use of the term "on opposites," to designate whether one means **threading a draft on opposites or weaving on opposites**. The Monk's

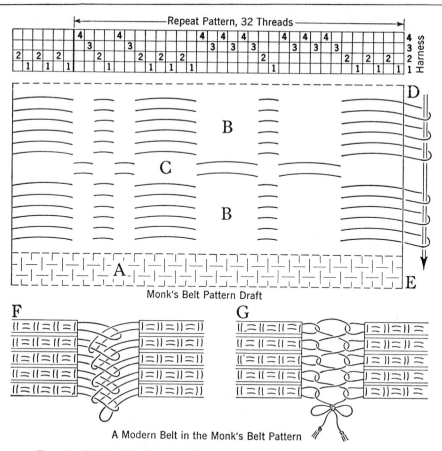

Fig. 120—Draft of the Monk's Belt, a useful conventional pattern from Europe.

Belt Pattern is a draft on opposites and is best woven by using the same two combinations as its two opposite blocks, i.e. harnesses 1 and 2 and harnesses 3 and 4. If the other two harness combinations of the Monk's Belt threading are used in alternation without Tabby, a fabric with a very interesting texture results. The weaving becomes: Use harnesses 2 and 3, followed by harnesses 4 and 1; repeat with one row of each combination, using a fine thread of the same size as the warp.

The weaver therefore finds that there are many interesting ways of weaving any pattern threading. He has now learned how to weave a pattern **twill-fashion, as-drawn-in, on opposites,** with or without Tabby, and also with any succession of harnesses desired to produce creative textures.

Checkerboard Overshot, a Useful Weave on Opposites

This weave is a pattern on two opposite blocks, similar to the Monk's Belt but even simpler, with both kinds of little blocks just the same size and alternating regularly to make small squares of pattern. It is adaptable to borders for doilies, towels, handkerchief cases, purses, book jackets, etc., as well as to narrow bands for upholstery edges, tie-backs for curtains, belts, and sandal straps. Woven as a solid all-over pattern surface, it is excellent for chair coverings, upholstery, pillows, screen covers, bags, and purses. The pattern may be made into columns of color by weaving harnesses 1 and 2 with one color and harnesses 3 and 4 with another color.

Threading: Harnesses 1, 2, 1, 2, 3, 4, 3, 4, and repeat.

Weaving: Use a Pattern weft and a Tabby weft. Follow each row of Pattern with a row of Tabby.

Weave harnesses 1 and 2, followed by Tabby. Repeat as desired, preferably to form small square blocks.

Weave harnesses 3 and 4. Repeat as desired, preferably to form small square blocks.

Alternate these two blocks as desired.

One can also omit the Tabby and weave with two wefts of different colors, as follows: Weave harnesses 1 and 2 with one color, and then weave harnesses 3 and 4 with the second color. Alternate the harness combinations.

Making a Modern Belt in the Monk's Belt Pattern

In Fig. 120 is shown a draft for a belt woven in the Monk's Belt Pattern. This draft shows how a long length may be woven crosswise of the loom instead of lengthwise. In this way one is able to make a belt on a warp planned for other things, thus saving both time and expense. The finished woven belt is shown in Fig. 32 at the upper left. To make a belt woven thus from selvage to selvage, a section of Tabby is first woven to be made into a hem; then the solid portion of the belt is made as wide as desired; and finally enough Tabby for a hem is added on the other edge. Weave the belt in one wide setting of a warp 30 in. to 36 in. wide; or weave it in two sections on a narrower loom on a warp of towel width, each section measuring about 16 in., **i.e.,**

half of the desired length of the belt. Put the two sections together, when woven, with interesting ties or knots, as indicated in Fig. 120 below the draft.

Warp Plan:
Warp: 24/3 or 16/3 cotton, or Perle 10/2
Threads per inch: 24
Width in reed: 17 in. (weaves down to 16 in.)
Total threads: 408
Weft: Tabby—Same as warp
  Pattern—Heavy yarn, such as Germantown; or Perle 3/2; or tufting cotton; or crochet cotton used triple; or any heavy cotton
Colors: Use two colors

Threading Plan: Patterns that lend themselves to this type of belt are those of short overshot. The Monk's Belt Pattern is especially good, and the Rosepath, Diamond, and Honeysuckle Patterns, as well as many others, can be used. In threading, use selvages threaded in the Twill weave; i.e., use harnesses 1, 2, 3, 4, etc. at both the right and left sides. Repeat the pattern all across.

Weaving the Belt: See the sections marked **A**, **B**, and **C** in Fig. 120.

A. Weave ½ inch or more of plain Tabby for the hem. Follow this with four rows in Twill weave, using harnesses (1 and 2), (2 and 3), (3 and 4), and (4 and 1).

B. Use a pair of harnesses giving an attractive overshot, such as harnesses 1 and 2 in the Monk's Belt or harnesses 4 and 1 in the Honeysuckle, Rosepath, or Diamond. Repeat this for a width of ½ inch or more in the first color.

C. Use the opposite pair of harnesses, such as harnesses 3 and 4 in the Monk's Belt or harnesses 2 and 3 in the Honeysuckle, Rosepath, or Diamond, with a color darker than the first. These opposite treadlings in two contrasting colors make a smart design.

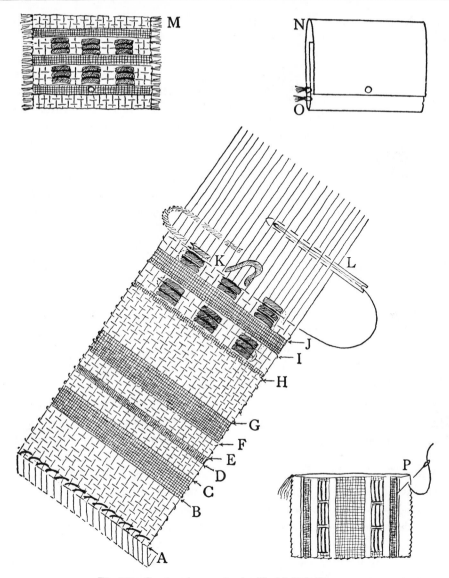

Fig. 121—Scarf and purse in the Monk's Belt Pattern.

Then repeat a wide section of **B**, and follow it with a narrow section of **C**, for the desired width. Finish with section **B** and Tabby **A** on the other edge.

Making the Belt: If the belt is all in one piece, simply sew it to a buckle, or tie colored threads like the pattern threads to the selvages to make a fringe. For a belt consisting of two pieces to be joined, make up each piece as follows: Set the warp 1 in. wider than the final width of half the belt. Separate the last two threads of the warp at each side, leaving a 1-in. space **D** between them and the rest of the warp. Weave around these last two threads every fourth row, to make loops of weft **E** for tying the belt. Weave both halves alike, and then join the sections by slipping the loops through one another, as at **F**. Lace the opposite ends with a cord made of the heavy weft, as at **G**.

Making a Scarf and a Purse in the Monk's Belt Pattern

In Fig. 121 are shown a narrow scarf and a purse woven in the Monk's Belt Pattern, the draft for which is given in Fig. 120. The same draft can also be used for a wider warp for a table mat or a doily.

Planning the Warp: The warp for one scarf and a purse like those in Fig. 121 should have a total length of 2 yd (38 in. for the scarf, 18 in. for the purse, and 16 in. for shrinkage and waste at the ends). If making a number of them, add 5 ft for each scarf and purse.

Plan a scarf as sketched in Fig. 121. Use three colors of wool, such as tan, green, and brown. Make the warp 8 in. wide, using tan wool. This should be of medium weight set at 16 threads per inch, a total of 128 threads being required.

Weaving the Scarf: Use three stick-shuttles, a separate one for each color. Follow the letters in Fig. 121 for each section.

A to B: 2 in. of tan, Plain Weave, using harnesses (1 and 3) and (2 and 4)

B to C: 1 in. of green, Plain Weave, using harnesses (1 and 3) and (2 and 4)

C to D: ¾ in. of tan, Plain Weave

D to E: ¼ in. of green, Plain Weave

E to F: ¾ in. of tan, Plain Weave

F to G: 1 in. of green, Plain Weave

G to H: 2 in. of tan, Plain Weave

At H: 2 rows of Plain Weave in dark brown, ending on harnesses (2 and 4)

H to I: ¾ in. of Pattern Weave in brown, as described in detail later

I to J: ½ in. of green, Plain Weave

J to K: ¾ in. of Pattern Weave

At K: Add 2 rows of Plain Weave in dark brown

The rest of the scarf may be Plain Weave in tan.

Making Sections from H to K: The section of Pattern Weave from H to I is made in the following manner:

Weave a Pattern row with heavy brown thread on harnesses 1 and 2.

Weave Tabby in tan on harnesses 1 and 3.

Weave another Pattern row with brown on harnesses 1 and 2.

Weave Tabby in tan on harnesses 2 and 4.

Weave another Pattern row with brown on harnesses 1 and 2.

Weave Tabby in tan on harnesses 1 and 3.

At I, weave Tabby, using harnesses 2 and 4 alone; and follow with ½ in. of Tabby from I to J, using harnesses 1 and 3 and 2 and 4 alternately and ending on 2 and 4.

Now start at J and weave from J to K by proceeding in the manner just described for the section from H to I. Then, at K, add two Pattern rows of dark brown on harnesses 2 and 4 and 1 and 3; and weave one row of fine Tabby in tan on harnesses 2 and 4.

Complete the rest of the scarf by weaving Tabby in plain tan with the shuttle L. Use harnesses 1 and 3 and 2 and 4.

Making the Purse to Match the Scarf: For the purse shown in Fig. 121 at M, use the piece of weaving 18 in. long and 8 in. wide, with the same pattern as that described for the part of the scarf from G to the end. Fold it over, as at N; and then tie a fringe on the sides, as at O.

For the purse in the lower corner of Fig. 121 at P, make the piece of weaving only 14 in. long and 8 in. wide. Fold the piece double, and sew the sides together with a needle and thread. Put a zipper across the opening at the top.

(*Courtesy of Lily Mills, Shelby, N. C.*)

This beautiful bridge cloth in the Monk's Belt Pattern was made of red, white, and blue mercerized cottons on a small loom. The full-size cloth was made by joining four small woven squares together, and the tea napkins were made by cutting one square into four smaller squares and fringing at the edges. Full-size towels may be woven on the same warp.

31—Practical Overshot Patterns

The Uses of Overshot

THE beautiful figurations of our Overshot Pattern Weaves can be combined in many original ways to form allover textures or borders to be used on table linens, towels, runners, and draperies, as well as wearing apparel such as scarves, dress trim, belts, and jackets. Repeated patterns of short Overshot can be used effectively for upholstery and pillow and coverlet textures. Patterns can be woven as drawn in or with any succession of pattern groups so that the pattern is subtly hidden with the texture. With a creative use of color and texture, an Overshot Pattern may be completely transformed into a modern fabric. Many weavers today tend to conceal the basic pattern form and embellish it with new treadling successions and color changes in such a way that the pattern acts more as a basic groundwork upon which to paint with thread than as a design in itself. In other words, the pattern becomes the means to an end, not the end itself.

Overshot Draft Designs

The three textures characteristic of Overshot Pattern Weaves were explained in Lesson 28. There are hundreds of ways in which the pattern motifs can be designed and threaded on a four-harness loom. The size of the motifs, the connections between them, and the succession of the blocks can all be varied to make fascinating developments and figurations.

The Diamond and Monk's Belt families (Lessons 29 and 30) give some idea of the variations possible.

Just as there is no limit to the ways in which notes of music can be combined to make new melodies and harmonies, the possibilities of combining thread notations on a four-harness staff to make new weaving patterns are endless. The key pattern or the line of the draft as it ascends and descends may be compared to the melody. The development of the pattern into its many forms may be compared to the harmony. There are hundreds of historic American patterns in books, and many drafts are available from European sources. Hundreds more are nascent in the minds of potential weavers. Any weaver, if he learns the system of draft writing, can create his own pattern drafts.

In Lesson 32, you can see how to group the pattern units for varying effects. In this lesson, various types of Overshot Weaves, chosen because of their practical nature as well as their beauty, will be given.

Ways of Weaving Overshot

You can make your own decision as to the succession of the pattern notes in your "melody" draft. After this is decided, there is still a world of choice in the weaving of the pattern.

There are many ways in which systems can be established for weaving Overshot

210

in different ways. Units can be woven as drawn in (explained on page 192) or Rose-fashion or Star-fashion (pages 237, and 238). A pattern can be woven in relief, as in Honeycomb (page 236), "on Opposites" (page 204), or without tabby, using another pattern row to bind each previous pattern row, a method known as "Bound Weaving" (page 249).

Textures to Use

In Overshot, the pattern rows are almost always woven with heavier thread than the warp. The warp and tabby are usually about the same weight, but this is a matter of choice. There are delightful varieties of yarn of subtle finish and color tone that prove valuable in creating new texture effects. In addition to cottons, linen, wools, and silks, there are many more yarns to work with. These include varieties of Nylon, Rayon, Orlon, Dacron, Acrilon, and so on, as well as combinations of natural threads and synthetics. The weaver is inspired by the many yarn samples furnished by thread companies, and his experiments on his fabric pallette often reward him with unexpected surprises.

Characteristics of the Honeysuckle Pattern

The Honeysuckle Pattern, Figs. 122 and 123, is a charming, useful, and popular pattern of short repeating motifs. It consists of an oval-shaped figure alternating with a cross, as shown in the sketches above the draft in Fig. 123. Honeysuckle, which seems to be of American origin, is a combination of small Old-World motifs. Its quaint little borders go well with Colonial furnishings. It may also be woven as an all-over repeat to be used for upholstery (see Fig. 122, Pattern No. 3). Honeysuckle admits of

more variation than any of the small-motif patterns.

It can be modernized by weaving only three of the blocks. In addition, Honeysuckle can be woven on Opposites, as a texture without tabby, or as lace with an intermittent second tabby.

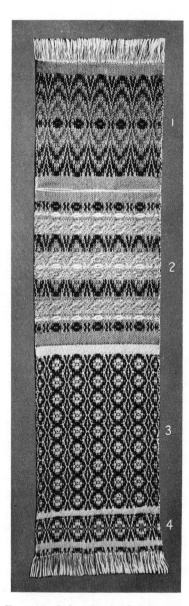

Fig. 122—A length of fabric in the Honeysuckle Pattern, planned for purses, runners, table mats, book jackets, etc.

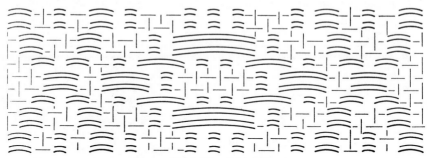

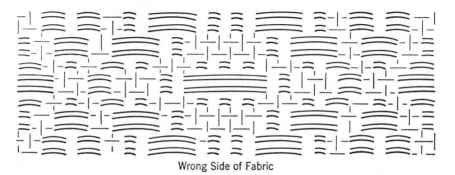

Right Side of Fabric

Wrong Side of Fabric

Fig. 123—Honeysuckle Pattern draft.

Authentic Weaving of the Honeysuckle Pattern, or Weaving as Drawn in

First weave this versatile pattern as drawn in; then study its pattern combinations to see its many possibilities. For weaving the pattern as drawn in, consult the draft in Fig. 123 and, starting at the right side, take each harness group the designated number of times, as follows:

Harnesses 1 and 2: Weave with pattern thread 3 times, following each Pattern row with a row of Tabby.
Harnesses 2 and 3; Weave 3 times
Harnesses 3 and 4; Weave once
Harnesses 4 and 1; Weave once

Harnesses 1 and 2; Weave once
Harnesses 2 and 3; Weave 2 times
Harnesses 1 and 2; Weave once
Harnesses 4 and 1; Weave once
Harnesses 3 and 4; Weave once
Harnesses 2 and 3; Weave 3 times
Harnesses 1 and 2; Weave 3 times
Harnesses 4 and 1; Weave 6 times

If you wish an all-over pattern surface, repeat all. If finishing a border, regard the last treadling combination of harnesses 4 and 1 woven 6 times as the center; and reverse from there.

Weaving Articles in the Honeysuckle Pattern

In Fig. 122 is shown a length of fabric in the Honeysuckle Pattern, planned for purses, runners, hot mats, upholstery material, bell pulls, and bookmarks. Four variations are illustrated.

Warp Plan:

Warp: 8/4 carpet warp or bedspread cotton
Threads per inch: 16
Width: 12 in.
Total threads: 192
Weft: Pattern—Tufting cotton or crochet cotton double; or coarse 4-strand cotton Tabby—Same as warp.

1. Purse or Mat—Repeated Oval Pattern: This is Pattern No. 1 in Fig. 122. Choose three blending colors for the pattern thread, one dark, one medium, and one light; follow each row of Pattern with Tabby, same weight as warp.

Weaving Plan:

Background: Weave 1 in. of Plain Weave.
Pattern:
　*Harnesses 4 and 1—(4×) i.e. 4 times
　Harnesses 1 and 2—(4×)
　Harnesses 2 and 3—(4×)
　Harnesses 3 and 4—(4×)
　Repeat from asterisk once, dark color
　Repeat from asterisk once, medium color.
　Repeat once more with the light color.
Center:
　Harnesses 4 and 1—(2×) dark color
　Harnesses 1 and 2—(2×) dark color
　Harnesses 4 and 1—(2×) dark color
Beyond Center:
　*Harnesses 3 and 4—(4×)
　Harnesses 2 and 3—(4×)
　Harnesses 1 and 2—(4×)
　Harnesses 4 and 1—(4×)
　Repeat from asterisk once, light color.
　Repeat from asterisk once, medium color.
　Repeat once more with the dark color.
Background: Weave 1 in. of Plain Weave.

2. Three-Color Table Piece: The pattern for this section is shown in Fig. 122, No. 2. For the pattern thread choose three shades of the same color—dark, medium, and light. For the Plain Weave use a background color.

Weaving Plan:

End: 1 in. to 2 in. of Plain Weave
Rosette band next to end: Dark on Hs. 4 and 1 (2×); Hs. 1 and 2 (2×); Hs. 4 and 1 (2×)
Plain Weave: 4 rows
Narrow light band: Light on Hs. 4 and 1 (once); Hs. 1 and 2 (once); Hs. 4 and 1 (once)
Plain Weave: 4 rows
1-in. band: Medium shade on Hs. 4 and 1 (2×); Hs. 1 and 2 (2×); Hs. 2 and 3 (2×); Hs. 1 and 2 (2×); Hs. 4 and 1 (2×)
Plain Weave: 4 rows
Center: (all three colors)
　Dark on Hs. 4 and 1 (3×); Hs. 1 and 2 (3×); Hs. 2 and 3 (3×); Hs. 3 and 4 (3×)
　Medium on Hs. 4 and 1 (2×); Hs. 1 and 2 (2×); Hs. 2 and 3 (2×); Hs. 3 and 4 (2×)
　Light on Hs. 4 and 1 (once); Hs. 1 and 2 (once); Hs. 4 and 1 (once)
　Medium on Hs. 3 and 4 (2×); Hs. 2 and 3 (2×); Hs. 1 and 2 (2×); Hs. 4 and 1 (2×)
　Dark on Hs. 3 and 4 (3×); Hs. 2 and 3 (3×); Hs. 1 and 2 (3×); Hs. 4 and 1 (3×)

After the center is completed, weave the same sections on the other side, in reverse order. Weave each individual section as it is written from the beginning of the directions to the end; i.e., do not reverse the directions within any one section, but reverse the order of the sections.

3. Upholstery Material: This design is shown in Fig. 122, section No. 3. Such material is also useful for a school bag, knitting bag, or porch pillow. For the pattern, use only one color. The illustration shows a narrow width; for wide material add more warps and pattern repeats.

Weaving Plan:

End: 1 in. Plain Weave background color
Pattern: Hs. 4 and 1 (2×); Hs. 1 and 2 (2×); Hs. 2 and 3 (2×); Hs. 3 and 4 (2×); Hs. 4 and 1 (2×); Hs. 3 and 4 (2×); Hs. 2

and 3 (2×); Hs. 1 and 2 (2×)
Repeat all as far as desired
At end, add Hs. 4 and 1 (2×)

4. Bell Pull, Small Purse, or Bookmark:
For section No. 4 in Fig. 122, use only one or two colors for the pattern thread.

Weaving Plan:

End: 1 in. Plain Weave background color
Pattern: Hs. 4 and 1 (3×); Hs. 1 and 2
  (3×); Hs. 2 and 3 (3×); Hs. 3 and 4 (3×)
Center: Hs. 1 and 2 (2×)
Pattern: Hs. 3 and 4 (3×); Hs. 2 and 3
  (3×); Hs. 1 and 2 (3×); Hs. 4 and 1 (3×)

WEAVING AN OVERSHOT PATTERN SAMPLER

An interesting way to acquaint yourself quickly with many Overshot Patterns is to plan a succession of different drafts on the same loom, with several repeats of each. This forms a composite fabric from which countless designs and textures can be derived. Below are thirteen such patterns to be threaded in their given order, with a narrow band of Twill following each one to separate it from the next. The separation is still further

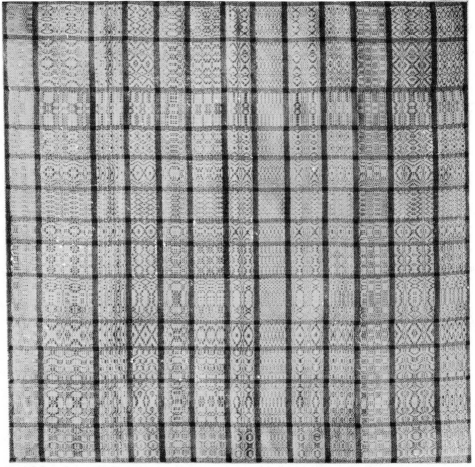

(Courtesy Mrs. Charles Price)

Fig. 124—A pattern sampler with thirteen successive patterns woven in thirteen different ways, making a total of 169 different design effects.

DIRECTIONS FOR THREADING AN OVERSHOT PATTERN SAMPLER

Thirteen Small and Miniature Overshot Patterns

Warp: 163 threads Dark 20/2
803 threads Light 20/2

Reed: 15 dents per inch
2 threads per dent
width in reed—32¼ inches

Weft: Pattern—6-strand floss or Perle 5
Tabby—Dark and Light 20/2 (as in warp)

Threading of Sampler: from right to left. Standard tie-up, page 168

Pattern	Threading Plan	Color	Threads
Twill Border	Hs. 4,1,2,3 (3×)	Dark	12
Small Star	4,3,2,1,2,1,2,3,4,1,4,3,2,3,2,3,4,1 (3×)	Light	54
Twill	2,3,4,1,2,3,4,1,2,3,4,1	Dark	12
Maltese Cross	2,1,4,1,2,1,2,3,2,3,4,3,4,1,4,1,2,1,4,3,2,1,2,3,4,1,2,1,4,1,4, 3,4,3,2,3,2,1,2,1,4,1 (2×)	Light	84
Twill	2,3,4,1,2,3,4,1,2,3,4,1	Dark	12
Crackle	4,3,2,1,4,3,4,1,4,3,4,1,4,3,4,1,2,3,4,1,2,1,4,1,2,1,4,1,2,1	Light	60
Twill	2,3,4,1,2,3,4,1,2,3,4,1	Dark	12
Weaver's Fancy	4,3,2,1,4,3,4,1,2,1,2,1,4,3,4,1,2,3 (3×), and H. 4 at end	Light	55
Twill	1,2,3,4,1,2,3,4,1,2,3	Dark	11
Honeysuckle Twill	4,3,2,1,4,3,2,1,4,3,4,3,2,3,2,1,2,1,2,1,2,3,2,3,4,3,4,1,2,3,4, 1,2,3 (2×), add H. 4	Light	69
Twill	1,2,3,4,1,2,3,4,1,2,3	Dark	11
Rosepath Variation	4,3,2,3,4,1,2,1,4,3,2,3,4,1,2,1 (3×), add 4,3,2,3,4,1,2,1	Light	56
Twill	2,3,4,1,2,3,4,1,2,3,4,1	Dark	12
Honeysuckle	4,3,2,1,4,3,4,3,2,3,2,1,2,1,2,1,2,3,2,3,4,3,4,1,2,3 (2×), add H. 4	Light	53
Twill	1,2,3,4,1,2,3,4,1,2,3	Dark	11
Rose Pattern	4,3,4,3,2,3,2,3,4,3,2,3,2,3,4,3,4,1,2,1 (3×)	Light	60
Twill	2,3,4,1,2,3,4,1,2,3,4,1	Dark	12
Lovers Knot	4,1,2,3,4,1,4,3,2,1,2,3,2,1,2,3,4,3,4,1,4,1,4,3,4,1,4,3,4,1,4, 1,4,3,4,3,2,1,2,3,2,1,2,3,4,1,4,3,2,1,4	Light	51
Twill	1,2,3,4,1,2,3,4,1,2,3,4	Dark	12
Russian Diaper	1,2,1,2,3,2,3,4,3,4,1,4,1,2,1,2,1,4,1,4,3,4,3,2,3,2 (2×)	Light	52
Twill	1,2,3,4,1,2,3,4,1,2,3	Dark	11
Miniature Monk's Belt	4,3,4,3,4,3,2,1,4,3,2,1,2,1,2,1,4,3,2,1 (3×)	Light	60
Twill	2,3,4,1,2,3,4,1,2,3,4	Dark	11
Miniature Whig Rose	1,2,3,4,1,2,3,2,1,2,3,2,1,4,1,4,3,4,3,4,1,4,3,4,1,4,3,4,3,4,1, 4,1,2,3,2,1,2,3,2,1,4,3,2 (2×), add H. 1	Light	89
Twill	2,3,4,1,2,3,4,1,2,3,4,1	Dark	12
Twill Miniature	4,3,2,1,2,3,2,1,2,3,2,1,2,3,4,1,2,3,4,3,2,3,4,3,2,3,4,3,2,1, (2×)	Light	60
Twill Border	2,3,4,1, (3×)	Dark	12

966

215

marked by having the patterns threaded in light color warp and the Twill divisions in a dark color warp. If each of these patterns is woven according to its threading, or as drawn in, all the other patterns unfold in fascinating and unexpected forms which can be used in any way desired. (Look at the pattern sampler in Fig. 124.)

Weaving the Sampler

Weave the sampler as drawn in. Directions are given on page 192.

For pattern sections, use the light pattern thread and bind with the dark colored Tabby. For the Border and Twill bands, use the dark pattern thread and bind with the light Tabby, or vice versa.

Start with Twill Border, and weave: Hs. 4-1, 1-2, 2-3, 3-4. Repeat 2 times. Follow each row with Tabby.

Pattern No. 1, Small Star. Weave as drawn in: Hs. 3-4 (1✕), 2-3 (1✕), 1-2 (4✕), 2-3 (1✕), 3-4 (1✕), 4-1 (2✕), 3-4 (1✕), 2-3 (4✕), 3-4 (1✕) 4-1 (2✕). Follow each row with Tabby. Repeat to square the threaded section of this particular pattern, about 2½ inches.

Twill Band. Weave Hs. 1-2, 2-3, 3-4, 4-1. Repeat 2 times.

Pattern No. 2, Maltese Cross. Weave as drawn in, and so on.

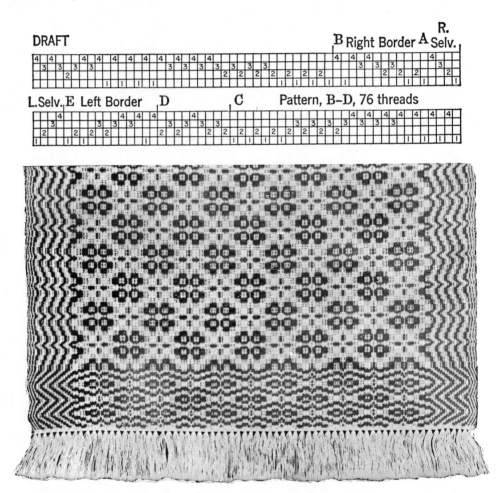

Fig. 125—"Four Petals" Pattern with side borders.

Square each pattern, weaving as much of it along the warp as was threaded across the warp. Many different design effects results from different threadings along any one horizontal row of woven blocks.

Continue in this manner, taking the patterns in order, weaving each as drawn in, and making the height of each equal to its width. Follow each block with a Twill band to separate it from the adjacent block.

If you prefer, you can weave the Border and Twill sections without Tabby since woven twill-fashion, the rows bind one another. Repeat Hs. 1-2, 2-3, 3-4, and 4-1.

A FLORAL PATTERN

The draft of alternating Star and Rose motifs shows how two different units may be balanced in a pleasing pattern. The arrangement is best woven as drawn in, with only one color; otherwise its allover effect is broken up. If you wish to use two colors, change the color when passing from one area (a) to the other area (b). One can also use parts of the pattern for a conventional border (c) and one with a twill effect (d). There are two definite centers to the draft, marked C-1 and C-2. Reverses are made from these points.

The pattern weaves into a lovely allover surface design useful for pillows, hangings, and couch throws. For coverlets, repeat A-B more times. It is effective woven as Honeycomb, p. 234.

Warp Plan

Warp: 20/2 or 24/3 Cotton
Weft: Pattern: 5/2 or 10/3 Cot. Tabby, like warp.
Thds. per in: 30. Width: 19 in.

Threading Plan

Selvage, 4 thds. 6 times	24
Pattern, A–B, (242) 2×	484
Last time, A–D only	36
Left Selvage, (4) 6×	24
Total Threads	568

Weaving Plan (Counterbalanced)

Border:	1st Motif, Cont.
Hs. 2-3, 1×	Hs. 1-2, 2×
3-4, 1×	4-1, 6×
4-1, 1×	1-2, 6×
1-2, 1×	2-3, 1×
Repeat 6×	3-4, 2× (C-1)
	Reverse to (*)

Pattern:	
1st Motif	2nd Motif
*Hs. 2-3, 6×	**Hs. 1-2, 6×
3-4, 6×	4-1, 2×
4-1, 6×	1-2, 6×
1-2, 6×	4-1, 6×
2-3, 6×	3-4, 2×
3-4, 6×	4-1, 6×
4-1, 2×	3-4, 6×
3-4, 6×	1-2, 2× (C-2)
4-1, 6×	Reverse to **

PATTERN DRAFT FOR RUNNERS, PILLOWS AND COVERLETS   A Selv.

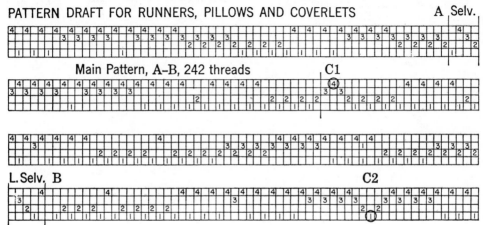

Main Pattern, A–B, 242 threads   C1

L. Selv. B   C2

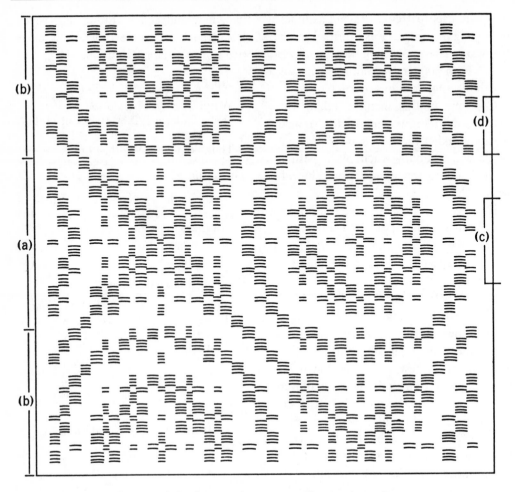

Fig. 126—A floral pattern for runners, pillows, and coverlets.

THE HUMMINGBIRD PATTERN

Here is a pattern of versatile beauty, offering many weaving variations. The radiating wings surround a lovely smaller motif, making possible borders of oval outline. The pattern shows its full wing spread when woven as drawn in (see drawing, page 219).

"Hummingbird" is excellent for borders on linens, guest towels, and dainty gifts. The pattern is planned with an effective side border for runners, mats or drapes. For upholstery, simply omit border A-B in threading, and start with a selvage, Hs. 4, 3, 2, 1. Then repeat pattern B-D as desired. End with Hs. 2, 3, 4, 1. For a bathmat repeat B-D less times.

Warp Plan for 18-in. doiley with border.

Warp: 20/2 or 24/3 Cotton. Tabby, same.
Weft: Pattern: 5/2 or 10/3 Cotton
Threads per in: 30. Total Threads: 561

Threading Plan	Threads
Selvage, (4) 6×, -24; Border A–B 63	87
Pattern B–D (44), 8 times	352
Add B–C only	35
Border backwards, B–A, 63;	
Selv. 6×, 24	87

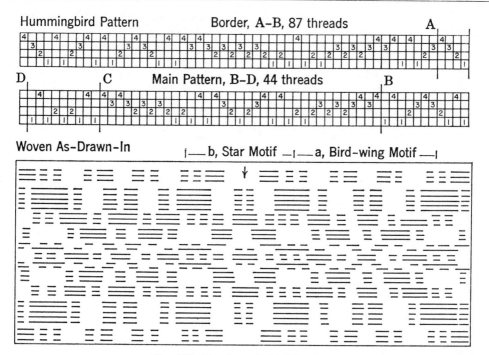

Fig. 127—The Hummingbird Pattern.

No. 2. Oval
Border

Hs. 1-2, 1×
    2-3, 1×
    3-4, 1×
    4-1, 1×
    1-2, 2×
    2-3, 2×
    3-4, 2×
    (4-1, 4×)
Center;
    Reverse

No. 3. Wing Border

Hs 1,2, 2×; 4 rows tabby
    4-1, 3×   (Follow
    3-4, 3×   each row
    2-3, 3×   with one
    1-2, 3×   row tab.)
    4-1, 3×
    3-4, 1×   Reverse
    2-3, 1×   from cen-
***(1-2, 2×)   ter ***

4-1, 4×   1-2, 1×   4-1, 3×
1-2, 3×   2-3, 1×   1-2, 4×
2-3, 5×   3-4, 2×   4-1, 3×
3-4, 3×   2-3, 1×   Repeat as de-
4-1, 3×   1-2, 1×   sired. At end
1-2, 1×   4-1, 3× ** finish at *.
            End of Border   Add border
                            backwards **

The **Chariot-Wheel Pattern** is one of
the old Colonial favorites for coverlets,
pillows, and runners. It comes in several
forms—single wheels with table, double
wheels, and single wheels with cross. The
pattern for this last-named form is shown
in Fig. 128. It consists of separate wheels
joined by diagonal crosses evenly spaced
between the wheels.

Warp Plan for a Coverlet Panel:
Width of material on loom: 32 in.
Number of threads per inch (2 per
    dent): 32
Reed: 16-dent
Warp thread: 20/2 ply cotton
Pattern weft: Crochet cotton 10/3 or

Weaving Plans

1. As Drawn In
Border:
Hs. 1-2, 1×
    2-3, 1×
    3-4, 1×
    4-1, 1×
Repeat all 6×
Hs. 3-4, 1×
    2-3, 1×
    1-2, 1×
    4-1, 3×
    3-4, 3×
    2-3, 5×
    1-2, 3×

Border, Cont.
    2-3, 1×
    3-4, 2×
    2-3, 1×
    1-2, 1×
    4-1, 3×
    3-4, 1×
    2-3, 1×
    1-2, 1×
    4-1, 2×
    1-2, 1×
    2-3, 1×
    3-4, 1×
    4-1, 3×

Center:
Hs. 3-4, 3×
    2-3, 5×
    1-2, 3×
    4-1, 3×
    3-4, 1×
    2-3, 1×
    1-2, 2×
    2-3, 1×
    3-4, 1×
    4-1, 3×
    1-2, 3×
    2-3, 5×
 * 3-4, 3×

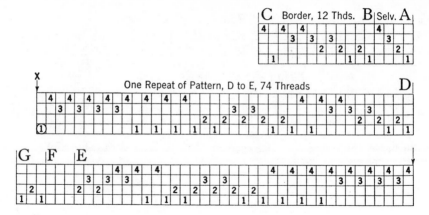

Perle 5, or 2-ply wool yarn

Tabby weft: Same as warp

Total number of threads: 1029 (if this number exceeds the number allowed for the width of the reed, take out one repeat of selvage at each side, making 1021 threads)

Weave two or three panels, and sew them together.

Plan 1: Threading Plan for a 32-in. Panel with a Border on Each Side. Use the following plan, which is also suitable for drapes and runners:

	Threads
Selvage A–B: 4 threads, 2 times	8
Border B–C: 12 threads, 2 times	24
Pattern D–E: 74 threads, 13 times ...	962
Add F–G	8
Border reversed C–B, 2 times	24
Selvage reversed B–A, 2 times	8
Total	1029

Plan 2: Threading Plan for a 32-in. Coverlet Panel with a Border on Only One Side. For each of two panels which are to be attached at a central seam to form a coverlet 64 in. wide for a single bed, use the following:

	Threads
Selvage A–B: 4 threads, once only ...	4
Border B–C: 12 threads, 2 times	24
Pattern D–E: 74 threads, 13 times ..	962
D to X only (see H.1 in circle, at center of wheel)	39
Total	1029

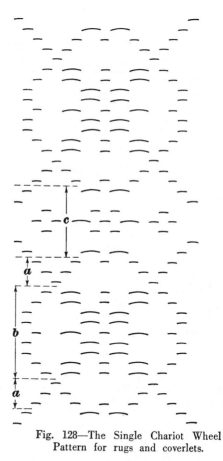

Fig. 128—The Single Chariot Wheel Pattern for rugs and coverlets.

Plan 3: Threading Plan for a 30-in. Coverlet Panel Without Borders. For a panel to be inserted between two side panels to form a full-width coverlet 90 in. wide, thread a center panel with no borders, as follows:

Threads

Starting at **X** (thread in circle on H. 1),
thread Pattern from **X** to **E** 36
Repeat entire Pattern from **D** to **E**, 74
threads, 12 times 888
Finish with Pattern from **D** to **X** only 39
_____
Total 963

NOTE: It is possible to thread this center panel quite easily from the threading of the side panels by Plan 2. Simply leave in 12 complete repeats of the Pattern from **D** to **E**. At the right side of this, thread the 36 threads from **E** to **X**. At the left side, thread the 39 threads from **D** to **X**. Unthread the unused warp threads, tie them in a slip knot in back of the heddles, and leave them unused during the weaving of this panel. The 963 threads make the warp 30 in. wide.

Warp Plan for a Rug to Match Coverlet:
Width of Material: 30 in.
Threads per inch: 12
Total threads: 363
Warp: 8/4 Carpet warp
Weft:
Pattern—Rug yarn or rags, all one color
Tabby—Same as warp

Threading Plan for the Rug:

Use Plan 1 for a panel with borders, but reduce the number of Pattern repeats; i.e., repeat the pattern **D-E**, 74 threads 4 times only. For a wider rug, add one repeat for each additional 6 inches of width.

Weaving Plan:

	FOR COVERLET PANEL	FOR RUG
Border: Repeat as desired		
Hs. 1 and 2	(3×)	(2×)
Hs. 2 and 3	(3×)	(2×)
Hs. 3 and 4	(3×)	(2×)
Hs. 4 and 1	(3×)	(2×)

Main Pattern (Fig. 129):

Section (a):		
Hs. 1 and 2	(3×)	(2×)
Hs. 2 and 3	(4×)	(2×)
Hs. 1 and 2	(3×)	(2×)
Section (b):		
Hs. 4 and 1	(7×)	(4×)
Hs. 3 and 4	(7×)	(4×)
Hs. 4 and 1	(2×)	(2×)
Hs. 3 and 4	(7×)	(4×)
Hs. 4 and 1	(7×)	(4×)
Section (a):		
Hs. 1 and 2	(3×)	(2×)
Hs. 2 and 3	(4×)	(2×)
Hs. 1 and 2	(3×)	(2×)
Section (c):		
Hs. 4 and 1	(3×)	(2×)
Hs. 3 and 4	(3×)	(2×)
Hs. 2 and 3	(3×)	(2×)
Hs. 1 and 2	(3×)	(2×)
Hs. 2 and 3	(3×)	(2×)
Hs. 3 and 4	(3×)	(2×)
Hs. 4 and 1	(3×)	(2×)

Section (a) forms the base of a wheel and the small rose; section (b) forms the star within the wheel; and section (c) forms the diagonal cross between wheels. Keep repeating the motifs in the order given as far as desired: (a), (b), (a), (c). Then weave the border backward.

Weaving Plan for Special Border: By weaving certain parts of the pattern, one can develop attractive borders for use at the bases of drapes or the ends of bureau scarves and runners to match the rug and the coverlet. Two such borders follow:

1. Weave section (b) alone.

2. Weave section (a), then section (c), and section (a) again.

32–Designing Overshot Drafts

GENERAL PROCEDURE IN DESIGNING DRAFTS

THE principles given in Lessons 28 and 29 on the writing of drafts to make patterns for four-harness weaves may be applied to the making of many beautiful textures for fabrics. The weaver will find hundreds of four-harness patterns already worked out in good books on weaving, such as those listed in the Bibliography at the end of this book. These patterns are given in clear form and often are illustrated.

In Fig. 129 are shown two sturdy table mats and a napkin in a conventional pattern. The warp of the mats is carpet warp set at 16 threads per inch; the Tabby weft is the same, and the Pattern weft is tufting cotton. The napkin has fine texture. Its warp is 24/3 cotton set at 30 threads per inch, its Tabby weft is the same, and the Pattern weft is crochet cotton of colors matching those in the mats.

Writing One's Own Pattern Drafts

It is possible and most interesting to learn to make one's own patterns. Here are some rules to observe in writing drafts of typical four-harness Overshot Patterns with adjacent blocks, such as Diamond, Honeysuckle, and the patterns in this lesson.

Rule 1: Follow Odd Threads with Even and Even with Odd. In writing the draft, all threads designated on odd-numbered harnesses must be followed by threads on even-numbered ones; and all even-numbered threads must be followed by odd-numbered ones; i.e.,

Follow H. 1 or H. 3 by H. 2 or H. 4
Follow H. 2 or H. 4 by H. 1 or H. 3

If this rule is adhered to, the treadling combinations of harnesses 1 and 3 and 2 and 4 will always make Tabby.

Rule 2: Plan Blocks of Reasonable Size. The notes in any one block written on two adjacent harnesses, such as block (1, 2, 1, 2), should not be prolonged too far. In rugs, the block should not be over 1 in. long. Therefore, if the warp is set at 16 threads per inch, any one block should not contain more than sixteen threads, and twelve threads would be better. A draft consisting of twelve threads in a certain block would read as follows: 1, 2, 1, 2, 1, 2, 1, 2, 1, 2, 1, 2. It might then progress to harness 3 and read Hs. 3, 2, 3, 2, 3 and so on. In towels, linens, pillows, coverlets, etc., with the warp set at 30 or 32 threads per inch, the blocks in the draft should not extend for more than ½ in. or 16 threads, and a bit less than this would be better.

Rule 3: Mark Each Reverse Note with a Circle. When reversing a pattern draft to make a center, as in the Herringbone drafts in Fig. 112, **B** to **F**, mark the reverse note with a circle, and then retrace each step taken, making the left side like the right. This gives an extra note on one of the harnesses, making an odd number

Fig. 129—Sturdy table mats and napkin in a conventional pattern.

of notes in the reversing block, such as Hs. 1, (2), 1; or Hs. 4, (1), 4; or Hs. 4, 1, (4), 1, 4.

Rule 4: For a Pattern on Adjacent Blocks, Use a Thread in Common. A large number of four-harness Overshot Patterns are written on adjacent blocks. This means that in these drafts there is a connection, or thread in common, be-

tween any two blocks that occur next to each other on the draft. Such patterns are the Diamond, the Honeysuckle, and a great many patterns of larger size like those in this lesson.

The manner in which patterns **on** adjacent blocks are written is clearly shown in the Stepladder Pattern in **Fig.** 116 (see the blocks surrounded by the dotted lines). The (1 and 2) block of four threads ends on harness 2, but this is also the beginning of the next block (2 and 3), which picks up the note on harness 2 and uses it as one of its own notes. In other words, harness 2 is common to both blocks. Likewise, the (2 and 3) block ends on harness 3, but this is the beginning of the next block (3 and 4). This note in common makes an overlapping both in threading and in weaving the pattern, and the result is that the progression between blocks is gradual and pleasing.

Follow this method, then, in writing this type of pattern, taking the last note in any one combination as the first note of the new combination. Having found what the first note in the new combination is to be, to find the second note apply Rule 1, according to which an even note is followed by an odd, and an odd is followed by an even. Examples are:

If the first note of the new block is on H. 1, it can combine with H. 2 or H. 4, making block 1 and 2 or block 4 and 1.

If the first note of the new block is on H. 2, it can combine with H. 3 or H. 1, making block 2 and 3 or block 1 and 2.

If the first note of the new block is on H. 3, it can combine with H. 4 or H. 2, making block 3 and 4 or block 2 and 3.

If the first note of the new block is on H. 4, it can combine with H. 1 or H. 3, making block 4 and 1 or block 3 and 4.

Note that Rule 4 for adjacent blocks does not hold for patterns on opposites (see Rule 5).

Rule 5: For a Pattern on Opposites, There Is no Note in Common. Some patterns are written on opposite blocks instead of on adjacent ones. Such a pattern is the Monk's Belt in Fig. 120, which weaves into small separate square figures that have no connecting link or note in common. In writing pattern drafts of this type, follow Rules 1, 2, and 3, but not Rule 4. In such drafts, the last note of any one block, such as H. 2 in the (1 and 2) block, is not used in the new block. Instead, the next block uses two entirely different harnesses, and these of course must be the two opposite harnesses, such as Hs. 3 and 4. Thus, in patterns "on opposites," which produce little separate squared effects as in the Monk's Belt, use the following directions:

Follow the (1 and 2) block with the (3 and 4) block

Follow the (2 and 3) block with the (4 and 1) block

Follow the (3 and 4) block with the (1 and 2) block

Follow the (4 and 1) block with the (2 and 3) block

Checkerboard Overshot

One of the simplest and most useful of patterns on Opposites is the **Checkerboard Overshot.** This is nothing more nor less than a block on Hs. 1-2, followed by a block on Hs. 3-4. Thread Hs. 1-2 two, three, or four times, and follow with Hs. 3-4 the same number of times. One block may be woven with one color, the opposite block with a second color.

You can also make a pattern of four blocks as follows: Hs. 1-2 four times; Hs. 3-4 four times; Hs. 1-2 four times. Then Hs. 2-3 four times; Hs. 4-1 four times; Hs. 2-3 four times. Repeat all. Weave in the same order, squaring each block.

This pattern is suitable for upholstery, textured coverlets, towel borders, purse designs, and heavy drapes and rugs. Both threadings given above turn out beautifully when woven as Honeycomb (page 234). This is especially good for counterpanes in tones of white or for bathmats. Effective too is a rug with fine pattern thread dark, heavy tabby outlines, light.

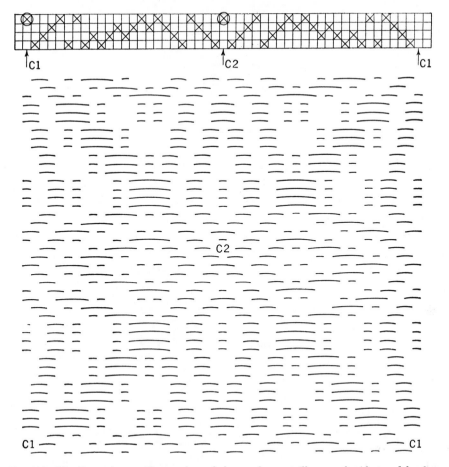

Fig. 130—The Remembrance Pattern for upholstery, drapes, pillows, and wide towel borders.

Making a Threading Plan

The **Remembrance Draft** is a simply designed pattern. Its two reverse points are quite visible at C1 and C2 in the draw-down above.

Centering the Pattern Between Borders: In the case of some drafts it is possible for the weaver to plan so that the number of warp threads in one repeat of the pattern goes evenly into the total number of warp threads, making each side of the woven fabric appear the same. If desired, one can add a certain number of selvage threads at the right and left sides. A selvage edge is formed by threading one or more repeats of the Twill (Hs.

1, 2, 3, 4) at the **beginning** and **ending** of the pattern threading.

Simple Pattern Repeats: Some patterns are written from center to center. In such a case one can simply divide the number of threads in the Pattern repeat into the total number of warp threads. Consider, for instance, the Remembrance Pattern in Fig. 130, which consists of 48 threads. The two alternating centers of the pattern are marked C1 and C2 in the sketch. The draft can be repeated as many times as desired, and selvage may be added at the beginning and end of the threading. If there are 400 threads in our warp, divide this by 48 to get 8 repeats with

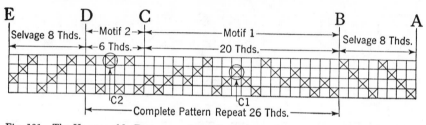

Fig. 131—The Honeysuckle Pattern used as a basis for making a typical threading plan.

16 threads left over. Use 8 threads for selvage at the right and 8 at the left.

Patterns of Two Alternating Motifs: Most patterns consist of two separate motifs, which alternate throughout the draft. For instance, in the Honeysuckle Pattern in Fig. 131, one can clearly see two successive motifs: motif 1 from **B** to **C**; and motif 2 from **C** to **D**. The center note of each motif is enclosed in a circle. The complete pattern of motifs 1 and 2 consists of 26 threads. It would be best to thread this pattern in such a way as to have it end as it began, **i.e.,** with motif 1. To do this, repeat the entire pattern (motifs 1 and 2) a certain number of times, and then add motif 1. If the warp consists of 400 threads, 15 repeats of 26 threads (390 threads) will not leave enough warp for another repeat of motif 1 of 20 threads. Therefore, repeat the entire pattern only 14 times, using 364 threads; add one repeat of motif 1 (20 threads), using 384 threads; and thread the remaining 16 threads as selvage or border. Our threading plan will therefore read as follows:

	Threads
Selvage at right (**A to B**)	8
Pattern: Motifs 1 and 2 (**B to D**), 26 threads, 14 times	364
Add motif 1 (**B to C** only)	20
Selvage at left (**D to E**)	8
Total	400

NOTE: After adding motif 1, finish at **C**, skip to **D**, and thread from **D** to **E**.

Arranging the Selvage: Note that our pattern in Fig. 131, beginning at **B**, reads from right to left. The warp notes or crosses seem to proceed from H. 1 to H. 4, rising upward gradually on the draft bars. Starting with block (1, 2, 1, 2), they proceed to block (2, 3, 2, 3), and then to block (3, 4) and to block (4, 1). If the selvage is made to ascend in the same direction, it results in a line flowing in the same direction when woven. Therefore, we plan our selvage to read (1, 2, 3, 4), (1, 2, 3, 4). Likewise, at the left side, where the notes seem to descend from H. 4 to H. 1 at point **C**, we plan the selvage to read (4, 3, 2, 1), inserting an extra 1 before the 4 to complete the block at **C**, just before we add the selvage.

Number of Repeats: For narrower or wider warps, simply add or subtract one or more repeats of the complete pattern from **B to D**.

Miniature Patterns

Miniature patterns are condensed drafts of larger Overshot Patterns. Just as a Twill Pattern or a Herringbone Pattern may be enlarged to a pattern with longer overshot spaces by taking the small 2- or 3-thread blocks, such as Hs. 1 and 2, and enlarging them to 4- or 5-thread blocks, such as Hs. 1, 2, 1, 2, in the same way we may reduce 4- or 5-thread blocks to 2- or 3-thread blocks. We may also alter blocks of still larger size to be half as large in the miniature.

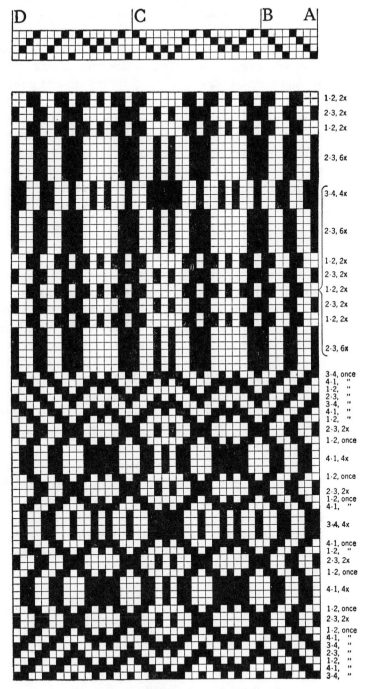

Fig. 132—Tiny Wheel Pattern for bookmark.

In miniature patterns the blocks extend for a very short space and the resulting length of pattern weft showing is not very prominent. They form most attractive tiny motifs and are useful for all kinds of small hand-woven things, such as bookmarks, belts, sandal straps, curtain tie-backs, fine textures for purses, delicate borders for towels or doilies, and also very durable and unusual textures when repeated for upholstery fabrics.

The weaver himself can design miniature patterns by altering regular four-harness Overshot Patterns. The blocks must occur in the same succession as in the pattern proper, and the method of connecting the blocks must be the same; but any large block of four or more threads may be reduced at will. For instance, in the Single Chariot Wheel in Fig. 129, the first block, Hs. 1, 2, 1, 2, can be reduced to a 2-thread block, Hs. 1, 2; the next block, Hs. 2, 3, 2, 3, can be reduced to Hs. 2, 3; and the same plan can be consistently carried out all through the pattern. When one reaches an 8-thread block, such as that on Hs. 1, 4, 1, 4, 1, 4, 1, 4, he can simply reduce this to Hs. 1, 4, 1, 4; and one can reduce the 9-thread block, Hs. 4, 3, 4, 3, 4, 3, 4, 3, 4, to a 5-thread block, Hs. 4, 3, 4, 3, 4. Blocks with an even number of notes will have an even number of notes, although fewer, in the miniature; and blocks with an odd number of notes will have an odd number in the miniature. Also one must always make the beginning and ending notes of the reduced block exactly the same as those of the larger block. To set off the miniature pattern at both the right and left sides, use one or more repeats of the Twill as a selvage border.

The Tiny Wheel Pattern in Fig. 132 is a simple and practical miniature pattern with Twill borders. In the diagram the 18-thread motif B–C is shown only once. However, as planned for a bookmark, the pattern contains 60 threads and the motif B–C is repeated. Also, one may repeat this motif as far as desired to make an all-over texture for a purse, a pillow, or upholstery.

The treadling in the diagram is for a rising shed on a jack loom. For the same effect on a counterbalanced loom in which there is a sinking shed and the harnesses are lowered—instead of being lifted—to make the shed, simply change the harness combinations given in the diagram to their opposites, as follows: Change Hs. 1-2 to Hs. 3-4; Hs. 2-3 to Hs. 4-1; Hs. 3-4 to Hs. 1-2; and Hs. 4-1 to Hs. 2-3. In the diagram the pattern is shown woven from the base of the page upward. It starts with a Twill border at the base in the first 8 rows of weft, proceeds to the formation of the Tiny Wheel, and continues with the weaving included by the bracket in the treadling schedule.

If desired, one or more additional Tiny Wheels can be woven into the design, or the section covered by the bracket can be repeated as far as necessary. To finish with the same design used at the start, end the last repeat of the bracketed section with the group consisting of Hs. 2 and 3 woven 6 times shown near the upper end of the bracketed section in Fig. 132.

Warp Plan:

Warp: 20/2 cotton
Threads per inch: 30
Width: 2 in.
Total threads: 60 (one spool of 60 ends of warp may be used)
Weft:
Pattern: Mercerized cotton No. 10; or Silkateen; or any thread of similar size, such as very fine 2-ply wool
Tabby: Same as warp

Threading Plan:

For a 2-in. band, thread the pattern as given in Fig. 132 from **A** to **C**; then repeat the 18-thread motif **B–C**; and finish with the first unit of the pattern and the left selvage **C–D**.

For a wider fabric, thread the selvage **A–B**; follow with the motif **B–C** repeated as far as desired; and finish with the first unit of the pattern and the left selvage **C–D**.

Weaving Plan:

Follow the combinations given in Fig. 132, proceeding upward from the bottom of the diagram.

PERSONALIZED DRAFTS

Every weaver desires to create patterns according to his own liking. However, the necessary confidence is often lacking. Here is a way in which you can find a clue to designing your own drafts. Instead of merely weaving traditional patterns, you can become an amateur fabric designer.

Simply make a code between the alphabet and the notes of the draft and replace one with the other. Read the name on the draft using the designated harness number for each letter. Delightful and unusual paterns will result.

CODING THE ALPHABET

Here are three ways of coding the alphabet.

Method No. 1

a b c d e f g ..... H. 1 (all these letters will be written on H. 1)

h i j k l m n ...... H. 2

o p q r s t   ...... H. 3

u v w x y z   ...... H. 4

Now make a draft of the name MARY SMITH. Mark harnesses on graph paper.

M ...... H. 2

A ...... H. 1; add H. 4

R ...... H. 3

Y ...... H. 4

S ...... H. 3

M ...... H. 2; add H. 1

I ...... H. 2

T ...... H. 3

H ...... H. 2

Now you will note that there would be a flat, Hs. 1 and 3 (both odd harnesses) between the "A" and "R" of MARY. Therefore, we add H. 2 or H. 4. We will choose H. 4. There is also a flat betwen two notes, H. 2, of the "M" and "I" of SMITH. Here H. 1 or H. 3 can be inserted. Suppose we make it H. 1. (There is no rule. You can add the note that seems to look most interesting.) The finished draft, reading from right to left, will be:

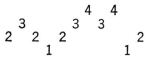

Add a reverse to this from last note on H. 2 (in circle), continuing right to left, as shown in the draft below.

Add H. 3 at end so you will be ready to begin on H. 2 without a flat.

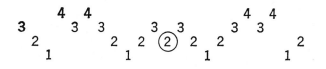

③₂ 4 3 3 3 3 3 4 4 4 3 3 2 2
        2   2   1   1 2

Method No. 2

Write the letters in columns and follow the same procedure of drafting:

Harness	1	2	3	4
	a	b	c	d
	e	f	g	h
	i	j	k	l
	m	n	o	p
	q	r	s	t
	u	v	w	x
	y	z		

Method No. 3

Still another way of coding drafts is to let each letter represent a block instead of just a simple harness figure.

a b c d e f g .... Hs. 1 and 2
h i j k l m n ..... Hs. 2 and 3
o p q r s t   ..... Hs. 3 and 4
u v w x y z   .....Hs. 4 and 1

In transferring a name to a draft by this method you need not add any extra notes. If a flat occurs, you turn the combination around and it disappears. For instance, instead of progressing from H. 1 to 2, you go from H. 2 to 1.
To write MARY SMITH by this method you then have:

M ...... Hs. 2 and 3
A .... Hs. 1 and 2
R .... Hs. 3 and 4
Y .... Hs. 4 and 1

S .... Hs. 3 and 4
M ...... Hs. 2 and 3
I .... Hs. 2 and 3
T ...... Hs. 3 and 4
H ...... Hs. 2 and 3

and you would write the draft, right to left, as shown at the top of the page.

Reversing this on H. 3 in circle, you have the draft shown at the bottom of this page.

Note: The extra note on H. 1 provides a means for repeating the pattern.

This draft gives you a table at the center and has more character than the draft written by Method 1. Note how the blocks were turned around as on "A" in "MARY" from Hs. 1 and 2 to Hs. 2 and 1 to avoid flats.

Possibilities of Coded Names and Numbers

There is no limit to the kinds of coding you can do. You can code the names of flowers, of birds, of states, of short mottos, of the names of friends, of greetings such as "Happy Birthday," and so on. One weaver I know opens her phone book to any page and reads down the exchange numbers that are in a vertical row and puts these numbers right on the draft.

Harnesses	1	2	3	4
Exchange Numbers	8	2	4	7

1, etc. (Write

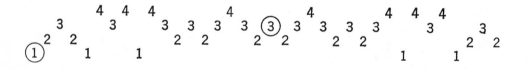

left to right in order in which they appear vertically in book.)

An example of a phone book series would be:

Williams, Jas. R. ...... HI 8-2125
Williams, John ...... MO 2-4321
Williams, L. P. .... WI 4-8761
Williams, Paul .... FR 7-6311
Williams, Ralph ..... MO 1-4119

Simply take the 8, 2, 4, 7, place under Hs. 1, 2, 3, 4 and continue down the line. Do not take the four numbers following the exchange number (the 2125 following Hi-8).

Many beautiful patterns are the result of these codes. Draft them down on graph paper by the method given in Fig. 116.

Fig. 133—Summer coverlet in the Bowknot Pattern, white cotton warp, 20/2; pattern, gray linen weft, 30/2. Notice the well balanced figures.

33—Ways of Weaving Overshot

OVERSHOT Patterns are usually woven with various successions of two-treadle combinations, such as Hs. 1-2, 2-3, 3-4, 4-1. Below are other ways of adding variety to patterns.

THREE AND ONE COMBINATIONS

Most Overshot Patterns can also be woven by using three of the harnesses together, Hs. 1-2-3, Hs. 2-3-4, Hs. 3-4-1, Hs. 4-1-2. The result is a pattern of large skips and stronger color appearance. If any one of the combinations produces too large a skip to be practical, simply use the others. On Jack looms or wide-shed counterbalanced looms, you can also treadle H. 1 alone, H. 2 alone, H. 3 alone, H. 4 alone.

By combining any of the above in various ways, you obtain new texture and design effects. On looms of direct tie-up, with each harness tied directly to the treadle of the same number, you can make any of the above twelve combinations plus the two Tabbies, Hs. 1-3 and Hs. 2-4.

OVERSHOT AS TEXTURE

Another method of weaving Overshot is to use your pattern purely as an allover texture. Experiment with treadle successions until the pattern is a subtle suggestion buried within the threads. One way to achieve this is to use the same thread for both Pattern and Tabby.

LAYING-IN ON A PATTERN THREADING

Choose certain portions of the pattern and carry the pattern thread to the boundaries of these portions only. (The tabby is constant.) Each section has its own pattern thread which travels back and forth for successive rows, and the reversing threads can form color accents for the pattern at their nodes. Vertical pattern borders can be made in this manner.

LACE WEAVES ON SHORT OVERSHOT PATTERNS

You can make a lacey textural weave by treating Overshot somewhat like Bronson. Hold out one of the harnesses for several rows and bind with Tabby.

H. 3 alone, Tabby 2-4
H. 3 alone, Tabby 2-4
Hs. 1-3, Tabby 2-4
or
H. 2 alone, Tabby 1-3
H. 2 alone, Tabby 1-3
Hs. 2-4, Tabby 1-3

Best results are obtained by using only one weft for both the Pattern and Tabby.

WEAVING WITH DIFFERENT COLOR SUCCESSIONS

Some patterns should be woven with only one color against a background so that they will not lose their pattern effect. Such a pattern is shown in Fig. 105. This pattern is too intricate to be broken up into colors. On the other hand, some patterns work out very effectively when woven with two or three colors or with shades of colors.

In changing colors you organize a pattern into areas, and weave one area in one color, another in a second color. If the pattern is very simple, it is easier to work in two or three colors. In Pattern B, Fig. 142, the shaded portions can be in one color and the light portions in another. In Fig. 117, the dark diamonds can be done in one color and the light portions in another. In Fig. 108, a clever balance of lights and darks serves to enhance the pattern.

WEAVING AS CRACKLE

Overshot Patterns can be changed to Crackle Weave by substituting the Crackle block units for the regular Overshot units printed in the draft. See page 250.

WEAVING STAR-FASHION OR ROSE-FASHION

Overshot may be woven Star-fashion by weaving as drawn in, or Rose-fashion with reverse treadling. See page 237.

WEAVING AS HONEYCOMB

This method produces the same pattern outlines as the Overshot, but in a relief texture with the pattern blocks appearing as small pits below the tabby. Since there are long floats of pattern thread on the back of the fabric, the Honeycomb method is used for articles on which the back is not seen—upholstery, pillows, and so on. Full directions are given on page 236.

BOUND WEAVING

This is a way of weaving Overshot that brings out the pattern in a more subtle and often more textural way than by following each row with tabby. Instead of tabby, you should use another thread of about the same size as the pattern, but of a different color to set it off. Use the opposite shed, not a tabby shed. Bound Weave came originally from the Scandinavians. There are several ways of interpreting the weave.

Method No. 1: "On-Opposite" Treadling

In this method, you use the opposite treadle combination in place of Tabby. If you are putting in Hs. 1-2 in one color, you use the opposite, or Hs. 3-4, in a contrasting color to show off the first color.

Hs. 1-2 . . . . . . Color 1
Hs. 3-4 . . . . . . Color 2

Repeat this just as many times as desired. The Pattern treadling is always followed by opposite treadling in another color or texture. This simply acts as a binder to the first thread.

Follow with next block, such as

Hs. 4-1 . . . . . . Color 1
Hs. 2-3 . . . . . . Color 2

Or make another progression of Hs. 2-3 followed by Hs. 4-1.

If your binding row interferes with the next pattern combination, omit the binding row. For example, if you are weaving Hs. 1-2 (C. 1) and Hs. 3-4 (C. 2) and wish to proceed to Hs. 3-4 (C. 1) and Hs. 1-2 (C. 2), simply omit the last Hs. 3-4 (C. 2) and proceed to the new Hs. 3-4 (C. 1).

Always follow 1-2 by 3-4, 2-3 by 4-1, 3-4 by 1-2, 2-3 by 4-1. Use the pattern successions that seem effective. Repeat or reverse as desired.

Method No. 2: Adjacent Treadling, Two Harnesses Together

You can use the treadle combinations in adjacent order and vary the effects by color changes. The simplest way is to weave as Twill, Hs. 1-2, 2-3, 3-4, 4-1, using two colors in the following way.

Hs. 1-2, Color 1; Hs. 2-3, Color 2;

Hs. 3-4, Color 1; Hs. 4-1, Color 2; and repeat.

You can also use a different color or shades of color for each treadle combination.

Hs. 1-2, Color 1 (Darkest); Hs. 2-3, Color 2 (Dark)

Hs. 3-4, Color 3 (Medium); Hs. 4-1, Color 4 (Light)

Continue to repeat the treadles and colors in the same succession until you wish a change of design. Then change the color order, but not the order of the treadles. Keep on weaving as Twill or Reverse Twill.

Method No. 3: Three Harnesses Against One

Follow the same successions and color routines described for Methods 1 and 2, but use three treadles at a time.

For Opposite Combinations:

Hs. 1-2-3 together, Color 1; H. 4 alone. Color 2;

Hs. 2-3-4 together, Color 1; H. 1 alone, Color 2;

Hs. 3-4-1 together, Color 1; H. 2 alone, Color 2;

Hs. 4-1-2 together, Color 1; H. 3 alone, Color 2.

For Adjacent Succession:

Hs. 1-2-3 together, Color 1; Hs. 2-3-4 together, Color 2;

Hs. 3-4-1 together, Color 1 (or Color 3);

Hs. 4-1-2 together, Color 2 (or Color 4).

On Jack looms and wide-shed counter-balanced looms, you can also treadle H. 1 alone, H. 2 alone, H. 3 alone, H. 4 alone, with desired color changes. This is the opposite of Three Against One.

Bound Weaving is very effective for Twill, Herringbone, or Diamond. Many successive color changes can be used. In these you usually follow the succession of adjacent blocks, each followed by its opposite.

Hs. 1-2, Color 1; Hs. 3-4, Color 2; repeat as desired

Hs. 2-3, Color 1; Hs. 4-1, Color 2; repeat as desired

Hs. 3-4, Color 1; Hs. 1-2, Color 2; repeat as desired

Hs. 4-1, Color 1; Hs. 2-3, Color 2; repeat as desired

When Bound Weaving is woven as drawn in, the binding rows form a subtle design which looks like a shadow against the regular pattern rows.

THE HONEYCOMB TECHNIQUE

Texture of Honeycomb

Certain Overshot Patterns are more suitable for the Honeycomb Technique than others. The texture of Honeycomb is what the name implies, and might be described as "relief weaving," with the Pattern blocks appearing as sunken spots or pits between heavy ridges of Tabby thread. Thus, in Honeycomb the Pattern blocks appear below the surface of the Tabby instead of above it, as in Overshot Weaving. This effect is brought about by using a fine thread for the Pattern and a heavy thread for the Tabby instead of the usual heavy Pattern thread and fine Tabby thread. At those points between the fine texture Pattern blocks where ridges of Tabby show, the texture appears somewhat like a warp-surface fabric with the heavy weft threads making horizontal ridges through closely set warp threads. The same color may be used for the Pattern and Tabby threads, since the contrast of fine and heavy textures and the raised and sunken surfaces bring out a strong contrast of lights and shadows to set off the desired pattern. Different colors are equally effective. The Tabby thread can be very much heavier than the warp and Pattern threads.

The Honeycomb Weave makes a beautiful coverlet texture, often being woven in tones of white or cream. It is excellent for purses, table runners, and pillows; while bath mats and rugs in Honeycomb are unusually lovely.

Designing Honeycomb Patterns

There are many Overshot Patterns suitable for weaving the Honeycomb way. One should not select those with pattern blocks of too great length, for this creates a long span between the blocks on either side of the long block and, because of the nature of the weave, causes impractical loops on the under side of the fabric. For fine fabrics, such as those threaded at 30 to 36 threads per inch, the pattern blocks when woven should not measure over ⅝ inch; and for coarse drapes, purses, mats, etc., set at from 10 to 20 threads per inch, the blocks should not measure over 1¼ inches long, unless one has recourse to the method of tie-downs described in the next paragraph.

The best results are obtained by choosing those patterns in which there is not too great a span before the reappearance of each harness. For instance, if weaving an Overshot Pattern as Honeycomb, where there is a Table made up of harnesses 1 and 2 and harnesses 2 and 3, there is obviously no recurrence of har-

ness 4 for quite a space. To avoid this, in planning a design for Honeycomb, one slips a "pass-through" warp thread into the draft. In this case this thread would occur on harness 4, and the Table would be interrupted as follows: Hs. 1, 2, 1, 2, 3, 2, 3, (4), and repeat. This one note on harness 4 will catch the fine Pattern weft where necessary to avoid its long weft loops on the wrong side of the fabric.

In designing patterns for Honeycomb especially, remember the two points just mentioned: first, to limit the length of the pattern blocks; and, second, to insert frequent "tie-down" threads. There is one more point to observe: In the draft do not let the warp threads of a block change their direction, but have the pattern notes of all the blocks run in the same direction. This will avoid blocks with an uneven number of threads at reverse points. In Overshot, one reverses at will, making blocks of an odd number of threads. For example, in such patterns as the Diamond, one would thread Hs. 1, 2, 1, 2, 3, 2, 3, 4, 3, 4, 1, (4), 1, 4, 3, 4, 3, 2, 3, and 2, and repeat, the reverse thread being in parenthesis. For Honeycomb this would be written: Hs. 1, 2, 1, 2, 3, 2, 3, 4, 3, 4, 1, 4, 1, (2), 3, 4, 3, 4, (1), 2, 3, 2, 3, and (4), and repeat. Here the threads in parentheses not only serve as tie-down threads but make the blocks of the second half of the Diamond run in the same direction as those of the first half. Write both these patterns down on graph paper, and note the similar succession of the blocks with the difference in connecting them. In the draft you have written, put circles around the tie-down threads and note that there is the same succession of blocks in both the Overshot version and the Honeycomb version. Thus, you can rewrite Overshot drafts as Honeycomb.

Method of Weaving Honeycomb

Honeycomb is woven quite differently from Overshot. In Overshot, one weaves each harness combination, such as harnesses 1, 2, 1, 2, by treadling both harnesses at the same time, i.e., Hs. 1 and 2 together, and weaving through with a heavy Pattern thread. Each Pattern row is followed by a row of fine Tabby thread. In Honeycomb one weaves each harness combination, such as harnesses 1, 2, 1, 2, by treadling each harness singly, i.e., H. 1 alone, H. 2 alone, H. 1 alone, and H. 2 alone. One weaves through each shed with a fine Pattern thread of about the same weight as the warp. If the block being woven consists of four threads on the draft, such as harnesses 1, 2, 1, 2, one weaves four or more rows of the fine Pattern thread through the single sheds, or enough rows to make the block being woven into a square. No Tabby is woven until after the Pattern block is completed. Then one weaves two rows of Tabby on harnesses 1 and 3 and harnesses 2 and 4 with the heavy Tabby thread. These two rows outline the Pattern block just woven and take on a curving contour as they are beat down against it. One usually weaves more Pattern weft rows than there are warp threads in any one block, to make the block square; for the weft rows beat down considerably when of fine thread. For instance, instead of just four rows for block 1, 2, 1, 2, one may find it necessary to weave six or eight.

When weaving the Honeycomb way, the best results are obtained from weaving the pattern as-drawn-in. Starting at the right of the draft, weave each block in succession, and follow each complete woven Honeycomb block with two rows of Tabby. When weaving only one harness on a counterbalanced loom, always remember to even up the other three harnesses with the palm of the hand.

As an example, use the Diamond Pattern, Fig. 118: Hs. 1, 2, 1, 2, 3, 2, 3, 4, 3, 4, etc., consisting of a 4-thread block on Hs. 1 and 2, followed by a 4-thread block on Hs. 2 and 3, followed by a 4-thread block on Hs. 3 and 4, and so on. First weave the 1 and 2 block, weaving H. 1, then H. 2, then H. 1, then H. 2, until this little block at the furthest right side of the draft forms a square. Follow with two rows of Tabby: Hs. 1 and 3 and Hs. 2 and 4. Next, weave the 2 and 3 block, weaving H. 2, H. 3, H. 2, H. 3, etc. until this block forms a square. Follow with two rows of Tabby: Hs. 1 and 3 and Hs. 2 and 4. Next weave the 3 and 4 block, weaving H. 3, H. 4, H. 3, H. 4, etc. until this block forms a square. Follow with two rows of Tabby: Hs. 1 and 3 and Hs. 2 and 4. Continue thus, weaving all the blocks in succession.

We have given a pattern with small blocks for illustration of the principles of weaving the Honeycomb way, but actually four-thread blocks do not show up much in Honeycomb unless they are of carpet warp set at 12 or 16 threads per inch. If using fine thread, choose patterns having blocks of six or more threads, in which the fine Pattern thread will have more chance of forming a sizable block that will not be hidden so much by the heavy Tabby rows.

Honeycomb woven as drawn in results in the same design as the Overshot Pattern having the same draft notation; but in Honeycomb the effect of the fine colored Pattern blocks is set off by the heavy Tabby ridges, and in the Overshot the heavy Pattern threads stand above the Tabby which forms the background only. Honeycomb may therefore be woven on the same threadings as many of our Overshot Patterns.

WEAVING STAR-FASHION AND ROSE-FASHION

A Star design is caused by alternating two blocks in such a way as to make a figure having four corners and a center, Stars may occur anywhere in a draft; however, they are seldom used in the border. A Star is composed of an odd number of blocks, as five, seven, or nine. In a draft reading from right to left, a typical Star is as follows: Hs. 1, 2, 1, 2, 1, 2, 3, 2, 3, 2, (1), 2, 3, 2, 3, 2, 1, 2, 1, 2, 1; the center is in parenthesis. Write this notation out on graph paper to see it more clearly.

The first block is: Hs. 1 2, 1, 2, 1, 2
The second block is: Hs. 2, 3, 2, 3, 2
The third block is: Hs. 2, 1, 2 (this is also the center block)
The fourth block is: Hs. 2, 3, 2, 3, 2
The fifth block is: Hs. 2, 1, 2, 1, 2, 1

This Star threading may be woven either as a Star or as a Rose, the result depending on the order of treadling.

Weaving Star-Fashion

To form a Star one weaves the blocks in order, or as-drawn-in, as follows:
First block: Hs. 1 and 2 (5×)
Second block: Hs. 2 and 3 (4×)
Third block: Hs. 1 and 2 (2×)
Fourth block: Hs. 2 and 3 (4×)
Fifth block: Hs. 1 and 2 (5×)

Weaving Rose-Fashion

One may also weave the portion of the draft just considered into a Rose-like figure, with no sharp-pointed effects at the corners. To do this, one simply changes the blocks around, weaving the 1 and 2 block in place of the 2 and 3 block, and weaving the 2 and 3 block in place of the 1 and 2 block; but one weaves each block the number of times specified for the other notation in the original Star. For instance, one weaves the 2 and 3 block first, but gives it the number of rows planned for the 1 and 2 block of the Star. Then one weaves the 1 and 2 block second, giving it the count of the block that was used second in the Star; and so on. Simply change the numbers of the blocks around in the former weaving directions for the Star, and weave as follows:

First block: 2 and 3 (5×)
Second block: 1 and 2 (4×)
Third block: 2 and 3 (2×) (center block)
Fourth block: 1 and 2 (4×)
Fifth block: 2 and 3 (5×)
The rule to follow in changing a pat-

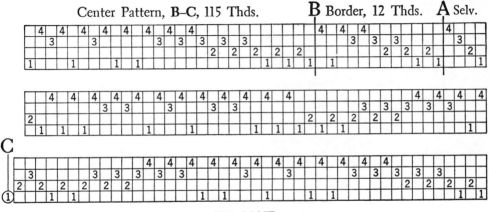

Center Pattern, B–C, 115 Thds.   B Border, 12 Thds.   A Selv.

THE DRAFT

tern woven Star-fashion to one woven Rose-fashion is:

1. Write down the succession of the two types of blocks found in the draft as if they are to be woven Star-fashion.
2. Write down the number of times each block is to be woven.
3. To weave Star-fashion, i.e., as drawn in, follow this succession. This will make your pattern come out as a Star, and the rest of the Overshot Pattern will likewise be woven authentically, showing the true diagonals of successive blocks.
4. To weave the same pattern Rose-fashion, change the order of the two blocks in the Star draft you have just made, but keep the same count as for the other block or the Star. At other points in the pattern, the two blocks occurring in the Star may also be reversed in this way.

An example of a pattern woven Rose-fashion is shown in Fig. 142 at **D**.

A Rose-and-Star rug with attractive twill border makes a pleasing pattern either with dark warp and light weft, or light warp and dark weft. Tabby is 8/4 carpet warp. (See draft, page 237.)

Read pattern straight through to **C**; then reverse, but thread the 1 in circle once only. (See woven runner below.)

Warp Plan

Warp: 8/4 colored
Weft: White rags
Threads per inch: 12
Width: 28 in.; weave down to 26 in.
Total number of threads: 333

Threading Plan

Selvage	4
Border (**A–B**), 12 threads, 4 times	48
Pattern (**B–C**)	115
Reverse of pattern, leaving out center thread **C**	114
Border backward, 12 threads, 4 times .	48
Selvage harnesses 4, 3, 2, 1	4
Total	333

Weaving Plan

(Follow each Pattern row with Tabby)

Border:		Motif **b**	
1–2	2×	4–1	3×
2–3	2×	3–4	2×
3–4	2×	4–1	1×
4–1	2×	3–4	1×
Repeat 4 times		4–1	1×
		3–4	2×
Pattern:		4–1	3×
Motif **a**			
1–2	3×	Motif **c**	
2–3	3×	(center)	
3–4	3×	(Same as	
4–1	2×	Motif a)	
3–4	1×		
4–1	1×	Motif **d**	
3–4	1×	(center)	
4–1	2×	2–3	once
3–4	3×	1–2	once
2–3	3×	2–3	once
1–2	3×		

A Rose-and-Star runner, showing an adaptation of the Rose-and-Star principle, using two colors.

Weave border; then weave motifs * **a, b, c, d, c, b*, a**; then weave border backward. For longer rug, repeat between asterisks and then add motif **a**.

34–Special Four-Harness Techniques

THERE are some weaves that vary from the regulation Overshot Weave. Three of the most popular of these are the **Summer and Winter**, the **Bronson Weave** or **Lace Weave**, and the **M's and O's**, which are shown in Fig. 136. In these weaves the rule for following odd harnesses with even ones and following even harnesses with odd ones, when writing the draft, is not adhered to. All these three weaves are written in two-block form; that is, they may be reduced to two units, which are shown separately in Fig. 136. For instance, in the Summer and Winter Weave, the two units are: Unit (a)—Hs. 1, 3, 2, 3; Unit (b)—Hs. 1, 4, 2, 4. These units alternate regularly throughout the pattern, but either one may be repeated as often as desired. The two units for the Bronson Weave are: Unit (a)—Hs. 1, 3, 1, 3, 1, 2; Unit (b)—Hs. 1, 4, 1, 4, 1, 2. The two units for the M's and O's Weave are: Unit (a)—Hs. 1, 3, 1, 3, 2, 4, 2, 4; Unit (b)—Hs. 1, 2, 1, 2, 3, 4, 3, 4. Any one of the three patterns can be easily written and woven when it is regarded as consisting merely of two independent units which alternate.

In Fig. 136, all three techniques—the Summer and Winter, Bronson, and M's and O's—have been written with the same number of unit repeats, so that in weaving them the same design results. This design, woven, appears as in Fig. 142 at **C**. Although each of these patterns may thus be planned to present the same proportions and balance between their light and dark sections, yet the kind of weave and the texture resulting from each is much different. The Summer and Winter Weave consists of a surface of Pattern weft threads bound down by every fourth warp thread, and the pattern is set off by a background of binding Tabby. The Bronson technique weaves into attractive lace units, with the weft forming skips on the right side and the warp forming similar skips on the wrong side; the two Tabby sheds are used at intervals to bind down the lace units. The M's and O's Weave results in sections of Tabby alternating

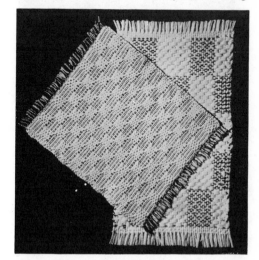

Fig. 134—Two mats in black and white. Above, Checkerboard design in M's and O's, woven with silk stockinette rayon on a black and white warp. Below, warp of rayon at 4 per inch, crossed with black and white rayon in Summer and Winter blocks.

with sections of a more open lace-like fabric, and these two contrasting textures are combined to form attractive figures. The following detailed directions for threading and weaving these three techniques should prove a reliable guide for their mastery.

Other special techniques in four-harness weaving are the **Crackle Weave**, the **Waffle Weave**, the **Matta Weave**, and the **Double Weave**. These four have the same Tabby system as Overshot, but they are distinctive enough in other ways to be classified as separate techniques.

While the Crackle Weave (pages 247-251) has the same alternation of harnesses as Overshot (odd following

(Courtesy Josephine Del Deo)

Fig. 135—Two textural mats. Above, banana stem strips, palmetto fibers, and jute yarn alternate in a soft-toned mat on a multi-colored pastel carpet warp. Below, Waffle Weave woven with strips of brown leather on white carpet warp, planned for a room divider.

even, and even following odd) and the pattern rows are followed by a binding tabby, the harness combinations of the two are quite different. In Overshot, the blocks of the draft are on two harnesses, such as Hs. 1-2-1-2. In Crackle, however, each block covers three harnesses, such as Hs. 1-2-3-2.

While Waffle Weave is threaded on four harnesses with odd notes following even and you can always weave tabby on alternate harnesses, Hs. 1-3 and 2-4, you use only one weft and do not follow pattern rows with tabby. Instead, you weave an allover fabric with ridges of textural design above lower portions of Plain Weave.

Matta Weave is similar to Log Cabin (page 104), but is threaded on four harnesses instead of two. Two or more colors are used in the warp. These are set so close that the design shows in the warp instead of a Pattern weft.

Double Weave is a way of weaving a Twill threading or a variation of Twill. By this method, you can weave two fabric surfaces at the same time, weave a fabric double the width of the warp, or weave a tubular fabric.

THE SUMMER AND WINTER WEAVE

Use of Summer and Winter Weave

The Summer and Winter Technique results in a closely knit weave, the pattern threads of the weft being bound under the warp at every fourth thread. With this frequent "tie-down" there may be a long repetition of the same block to make a span of color for any desired length. This is different from the Overshot Technique, in which the pattern weft threads skip across the entire width of each block and the blocks are limited in size.

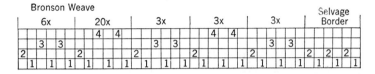

Fig. 136—Three unusual techniques worked out in the same design.

Because of its closely bound texture, the Summer and Winter Weave is found very useful for upholstery, coverlets, couch pillows, table linen, and many other household fabrics subjected to hard wear or frequent washing. It makes splendid rugs and seat mats. Summer and Winter coverlets and pillows, threaded with fine cotton warp and woven with a pattern weft of fine soft wool, are very beautiful.

The pattern surface of the finished weaving consists of square blocks of varying sizes, which may be proportioned at will. Wherever the pattern weft produces a dark ground on one side of the fabric, it leaves a light ground directly beneath it on the opposite side, and vice versa. In four-harness Summer and Winter there are only two alternating blocks, designated in Fig. 136 as Unit (a) and Unit (b). If Unit (a) is dark on one side, Unit (b) is found to be light on this side. One can therefore form beautiful contrasts of pattern and background, one side being predominantly dark and the other side light. This fact may have given rise to the name of the technique, for it is said that in Colonial days our practical ancestors used the light side in summer and the dark side in winter, when there may have been more hard usage and soil.

Designing Summer and Winter Patterns

The best way to design a Summer and Winter Pattern is to use a piece of graph paper, map out a square or oblong center, and surround this with alternating dark or light blocks in the sizes desired, more or less in the manner shown in Fig. 142 at C. One can also plan a linen or upholstery pattern consisting of the same repeat all across the fabric, with a series of dark and light blocks in varying sizes.

After getting the desired proportions and alternations of the dark and light blocks on the graph paper and shading them in, write the draft for the four harnesses. Plan all the dark parts of the design for Unit (a), Fig. 136, or Hs. 1, 3, 2, 3; and all the light parts for Unit (b), or Hs. 1, 4, 2, 4. To find out how many times to repeat each unit to cover the space desired before changing to the other unit, figure how much space one unit will take up. If the warp is set at 20 threads per inch, one unit of four threads will take up 1/5 inch and it will take five repeats of a unit to make an inch of weaving.

Method of Weaving Summer and Winter

Summer and Winter is woven with the use of two threads, a pattern thread and a tabby thread. The pattern thread should be of about the same weight as the warp, or very little heavier; the tabby thread should be somewhat finer than the warp. Tabby alone is woven by alternating sheds 1 and 2 with sheds 3 and 4. In Summer and Winter the textural appearance of the finished cloth depends on which Tabby shed follows the first row of each unit or block. There are several ways in which Summer and Winter may be woven.

(1) The usual succession of pattern and tabby threads, which produces the traditional Summer and Winter texture, is:

Unit (a):

Pattern on Hs. 1 and 3, followed by Tabby on Hs. 1 and 2
Pattern on Hs. 2 and 3, followed by Tabby on Hs. 3 and 4

Pattern on Hs. 2 and 3, followed by
  Tabby on Hs. 1 and 2
Pattern on Hs. 1 and 3, followed by
  Tabby on Hs. 3 and 4

Unit (b):
  Pattern on Hs. 1 and 4, followed by
    Tabby on Hs. 1 and 2
  Pattern on Hs. 2 and 4, followed by
    Tabby on Hs. 3 and 4
  Pattern on Hs. 2 and 4, followed by
    Tabby on Hs. 1 and 2
  Pattern on Hs. 1 and 4, followed by
    Tabby on Hs. 3 and 4

(2) An entirely different effect is obtained by weaving as follows:

Unit (a):
  Pattern on Hs. 1 and 3, followed by
    Tabby on Hs. 3 and 4
  Pattern on Hs. 2 and 3, followed by
    Tabby on Hs. 1 and 2
  Pattern on Hs. 2 and 3, followed by
    Tabby on Hs. 3 and 4
  Pattern on Hs. 1 and 3, followed by
    Tabby on Hs. 1 and 2

Unit (b):
  Pattern on Hs. 1 and 4, followed by
    Tabby on Hs. 3 and 4
  Pattern on Hs. 2 and 4, followed by
    Tabby on Hs. 1 and 2
  Pattern on Hs. 2 and 4, followed by
    Tabby on Hs. 3 and 4
  Pattern on Hs. 1 and 4, followed by
    Tabby on Hs. 1 and 2

(3) One can also weave the harness combinations singly instead of in pairs. This is often done when using a heavy pattern weft, as for rugs or bath mats, for this material is too heavy for the usual four pattern rows per unit. The method of weaving is as follows:

Unit (a):
  Pattern on Hs. 1 and 3, followed by

Tabby on Hs. 1 and 2
Pattern on Hs. 2 and 3, followed by
  Tabby on Hs. 3 and 4
Repeat as desired

Unit (b):
  Pattern on Hs. 1 and 4, followed by
    Tabby on Hs. 1 and 2
  Pattern on Hs. 2 and 4, followed by
    Tabby on Hs. 3 and 4
  Repeat as desired

(4) One can also repeat any one harness combination as desired, each row being followed by Tabby. This method produces effects in columns, as follows:

  Pattern on Hs. 1 and 3, followed by
    Tabby on Hs. 1 and 2
  Pattern on Hs. 1 and 3, followed by
    Tabby on Hs. 3 and 4
  Follow this with Pattern on Hs. 2 and 3 for a section; on Hs. 1 and 4 for a section; on Hs. 2 and 4 for a section. Each row of Pattern is always followed by its Tabby. Four columnar effects are thus possible, giving pleasing block formations.

THE BRONSON WEAVE

Features of Bronson Weave

The Bronson Weave probably came originally from northern Europe, where it is still used as a lace weave today. In the Bronson Weave a single weft thread is used to weave both the lace sections and the Tabby sections between them, and Bronson is therefore known as a **one-thread weave**. In the sections of lace, the weft skips over short groups of warp threads and, after several rows of skips, two rows of Tabby are used to bind down the warps. Where the weft-skips occur on the right side, warp-skips appear on the wrong side. The draft is written with every other thread on harness 1 (see Fig. 136). Tabby is therefore woven by alternating harness 1 alone for the first shed, with the other three harnesses woven together for the second shed.

Designing Bronson Weave Patterns

Bronson Weave Patterns are planned with sections of lace set off by sections of Tabby. The Tabby sections may be used alone to form borders or to make Plain Weave sections between the lace sections. There are two lace blocks possible when Bronson is threaded on a four-harness loom. Thus, we may have three different effects in the weaving: the Tabby, the first lace, and the second lace.

Tabby is threaded (either as side borders or between lace sections) on Hs. 1, 2, 1, 2, etc.

Unit (a), the first lace, is threaded on Hs. 1, 3, 1, 3, 1, 2

Unit (b), the second lace, is threaded on Hs. 1, 4, 1, 4, 1, 2

There are six threads of each unit, repeated as far as one wishes this block to extend in the design. Unit (a) consists of four threads of lace on Hs. 1, 3, 1, 3 followed by two threads of Tabby on Hs. 1, 2; Unit (b) consists of four threads of lace on Hs. 1, 4, 1, 4 followed by two threads of Tabby on Hs. 1, 2. These two rows of Tabby act as a tie-down between the lace sections.

If the Tabby on Hs. 1 and 2 occurs in this way as a tie-down only between the successive lace blocks on Hs. 1 and 3 and Hs. 1 and 4 or at the right and left selvages outside of the lace to frame it, the weave is known as **Lace Bronson**. If, on the other hand, the Tabby on Hs. 1 and 2 is repeated to form a third block, and this takes its place at intervals as a unit

of four or more threads along with the other two blocks, thus making whole sections of Tabby between spots of lace, the weave is known as **Spot Bronson.**

Articles planned in Bronson Weave usually have sections of Tabby acting as borders at the right and left selvages. These may extend for several inches, if desired. Simply repeat harnesses 1, 2, 1, 2, etc. for the desired space. The central lace portion is planned to consist of as many repeats of either lace block as desired. As in Summer and Winter, one alternates the units to give the two possible lace effects. For Unit (a), called the first lace, one repeats harnesses 1, 3, 1, 3, 1, 2 as far as desired; and for Unit (b), called the second lace, one repeats harnesses 1, 4, 1, 4, 1, 2 as far as desired. Either unit may follow the other directly; or, after several repeats of a unit, one may add an inch or so of Plain Weave by repeating the Tabby threading on Hs. 1, 2, 1, 2, etc. as desired, before proceeding to the other unit again. A Bronson Pattern therefore results in a pleasing alternation of different lace effects, either set off by Plain Weave or forming continuous lace with Tabby at the edges only. Thus, one can design lace borders to be woven on all four sides of doilies, or lace panels for drapes, or lace coverlets with columns of lace alternating with columns of Plain Weave.

Method of Weaving Bronson

The usual method of weaving Bronson is to use a single weft for both lace and Tabby rows. Either unit when woven results in lace sections in certain parts of the article. There is a way, too, of weaving both lace units together to give a combined lace effect all across the piece.

Tabby: For Plain Weave only, treadle H. 1 alone, followed by Hs. 2, 3, and 4 together.

Alternate these two sheds.

First Lace, or Unit (a): Treadle Hs. 1 and 3, followed by Hs. 2, 3, and 4 together.

Repeat these two sheds two to four times, making four to eight rows of weaving. The object is to weave just enough rows to make each unit of six warp threads into a perfect little lace square.

Follow this lace section with two rows only of Tabby, i.e., H. 1 alone followed by Hs. 2, 3, and 4 together.

Repeat all as desired.

Second Lace, or Unit (b): Treadle Hs. 1 and 4, followed by Hs. 2, 3, and 4 together.

Repeat these two sheds two to four times, making four to eight rows of weaving.

Follow this lace section with two rows only of Tabby, i.e., H. 1 alone followed by Hs. 2, 3, and 4 together.

Repeat all as desired.

Combined Lace, or Units (a) and (b) Together: Treadle Hs. 1, 3, and 4 together, followed by Hs. 2, 3, and 4 together.

Repeat these two sheds two to four times, making four to eight rows of weaving.

Follow this lace section with two rows only of Tabby, i.e., H. 1 alone followed by Hs. 2, 3, and 4 together.

Repeat all as desired.

Weaving Bronson with Two Wefts, a Pattern Thread and a Tabby Thread

It is possible to weave Bronson like an Overshot Pattern Weave for an entirely different effect. This method is used for heavy articles, rugs, mats, and pillows. Choose a heavy Pattern yarn for the best effects, with Tabby thread of the same weight as the warp. Weave either of the lace blocks as a regular repeat, followed first by one Tabby shed and then by the other.

First Lace, or Unit (a): Treadle harnesses 1 and 3 (Pattern thread), followed by H. 1 alone (Tabby thread).

Treadle harnesses 1 and 3 (Pattern thread), followed by Hs. 2, 3, and 4 together (Tabby thread).

Repeat as desired.

Second Lace, or Unit (b): Treadle Hs. 1 and 4 (Pattern thread), followed by H. 1 alone (Tabby thread).

Treadle Hs. 1 and 4 (Pattern thread), followed by Hs. 2, 3, and 4 together (Tabby thread).

Repeat all as desired.

Weaving Bronson on a Jack Loom

The foregoing treadlings are given for a counterbalanced loom. If your loom is a jack loom, thread as shown in Fig. 136, but substitute the treadlings in the second group in the following list for those in the first group.

COUNTERBALANCED LOOM TREADLING

Lace
Treadle 1: Harnesses 1 and 3
Treadle 2: Harnesses 1 and 4
Treadle 3: Harnesses 1, 3, and 4
Tabby
Treadle 4: Harness 1 alone
Treadle 5: Harnesses 2, 3, and 4

JACK LOOM TREADLING

Lace
Treadle 1: Hardnesses 2 and 4
Treadle 2: Harnesses 2 and 3
Treadle 3: Harness 2 alone

Tabby
Treadle 4: Harnesses 2, 3, and 4
Treadle 5: Harness 1 alone

THE M'S AND O'S WEAVE

Units of the M's and O's Weave

The M's and O's Weave is a traditional Colonial Pattern Weave used for linens. This type of pattern is also employed in Scandinavia, where it is woven in very stunning heavy effects. It consists of an alternation of two units, and its effect is that of Tabby sections alternating with texture sections. Like Bronson, M's and O's is woven with a single weft thread and is called a one-thread weave. There is no perfect Tabby; but, by alternating harnesses 2 and 3 with harnesses 4 and 1, one can obtain a close weave somewhat like tabby.

The first block, or Unit (a), is composed of a succession of harnesses 1 and 3 and harnesses 2 and 4, combined in an 8-thread block: Hs. 1, 3, 1, 3, 2, 4, 2, 4; or in a 4-thread block: Hs. 1, 3, 2, 4. The 4-thread block is less frequently used. The second block, or Unit (b), is composed of a succession of harnesses 1 and 2 and harnesses 3 and 4 combined in an 8-thread block: Hs. 1, 2, 1, 2, 3, 4, 3, 4; or in a 4-thread block: Hs. 1, 2, 3, 4, the smaller block again being less used. In any one pattern, however, one usually follows the same count for both blocks, such as 8 threads in Unit (a) and 8 threads in Unit (b).

Because of the character of the two units, each having the same succession of harnesses as that used for certain Tabby systems, the M's and O's Weave may be said to be a combination of two Tabby systems. A plain Weave or Tabby texture is thus secured by treadling Hs. 1 and 2 and Hs. 3 and 4 for those parts

threaded to Unit (a), i.e., the block on Hs. 1, 3, 1, 3, 2, 4, 2, 4; and by treadling Hs. 1 and 3 and Hs. 2 and 4 for those parts threaded to Unit (b), i.e., the block on Hs. 1, 2, 1, 2, 3, 4, 3, 4.

Designing M's and O's Patterns

Like Summer and Winter and Bronson, the M's and O's Pattern may be worked out in different designs by planning various proportions of the unit repeats, and alternating them as desired. The pattern is planned in such a way that when one unit weaves Tabby texture the other shows as a texture weave; and, while the second unit weaves as Tabby, the first unit shows as a texture weave in the intervening spaces.

To plan a wide section of Plain Weave or Tabby on the draft, one therefore repeats either one of the units for a space, and sets this off by shorter repeats of the other unit. For instance, a traditional Colonial M's and O's Pattern with a good balance of the units and a resulting lovely all-over pattern figure results from the following threading:

One repeat of Unit (a): Hs. 1, 3, 1, 3, 2, 4, 2, 4 (8 threads in the draft)
One repeat of Unit (b): Hs. 1, 2, 1, 2, 3, 4, 3, 4 (8 threads in the draft)
One repeat of Unit (a): Hs. 1, 3, 1, 3, 2, 4, 2, 4 (8 threads in the draft)*
Three repeats of Unit (b): Hs. 1, 2, 1, 2, 3, 4, 3, 4 (24 threads in all)
Repeat these 48 threads all across the warp. When finishing the piece, end at the asterisk.

Method of Weaving M's and O's

Since M's and O's is a one-thread weave, it is necessary to use only one weft thread in weaving, and this saves time and enables a person to weave easily. The weft should be somewhat heavier than the warp, but not too heavy. Good settings for both Bronson and M's and O's are:

For Very Fine Fabrics:
Warp:
Cotton, 20/2 or 24/2 or 24/3
Linen, 40/2 or 50/2
Weft:
Cotton, Perle 10/2 or 10/2 colored
Linen, 30/2 or 40/2 or 18/1
Threads per inch: 30 to 36

For Coarse Towel Effects:
Warp:
Cotton, 16/4 or 16/3 or 10/2
Linen, 20/2 or 25/2 or 30/2
Weft:
Cotton, 5/2 or 10/3 or 6-strand
Linen, 10/2 or 18/2 or 20/2 or floss
Threads per inch: 20 to 24

For Heavy Bath Mats and Upholstery:
Warp:
Cotton, 8/4
Linen, 10/5
Weft:
Rug-weave yarn or rug yarn
Tufting cotton or jute
Threads per inch: 12 or 16

Plain Surface Background: The nearest one can approximate Tabby texture is to alternate harnesses 2 and 3 with harnesses 4 and 1 and to repeat.

First Texture or Unit (a): Treadle harnesses 1 and 3, followed by harnesses 2 and 4.

Alternate these two sheds for the desired space.

Second Texture or Unit (b): Treadle harnesses 1 and 2 and harnesses 3 and 4.

Alternate these two sheds for the desired space.

Traditional Colonial M's and O's Pattern: For this pattern, weave as follows:

Hs. 1 and 3, then 2 and 4; Repeat 8 to 10 times

Hs. 1 and 2, then 3 and 4; Repeat 8 to 10 times.

Hs. 1 and 3, then 2 and 4; Repeat 8 to 10 times.*

Hs. 1 and 2, then 3 and 4; Repeat 20 to 30 times.

Repeat all as desired. When finishing the piece, end at the asterisk.

THE CRACKLE WEAVE

The Crackle Weave, known in Sweden as "Jamtlandsvaev," was given its American name because its background resembles the crackle of pottery. See Figs. 137 and 138. The Crackle Weave produces a texture similar to the Summer and Winter Weave in that the Pattern weft is closely tied into the fabric and there are no long floats or skips. This produces a fabric of excellent wearing qualities suitable for rugs, mats, pillow tops, upholstery, screens, panels, and purses. As there are no skips in the pattern, blocks may be made as large as desired. Both modern and Colonial patterns are therefore possible in this weave.

The Crackle Weave is particularly effective for rugs. In making rugs, set the warp at 12 ends to the inch instead of 15 to the inch (a setting sometimes used for rugs in Overshot). For weft, use cotton roving, wool rug yarn, or cotton chenille. If the material used is not too coarse, use it double for the Pattern rows and single for the Tabby rows.

In Crackle Weave each pattern shed weaves across two blocks, giving an overlapping effect. In Summer and Winter Weave the blocks may overlap or not, according to the designer's choice. In

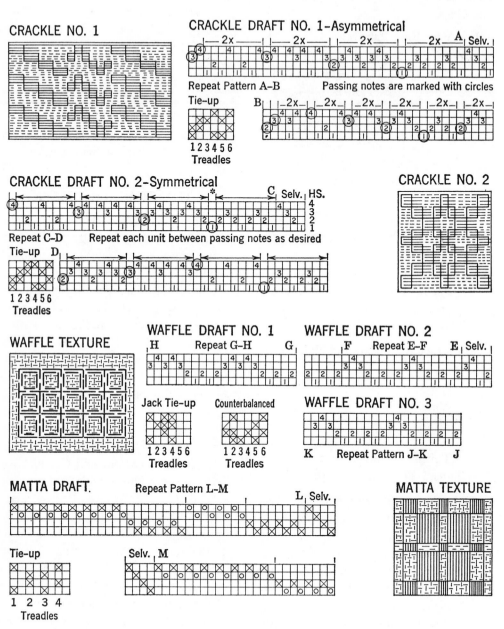

Fig. 137—Drafts and textures of Crackle Weave, Waffle Weave, and Matta Weave.

Crackle Weave, however, the overlapping effect always occurs. This somewhat limits the pattern possibilities. While many patterns that would require six harnesses in Summer and Winter Weave may be woven on four harnesses in Crackle Weave, it is not true that any six-harness Summer and Winter pattern can be translated to Crackle Weave.

Crackle is considered a very practical variation of the four-harness weaves. Each of its four-harness combinations, however, is made up of two regular pairs of harnesses instead of one to cause the overlapping effect. The four units are Block 1: Hs. 1, 2, 3, 2; Block 2: 2, 3, 4, 3; Block 3: 3, 4, 1, 4; and Block 4: 4, 1, 2, 1. Each unit may be repeated as long as desired for a large block effect, but there must be a proper connection between changes.

WAYS TO WEAVE CRACKLE

Weave as Overshot

Crackle may be woven just like Overshot, using the first two harnesses of each group, such as Hs. 1 and 2, 2 and 3, 3 and 4, or 4 and 1. The combinations overlap and show at various points. Lovely color blends may be achieved because any one block, such as Block 1, Hs. 1, 2, 3, 2, is composed of two blocks. When it is woven as Hs. 1 and 2, the 1 and 2 Block shows here as well as in Block 4, Hs. 4, 1, 2, 1. Likewise, when Block 2, Hs. 2, 3, 4, 3, is woven, there is a visible weft across Hs. 2, 3 of Block 1, as well as Hs. 3, 4, 3 of its own block. They are all interlocked and the result is a blending of colors.

When any block is woven as Overshot, such as Hs. 1 and 2 of Block 1 (Hs. 1, 2, 3, 2), the extra note on a third harness, in this case H. 3, acts as a tie down. In

Block 2 (Hs. 2, 3, 4, 3) it is H. 4, and so on. This fact enables you to form motifs of any length in the design.

Different Colored Tabbies

An unusual effect is obtained by weaving with the same colored pattern weft, but with different colored tabbies, such as one color on Hs. 1 and 3, and another on Hs. 2 and 4.

Still another way is to weave one inch of one color, a half inch of another, etc.

Weave as Bound Weave

In this method, each row of Pattern, instead of being followed by Tabby, is bound in by the opposite Pattern combination, with another color of weft being used. This method is used a great deal in Overshot and is particularly effective for widely set Rosepath or Herringbone.

Harnesses 1 and 2 are woven with a pattern filler, and are followed by the opposite combination, Hs. 3 and 4, with another color pattern filler or thread a bit lighter in weight. Harnesses 2 and 3 are followed by Hs. 4 and 1; Hs. 3 and 4 by Hs. 1 and 2; and Hs. 4 and 1 by Hs. 2 and 3.

This Crackle treadling is just the same as in Overshot, but you may want to try using a different set of colors for each combination and its binding pattern row.

Weave in the Italian Manner

Patterns in Crackle Weave can be woven in the Italian manner without a Tabby. This method is particularly good for upholstery fabrics and also for decorative articles such as pillows, runners, purses, and heavy draperies. This method is not confined to patterns in the Crackle Weave, however. Overshot Patterns may also be woven in the same way, but if

Patterns with long skips are used, the resulting fabric will be very loosely integrated and will have poor wearing qualities. These drawbacks do not occur in Crackle Weave.

Italian Method: For the Italian method three colors may be used—a Pattern color (P), in a yarn somewhat coarser than the material used for background, and two background colors (a) and (b). A single color may be used for background if preferred. However, the play of color is particularly attractive when three shades are used.

For Block 1 (Hs. 1, 2, 3, 2) weave:

Hs. 1-2, Pattern, Color (P)

Hs. 2-3, Background, Color (a)

Hs. 1-2, Pattern, Color (P)

Hs. 4-1, Background, Color (b)

Repeat as desired to square the block. End on Hs. 1-2 (P).

(Note that in each block a pattern row, Hs. 1-2, is followed by its adjacent combination in a background color, Hs. 2-3. Then the next pattern row, Hs. 1-2, is followed by the opposite of this adjacent, Hs. 4-1. The same system is followed for all of the blocks.)

For Block 2 (Hs. 2, 3, 4, 3) weave:

Hs. 2-3 (P); 3-4 (a); 2-3 (P); 1-2 (b). Repeat. End on Hs. 2-3 (P).

For Block 3 (Hs. 3, 4, 1, 4) weave:

Hs. 3-4 (P); 4-1 (a); 3-4 (P); 2-3 (b). Repeat. End on Hs. 3-4 (P).

For Block 4 (Hs. 4, 1, 2, 1)

Hs. 4-1 (P); 1-2 (a); 4-1 (P); 3-4 (b). Repeat. End on Hs. 4-1 (P).

The Pattern may be developed in this fashion as drawn in, or each shed may be woven with the same number of repeats. This is particularly interesting in Patterns of the modern style.

For best results, the warp should be set as for Overshot, and the weft material should not be very coarse. However, the warp should not be set too far apart or the weft should not be so fine that the warp will be completely covered. Weaving in the Italian manner is not recommended for rugs.

How To Write Crackle Drafts

Crackle Harness Combinations: The four combinations used in Crackle Weave are given at the left, with corresponding groups at the right. Note that the Crackle combinations are like the Overshot, but with a third harness added.

	Crackle	Both Are Woven Overshot
Block 1 (1, 2, 3, 2)	Hs. 1 & 2	Hs. 1 & 2
Block 2 (2, 3, 4, 3)	Hs. 2 & 3	Hs. 2 & 3
Block 3 (3, 4, 1, 4)	Hs. 3 & 4	Hs. 3 & 4
Block 4 (4, 1, 2, 1)	Hs. 4 & 1	Hs. 4 & 1

Writing the Draft: It is difficult to write Crackle drafts for two reasons. First, if the blocks follow each other directly, they create a "flat," two threads in succession on the same set of harnesses. Second, there can be no blocks of more than three notes without a tie-down by a fourth note. Therefore, it is correct to write Hs. 1, 2, 3, 2 but not Hs. 1, 2, 1, 2. If the succession of the blocks makes four threads come up on the same two notes, you have to alter the draft because it is the grouping of three warps tied down by a fourth that makes the Crackle texture. The selvage is written the same as in Overshot, Hs. 1, 2, 3, 4 or Hs. 4, 3, 2, 1.

Avoiding Flats: In making a draft it is obvious that some of the blocks cannot follow each other as they are given here. Block 1 ends on H. 2 and Block 2 begins on H. 2. This would make a flat. Therefore, you have to add a passing note. This can be the first note of the block you are

Fig. 138—Crackle Weave pillows.

finished with. If you have been repeating Block 1 (Hs. 1, 2, 3, 2), add H. 1 before going on to Block 2. See Figure 137 with inserted notes in circles. In progressing, after Block 2, the connecting note can be H. 2; after Block 3, H. 3; and after Block 4, H. 4.

Avoiding Too Large a Block: The above rule holds except when passing to an opposite block. The opposite block of Block 1 is Block 3; the opposite of Block 2 is Block 4.

To progress between blocks on opposites, add both the passing note and another note to avoid the group of four in a block. Thus in going from Block 1 (Hs. 1, 2, 3, 2) to Block 3 (Hs. 3, 4, 1, 4), add H. 1 after its last note, H. 2, and then another note to get up to H. 3 of Block 3. This must be in the same line of progression, and will therefore be H. 2. The complete connection will be Block 1 (Hs. 1, 2, 3, 2); an added H. 1; then H. 2; and then Block 3 (Hs. 3, 4, 1, 4).

Apply the same rule to all the blocks, as follows:

To progress from Block 2 to Block 4: After Block 2 (Hs. 2, 3, 4, 3), add H. 2 if going to the adjacent blocks (Blocks 3 or 1); but H. 2 and also H. 3 if going to Block 4 (Hs. 4, 1, 2, 1).

To progress from Block 3 to Block 1: After Block 3 (Hs. 3, 4, 1, 4), add H. 3 if going to Blocks 4 or 2; but H. 3 and also H. 2 if going to Block 1 (Hs. 1, 2, 3, 2).

To progress from Block 4 to Block 2: After Block 4 (Hs. 4, 1, 2, 1), add H. 4 if going to Blocks 1 or 3; but H. 4 and also H. 3 if going to Block 2 (Hs. 2, 3, 4, 3).

In learning the four Crackle Weave blocks, it helps to note that each block, such as Block 1, starts its notation on the same note, H. 1, Block 2 on H. 2, and so on. You may find Crackle drafts written with other note successions in some books. Follow them for their particular context. However, the above system is the most logical to understand and follow in writing your own drafts or transposing Overshot designs to Crackle Weave.

	Jack Harnesses	Treadles	Counterbalanced Harnesses
Plain-Weave Background:	Hs. 1–3, then 2–4		Hs. 1–3, then 2–4, end on 1–3
Ridge:	H. 3 alone	2 alone	Hs. 1–2–4
	Hs. 4–1	1 alone	Hs. 2–3
	H. 3 alone	2 alone	Hs. 1–2–4
Pocket:	Hs. 2–4	5	Hs. 1–3
	Hs. 1–3–4	4	H. 2 alone
	Hs. 2–3–4*	3*	H. 1 alone*
	Hs. 1–3–4*	4*	H. 2 alone*
	Hs. 2–3–4	3	H. 1 alone
	Hs. 1–3–4	4	H. 2 alone
	Hs. 2–4	5	Hs. 1–3

Alternate ridge and pocket. Finish with ridge and add Plain Weave at the end. If the pocket is too large, omit the two rows marked with an asterisk.

THE WAFFLE WEAVE

The Waffle Weave is a textured weave with a Honeycomb effect. Its woven surface consists of depressed squares of tabby imbedded within outlining ridges of texture in relief. The whole effect resembles the markings of a waffle iron. The weave is useful for drapes, fancy purses, screens, coverlets, pillows, and hangings, as well as washcloths and bath towels. It makes an ideal absorbent texture if the warp and weft are of soft unpolished cotton. Woven with sturdy linen closely set, it becomes a modern upholstery fabric.

Varying effects are given by adding warp threads of interesting color and texture at raised sections, and by accenting the divisions when weaving with equally textured wefts. In the draft given in Fig. 137, the reverse points can be used for these texture threads, and texture can also be added to the rows of the ridge for accent. Try Waffle with two tones or different colors, one for the imbedded pockets, the other for the ridges. Soft tones of white, ivory, ecru, and cream are stunning.

Warp Plan

For a heavy texture, use 5/2 or 10/3 cotton, or 20/2 linen, set at 18 or 20 per inch. For the ridges, use the same thread in another color or a heavier thread in the same color. For bath-towel texture, use carpet warp, set at 15 per inch, or 16/4 dull cotton, set at 30 per inch.

Threading

Selvages are Hs. 2, 1, 4, 3. Repeat the pattern continuously.

Weaving Plan

A Jack loom is best for Waffle, but if your loom is counterbalanced, simply treadle as directed, evening up the harnesses when making a one-against-three shed so that all three harnesses will lie level. Do this with the flat of your hand on top of the harnesses.

THE MATTA TECHNIQUE

Matta is quite like Log Cabin (with two colors alternating, see page 104), except that the principle is worked out on four harnesses instead of two, and the warp must be set closely to produce a warp-face texture. The technique is used a great deal in Scandinavian countries to make sturdy mats, pillows, rugs, and bedspreads.

Matta depends on the use of two colors alternating with each other with an occasional shift of each color to another shed. For instance, in the draft shown in Fig. 137, the dark color (X) starts out on Hs. 1-2, which puts the dark on both the 1-3 and 2-4 sheds. Then the light color (O) takes over on Hs. 3 and 4. Later the dark color will be on H. 1 and the light on H. 2. This gives a light color on the 2-4 shed and a dark color on the 1-3 shed. Next comes the Hs. 3-4, with light on H. 3 and dark on H. 4. This reverses the colors of the sheds, putting light color on the 1-3 shed and dark color on the 2-4 shed. The draft continues in this manner with various reversings. You can readily see that at points where this shifting occurs, a different color rises to the upper surface of warp threads when the shed is made. This causes a change both in the pattern and the color of the woven blocks.

To make the changes of warp colors more apparent, weave with a heavy yarn. Since the warps are always set close together to form a warp-face texture, one set of warps will become prominent by using first a heavy weft and then a fine weft, and alternating. To bring up the other set of warps or opposite colors, weave in an extra row with the heavy yarn. This will put the fine weft on the other shed and show up the new set of colors under the heavy yarn.

Warp Plan

The entire effect depends upon the warp and its setting. Select two colors that set off each other and a thread that will make the weight of fabric you desire when set close in the reed. Carpet warp or 5/2 cotton should be set at 20 to 24 per inch; 10/2 at 30 to 36 per inch; or 3/2 at 15 per inch.

Threading Plan

Thread the selvage, Hs. 1, 2, 3, 4. Repeat L to M as desired. Add L through asterisk, then selvage.

Weaving Plan

There are four possibilities of harness combinations: Hs. 4-1 alternating with Hs. 2-3, fine or heavy coming first; Hs. 1-3 alternating with Hs. 2-4, fine or heavy coming first.

Think out ways of combining these with various interchanges of color. For example:

A. Use a heavy weft alternating with a fine one on Hs. 1-3; 2-4. End on Hs. 1-3, heavy.
B. Follow this with heavy on Hs. 2-3; fine on Hs. 4-1. Repeat. End on Hs. 2-3, heavy.
C. Follow this with heavy on Hs. 4-1; fine on Hs. 2-3. Repeat. End on Hs. 4-1, heavy.

Reverse this series or repeat it.

SYNCOPATION

Syncopation is a novel variation of pattern weaving. Introduced to this country through the activities of the Canadian Handicraft Guild, it came originally from Scandinavia. In this weave the overshot system is repeated twice with alternating threading notes, first from one system then from the other.

A syncopated variation can be made from any regular overshot draft. The technique requires two alternating warp colors, such as black and white, red and blue, brown and yellow, or cream and rust. Contrasting colors are better than two shades of the same color, unless there is a marked difference, such as between tan and dark brown. The weave was originally planned as a complete warp-face weave, and was often used for belts. However, with equally balanced warp and weft, it forms an interesting fabric texture for suiting, draperies, blankets, and so on.

Planning the Pattern: Take any simple Overshot pattern—twills or their variations are excellent. Mark this pattern on graph paper, as shown in the diagram at A, and leave an empty graph square after each note, as indicated. This completes one repeat of the overshot pattern. All warp threads for this first part of pattern are of the first color.

The object now is to fill the empty squares with a second repeat of the overshot draft, which we will call the second part of pattern, with warp threads planned in a second color. For this second part we have used crosses, but colored crayon or red ink may also be used. Follow each number of the first part with the opposite in its own tabby combination. The tabby combinations are Hs. 1 and 3, Hs. 2 and 4. Therefore H. 1 will be followed by H. 3; H. 2 by H. 4; H. 3 by H. 1; and H. 4 by H. 2.

Part A of the diagram, Hs. 1, 2, 3, 4, 1, 2, 3, 4, 3, 2, 1, 4, 3, 2, is now enlarged to the double interpretation shown at Part B: H. 1, (3); H. 2, (4); H. 3, (1); H. 4, (2); and so on. Continue thus, reading the draft, as usual, from right to left. You will note that when finished

either part of pattern may be read off alone, omitting the alternate notes, and each part will form a complete twill pattern.

Threading Plan: Thread the pattern consecutively from right to left. All the warp threads of the first part (shown by numbers) will be in the first color; all warp threads of the second part (shown by crosses) will be in the second color. For instance, the pattern below at B would be threaded left to right (see table at bottom of page).

SYNCOPATION TECHNIQUE
A–1st OVERSHOT SYSTEM

B–2nd or ALTERNATE SYSTEM

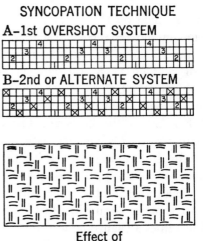

Effect of
Reverse Twill Threading Above

Weaving Plan: Weave as a twill or its reverse. Hs. 1 and 2, Hs. 2 and 3, Hs. 3 and 4, Hs. 4 and 1. Repeat or reverse. The tabby is regular: Hs. 1 and 3, Hs. 2 and 4. Different effects are achieved by using all one-color thread as weft, two colors, or several colors in succession. The unique surface design is given more by the alternation of colors and textures in warp and weft than by the threading.

Harness 1, 1st color, dark	H. 3, 2nd color, light
H. 2, 1st color, dark	H. 4, 2nd color, light
H. 3, 1st color, dark	H. 1, 2nd color, light
H. 4, 1st color, dark	H. 2, 2nd color, light

DOUBLE WEAVING ON A FOUR-HARNESS LOOM

Double Weaving (Fig. 139) consists of weaving two surfaces of material at one time on the same loom. With a Twill threading on a four-harness loom, three types of Double Weave can be produced, (1) two separate surfaces, (2) double-width material, and (3) tubular material.

1. Two separate surfaces of material are woven at the same time. Each has its own surface with separate selvages, and is entirely apart from the other.

2. Double-width material is made by weaving a fabric twice as wide as the usual width possible on a loom. There is a fold of material at one side and the two selvages at the other side. When the material is taken off the loom, the fold forms the center, and the cloth is double the width of the warp.

3. Tubular material results when two separate surfaces, one above and one below, are joined at both selvages to form a circular tube of cloth like a sweater or stocking.

The Threading

The Twill threading shown at **A** in Fig. 139 can be used for each type. When the loom is threaded in this manner, you can make a sampler to show all three types. For beginners, it is best to use two colors, as shown at X (dark) and O (light). In this way, the upper and lower surfaces will contrast. See draft and tie-up, Fig. 139.

Weaving a Plain Weave Ground

Since the threading is Twill, you can make Plain Weave by simply treadling Hs. 1 and 3 against Hs. 2 and 4. This produces a mottled Tabby. You can also treadle Hs. 1 and 2 against Hs. 3 and 4 to produce a Basket Weave with two

warps light against two warps dark. Either of these textures can be used at the start and finish of the three textures described above.

General Method Used

To provide for the two fabric surfaces, the warp threads must be set twice as close as for regular weaving. In every four adjacent threads of warp, two are used for the upper surface and two for the lower surface. The four sheds used are shown in Fig. 139.

In Rows 1 and 2, the dark surface is shown woven above, while the light warps fall below and are left untouched as the weft passes through the two dark sheds. In Row 1 (see separate sketch), the first of each pair of dark threads is up and all other threads are down when the weft weaves through from right to left. In Row 2, the second of each pair of dark threads is up and the other dark thread, as well as the light threads, is down when the weft goes through from left to right. In Row 3, the first of each pair of light threads, as well as the dark threads, is up when the weft goes through from left to right. In Row 4, the second of each pair of light threads, as well as all dark threads, is up when the weft goes through from right to left. (The direction in which each weft moves is given here for clarity. This applies to the weaving of two separate surfaces.)

Weaving Two Separate Surfaces: This method enables you to weave two identical sections, or panels, one above the other. You can plan stripe designs in both warp and weft, but no Overshot designs.

Use two shuttles, one light and the other dark, to match lights and darks of the warp. Start each one from opposite

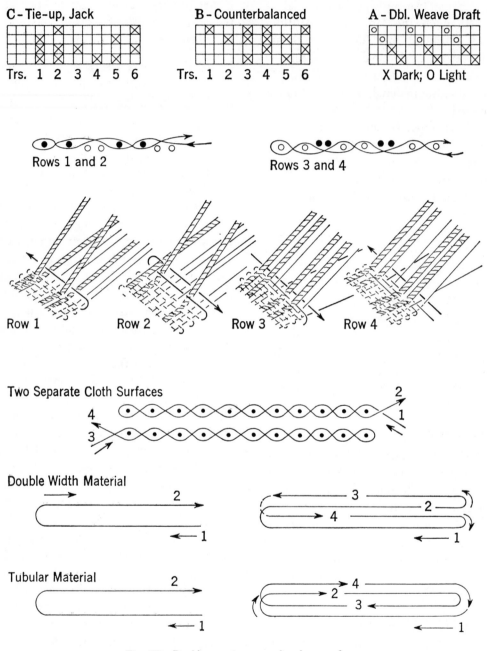

Fig. 139—Double weaving on a four-harness loom.

sides in order to avoid locking at the edges. This was the method just described. It is shown in the separate sketches of Rows 1, 2, 3, and 4, Fig. 139.

See diagram of "Two Separate Cloth Surfaces," Fig. 139.

Row 1. Treadle 4: (Counterbalanced (CB), Hs. 2, 3, 4; Jack, H. 1) Weave with dark thread, right to left, upper surface.

Row 2. Treadle 3: (CB, Hs. 1, 3, 4; Jack, H. 2) Weave with dark thread, left to right, upper surface.

Row 3. Treadle 2: (CB, H. 3; Jack, Hs. 1, 2, 4) Weave with light thread, left to right, lower surface.

Row 4. Treadle 1: (CB, H. 4; Jack, Hs. 1, 2, 3) Weave with light thread, right to left, lower surface.

This finishes two tabby rows dark on upper surface, and two light on lower surface. Drop light weft thread and weave Rows 1 and 2 dark, above. Then drop dark weft and weave Rows 3 and 4 light, below. Continue to alternate in this manner. For each two rows above, there should be two rows below.

Weaving Double-Width Material: With this technique, you can weave cloth double the width of the loom. Designs in stripes may be made by changing the color of thread as desired, or a warp of stripes may be used with weft stripes to form plaids. Only one shuttle and either dark or light thread are used.

If you have a narrow loom and wish cloth twice as wide, you can utilize this method. However, you must be careful to avoid streaks at the edges where the fold occurs and also to avoid narrowing in. If the edges are too loose, a streak will also show at the fold. It is helpful to put a cord at the folding edge, running it from the warp roller straight through to the cloth roller. It is *not* threaded through a heddle. You simply weave around it. The cord is on the fold side of the material only.

To weave double width, weave back and forth across the upper fabric and then back and forth across the lower fabric. The fold and cord may be on either selvage but is at left here.

See diagram for "Double-Width Material," Fig. 139. Use only one shuttle.

Row 1. Treadle 1: (CB, H. 4; Jack, Hs. 1, 2, 3) Weave from right to left on lower surface.

Row 2. Treadle 3: (CB, Hs. 1, 3, 4 together; Jack, H. 2) Weave from left to right on upper surface.

Row 3. Treadle 4: (CB, Hs. 2, 3, 4 together; Jack, H. 1) Weave back on upper surface from right to left.

Row 4. Treadle 2: (CB, Hs. 3; Jack, Hs. 1, 2, 4) Weave left to right on lower surface.

This finishes four rows of fabric. The shuttle is carried through from side to side. Two rows of fabric will show on the upper surface and two on the lower surface. Both are connected at the left selvage. The rows start at lower right, go around the left selvage to upper right, then reverse to left selvage, and go around this to the lower surface and back to the starting point. From here, start weaving another round.

Weaving Tubular Material: By this method, a pillow or enclosed object, such as a bag, can be made right on the loom. Again, avoid drawing in at the selvages. Stretch a taut cord at each side to weave around. Weave one row across the top, then one row across the bottom, and keep weaving round and round with only one weft.

See the diagram for "Tubular Material," Fig. 139.

Row 1. Treadle 1, weave from right to left on lower surface.

Row 2. Treadle 3, weave from left to right on upper surface.

Row 3. Treadle 2, weave from right to left on lower surface.

Row 4. Treadle 4, weave from left to right on upper surface.

Continue as shown in the diagram. Row 1 starts at arrow. Row 2 carries weft around to upper surface. Row 3 carries weft around selvage at right to lower surface again. Row 4 finishes around to upper surface.

A Seamless Bag: To make a seamless bag right on the loom, weave a tabby heading, both surfaces together, which will form the base of the bag. Then weave a circular section for the open bag. When you reach the top, keep weaving in this circular fashion to make a part to turn over for shirring cord. Take the bag off the loom. The base will be closed and the top will be open for hemming.

A Closed Pillow: To make a pillow or pin cushion, weave a heading with all warps together for the base. Next follow directions for the Tubular method of weaving and continue as desired for the pillow part. Open the shed between the two fabrics, and stuff the pillow. Weave the top shut with a few rows of tabby. There must be a wide space between the front beam and reed or there will be no room to weave and stuff the pillow before bringing the warp forward.

35—Multi-Harness Weaves

Transition Between Four-Harness and Multi-Harness Weaves

THE MORE harnesses one employs in developing a design, the greater the number of pattern variations possible. Although four-harness looms offer a lifetime of interest, many weavers seek the creative potentials of multi-harness patterns. In addition to various unique weaves, the following standard techniques may be developed into multi-harness formations: Twill, some Overshot patterns, Double Weave and Damask, Summer and Winter and Bronson Weave.

Multi-Harness Twill

This offers infinite variations. Twill can be written in drafts of five, six, seven, eight, or more harnesses. One can plan repeats as shown on page 260 in the draft at A-B; reverses, B-C; or combinations, C-D. The Point Twill, B-C, weaves into attractive crosses, diamonds, and triangles. For the Twill design, C-D, use the tie-up given, and weave treadles in the following order:

Design 1. Trs. 1,2,7,6,5,4,3,2,3,4,5,6,7,2.
  Repeat all; at end add Tr. 1.
Design 2. Trs. 1,2,3,4,5,6,7,6,5,4,3,2.
  Repeat all; at end add Tr. 1.
Design 3. Trs. 7,6,5,4,3,2,1,2,3,4,5,6.
  Repeat all; at end add Tr. 7.

Multi-Harness Overshot

Drafts of three blocks (Hs. 1-2, 2-3, 3-4) can be written for six harnesses with interesting texture effects. Keep Hs. 1-2 the same; change Hs. 2-3 to 3-4; change Hs. 3-4 to 5-6. For transition blocks one can use all units: Hs. 1-2, 2-3, 3-4, 4-5, 5-6, 6-1. To weave, combine two harnesses of any block with any other single harness:

Hs. 1,2,3; 1,2,4; 1,2,5; 1,2,6; or
Hs. 3,4,5; 3,4,6; 3,4,1; 3,4,2; or
Hs. 5,6,1; 5,6,2; 5,6,3; 5,6,4; etc.

Four harness drafts of four blocks can be written on eight harnesses. Keep Hs. 1-2 the same; change Hs. 2-3 to Hs. 3-4; change Hs. 3-4 to Hs. 5-6; change Hs. 4-1 to Hs. 7-8. To weave, combine the two harnesses of any unit with one harness each from the two other units.

Hs. 1,2,5,7; or Hs. 1,2,6,8;
Hs. 3,4,5,7; or Hs. 3,4,6,8;
Hs. 5,6,1,3; or Hs. 5,6,2,4;
Hs. 7,8,1,3; or Hs. 7,8,2,4.

Multi-Harness Damask

An eight-harness Twill draft can be woven as Double Twill, Double Weave, or Damask by altering the tie-up. (See draft.)

Multi-Harness Summer and Winter

This is written and woven by the same principle as four-harness drafts, with an extra harness for each added block. For two blocks (4-H.) we have Units 1,3,2,3; 1,4,2,4; for three blocks (5-H.) add Unit 1,5,2,5; for four blocks (6-H.) add Unit 1,6,2,6; for five blocks (7-H.) add Unit 1,7,2,7; for six blocks, (8-H.) add Unit 1,8,2,8. Tabby is Hs. 1-2 versus all other harnesses. Weave the units singly, Hs. 1,5; 2,5; 2,5; 1,5; etc., or in combinations, Hs. 1,3,7; 2,3,7; 2,3,7; 1,3,7; etc. Tabby after each pattern row (see page 263).

Multi-Harness Bronson

This is written and woven by the same principle as four-harness drafts, but with added units on more harnesses. For two blocks (4-H.) we have Units 1,3,1,3,1,2; 1,4,1,4,1,2; for three blocks (5-H.) add Unit 1,5,1,5,1,2; for four blocks (6-H.) add Unit 1,6,1,6,1,2; for five blocks (7-H.) add Unit 1,7,1,7,1,2; for six blocks (8-H.) add Unit 1,8,1,8,1,2. Tabby is Hs. 1 alone versus all other harnesses, Hs. 2,3,4,5, 6,7,8, if all eight are used. Weave units singly: Hs. 2,7; then H. 1. Repeat these two rows; add alternate tabbies. Combinations can contain several harnesses: Hs. 2,3,5,6,7; then H. 1; repeat; add alternate tabbies. (See page 262.)

Eight-Harness Damask Design

On an eight-harness loom it is possible to weave Damask designs of two blocks, and these may be planned in various pleasing proportions. The first block is threaded on harnesses 1,2,3,4; the second block on harnesses 5,6,7,8. In the weaving directions below, Block 1 means treadle 1,2,3,4 in succession; Block 2 means treadle 5,6,7,8. The warp is closely set, and a linen weft of the same weight beat firmly brings out the texture.

Warp Plan:

Warp: 20/2 Cotton or 40/2 Linen.
Weft: Fine linen 20/1 or 40/2.
Threads per inch: 36
Width: 14 in.

Threading Plan:

	Threads
Border a-b (8 threads) 5 times ..	40
b-c (68 threads); repeat twice ..	136
c-d (center) follow draft	136
b-c (68 threads); repeat twice ..	136
Border a-b (8 threads) 5 times ..	40
total	488

Weaving Plan for Damask Linen Mat:

Following Damask tie-up above,
Treadle Block 1 (Trs. 1,2,3,4) then Block 2 (Trs. 5,6,7,8). Repeat 5x.
*Treadle Block 1, 3x.
Treadle Block 2, 10x.
Treadle Block 1, 3x.
Treadle Block 2, once.
Repeat all from (*) asterisk.
Center: Treadle Block 1, then Block 2, once.
Treadle Block 1, 30 times.
Reverse the treadling from this center.

DAMASK DESIGN, EIGHT-HARNESS WEAVE

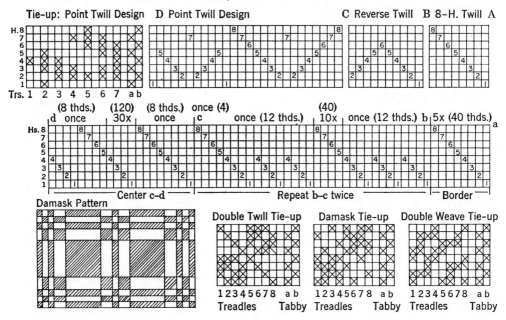

Eight-Harness Bronson Lace in Modern Design

This Bronson threading for an eight-harness loom has an uneven balance to provide for the weaving of mats or runners of asymmetrical design. Each section of the draft (separated in the sketch by vertical arrows) can be repeated as many times as desired to form proportions other than those given here. Many other tie-ups are possible.

This same design can be worked out in the Summer and Winter texture by replacing the Bronson units with the Summer and Winter units and by using a Summer and Winter tie-up. Thus, replace Bronson Block: Hs. 1, 3, 1, 3, 1, 2, with Summer and Winter Block: Hs. 1, 3, 2, 3; replace Hs. 1, 4, 1, 4, 1, 2, with Hs. 1, 4, 2, 4; and Hs. 1, 5, 1, 5, 1, 2 with Hs. 1, 5, 2, 5, and so on. (Weave the Summer and Winter threading according to the directions on pages 242, 261.)

Warp Plan: *Fine:* Cotton 20/2 or linen 40/2 set at 30 per inch. *Medium:* cotton 10/2 or linen 40/3 or 30/2 set at 24 per inch. *Coarse:* Cotton 5/2 or 10/3 or linen 20/2 set at 15 to 18 per inch.

Threading: Thread from right to left. Add Hs. 1, 2, 1, 2 for selvage.

Weaving Plan: Design I. See Tie-Up and Design I. Use only one weft, somewhat heavier than warp.

Section a: Tr. 3; then Tab. A; repeat; Tab. B; then Tab. A. Repeat these 6 rows as desired.

Section b: Tr. 2; then Tab. A; repeat; Tab. B; then Tab. A. Repeat these 6 rows as desired.

Section c: Tr. 1; then Tab. A; repeat; Tab. B; then Tab. A. Repeat these 6 rows as desired.

Weaving Plan: Design II. See Tie-up and Design II. (Repeat the 6 rows of each section as desired.)

Section d: Tr. 1; then Tab. A; repeat; Tab. B; then Tab. A.

Section e: Tr. 2; then Tab. A; repeat; Tab. B; then Tab. A.

Section f: Tr. 3; then Tab. A; repeat; Tab. B; then Tab. A.

Section g: Tr. 4; then Tab. A; repeat; Tab. B; then Tab. A.

Section h: Tr. 5; then Tab. A; repeat; Tab. B; then Tab A.

Section i: Tr. 6; then Tab. A; repeat; Tab. B; then Tab A.

Weaving Plan: Design III. See Tie-up and Design III. (Repeat the 6 rows after each section as desired.)

Section j: Tabby only, as desired; Tr. B; then Tr. A.

Section k: Tr. 5; then Tab. A; repeat; Tab. B; then Tab. A.

Section l: Tr. 4; then Tab. A; repeat; Tab. B; then Tab. A.

Section m: Tr. 3; then Tab. A; repeat; Tab. B; then Tab. A.

Section n: Tr. 2; then Tab. A; repeat; Tab. B; then Tab. A.

Section o: Tr. 1; then Tab. A; repeat; Tab. B; then Tab. A.

Pine Tree, Diamond, and Triangular Figures From an Eight-Harness Summer and Winter Draft

A practical eight-harness draft, from which borders of pine trees as well as over-all patterns of triangles or diamonds can be devised, is useful in making household fabrics and occasional gifts. Christmas cards may be made by weaving a strip of pine trees, cutting them apart to form separate green trees, and mounting these on cards.

Warp Plan: For a firm pattern texture, set 10/2 cotton warp at 20 per inch, and use 3/2 pattern weft bound with 20/2 tabby, which sinks into the texture and does not show. For linen, set 40/2 at 24 per inch; pattern 20/2 linen; tabby 40/2.

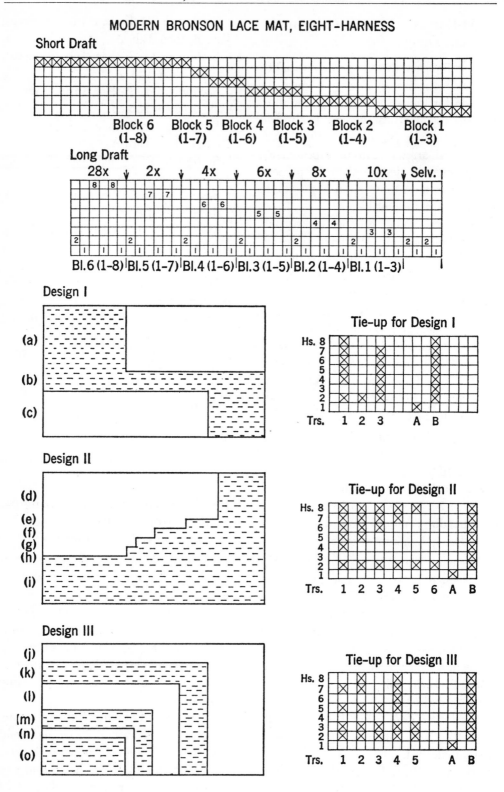

MODERN BRONSON LACE MAT, EIGHT-HARNESS

Short Draft

Block 6   Block 5   Block 4   Block 3   Block 2   Block 1
(1–8)   (1–7)   (1–6)   (1–5)   (1–4)   (1–3)

Long Draft

28x   2x   4x   6x   8x   10x   Selv.

Bl.6 (1–8) | Bl.5 (1–7) | Bl.4 (1–6) | Bl.3 (1–5) | Bl.2 (1–4) | Bl.1 (1–3)

Design I

(a)
(b)
(c)

Tie-up for Design I

Hs. 8 7 6 5 4 3 2 1
Trs.   1   2   3   A   B

Design II

(d)
(e)
(f)
(g)
(h)
(i)

Tie-up for Design II

Hs. 8 7 6 5 4 3 2 1
Trs.   1   2   3   4   5   6   A   B

Design III

(j)
(k)
(l)
(m)
(n)
(o)

Tie-up for Design III

Hs. 8 7 6 5 4 3 2 1
Trs.   1   2   3   4   5   A   B

DRAFT: EIGHT-HARNESS SUMMER AND WINTER DIAMOND AND PINE TREE

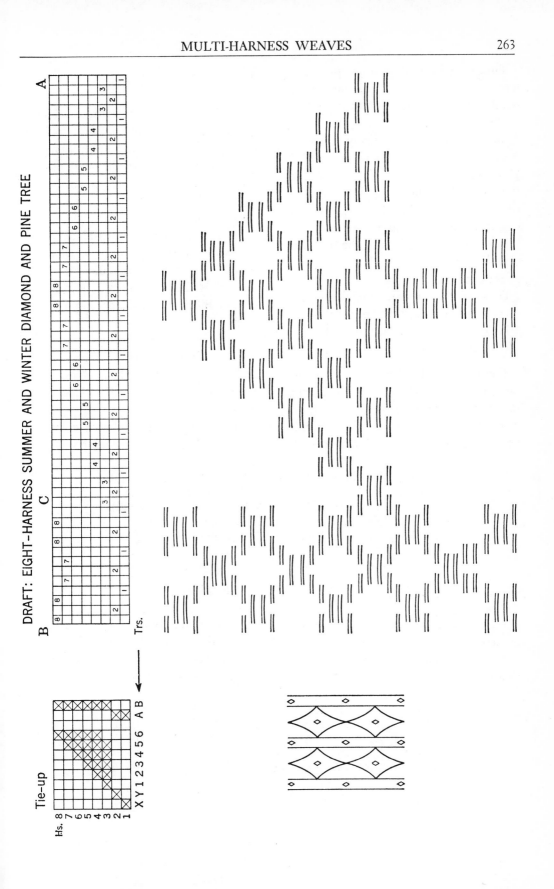

Threading Plan: Repeat complete pattern, A and B, 56 threads, the desired number of times. Add pattern from A to C only, 44 threads.

Weaving Plan: The tie-up gives six treadles in addition to the tie-up on H. 1 (X) and that on H. 2 (Y), plus A and B tabbies. By combining the X and Y treadles with treadles 1 to 6, you can weave the Summer and Winter texture.

For instance, for Block 6 (the treadling combination on Treadle No. 6), weave as follows:

Tr. X and Tr. 6 together, then Tabby A
Tr. Y and Tr. 6 together, then Tabby B
Tr. Y and Tr. 6 together, then Tabby A
Tr. X and Tr. 6 together, then Tabby B

For any other treadling proceed in the same manner, weaving 8 rows including tabby for each pattern block. Simply replace Tr. 6 with the particular treadle you wish to weave. Abbreviate as follows:

Variations

All-Over Diamond Pattern; Hour-Glass Pattern. Weave a purse, pillow-top, or runner with the lovely Summer and Winter texture in diamond design. For a dressy evening bag, you might use white perle pattern thread and gold or silver tabby.

Weave eight rows of each block in the following succession: Block 1, Block 2, Block 3, Block 4, Block 5, Block 6, Block 5, Block 4, Block 3, Block 2. Repeat all, or add Block 1 at end to complete diamond.

For the hour-glass pattern, treadle as follows: Block 5, Block 4, Block 3, Block 2, Block 1, Block 2, Block 3, Block 4. Repeat all, or finish with Block 5, as desired.

For units of design between diamonds or hour glasses, tread Block 6.

Block 5:   Tr. X and 5; A; Y and 5; B; Y and 5; A; X and 5; B.
Block 4:   Tr. X and 4; A; Y and 4; B; Y and 4; A; X and 4; B.
Block 3:   Tr. X and 3; A; Y and 3; B; Y and 3; A; X and 3; B.
Block 2:   Tr. X and 2; A; Y and 2; B; Y and 2; A; X and 2; B.
Block 1:   Tr. X and 1; A; Y and 1; B; Y and 1; A; X and 1; B.

WEAVING THE PINE TREE

Plain weave: Tr. A, then Tr. B. Repeat as desired.

Base under stem of tree: Block 4, 8 rows as given above.

Stem of tree: Block 5, 8 rows as given above. Repeat for 8 more rows.

Tree: Follow 8-row block plan below.

Design between trees: Treadle Block 6.

Block 1:   Tr. X and 1; A; Y and 1; B; Y and 1; A; X and 1; B.
Block 2:   Tr. X and 2; A; Y and 2; B; Y and 2; A; X and 2; B.
Block 3:   Tr. X and 3; A; Y and 3; B; Y and 3; A; X and 3; B.
Block 4:   Tr. X and 4; A; Y and 4; B; Y and 4; A; X and 4; B.
Block 5:   Tr. X and 5; A; Y and 5; B; Y and 5; A; X and 5; B.

36—The Handweaver's Approach to Color

WE LIVE in a wonderful world of color. In Nature we see color miracles created for our enjoyment and use. Exquisite color schemes are found in the flowers, the skies, the wings of birds and butterflies, the fields and rivers, oceans and sands, grasses and trees, and in that lovely filmy whisper of divine fabrication, the rainbow.

Man has been intrigued since the beginning of time by this lavish display of color. He has tried to search out the fugitive secrets on Nature's palette and to transfer them to his own surroundings. The artist, the decorator, the architect, the stylist, and the weaver, all require a skillful use of color, whether it be expressed in paints, dyes, yarns, wood, metal, or stone. Even the homemaker and restaurant chef must know something about color to add beauty and appeal to the foods they prepare.

The weaver is especially conscious of color. In fact, color is the very soul of handwoven fabrics. In no other art can the colors be mixed with greater ease. The weaver's warp lies before him like a canvas, and on this he can paint to his heart's content. As the warp and weft combine, each color retains its identity and is not lost in a completely new third color, as happens when two paints are mixed. Instead, the eye itself puts the colors together unconsciously, and the designer is rewarded with ever new and subtle tones.

The most intelligent approach to the world of color is to learn all you can about the laws evolved by man, and then to make your own firsthand observations of the greatest color artist of all, Mother Nature. This approach was followed by students of the weaving department of the University of Kansas who made sequences of warp colors on cards by choosing the key colors in natural scenes or in the actual flower or pod forms found in Nature. To make use of these color harmonies, they assembled all the textures and colors of yarn available in the studio, and then used their own originality in arranging them in the desired order and proportions by wrapping the yarns around small cards. Bright colors or textures were used in lesser quantities as accents.

This direct approach to color through natural sources is most valuable to the handweaver. It is also helpful to make a color wheel showing the interrelationship of the colors and a handwoven color sampler showing how warps and wefts react upon each other.

Making the Color Wheel

First of all, you should know the primary colors and the colors obtained by combining them. By arranging them in a circle, you can see clearly how the primary colors are combined to produce the secondary colors. Furthermore, complimentary colors will appear opposite

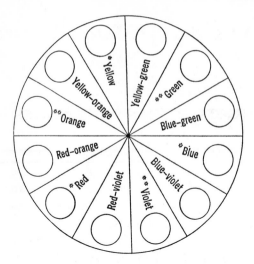

Fig. 140.—In this color wheel the primary colors are signified by an asterisk, and the secondary colors by a double asterisk. The unmarked colors are the intermediate colors.

each other on the color wheel. It is helpful to have these apparent for possible use.

The Primary Colors: Red, yellow, and blue, marked with an asterisk on the color wheel in Fig 140, are known as the **primary** colors because they cannot be made by a combination or mixture of any other colors. These three colors and black are really the foundation for many other colors and are used in all fundamental studies of art.

The Secondary Colors: Green, orange and violet, marked with two asterisks on the color wheel, are the **secondary** colors. They are made by mixing equal parts of the primary colors in the following manner:

Red and yellow make orange.
Red and blue make violet.
Blue and yellow make green.

The Intermediate Colors: In addition to the three primary and three secondary colors, there are six **intermediate** colors on a 12-color wheel. These are produced

by the addition of small extra amounts of one of the primary colors to a secondary color. For instance, if you add an extra amount of red to orange, you have red-orange. This is called a "hue" of orange. In this manner, you can also get yellow-orange, yellow-green, blue-green, red-violet, and so on. In water color, paint small circles of the colors described.

Weaving a Color Sampler

Now that you have learned how to combine primary colors to make other colors, you can put this knowledge to use in weaving a color sampler. (See Fig. 141.) This will test the effects of using certain colors in the weft and others in the warp.

Arrange twelve thread colors similar to those in your water-color wheel across your warp. With two inches of each, your warp will be 24 inches wide. Now plan to weave with the same succession of colors. A convenient size thread is 10/2 or Perle 10, which comes in many beautful colors and shades, and makes a very gradual color series possible. The result will be a color sampler with 144 different color effects in two-inch squares. This sampler can be used for reference in obtaining certain color tones.

The color sampler shown in Fig. 141 was first worked out on paper and then woven with the same succession of colors as in the warp. The effective results of the combinations prove that the weaver is most fortunate in the ease with which colors can be blended on the loom. The warp threads always carry their color over the entire web, as if one tone were lightly brushed over all. While the wefts give changing colors, the warp threads literally tie the whole together, subduing any harsh accents.

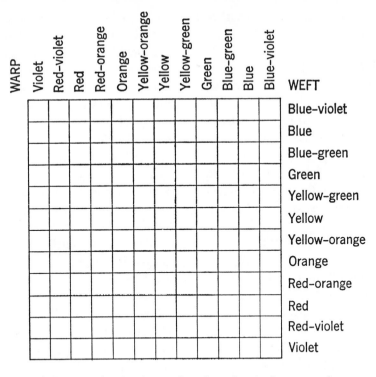

Fig. 141—A color chart with twelve colors in the warp and the same twelve colors in the weft. This weaves into 144 squares of different color effects.

Attributes of Color

There are also certain attributes of color resulting from the addition of light or dark or other colors. These are color tone, color intensity, and color value.

Color Tone: By "**tone**" is meant the tints and shades of color. Light tones are termed "**tints,**" and dark or grayed tones are termed "**shades.**" The tints are obtained by adding white or water to a normal color. Shades are obtained by adding black or the color's complement, such as green to red.

Color Intensity: Intensity is the purity or brilliance of a color. Artists speak of a dull red and a brilliant red. Both are red, but one has been mixed with a little of its complement, a grayed color, a neutral gray, or some black, and it lacks the intensity of a pure color.

Color Value: Value is that quality of a color which indicates its relation to black and white. For instance, light red is considered near in value to white, while dark red is considered nearer in value to black. Of all the colors on the wheel, yellow is nearest to white in value, and violet is nearest to black.

Advancing and Receding Colors

Red, orange, and yellow seem to stand out and command attention. These colors are known as "**advancing**" colors. Some colors seem more subdued than others and give the effect of distance. Blue, green, and violet have this effect and are therefore called "**receding**" colors.

As a rule, it is well to remember that all cool colors can be classed as receding colors, and warm colors are definitely advancing colors.

Carrying Power

Some colors seem to carry farther than others and therefore have greater attractive power. Arranged in their relative order from greatest to least, yellow comes first, then orange, green, red, blue, and violet. When these colors are placed on white, the same order prevails except that yellow has the least attractive power.

Harmonies of Similar Colors

Color harmonies may be classified under two headings. "Monochrome" means one color. A monochromatic color harmony is one which is made up of tones, shades, and intensities of only one color. "Analogous" refers to similar and neighboring colors on the wheel. Blue-green, green, and yellow-green are analogous. All three contain both yellow and blue and are next to each other on the wheel. Red is a common element in such analogous colors as red-orange, and red-violet. One color running through the series ties them togetther.

Harmonies of Contrasting Colors

Complementary Harmony is produced by two colors opposite each other on the wheel. This is a harsh combination when used to full intensity. Therefore, mix a little of the complementary with each before combining. In weaving, an allover warp color softens two complementary colors.

Split-Complementary Harmony is made by the use of any color on the wheel with the color on each side of the complement, such as blue with red-orange and yellow-orange (orange being opposite blue on the wheel). The complement need not be primary; tints or

shades or both may be used. Work out examples from your color wheel.

A Double-Complementary Harmony is that made by two colors next to each other on the wheel used with two colors directly opposite them, such as red-violet and violet used with their opposites, yellow and yellow-green.

A Triadic Harmony contains three different colors which form an equilateral triangle on the wheel. These colors differ enough to give variety and completeness to the combination. Select the first color, then take each fourth one on the wheel to go with it. For example you might select green, violet, and orange. Use only one of these colors in its full intensity, and use tints or shades of the other two. This use of three colors is helpful in weaving because it gives something definite to start with.

Color and Color Balance

The artist considers the balance of his color when planning a composition. The weaver must also consider this if a successful color scheme is to result. Dark colors seem to be heavier than light colors. Therefore, if you are planning a drape, you place the darker colors closer to the base. If they are used with other colors, you use less of them to produce a good color balance. Pure colors also seem to carry more weight or accent, so you neutralize these or use less of them in order to preserve a color balance.

Balance does not mean that colors should have equal attraction. It does mean that a pleasing variety and good balance are possible by contrasting, accenting, tinting, or shading colors. Complementary colors can be balanced against each other. However, if the colors are pure, the severe contrast detracts from any other colors in the piece. It is best, therefore, to use these colors sparingly.

In other words, in planning your fabric, consider carefully the amount and position of the colors used, as well as their relationships to each other.

Psychological Significance of Color

Most people think of color in terms of sight, but it is known that color also gives a reaction to the touch and, to some individuals, to the smell. In general, the cool restful colors are green, blue, and violet; the stimulating colors, red, yellow, and orange. Rooms painted blue and then repainted yellow have been found to make people feel warmer. Decorators use red to give a feeling of warmth and pep, blue for rest and recuperation, yellow for uplift. Rooms decorated in dark colors are always more dismal than those with light colors.

Color combinations can please or irritate us, depending upon our own personal reactions. However, the following attributes of the different colors are generally sound for most people.

Blue is cold, formal, and suggests open spaces and distance. It can be used to balance a color scheme that seems to have too many luminous colors.

Green is cool, restful, and suggestive of growing things. It is a splendid background color for woven fabrics when bright colors are placed against it.

Yellow is the most luminous of all colors. It is cheerful and gay and has carrying power. It is excellent for giving light and airiness to rooms, and may be used effectively for sun curtains, screens, or lampshades.

Red is warm, rich, and aggressive. It is the color of energy as well as passion and violence. It attracts the eye and should be used only where emphasis is needed. It can overpower other parts of a design.

Orange is a decorative color, rich in its effect. It is a strong color which should be used sparingly in full strength.

Violet is a mysterious color, lovely when pale for quieting effects. It can be mournful if used to any great extent. It can be used most successfully for shadow effects.

37—Planning Borders

Types of Borders

JUST AS WE FRAME pictures to set them off and to enhance their beauty, we plan borders for our hand-weaving patterns to make them show to their best advantage. Sometimes the border itself has even greater interest than the pattern; again it is purely subsidiary to the pattern.

The type of border that comes at once to the mind of the weaver is the **horizontal border** woven across the warp at the ends of a runner or towel or at intervals along its length, at the bases of curtains, and in similar places. This type is readily woven from the threaded pattern in colors to enhance the effect of the entire article. However, borders that are **threaded into the loom** and show all around the four sides of the material, running along both the horizontal and vertical edges, are more difficult to plan, and it is possibly more valuable to know about them. Such a border is threaded at the sides, and a border design develops as a vertical column along the right and left selvages during the weaving of the pattern. This type may therefore be called the **vertical type border.** The horizontal parts of the border, or the parts across the top and bottom of the piece, are formed by weaving the part of the pattern that contains the vertical border as-drawn-in. When weaving hanging towels, draperies, wall panels, bell pulls, aprons, etc., weavers like to thread their looms in such a way that overshot borders will occur lengthwise of the material.

Borders Running Across the Material, or Horizontal Borders

Narrow bands of Pattern Weaving or planned sections of Laid-in or Lace Weaves are used for horizontal borders running across the material weft-wise. To secure pleasing proportions, it is a good plan to cut a smooth piece of newspaper or wrapping paper the shape and size of the final piece and, using heavy crayon, to sketch in the border. Then, lay out the possibilities of the pattern by first weaving each harness combination separately; and, from the pictures before you, make sketches of various ways in which you think the combinations will look well together. Remember that there are fourteen possibilities to choose from in treadling any four-harness Overshot Pattern: Harnesses 1 and 2; 2 and 3; 3 and 4; 4 and 1; 1 and 2 and 3; 2 and 3 and 4; 3 and 4 and 1; 4 and 1 and 2; 1 alone; 2 alone; 3 alone; 4 alone; and also the two Tabby sheds, namely, 1 and 3 and 2 and 4. Often a pleasing effect is produced by weaving a row of Tabby in heavy pattern thread at each side of a horizontal border. This row may be separated from the main pattern border by several rows of the fine Tabby thread, if a slight variation is desired.

Borders Running Lengthwise of the Material, or Vertical Borders

This kind of border acts as a framework to the pattern. In general, there are two ways to plan the pattern and its border.

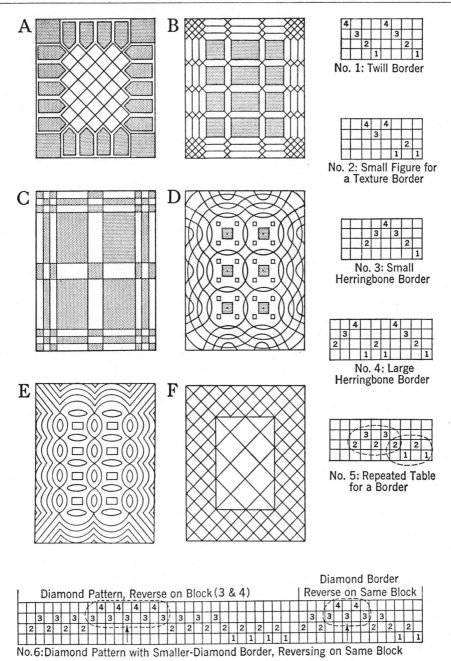

No. 1: Twill Border

No. 2: Small Figure for a Texture Border

No. 3: Small Herringbone Border

No. 4: Large Herringbone Border

No. 5: Repeated Table for a Border

Diamond Pattern, Reverse on Block (3 & 4)

Diamond Border Reverse on Same Block

No. 6: Diamond Pattern with Smaller-Diamond Border, Reversing on Same Block

Fig. 142—Several borders suitable to their respective patterns.

(1) Plan a border of a small repeated motif, with the central part of the article to hold the main interest and to consist of fairly large motifs. The border in this case is subsidiary, consisting of small repeated motifs, as shown in Fig. 142 at **C**

and **E**. The chief interest is in the center, and the border is merely its frame.

(2) Plan a wide border with motifs large in character, and make the center of small repeated motifs; in this case the interest is in the border, as in Fig. 142

at **A** and **F**. Sometimes one achieves a very lovely balance between the border and the pattern, each one setting off the other, as at **B** and **D**.

Small Repeated Border with Chief Interest in Large Center

Where the central part of the article is to hold the main interest and the border is to consist of small repeated motifs, suitable patterns for the borders are the Twill, Herringbone, and Diamond Patterns.

The simplest border to plan is the Twill, repeated as desired. The draft for such a border is shown in Fig. 142 at No. 1, and the effect is illustrated at **E**. This proves interesting, for each motif of the pattern changes to a Twill-like figure at the sides. Use it when desiring a border of fine texture lines. Simply thread Hs. 1, 2, 3, 4 at the right side, and repeat; then thread Hs. 4, 3, 2, 1 at the left side, and repeat. Before threading the left selvage, when the main pattern ends on either harness 2 or harness 4, insert an extra thread on harness 1 or harness 3 between the pattern and the selvage border. This avoids two adjacent threads on even harnesses, a succession which weaves as a **flat**, or brings two warp threads side by side on the same shed, thus spoiling the Tabby texture.

A draft for a border with fine texture lines is shown in Fig. 142 at No. 2; and drafts for small and large Herringbone borders are shown at No. 3 and No. 4. The Herringbone Pattern repeated at the sides of a woven piece makes a bird-like effect. If the pattern is woven twill-fashion, the border appears in zig-zag horizontal lines. If it is woven as drawn in, it forms small Diamond figures. Thread Hs. 1, 2, 3, (4), 3, and 2, and re-

peat; or thread Hs. 1, 2, 3, 4, (1), 4, 3, and 2, and repeat.

A draft for a Diamond border is shown in Fig. 142 at No. 6, and the effect is illustrated at **F**. A small Diamond often can be used effectively for the border, especially where the center is composed of large units, as in wide coverlets or rugs. Reverse the Diamond at the same block on which one of the main pattern units reverses. For instance, if there is a large cross reversing on a long (3 and 4) block, use this same form of the Diamond for the border, as in draft No. 6 in Fig. 142. Thus, thread blocks (1 and 2), (2 and 3), and (3 and 4); and reverse, as shown at the right in draft No. 6. Note that in the pattern itself the reverse block on harnesses 3 and 4 is a long one; but in the border all blocks are shorter than those in the pattern draft.

Wide Borders for Interest, with a Center of Small Repeated Motifs

Hand-woven articles of effective design may be planned with the center area of the article nothing more than a continuous repeat of a small insignificant motif, such as a 3-block or 4-block Diamond, or a series of small Stars and Roses, or simply two alternating blocks. The charm of this field of repeated motifs usually lies in the fact that it is set off by a wide border of simple design.

A very attractive type of border for patterns consisting of center repeats is formed by threading a wide Table at each side. Such a design is shown in Fig. 142 at **A** and the draft for the border is shown in No. 5. The two small blocks that alternate over a wide area for the sides and corners are obtained by taking two adjacent blocks occurring in the pattern and making a Table out of them, as shown.

Repeat these two alternating blocks for 5 to 8 inches for rugs and still further for coverlets.

Planning Borders for Summer and Winter, Bronson, and M's and O's

Effective borders for two-block patterns, such as the Summer and Winter Weave, Bronson Weave, and M's and O's Weave described in Fig. 136, may consist of a series of single units alternating with each other. This arrangement was used for the Summer and Winter border in Fig. 142 at **C**. After writing four selvage notes, Hs. 1, 3, 2, 4, start threading with Unit (**a**), follow with Unit (**b**), and then alternate one repeat of each to the width desired. Continue with the regular pattern plan in which these units are repeated many times to make larger pattern spaces for the fabric proper. Adapt this same plan of alternating single units for the border to the Bronson Weave and the M's and O's Weave.

A good border for these patterns also consists of simply a section of Plain Weave planned for a certain width at the edge of the fabric. This sets off the texture pattern occupying the center.

Borders Suitable for Certain Types of Patterns

The patterns with their borders shown in Fig. 142 should prove helpful as guides in planning table mats, doilies, runners, pillows, draperies, and coverlets. To obtain the right proportions between the pattern and the border, it is a good idea to make a rough sketch of the effect on a large piece of wrapping paper cut to the size of the finished article. Borders vary greatly in width. Coverlet borders may be as wide as 10 or 12 inches; in doilies the border should be fairly narrow, to leave enough main pattern at the center to act as a background for the plate. Borders for rugs, pillows, and drapes may be of any size desired.

Typical Borders for Household Fabrics

The coverlet pattern shown in Fig. 142 at **A** consists of a large Diamond figure set off by a border in a Table design. The Table consists of two small blocks repeated in alternation, as indicated in draft No. 5.

The pattern at **B** is suitable for a coverlet, rug, or doily. Its pattern of Tables and Crosses is set off by a Diamond border, such as that in draft No. 6.

At **C** is shown the Summer and Winter Pattern of Fig. 136 planned for a rug. Short spans of each block alternate to form the border; i.e., Hs. 1, 3, 2, 3 alternate with Hs. 1, 4, 2, 4. To make each unit wider, simply enlarge the 4-thread blocks to 8-thread or 12-thread blocks; thus, Hs. 1, 3, 2, 3, 1, 3, 2, 3 alternate with Hs. 1, 4, 2, 4, 1, 4, 2, 4. This same design arrangement may be adapted to a pattern with blocks on opposites, with the border formed by an alternation of Hs. 1, 2, 1, 2 and Hs. 3, 4, 3, 4.

At **D** in Fig. 142 is shown a bath mat or rug in the Whig Rose Pattern surrounded by a border formed by short repeated motifs of the pattern.

The Honeysuckle doily at **E** has a Twill border of the type indicated in draft No. 1. This turns into a zig-zag effect during the weaving of the pattern.

At **F** is a mat with large Diamonds or Crosses for the center framed by an extensive border of repeated small Diamonds. These are made to reverse on the same block as the large main Diamond figure, as indicated in draft No. 6.

Connecting a Border with the Main Pattern

Any one of the small drafts in Fig. 142 makes an excellent border. Also, any of the Herringbone Patterns of Fig. 112 may be used, but the weaver should choose one that has a reverse point on the same block as that on which the main pattern reverses. These patterns are suitable for extensive border repeats. Where the main pattern is large in character, a repeated Diamond may prove more effective than a Herringbone. Here, too, one should follow the rule of choosing a Diamond that has a reverse on the same block as the larger Cross or Diamond of the pattern. Where the pattern does not reverse Diamond-fashion, a Diamond or Herringbone border may be used in marked contrast to the character of the main pattern.

In connecting a border with the main pattern, one may begin the border on the same block as the pattern proper, or on the block of that portion of the pattern which has been taken out to act as a key for the border, as shown in Fig. 142 in draft No. 6, where the border starts on a 4-thread block (Hs. 1, 2, 1, 2) and a similar portion of the pattern starts on an 8-thread block of the same combination.

It is very important that the last note of the border and the first note of the main pattern be on opposite sheds; i.e., if the border ends on an even note, the pattern must start on an odd note, and vice versa. This will prevent a flat, or two adjacent warp threads weaving together on the same shed. This regulation is for Overshot Patterns, and not for the unusual techniques given in Fig. 136. In these techniques the same units used for the pattern may be used in narrow form for the border, or the border may simply be a certain width of Plain Weave.

Side Borders on Four-Harness Looms

Many weavers are interested in learning how to weave side borders in color. On a four-harness loom, it is possible to have a vertical side border design comprised of two alternating blocks, as shown in Fig. 143.

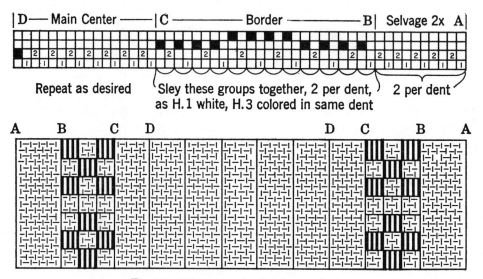

Fig. 143—Side borders for four-harness looms.

All the colored warps are marked as shaded squares in the draft, and all other warp threads are natural-colored background threads. The sections of Hs. 1, 2 are Plain Weave and underlie the border and form the fabric all across the warp. You will note that the tabby takes up two harnesses and the two blocks at sides, two more harnesses. (You cannot have a horizontal border in addition to a side border unless you are using a six-harness loom.)

Warp Plan: For Pattern (shaded squares, Fig. 143) use double the size thread as used for Tabby. (For example: Pattern (on Hs. 3, 4) Perle 5; Tabby (on Hs. 1, 2) Perle 10.)

Threading Plan: Make your own plan, threading tabby border **AB** where desired and in the width desired. In sleying, however, sley each pattern warp with the preceding tabby warp. If the warp is 10/2 cotton, for instance, sley two threads Hs. 1, 2 in one dent throughout, at two per dent in a 12-dent reed. When you come to added pattern threads, sley H. 1 with the first pattern thread which follows it (H. 3) in the same dent; then H. 2 with the next added pattern thread (H. 3), and so on, as shown in the draft (small brackets).

Weaving Plan: See table below.

Use only a single weft of the same color and size as the warp. If you wish, add accent-line stripes throughout the warp in the same color as the heavy Overshot border warp. You can also add heavy stripe lines at intervals in the weft as well, if outline plaids are desired. The heavy accent warps can be placed anywhere throughout the tabby warp on either harness. (See **D** of Fig. 143.)

Weaving Plan	Jack	Counterbalanced
Plain Weave:	H. 1 alone, then H. 2 alone	Hs. 1, 3, 4, then Hs. 2, 3, 4
First Block:	Hs. 1–3, then Hs. 2–3. Repeat as desired.	Hs. 2–4, then Hs. 1–4. Repeat as desired.
Second Block:	Hs. 1–4, then Hs. 2–4. Repeat.	Hs. 2–3, then Hs. 1–3. Repeat.

38—Various Draft Notations

Y OU should be familiar with the different ways in which drafts are written in weaving books in order to interpret them properly. Figure 145 shows the same pattern worked out in methods used today and in those found in Colonial and foreign drafts. A comparison of the various notations on the same pattern will be helpful.

Numbering the Harnesses

Some weavers number the harnesses of the loom from back to front, as written from the top down at (a) (1, 2, 3, 4) in Fig. 145. Others number from front to back, shown here at (b). Either method is

acceptable; weaving the pattern as drawn in produces the same results. However, be consistent and follow the method and numeration with which you start.

The Tie-Up

Again, the treadles may be numbered left to right on the loom, as at (c), in which case the tie-up should be numbered left to right (c'). They may also be numbered right to left as at (d), corresponding to the same direction in the tie-up (d'). Just be sure you always connect what you call Harness 1 with any mention of H. 1 in the tie-up or draft. If you have a direct tie-up, one harness to each treadle, be

Fig. 144—Two practical handwoven skirts. Left, Overshot Pattern woven with dark brown and white. Right, skirt in pink, black, and white, woven with 5/2 cotton on a 20/2 black warp set at 15 per inch.

very sure you connect Harness 1 to Treadle 1, and so on. For direct tie-up see page 278.

Methods of Writing Drafts (Fig. 145)

In this book the treadles are numbered from left to right, the tie-up from left to right, the harness from front to back of the loom, Harness 1 being in front, and Harness 1 of the draft also being directly in front of you.

Method No. 1: This is probably the clearest method from a visual standpoint. The graph squares are filled in as solid black units. In this and ensuing drafts, repeat pattern **A** to **B** as desired and then add **B** to **C**.

Method No. 2: Single lines in the graph squares designate the chosen harness. This notation is used a great deal in the Scandinavian countries. The tie-up is given either at right or left, and the weaving plan appears in a vertical column directly below it. This is a clear, consistent method and may be applied to any of the graph notations. The tie-up here is given at the right of the draft, as shown at **D**. Following this tie-up, Hs. 1 and 2 are tied to Treadle 1 (see crosses); Hs. 2 and 3 to Tr. 2; Hs. 3 and 4 to Tr. 3; and Hs. 4 and 1 to Tr. 4. The Tabby for this draft is Hs. 2 and 4 tied to Tr. 5; and Hs. 1 and 3 to Tr. 6. In most books, the Tabby is not written down, but taken for granted.

The selvage of the draft is also omitted in most Colonial and foreign drafts. You are supposed to know how to arrange this. It usually progresses in the order given by the first two blocks of the draft. In Fig. 145, Hs. 1 and 2 are followed by Hs. 2 and 3. This upward progression indicates Hs. 1, 2, 3, 4 as the selvage. If the first block is on Hs. 4-1 and the second on

Hs. 3-4, you would write the selvage 4, 3, 2, 1. The weaving directions are given in the vertical arrangement **E**, below tie-up **D**. Any note in the column below Tr. 1 means weave Tr. 1; any note below Tr. 2 means weave Tr. 2, and so on. Consecutive numbers, 1, 2, 3, 4, 5 indicate: 1, first weft row; 2, second weft row, and so on.

In some blocks, the draft and tie-up are given at the bottom of the page, and the column and weaving directions continue upward instead of downward. This makes no difference in the final result.

In the draft in question at column **E**, No. 1 in the column indicates first combination (either singly or repeated) is on Tr. 1. Number 2 indicates next combination on Tr. 2. Number 3 indicates next combination is on Tr. 1 again. In other words, the consecutive numbers indicate the order in which the rows follow. These may also be indicated as crosses or shaded squares, as shown at **F** and **G**. You keep track of these by their positions gradually descending in the column. If each combination is to be woven more than once, it may be so indicated at the right. Two times is written as $2\times$, three times as $3\times$, and so on, as shown at **E**.

Another notation is shown at **H**. Here the graph writer simply progresses downward in simple vertical lines. If a combination is to be woven several times, the several vertical lines are written down in the same square, as at **J**. In some notations the treadle number is written down in columns, as shown at **K**, instead of the consecutive numbers of the weft rows, shown previously at **E**. The above weaving notations in vertical columns can be applied to any of the drafts given here.

Method No. 3: This is the same as Method 1 except that crosses are used instead of solid squares. The weaver can easily see which harness is indicated.

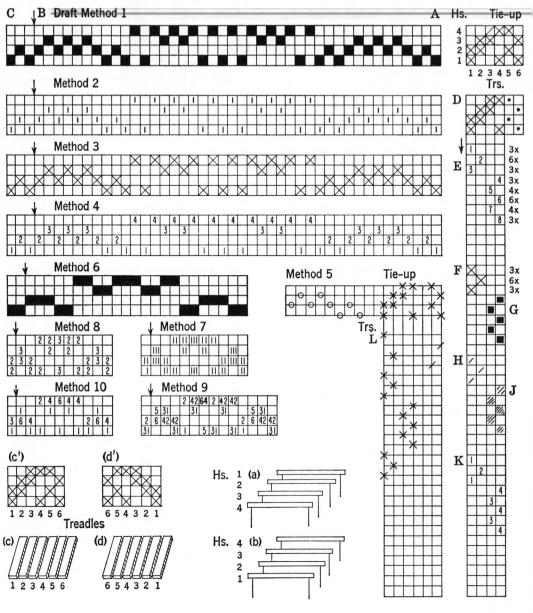

Fig. 145—Various draft notations.

Even on multiharness looms, the weaver gets used to the relation of the harnesses, which are all marked by crosses.

Method No. 4: Here the notes of the draft are numbered according to their harnesses to make it easy to thread the loom: #1, a thread on H. 1; #2, a thread on H. 2; #1, a thread on H. 1; #2, a thread on H. 2; #3, a thread on H. 3, and so on. These are just harness numbers, not the number of times to thread each note. Progress right to left no matter what the number, moving to the square at the left of each preceding square.

Method No. 5: This is a method used in some Scandinavian books. Only four lines of the graph are used instead of five. Each line represents a harness and the circles designate notes on the draft (Hs. 1,2,1,2,3,2,3,2, and so on).

The tie-up is given at the right with crosses also at the intersections of the lines, Tr. 1: Hs. 1 and 2, and so on. Likewise, the weaving plan **L**, below thé tie-up, is written on the lines, not between them. The first star indicates that you should weave a row of pattern on Tr. 1. Reading downward, this is followed by a dash on Tr. 6 for Tabby, a star on Tr. 2 for Pattern, and a dash on Tr. 5 for Tabby.

Tabby is not usually given, however. In Method 5, the weaving plan without Tabby is given below this short indication of Tabby. You can weave any treadle as many times as you desire, but each should be followed by Tabby.

Method No. 6: This is the profile system of writing a draft.

Each square on H. 1 refers to Block 1, Hs. 1 and 2.

Each square on H. 2 refers to Block 2, Hs. 2 and 3.

Each square on H. 3 refers to Block 3, Hs. 3 and 4.

Each square on H. 4 refers to Block 4, Hs. 4 and 1.

This draft then reads: 2 squares on H. 1 or Hs. 1-2 twice (Hs. 1,2,1,2); 3 squares on H. 2 or Hs. 2-3 three times (Hs. 2,3,2,3,2,3). Since Block 1 ended on H. 2, omit this at the start of Block 2. This kind of overlapping occurs in this method, but you should realize this and omit the duplicate harness note.

Method No. 7: In this method, a tiny vertical dash is used for each note on the draft. You can read this as Hs. 1,2,1,2; 3,2,3,2,3,2; 1,2,1,2,1,4 and so on. You will find the draft in Method 1 corresponds perfectly. At the end, one dash has been omitted to finish after last repeat on Hs. 1,2,1, without another H. 2 being added.

Method No. 8: This is a quicker way of writing Method 7. It shows that in the first vertical section at the right there are 2 notes on H. 1, 2 notes on H. 2, and so on, exactly as written in Method 7.

Method No. 9: This is the same as Method 7, except that instead of a dash, each note is given a number. This method is helpful because it shows on which harness each block begins and where it ends. Block 1 (Hs. 1,2,1,2) has four notes, and is therefore written 4,2. Block 2 has six notes, starts on H. 3 with #1, ends on H. 2 with #6, and is written

5,3,1

6,4,2.

Method No. 10: This is an abbreviated form of Method 9, with the first and last numbers of each block in their rightful places. The last number designates the number of warps in the group. For example, #4 in first group means four notes in this block, the fourth one ending on H. 2. In the next block, the first thread is placed on H. 3, the sixth on H. 2, and so on. This is a logical and easy method to write and to follow.

39—Thread Sizes, Counts, and Yardage, and costs of Hand-Woven Fabrics

‹‹‹

Sizes and Yardage per Pound of Weaving Threads

IT IS USEFUL to know how the different threads are given their **size numbers**, what the **ply of a yarn** means, and how to figure the **number of yards per pound** of thread. It is necessary for a weaver to know the number of yards per pound in the thread he is using, in order to estimate what fraction of a pound he needs for warp and weft and the resulting cost. The names of our American threads and their measurement date back to olden days in England. There are simple rules to follow for determining the properties of each kind of thread.

Thread Sizes of Cotton

A hank of cotton consists of 840 yards, and this is the unit of measure for cotton sizes. The **size** of the yarn, such as size No. 20, is figured by the **number of hanks** necessary to make a **pound.** For size No. 20, which is very fine, it takes 20 hanks 840 yards long, or 16,800 yards, to make a pound. After using the different sizes of threads, we grow accustomed to the feeling of size No. 20 as having a certain diameter when we roll it between our thumb and forefinger. **Size** then refers to the **thickness** of the strand of thread as well as to the **number of hanks** necessary

to make a **pound.** The **lower** the number, the **heavier** the yarn. Sizes No. 3 and 5 of cotton, and carpet warp 8/4 are coarse; sizes No. 20, 24/3, and 30/2 are fine, and have many more yards per pound than have the coarse threads.

It will be noticed that in some cases the size of a yarn is written as a fraction, such as size 24/3. The upper part of this fraction refers to the size of the yarn; the lower part refers to what is termed its "ply."

The Ply of Yarn

The **ply** of the yarn refers to its spinning construction. If it consists of a single strand produced by the first spinning of the fibers, it is called **singles yarn.** Such yarn has very little twist and should **not** be used for warp. The size of singles yarn is written as a whole number, such as size 16, size 20, or size 30.

Most weaving yarns consist of two or more of these single strands twisted together, and are therefore called **2-ply** or **2-strand, 3-ply, 4-ply,** etc. This number of the ply of a yarn is written as the part of a fraction under or after its size. Thus, we write size 20/2 ply or size 40/3 ply. If the words "size" and "ply" are left off, we have the number as it is usually given. Thus, cotton 20/2 means a yarn consisting of 2 strands of size 20; or carpet warp 8/4 means a yarn with 4 strands of size

8. The **ply** of a yarn, therefore, refers to the **number of strands** found in a cross-section of the yarn.

Figuring the Number of Yards per Pound of Cotton Yarn

If a cotton yarn is a **singles**, which has only one strand, you can find its yardage simply by multiplying 840, the number of yards in one hank, by its size, i.e., the number of hanks required for one pound. Thus, for size 20, the yardage is 840×20, or 16,800. If the yarn is a **ply-yarn**, or consists of two or more strands, it will be thicker and will therefore have less yardage per pound. For example, cotton 20/2, consisting of 2 strands of size 20, will have half as many yards as the regular singles 20. Therefore, to find its number of yards, we divide 16,800 (the yardage of singles 20) by 2, giving us 8,400 yards in a pound of cotton 20/2. Likewise, cotton 20/3, with 3 strands of size 20, will have one-third as many yards as the regular singles 20, or $1/3 \times 16,800$. In other words, there are 5,600 yards to a pound of cotton 20/3.

The rule for finding the number of yards in a pound of any size of cotton yarn is as follows: Multiply 840 by the count or size, and then divide by the ply. For instance, to find the yardage of cotton size 24/3, first multiply 840 by 24 and get 20,160; and then divide by 3 and obtain 6,720 yd per lb.

Thread Sizes of Linen

A **unit of linen** consists of 300 yards, and the size of a linen thread is figured by the number of 300-yard hanks that it takes to make a pound. Again, the lower the number of the yarn, the coarser its size. Size 10 obviously takes fewer hanks 300 yards long to make a pound than

does size 20; and size 20/3 linen takes one-third as many yards as singles size 20. The method of obtaining the yardage for linen is similar to that for cotton.

The rule is as follows: To obtain the yardage of linen thread, multiply 300 by the count and divide by the ply. For instance, to find the yardage of linen size 40/2, multiply 300 by 40 and divide by 2, getting 6,000 yd per lb.

Unit of Measure for Wools

It was past practice to regard a woolen skein as consisting of 256 yards, and the number of skeins which a pound of woolen fibers made when it was spun or drawn out to a certain size was known as the "count" of the yarn. Thus, if 1 pound of wool was drawn out to make ten skeins 256 yards long, this yarn was called a 10-skein yarn; it contained 2,560 yards. If the wool were spun still finer so that it made twenty skeins 256 yards long, it was called a 20-skein yarn; it consisted of 5,120 yards. The finer it was spun, the more skeins per pound it produced.

However, in the case of wools, we cannot rely on any definite count today, for various systems of counting were established in different parts of the world, and we find 200-yard, 300-yard and 400-yard skeins, as well as the traditional 256-yard skeins. Furthermore, wools stretch at different tensions, and it is hard to determine their exact yardage or count. Today wools are sold in 1-ounce, 2-ounce, and 4-ounce skeins or balls. The best method for obtaining the yardage per pound of a kind of wool is to measure off 1 ounce and to multiply this measured yardage by 16, the number of ounces in a pound. When measuring an ounce of wool in this way, be careful to stretch the yarn at a uniform tension as you proceed.

Unit of Measure for Silk

Silk is the one natural fiber in the world that comes already spun when found in Nature, for a strand of raw silk, issuing from the mouth of the silkworm, really consists of two filaments spun together. In a fine strand of sewing silk there are ten or more of these raw silk threads, all twisted together to make the strong usable thread. The filaments of silk have great tensile strength and will stretch somewhat before breaking. Silk is said to have a tensile strength equivalent to that of steel wire of the same weight; it has considerable elasticity also.

Silk is used less in weaving than any other fiber, and is rarely prepared especially for hand weavers. Its counts are given in the sewing silk trade. In the silk industry the weight, in drams, per 1,000 yards of silk gives the accepted count, which is spoken of as the "deniers" or measure of the silk in question. A dram is equivalent to $\frac{1}{16}$ ounce. In silks, as in all measurements of yarn and their counting and numbering, the higher the count the finer the yarn; for the count refers to the number of skeins or units per pound, and the finer the thread is spun, the more of these there will be. Thus, in silks, size No. 80 is much finer than size No. 50.

Measuring Raytones and Synthetic Threads

To guide one in using the many beautiful synthetic threads made today, as well as those yarns made by combining natural fibers with synthetic fibers, manufacturers of synthetic yarns generally state the number of yards per pound. If they do not, measure off 1 ounce and compute the yardage per pound.

The Texture of the Woven Piece

The question is often asked, "Can articles of fine dainty quality be woven on a large floor loom?" The **texture** of a piece of weaving depends on the **number of threads per inch** in the reed and on the **size of thread** used, and not on the size of the loom. Large looms can have either coarse or fine reeds to make either coarse or fine material. The same is true of small looms; the fabrics woven on them may be either coarse or fine according to the reed used. Texture has a very important effect on the beauty and durability of handwoven cloth.

Texture may be viewed from two aspects—touch and appearance. Handwoven articles have a distinctive "feel" because of the choice and manipulation of the yarns. You may have smooth wool suiting, silky stoles that cling to the body, downy blankets that envelop you with soft-textured warmth.

Viewed from a visible aspect, texture is equally important. It is not only what we feel, but what we see. Fabric colors and shades and the reflection of the woven threads give the handwoven its look— an impression in textiles comparable to the artist's expression on canvas. I have seen Herringbone textures that remind me of the peaked evergreens on a northwestern mountain and filmy handwrought laces that look like the fluffy white clouds in the sky.

There is a definite trend today in which the handwoven has its appeal because of a "blend" of factors, not because of any definite color or texture or pattern. In other words, many modern fabrics may be called impressionistic rather than definable. Certain selected color tones and texture tones in a particular setting com-

(*Courtesy Elsa Frielinghaus*)

Fig. 146—Plaid textures are as interesting as plaid colors. This heavy textured fabric is in tones of white.

bine to give the fabric that indefinable something that makes it pleasing or functional or both.

Although the handweaver may have something specific in mind when he begins to weave, he soon realizes that weaving any one object is merely a key opening the door to an expanding world of the formation of textile surfaces. He experiences increasing freedom because he is in control of the textures, the tones, the colors, the thread settings, and the pattern effects.

The Width of the Woven Piece

The width of cloth it is possible to weave on any loom depends on the width of the reed. The size of the loom is named by the width of the reed. Thus, a loom holding a 32-in. reed or weaving cloth of that width, is called a 32-in. loom. A wide reed can make cloth as wide as its own width less a small amount for shrinkage, and it can make any width of cloth less than this—even a small strip as narrow as a bookmark.

On a wide loom, one can weave the full width and any width narrower than this. On a 42-in. loom one can successfully weave belts 2 in. wide or table cloths or baby blankets 42 in. wide. If one has a narrow loom, however, one is definitely limited to articles within the range of the width of its reed.

Allowing for Shrinkage of Woven Material Crosswise or from Selvage to Selvage

On any loom, wide or narrow, always allow from 1 inch to 2 inches for shrinkage of the cloth between selvages when it is taken from the loom. The reed holds the cloth out to nearly its full width when it is being woven; but, as the material is wound on the cloth-roller, no longer near its reed, the warp threads are drawn closer together by the elasticity of the weft threads.

Some weavers use a device for spreading and holding the finished weaving out to full width. This is called a "temple," and it is an adjustable pair of bars fastened between the selvages of the cloth just in front of the unwoven warp threads. It helps considerably in preventing the elastic weft from drawing the warp threads in too far. However, the same result may be achieved by leaving the weft thread on a slant, as described in Lesson 6. In either case when the fabric is taken from the loom it is always quite a bit narrower than when held taut on the loom. This is the unavoidable shrinkage of hand-woven material.

The amount of shrinkage depends partly on the setting of the warp threads. If these are set far apart, the cloth will shrink more after weaving than if they are set close together. The shrinkage also depends on the character of the weft thread; if this is flexible and elastic in character, you must figure on greater shrinkage than otherwise. Some materials shrink a great deal more than others. Wools shrink more than cottons; cottons shrink more than linens, which are wiry and have practically no "give." A linen weft tends to hold the warp out to a greater width than does a cotton weft on this same warp. The shrinkage of the woven cloth from edge to edge is also controlled by the manner of laying in the weft rows. If the weaver is careful to leave each row on a slant to give the weft plenty of length when packed close with the beater, the material will shrink less than if he weaves his rows tightly from side to side.

Shrinkage Measured Lengthwise or Along the Warp Threads

It is neecssary to allow for a certain amount of shrinkage along the length of any hand-woven material after it is removed from the loom, where it was necessarily kept at some tension for its successful weaving. All threads, even the firmest and most wiry, have a certain amount of stretch to them. Moreover, all weft threads, even the finest, cause the warp to go over and under them as they are wedged down between the sheds, and this causes considerable take-up right along.

It requires some experience and the keeping of records over a long period of time to know exactly how much the various materials being made by a hand weaver shrink. It is customary to allow 12 to 15 per cent for loss in the length of rug warps; an inch per foot along the length of fine cotton warps being woven as doilies or towels; and as much as 8 or 10 per cent for loss of length on almost any type of hand-woven texture.

How to Figure the Cost of Finished Hand-Woven Material

The cost of a finished piece of hand-woven material is obtained as follows: First find the number of yards of thread in the **warp** and the number in the **weft**; figure what fraction of a pound each length is; and multiply that result by the price per pound. Then add the two products. If one plans to **sell** one's product, he should also add the **time value** for warping, threading, and weaving, as well as the overhead of his weaving room, including light, heat, and similar items of expense. After the total is found, he should add a percentage for profit.

How to Figure the Warp per Yard of Cloth: Count the number of threads across the warp, and take this as the number of yards of warp in 1 yard of cloth. If there are 400 warp threads, 1 yard of cloth will contain 400 yards of thread. Divide this into the number of yards per pound to get the fraction of a pound used. Then take this portion of the cost per pound.

How to Figure the Weft per Yard of Cloth: If the weft is of the same size and material as the warp, the cost of the weft is easy to figure when one is weaving Plain Weave, for there are about the same number of threads in 1 inch of weft as in 1 inch of warp. They should be evenly balanced for the best and most durable texture, and hence the amount of each can be estimated as about the same. Therefore, in one yard of cloth having 400 warp threads, there would be about 400 yards of weft thread, or a total of 800 yards of warp and weft.

If the weft material is different from that of the warp, figure as follows:

1. Count the number of threads of weft woven along 1 in. of warp; for ex-

ample, assume that there are 9 threads.

2. Count the number of inches across the warp, or the distance to be covered by one row of weft. Let this distance be 10 in.

3. To get the amount of weft thread to be used for 1 inch of weaving, multiply 10 inches for each time across by 9 threads of weft used in 1 inch. The product is 90 in., or 2½ yd, which is the length of weft required for 1 inch of weaving.

4. To get the amount of thread needed for weaving 1 yard of cloth, multiply the length used in 1 inch by 36, the number of inches in a yard. The result in this case is $2\frac{1}{2} \times 36$, or 90 yd.

5. To get the fraction of a pound required, consult the Thread Chart in Lesson 35 for the number of yards in 1 pound of this material. Suppose that we are using Homespun, which is not so heavy as Germantown and has 1,620 yd per lb. The weight needed for 90 yards of thread is $\frac{90}{1,620}$ or $\frac{1}{18}$ lb. Thus, the cost of $\frac{1}{18}$ lb (which is less than 1 oz) of Homespun would be added to the cost of the warp, to get the total cost of a finished yard of woven goods. If the Homespun is priced at $3.60 per lb, $\frac{1}{18}$ lb would cost $.20.

Allowing for Pattern Weft: When weaving with Pattern threads in addition to the Plain Weave background threads, one must add three items together to get the total cost of the material:

1. The total yardage and cost of the warp.

2. The total yardage and cost of the Tabby weft (usually the same as the warp).

3. The yardage and cost of the Pattern thread, figured as just described for weft material that is different from the warp.

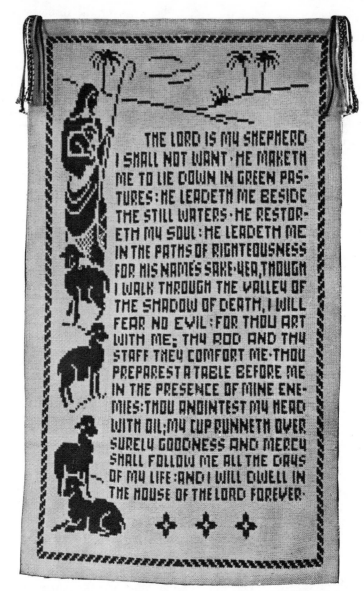

(Courtesy of Elva Slider)

A wall panel woven in the famous Double Weave supposed to have been invented in Finland, and hence called the "Finnweave." The effectiveness of this weave depends upon a perfect balance between warp and weft threads, each having the same count per inch. The panel was woven on a four-harness loom and is a delightful project for a month's creative work. The narrow band which holds the panel is an example of Egyptian card weaving.

40—Thread Chart of Warp Settings and Suitable Wefts

The Use of the Thread Chart

WHEN PLANNING a hand-woven fabric, an important consideration is the setting of the threads, or the number of threads per inch, in the finished fabric. The proper number depends both on the size and character of the threads used and on the texture desired.

For every kind of warp thread, there is a certain setting by the use of which the weft threads may be beat down across the warp threads to make a Plain Weave texture with the "count" or number of threads to an inch of weft the same as the number of threads to an inch of warp. This texture is known as a "fifty-fifty" balance of warp and weft threads. There is formed an even in-and-out grain like the texture of a linen handkerchief, and the fabric appears the same when viewed lengthwise or crosswise. The warp and the weft are equally exposed, and the character and color tone of one modify those of the other.

In the Thread Chart on pages 288 to 291, inclusive, we have attempted to give the perfect Tabby setting for each of the various warp threads. On either side of this mean or average setting are variations. Using fewer threads per inch produces a fabric with the warp threads set further apart. If the number is reduced enough, only the weft shows as it is beat down into the wide spaces and the fabric is known as **weft-surface fabric.** Increasing the number of threads per inch pro-

duces a fabric with the warp threads closer together. If they are so close that they practically touch and completely cover the weft threads, except at the selvages, the fabric is known as **warp-surface fabric.** In between the two extremes, there are many possible settings of any one kind of warp thread, and each setting will produce a different textural effect. However, it is generally conceded that the mean setting necessary for a "fifty-fifty" fabric is the one which looks the best, wears the best, and launders the best. This setting is possible not only for the Tabby Weave, either when used alone or when underlying a Pattern Weave, but also for the Twill and its variations; in fact, it may be used for the characteristic background texture of any threading.

One may feel safe in following the Thread Chart given here, and may even take the liberty to make changes that may seem desirable as soon as one becomes somewhat experienced and thread conscious. Just as one paints with threads to get color in weaving, one may also vary the counts in the warp and weft at will to achieve beautiful textures.

Plan of the Thread Chart

The Thread Chart on pages 288 to 291 shows the divisions into which finished hand-woven articles are usually grouped; i.e., it lists the various kinds of wearing apparel and household fabrics which prove practical either for one's own use

THREAD CHART OF PROPER THREAD SETTINGS FOR DURABLE HAND-WOVEN FABRICS

Wearing Apparel

Name of Article	Kind of Warp	Yards per Pound	Threads per Inch	Pattern Weft	Tabby Weft	Suitable Threadings
Suit and Dress Fabrics						
1. All Wool						
A. Fine: Dresses, Blouses, Scarves, Neckties, Kerchiefs	Fabri yarn / Weavewool / Fine 2- or 3-ply yarn / Fine Homespun	4800 / 4200 / 4000 / 3600	22 to 26 / 20 to 24 / 20 to 24 / 18 to 22	Preferably None	Single weft: Same yarn as warp, or yarn of same grist. Weft yarn may also be a bit heavier than warp.	1. Tabby planned for same number of weft threads as warp threads per inch. Designs planned in stripes, in plaids, or by the addition of texture threads. 2. Four-harness Twills and variations such as Rosepath, Herringbone, Three Twills, Goose-Eye, Shepherds' Check, and Dornick. 3. Bronson for fine or medium fabrics; also Log Cabin. 4. Eight-harness Twills and variations.
B. Medium: Skirts, Turbans, Blouses, Scarves, Neckties	Fabri yarn / Weavewool / Medium 2- or 3-ply yarn / Medium Homespun	4800 / 4200 / 3600 / 3200	20 to 24 / 20 to 24 / 18 to 22 / 16 to 20	Preferably None	Somewhat heavier than warp for medium texture.	
C. Coarse: Overcoats, Trousers, etc.	Woolspun / Coarse Homespun	2000 / appr. 1600	15 to 18 / 12 to 16	Preferably None	Same weight as warp.	
2. Linen Dress Goods (All or Half Linen)						1. If using Pattern and Tabby thread, choose very short overshots, such as Monk's Belt, Miniature Patterns, Small Diamond, Rosepath, and Tiny Rose. 2. For the best summer suiting effects, thread to Tabby or Twill and variations. Achieve design by planning color or texture stripes in warp or weft or both. Good threadings are Three Twills, Shepherds' Check, Dornick, Crepe, and Raindrops. 3. Fine openwork textures result from the use of Bronson. 4. Summer and Winter or Crackle may be used for firm texture suits and jackets. Note: Since cotton fabrics shrink more than linen, all-cotton fabrics may be expected to have the most shrinkage; half-linen fabrics, less; and all-linen fabrics, still less.
A. Fine	Linen 50/2 / Linen 40/2	7500 / 6000	32 to 40 / 30 to 32	Cotton Perle 10 / Fine Linen Floss	Same kind of thread as warp, or same weight.	
B. Medium	Linen 30/2 / Linen 25/2	4500 / 3750	24 to 30 / 20 to 24	Cotton Perle 5 / Linen Floss		
C. Heavy	Linen 20/2 / Linen 18/2	3000 / 2700	18 to 20 / 15 to 18	Cotton 10/3 / Linen 20/3 or 10/2		
3. Cotton Dress Goods						
A. Fine	Cotton 24/2 / Cotton Perle 20	10080 / 8400	32 to 40 / 30 to 36	Cotton Perle 10 / Spun Silk	Same kind of thread as warp, or same weight.	
B. Medium	Cotton 24/3 / Cotton 20/3	6720 / 5040	24 to 30 / 20 to 24	Cotton Perle 5 / Cotton 10/3 or 20/6		
C. Coarse	Cotton 10/3 or 20/6 / Cotton Perle 5	2800 / 2100	15 to 22 / 15 to 20	Cotton Perle 3 / Perle Floss		
4. Half Linen and Cotton (Cotton Warp; Linen Weft)						
A. Fine	Cotton 24/2 / Cotton 20/2	10080 / 8400	32 to 40 / 30 to 36	Cotton Perle 10 / Fine Floss	Linen 20/1 / Linen 40/2 or 50/2	
B. Medium	Cotton 24/3 / Cotton 20/3	6720 / 5040	24 to 30 / 20 to 24	Cotton Perle 5 / Cotton 10/3 or 20/6	Linen 14/1 / Linen 12/1	
C. Coarse	Cotton 16/3 / Cotton 16/4	4480 / 3360	18 to 24 / 15 to 20	Cotton Perle 3 / Heavy Floss	Linen 20/2 / Linen 10/1	
Knitting Bags, Purses						1. Summer and Winter or Crackle. 2. Texture Threadings: Crepe, Rosepath, Raindrops, etc. 3. One-Thread Weaves, such as Twill and variations; Bronson with Tabby. 4. Short Overshot Threadings. 5. Tabby, with Laid-in figures, monograms, etc.
A. Medium Weight	Cotton 24/3 / Cotton 10/2 / Linen 40/3	6720 / 4200 / 4000	20 to 28 / 20 to 24 / 18 to 24	Cotton Perle 5 / Cotton 10/3 or 20/6 / Wool, Medium	Same weight thread as warp.	
B. Heavy Weight	Cotton Perle 3 / Carpet Warp	1260 / 1200 to 1600	10 to 16 / 10 to 16	Cotton, 4-Strand Navy Cord / Coarse Wool / Silk or Linen Floss	Same weight thread as warp.	

Belts

Use	Warp			Weft	Weft Thread	Weaves / Remarks
A. Medium Weight	Cotton 16/3 Cotton 16/4 Cotton 10/3 or 20/6 Cotton Perle 5 Wool, Well Spun	4480 3360 2800 2100 1600 to 2000	20 to 26 18 to 24 16 to 22 15 to 20 16 to 20	Cotton Perle 3 Cotton Crochet Linen 20/3 Wool, Medium Homespun	Same weight as warp or somewhat heavier if only one weft is used.	1. Tabby and Twill. 2. Small Pattern Threadings. 3. Summer and Winter or Crackle. 4. International Belt Weaves: Hungarian, Peruvian, Canadian, etc. 5. Warp-surface textures (no reed). 6. Weft-surface textures with Tapestry or Laid-in figures. 7. Egyptian Card Weaving. 8. Inkle Loom Weaving.
B. Heavy Weight	Carpet Warp 8/4 Germantown Cotton Perle 3	1600 1500 1260	10 to 16 8 to 16 8 to 16	Tufting Cotton Navy Cord Heavy Yarn	Same weight as warp.	

Household Fabrics

Table Wear, Towels, Runners

Use	Warp			Weft	Weft Thread	Weaves / Remarks
1. All Linen (Good Quality)						1. Use all-over texture patterns, such as Twill, Herringbone, Rosepath, Bronson, M's and O's, Goose-Eye, Huck (these are known as "one-thread weaves," and also as "one-shuttle weaves"). 2. Short Overshot Patterns with Tabby, such as Stepladder, Tiny Rose, Walden-weave, Honeysuckle, Butternut, Monk's Belt, Raindrops, World's Wonder, Remembrance. 3. Summer and Winter, and Crackle. 4. Also weave as Tabby for pure linen texture.
A. Fine Texture: Table Cloths, Doilies, Guest Towels, etc.	Linen 50/2 Linen 40/2 (grey) Linen 20/1 Linen 35/2	7500 6000 6000 5250	36 to 40 32 to 36 32 to 36 30 to 32	Linen of heavier weight than warp; 18/2 or 20/2	Linen 35/1, 30/1, 25/1, or 20/1; or same thread as warp.	
B. Medium Texture: Tray Cloths, Dresser Scarves, Doilies, Towels	Linen 30/2 Linen 40/3 Linen 25/2	4500 4000 3750	28 to 30 26 to 28 24 to 26	Heavier than warp; 20/3, 18/2, or Floss	20/1, 18/1, or 16/1; or same thread as warp.	
C. Coarse Texture: Towels, Chair Sets, Runners	Linen 20/2 Linen 18/2 Linen 20/3	3000 2700 2000	20 to 24 18 to 20 15 to 18	Heavier than warp; 20/3, 10/2, or Linen Floss	16/1, 14/1, or 10/1; or same thread as warp.	
2. Half-Linen (Cotton Warp; Linen Weft)—A durable, economical and handsome texture						1. Suitable threadings for half-linen textures are the same as those listed for all-linen textures. 2. On cotton warps of fine, medium, or coarse weight, regular linen weft threads—natural, white, or colored—are effective. Twill patterns or variations and patterns of short Overshot may be woven twill-fashion or as drawn in. 3. Linen wefts of nubby texture are effective. 4. Weave borders in self-tone against same color backgrounds.
A. Fine: Same uses as 1A	Cotton 30/2 Cotton 24/2 Cotton 20/2 Cotton Perle 20	12600 10080 8400 8400	32 to 40 30 to 36 30 to 32 30 to 32	Cotton 5/2; Perle 5; Perle 10 dbl; Cotton or Linen Floss	Linen 35/1, 30/1, 25/1, 20/1, 50/2, or 40/2.	
B. Medium: Same uses as 1B	Cotton 24/3 Cotton 16/3 Cotton 10/2 Cotton Perle 10	6720 4480 4200 4200	24 to 30 22 to 26 20 to 24 20 to 24	Cotton 10/3, 20/6, or 6-Strand Floss; Crochet Cotton; Linen 15/2	Linen 20/1, 18/1, 16/1, or 14/1; Cotton same as warp.	
C. Coarse: Same uses as 1C	Cotton 16/4 Cotton 10/3 Cotton 5/2 Cotton Perle 5	3360 2800 2100 2100	18 to 24 15 to 18 15 to 18 15 to 18	Cotton Perle 3, Floss, 20/6 dbl, or 4-Strand; Linen 20/3	Linen 12/1, 10/1, or 20/2; Cotton same as warp.	
3. All Cotton (A serviceable texture, satisfactory for home fabrics)						Same as for all-linen and half-linen.
A. Fine	Cotton 30/2 Cotton 24/2 Cotton 20/2 Cotton 20/3 Cotton Perle 20	12600 10080 8400 8400 8400	36 to 48 32 to 40 30 to 36 30 to 32 30 to 36	Cotton Perle 10, 10/2, Floss, or 20/3; Crochet Cotton; Perleen	Cotton 30/2, 24/2, 20/2, 30/3, or Perle 20.	
B. Medium	Cotton 24/3 Cotton 20/3 Cotton 16/3 Cotton 10/2	6720 5600 4480 4200	24 to 30 20 to 24 18 to 24 18 to 24	Cotton Perle 5, 5/2, 10/3, or 20/6	Cotton 30/3, 24/3, 20/3, or 10/2.	Same as for all-linen and half-linen. For medium-weight and coarse-weight cottons with heavy Pattern wefts, one may also thread to patterns such as Orange Peel, Cleveland Web, Small Diamond, Winding Vine, Hazelwood, Solomon's Seal.
C. Coarse	Cotton 16/4 Cotton 10/3 Cotton 20/6 Cotton 5/2	3360 2800 2800 2100	18 to 24 16 to 20 16 to 20 15 to 18	Cotton Perle 3, 10/3 dbl, 8/4 dbl, or Crochet Cotton dbl; Tufting Cotton	Cotton 16/3, 16/4, 10/3, or 5/2.	

Name of Article	Kind of Warp	Yards per Pound	Threads per Inch	Pattern Weft	Tabby Weft	Suitable Threadings
Upholstery, Pillows						
A. Fine (Fine upholstery is the same as fine coverlets)	Cotton 24/3 Linen 30/2 Linen 40/3	6700 4500 4000	24 to 30 20 to 30 18 to 24	Linen Floss; Well Spun Silk; Homespun	Cotton 24/3 or 10/2; Linen 30/2 or 40/2; Wool, 2-ply	1. Use all-over patterns with close pattern figurations, such as the one-thread weaves: Twill, Herringbone, Goose-Eye, Rosepath, Wheat Stitch, Broken Twills, Waffle, Bronson with Tabby, Damask.
B. Medium Weight	Linen 20/2 Wool, 2-ply	3000 3000 to 3600	15 to 24 15 to 20	Cotton 10/3; Medium Wool, or Perle 3		2. Summer and Winter; Crackle; Honeycomb Weave.
C. Heavy Weight	Cotton 16/4 Linen 20/3 Homespun Wool Cotton 8/4	3360 2000 appr. 2000 1200	15 to 24 15 to 20 15 to 18 12 to 16	Cotton 10/3 dbl; Linen 10/2; Linen Floss; Heavy Twisted Wool Yarn	Cotton 16/3 or 16/4; Linen 16/2, 18/2, or 20/2; Homespun Wool; Cotton 8/4	3. Overshot Patterns with blocks of limited size, no longer than ¾ in. to ⅞ in. and with no more than 10 to 12 thds.
Draperies and Sun Curtains						
1. Side Drapes A. Fine	Cotton 24/2 Cotton 20/2 Cotton 30/3 Cotton 24/3 Linen 40/2	10080 8400 8400 6720 6000	32 to 36 30 to 32 30 to 32 24 to 30 24 to 30	Cotton Perle 5, 20/6, or 10/3; Cotton, Silk, or Linen Floss; Wool, 2-ply	Cotton 24/2, 20/2, Perle 20, 30/3, or 24/3; Linen 20/1.	1. Tabby and Twill and its variations; Rosepath, Waffle, Huck, Bronson, M's and O's; one shuttle-weaves, weft the same weight as warp or very little heavier. Also use texture wefts. Make designs by adding colored or texture threads in warp on weft; or by lace or Laid-in techniques.
B. Medium	Cotton 20/3 Cotton 16/3 Cotton Perle 10/2 Linen 30/2 Linen 40/3	5040 4475 4200 4500 4000	20 to 24 18 to 24 18 to 24 18 to 26 18 to 24	Cotton Perle 3, 10/3 or 20/6, or 20/3; Melium Floss; Wool, 3-ply	Cotton 20/3, 16/3, or 10/2; Linen 30/2, 40/3, or 14/1	2. Pattern borders of medium size Overshot blocks, such as Monk's Belt, Honeysuckle, Solomon's Delight, Cleveland Web, Winding Vine, Chariot Wheel. 3. Summer and Winter or Crackle Weave for firm textures. 4. Openwork weaves, such as Bronson, Swedish Lace, Gauze, Leno, Mexican Lace, Danish Medallion, Spanish Openwork, Waffle.
C. Coarse and Heavy	Cotton 16/4 Cotton 10/3 or 20/6 Linen 20/2 Linen 20/3	3360 2800 3000 2000	15 to 20 12 to 20 15 to 20 12 to 18	Cotton, Perle 3 or Heavy Nubbed; Linen, 20/6; Wool, 4-ply	Cotton 16/4, 10/3, or 20/6; Linen 20/2, 20/3, or 15/2	5. Laid-in Weaves. 6. Confité Knots; Boutonnée Tufts.
2. Sun Curtains A. Fine	Cotton 30/2 Cotton 24/2 Cotton 20/2 or Perle 20 Cotton 30/3 Linen 50/2 Linen 40/2 or 20/1	12600 10080 8400 8400 7500 6000	30 to 40 24 to 36 24 to 30 24 to 30 20 to 30 18 to 24	No Pattern thread. Use weft same weight as warp or somewhat heavier. Beat lightly to form more open texture than customary.	Use weft same weight as warp.	1. Tabby and Twill. Weave as an all-over simple texture. Achieve design by stripes or crossbars or Laid-in texture threads. 2. One-thread weaves, such as Bronson, M's and O's, Twill variations; Broken Twills; Texture Weaves.
B. Medium	Cotton 24/3 Linen 30/2 Wool, 2-ply	6720 4500 appr. 4000	20 to 24 18 to 24 15 to 20	Wefts of nubby texture or unusual character may be used; but choose simple effects.		3. Lace and Laid-in Weaves, such as Mexican, Gauze, Danish, Spanish, Leno, Greek Lace, Brooks Bouquet.
Rugs						
1. Pattern Rugs Standard Weight	Cotton 8/4 Cotton 3/2 Linen 20/6	1600 1260 1000	12 to 16 10 to 16 8 to 16	*Pattern Weft* Rug Filler; Wool Rug Yarn; Looper Clips; Evenly cut Jersey or stockings; Heavy selvages from textile mills; Carefully cut cloth rags.	*Tabby Weft*	1. Summer and Winter patterns (4 to 8 harnesses); Crackle Weave; Matta Weave. 2. Four-harness Overshot patterns, such as Diamond, Whig Rose, Wheel of Fortune, Block Work, Maltese Cross, Pine Bloom, Chariot Wheel, Pond Lily.
Heavy Weight	Cotton 8/4 dbl Linen 10/5	600 600	4 to 10 4 to 10		Use weft same weight as warp.	3. Tapestry Designs, using colored wefts all of about the same weight.

Article	Warp	Yds. per lb.	Threads per inch	Weft	Pattern Thread	Weaving
2. Bath Mats; Hot Mats						Same types of patterns as for Pattern Rugs, but of smaller character. For Overshot patterns, use small Diamond; Orange Peel; Queen's Delight; Sun, Moon, and Stars; Dog Tracks; The Patch Patterns, Honeysuckle, Butternut.
Light Weight	Cotton 10/3 Cotton 5/2	2800 2100	18 to 24 15 to 20	Same weight as warp.		
Medium Weight	Cotton 8/4 Linen 20/6	1600 1000	12 to 18 10 to 16			
3. Rag Rugs				No Pattern. One weft of cut rags from cheap cottons or used clothing; Selvages from mills; Silk stockings; Jersey underwear; Looper Clips; Woolen rags; Thin carpets cut into strips.		Use Tabby, Twill, Matta, Log Cabin. Achieve color and design by striped rag borders on plain warps and backgrounds; or striped warps producing plaid effects.
Standard Weight	Cotton 8/4 Linen 20/6	1600 1000	10 to 16 8 to 16			
Heavy Weight	Cotton 8/4 dbl Linen 10/5	800 600	8 to 12 6 to 10			
4. Pile Rugs	Cotton 8/4 dbl Linen 10/5	800 600	8 to 12 6 to 10	Wool Rug Yarns; Rug Worsted; Smyrna Yarn; Braided Wool; Germantown double or triple.	Like warp or heavier.	Use Tabby and Twill Threadings to produce Plain Weave background. Achieve design by colored figures against contrasting backgrounds or clipped surfaces against unclipped backgrounds.
Coverlets; Drapes, Runners, and Pillows to Match				Wool is traditional coverlet weft, and wool coverlets must be used with antiques.		1. Traditional Colonial 4-harness Overshot Patterns, such as Double Bowknot, Chariot Wheel, Governor's Garden, Whig Rose, Rings and Flowers, Queen's Delight, Kentucky Garden, Lover's Knot. 2. Patterns of close texture, such as Summer and Winter, Crackle. 3. Patterns planned for Honeycomb Technique. 4. 8-Harness Summer and Winter.
A. Fine	Cotton 24/2 Cotton 20/2 Linen 50/2	10080 8400 7500	32 to 36 30 to 32 28 to 32	Wool, 2-ply; Fine Homespun; Cotton Perle 5, 16/4, or 10/3.	Cotton 24/2 or 20/2; Linen 20/1	
B. Medium	Cotton 24/3 Linen 40/2 Linen 30/2	6720 6000 4500	24 to 30 24 to 30 20 to 26	Wool, Medium; Homespun; Cotton 10/3, Floss, or 20/6	Cotton 24/3 or 10/2; Linen 25/1 or 30/2	
C. Coarse	Cotton 16/3 Cotton 16/4 Linen 25/2	4480 3360 3750	18 to 24 16 to 22 18 to 24	Wool, heavy; Homespun; Cotton Perle 3; Crochet Cotton.	Cotton 16/3 or 16/4; Linen 25/2	
Blankets, etc.						1. Plain Weave with stripes in weft or in warp, or in both, forming plaids. 2. One-thread weaves, such as Twill, Herringbone, Goose-Eye, Rosepath, Three-Twills, Raindrops, Crepe; Small Texture Patterns, such as Bronson, M's and O's.
1. Regular Household Blankets						
A. Fine	Wool, 2-ply Fine Homespun Cotton, 20/6	4800 2800	20 to 24 18 to 20	No Pattern. Use weft like warp or wool a bit heavier.		
B. Medium	Wool, Shetland Wool, Homespun	2300 2000	15 to 18 15 to 16	Soft yarns, same weight as warp or a bit heavier.		
C. Heavy	Woolspun Germantown Coarse Homespun Knitting Worsted Peasant Wool	2000 1500 1200 1100 1000	12 to 16 8 to 12 8 to 10 6 to 8 6 to 8	Same yarn as warp or same weight and grist.		
2. Baby Blankets						1. Plain Weave with stripes or plaids in delicate pastel colors or texture threads. 2. One-thread weaves, such as Bronson, Twill, Herringbone, Rosepath, Raindrops; Small Texture Patterns, such as M's and O's, Lace Weaves. 3. Dainty Colonial Coverlet Patterns such as Whig Rose, Sweet-Briar Beauty, Four-Leaf Clover, Sugar Loaf, "Guess Me."
A. Fine	Fabri Yarn Weavewool	4800 4200	20 to 24 20 to 24	If Pattern thread is used: Shetland; Saxony; 2-ply Yarn	Same as warp or same weight and grist.	
B. Medium	Fine Peasant Yarn Crewell Wool Shetland	4000 appr. 3600	18 to 24 16 to 20	Yarn same weight as or slightly coarser than warp.	Same weight as warp.	
C. Coarse	Woolspun Germantown Homespun	2000 1500 1200	12 to 16 8 to 10 8 to 10	Yarn same weight as or slightly coarser than warp.	Same weight as warp.	
3. Sheets and Pillow Cases	Cotton 24/2 Linen 50/2	10080 7500	36 to 48 32 to 40	No Pattern thread.	Same thread or same weight thread as warp.	Plain Weave or Twill woven as Tabby.

or for sale. The Chart gives the names of the kinds of warps to use for each class of article, the number of yards per pound for each kind of warp, the number of warp threads per inch to set, suggestions for the kinds of Pattern and Tabby threads to use, and a group of practical threadings.

Certain fabrics, such as table linens and suitings, are usually planned as one-thread weaves. In such a weave, no separate Pattern weft is used, but there is a single weft which serves for both Pattern and Tabby. This manner of weaving is used not only for Tabby but also for many textures like the Twill and its variations and for unique weaves like the Bronson and M's and O's which when woven form a fine pattern surface of definite design without the addition of a separate Pattern thread. Everyone recognizes at sight the attractive grain of the Twill in serge cloth, or the lovely lights and shadows of the Herringbone Weave, whether this appears in towels or table linen or in the woolen cloth of a man's overcoat. In addition, the one-thread weaves are very practical and profitable to use, since one does not need to shift between two shuttles, and time and energy are thus saved. Where there is no separate Pattern thread, the space of the Chart usually given to suggestions for Pattern and Tabby threads is in some cases devoted to a description of the preferred kind of weft to use when one is weaving with only one thread.

For any thread given in the Chart, one may substitute a thread of the same grist or size and character, provided it also has the same structure. For instance, 40/2 and 20/1 linen are of the same size, 6,000 yards per pound; and one might think at first sight that they would be interchangeable. However, a "singles" or one-strand thread, such as the linen 20/1, is seldom used for warp, as it is not so well spun as a two-strand or two-ply thread and tends to fray and break as the beater passes back and forth over it. With rare exceptions, then, we save our singles threads for Tabby weft on a warp of the same size but having a two-strand structure. It is all right, for example, to use linen 40/2 for warp and to cross it with linen 20/1 as weft. A correct substitute for 40/2 warp would be 60/3 linen, equally firm and well spun and of the same size and number of yards per pound.

The same principle is true of singles wool yarn and of those two-ply wools which are too loosely spun to hold when stretched taut for warp or which might tend to fray when subjected to the friction of adjacent warp threads and the constant rubbing of the beater.

With these precautions, one may still make logical substitutions for the threads listed in the Chart. Thus, one may use cotton 20/6 ply in place of cotton 10/3 ply; cotton 20/4 ply in place of cotton 10/2 ply; and so on. One may also change the suggested settings slightly to achieve woven surfaces of either more open or closer texture. It may be preferable to place Fabri yarn at 20 threads per inch for soft shawls instead of at 24 per inch, the setting best for neckties.

The weaver should use the Thread Chart more as a guide to lead him into the varieties and beauties of hand-woven textures than as a set table of hard and fast rulings.

41—Practical Projects for Hand-Woven Fabrics

<!-- decorative border -->

Use of Hand-Woven Fabrics

A LOOM in a home is productive of the finest and most serviceable fabrics at the lowest cost. The quality and beauty of these fabrics excel in many ways those available in stores. Their texture and color may be such as to enhance the individuality and charm of the decorations. With a wide range of carefully graduated colors to choose from, the hand weaver creates material in the manner of the true artist, using his shuttle in ever-changing color and design as he paints with threads.

Not only can hand-woven articles be made to blend with any color scheme or act as an accent of unique beauty, but hand-woven fabrics have another quality which makes them stand alone in household value—they may be made in any size whatever to cover spaces of unusual shape. Instead of purchasing cut materials requiring hemming and a design adjustment, one plans exactly the right width and length for a mantlepiece, end table, or card table; or for book covers, wall hangings, or draperies. He designs them and weaves them with even, smooth selvages that lie flat and require no hemming. Sets of luncheon doilies may be made to fill the table surface to perfection; towels may be woven large or small to suit one's preference; coverlets and blankets may have that extra foot of length or width that gives them a look

of complete elegance rather than scantiness of coverage.

In Scandinavian countries, as well as in Canada and in some far-sighted communities of the United States and Mexico, it is the custom for the men to design and make furniture in the home or school shop and to cover this with fabrics woven by women or girls. Three projects may thus be united—carpentry, hand weaving, and upholstery. In Fig. 147 is shown upholstery material used on furniture made in a school shop.

Wearing apparel tailored from hand-woven fabrics is beyond compare in elegance, coloring, and distinction. Suitings, dresses, scarves, skirts, aprons, and neckties may all be designed for the express purpose of bringing out individual coloring and complexion.

Hand-woven fabrics may also be used to make attractive items suitable for gifts or to sell commercially. Their lovely colors and textures render them desirable for many purposes. Even the waste cuttings from hand-woven neckties, scarves, or suits may be used to cover small boxes, books, or cardboard trays, or simply made into small flower-vase mats or bookmarks.

On the pages following are some practical projects for the use of hand-woven pieces.

Specially Planned Guest Book

One of the most useful and interesting of gifts is a hand-woven book cover. One

Fig. 147—Handwoven upholstery material used on furniture made in a school shop.

can, of course, cut and sew a cover from any material; but a woven strip, planned just the right shape and size for a certain book, is superior. To create an unusual yet inexpensive guest book, purchase a simple notebook and add the hand-woven cover with its interesting design and rich-looking texture.

Plan and Proportions: In weaving the fabric for a cover, allow for shrinkage; and be sure to wash the fabric carefully and press it before making the cover, so that no further shrinkage will occur. Set the width of the warp, allowing ½ in. of regular shrinkage for each 6 in. of width, and allowing ¼ in. to provide for sewing edges and the thickness of the book cover.

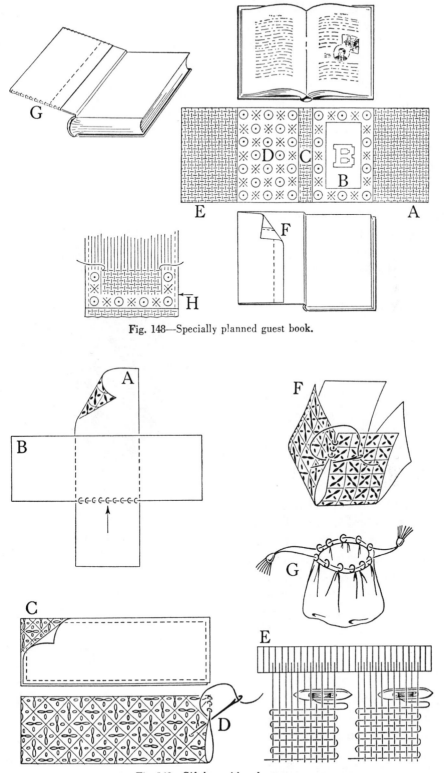

Fig. 148—Specially planned guest book.

Fig. 149—Gift bag with a dozen uses.

Weave section A, Fig. 148, of plain Tabby for the inside of the front cover; weave section B with a border of Pattern around an open space, where one can lay-in an initial if desired; weave section C in Pattern Weave or heavy Tabby, for the back of the book; weave section D of solid Pattern Weave to go over the back cover of the book; and weave section E like A, to turn under the back cover. Hem the ends of sections A and E back in a 1-in. hem, as at F; then fold section A back on B, and overcast their edges; and fold E back on D, and overcast the edges, as at G.

How to Weave the Center Front Panel: Weave as far as H, arrow, with solid Pattern Weave; then take separate pattern wefts at the right and left selvages and, for each row, lay-in these two wefts on the regular pattern shed, but only up to a certain point, which must be the same on each side. For each treadle combination you may have a different warp thread to reverse around; but you can plan the reverses within four warp threads so that the Pattern border will adhere to a fairly true vertical line. When the open space at the center reaches the desired point, proceed with solid Pattern Weave again. It is also possible to weave an initial by the laid-in method at the center of the front of the cover, as shown by the initial B; but this should not be done until one has made one cover and mastered the side border principle.

Gift Bag

The very useful bag in Fig. 149 may be used for cosmetics if lined with waterproof material; or it makes a smart looking handy bag for accessories when shopping. It is also excellent for holding sewing items. Two practical bags are shown in Fig. 150.

Make the bag of two strips of fabric, A and B in Fig. 150, woven as a solid pattern repeat. For the strips, divide a 13-in. warp into two equal parts each 6½ in. wide. Re-sley in the reed so that there is a space 2 in. wide between them at the

Fig. 150—Handwoven bags make useful containers. Braided handles may be woven right into the cloth for strength.

center of the reed, with no threads passing through (see E). One can weave the two strips side by side at the same time in this way, using two sets of shuttles. One can, of course, weave a single strip of material 13 in. wide and cut it into two equal pieces; but it is really easier and it makes a neater article to weave two separate strips, which can be made exactly alike and can have smooth selvages and planned borders.

Patterns to Use: For small bags of this kind, use small Overshot repeats, such as Diamond, Monk's belt, Tiny Wheel,

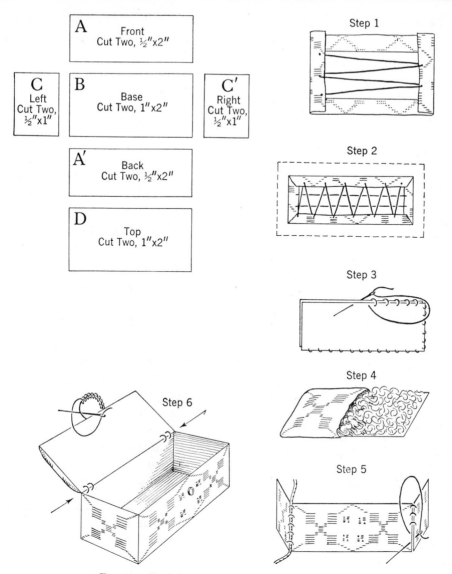

Fig. 151—Small box covered with handwoven material.

Cleveland Web, Butternut, Honeysuckle or Remembrance.

Directions for Making: Weave the two strips, **A** and **B**, 21 in. long and 6½ in. wide. When finished they will shrink down to 20 in. long and 6 in. wide. Cut two pieces of silk lining the same size (see **C**). Line both strips, turn to the right side, and whip the ends together, as at **D**. Lay the strips across each other, as at **A**, **B**, and attach them to each other

along the four edges of the double base, as at the arrow.

Fold up the adjacent edges and overcast them together on the outside with matching thread, as at **F**. When the bag is all closed around the side edges, attach celluloid or bone rings all around the top edge at intervals of 1½ or 2 in., as at **G**. Run cord, made in the same colors as the bag, through the rings. Also make tassels by knotting the cord at the ends.

Small Box for Trinkets

A unique and useful gift is a small box for rings and other jewelry. The procedure in making such a box and covering it with hand-woven fabric is illustrated in Fig. 151. It should be lined with silk.

The box may be made of any size from pieces of cardboard like those forming the backs of writing tablets. Six parts are needed for the box, each of which is made by covering an outside piece and an inside piece with cloth and sewing the two pieces together. The principles of making this box will be found very useful in constructing boxes of any shape or size, such as four-sided, six-sided, or eight-sided trays, small box-like scrap baskets, pencil boxes, utility holders, stamp boxes, and desk sets.

Cardboard for the Box: For the front A of the box, cut two pieces of cardboard ½ in. × 2 in.; and for the back A' cut two more similar pieces.

For the base B, cut two pieces 1 in. × 2 in.; and for the top D cut two more similar pieces.

For the left side C, cut two pieces ½ in. × 1 in.; and for the right side C' cut two more similar pieces.

Cloth for Covering the Cardboard: For covering the inside piece of cardboard for each part, use lining material. The outside pieces of cardboard for the front, back, sides, and top should be covered with hand-woven fabric or attractive belting. This same material may also be used for the outside piece of cardboard for the base, but that piece may be covered with the lining material, if desired.

The required sizes of the pieces of covering material are as follows: For the front and the back, 1 in. × 2½ in.; for the base and the top, 1½ in. × 2½ in.; for each side, 1 in. × 1½ in.

Steps 1 and 2: Covering the Pieces of Cardboard. After the pieces of cardboard and covering material have been cut, cover the cardboard by proceeding in the following manner: Lay the piece of covering material on a table with the right side of the material down. Fold the short edges over the cardboard, as shown in the diagram for Step 1, and sew these edges together. Then, fold the long edges over, as shown in the diagram for Step 2, and stitch those edges together. This procedure is used for all except the outside piece for the top.

Step 3: Sewing Pieces of Each Part Together. Sew together the two pieces for each of the parts of the box, using overcasting stitches, as shown in the diagram for Step 3.

Step 4: Stuffing Top. Before covering the outside piece for the top section of the box with the hand-woven material, add some cotton batting or kapok, as shown in the diagram for Step 4, to make a soft padded covering. Then, sew the outside and inside pieces for the top together as described in Step 3.

Step 5: Stitching Parts Together. Stitch the parts for the four sides together to form the bottomless and coverless box, as shown in the diagram for Step 5, and then stitch the sides to the base. Use overcasting and, to conceal this stitching, insert a twisted bit of thread-rope made in the same colors.

Step 6: Attaching Cover. Attach the padded cover to the back of the box with two heavy threads at each end in the manner shown in the diagram for Step 6 (the arrows point toward these threads). Then, use the same kind of heavy thread to make a loop on the cover for holding the lid down. Cover the thread with button-holing, and add a small decorative

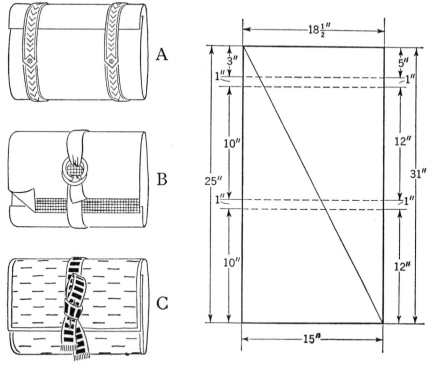

Fig. 152—A folder for linens.

button on the front of the box. The box can be kept closed by slipping the loop on the cover over the button on the front.

Folder for Linens

One of the housekeeper's problems is to keep lovely linens fresh and smooth as they come from the ironing board, so that at any time she can feel confident of finding an unwrinkled layout.

The hand weaver is especially linen-conscious and knows how important it is to take the proper care of articles made from this unusual and valuable fiber. Any weaver will appreciate the practicality of making a folder for mats and doilies like that shown in Fig. 152. This linen case also makes a useful gift for a friend; a pretty case in which to store linens is more than welcome.

One of the peculiar advantages of hand-woven fabrics is that their edges are smooth and finished by virtue of the selvage, and require no hemming at the sides. Hence, a folder like that shown here requires for its making just a single strip of fairly heavy hand-woven material hemmed at the ends only. We give two sizes: one measures 10 in. by 15 in. when finished, and is shown in the lower left diagonal of the sketch; the other measures 12 in. by 18 in. and is shown at the upper right of the same sketch. Follow the dimensions in the respective triangles. The spaces between the dotted lines are placed to provide for the thickness of the pile of linen stored within the case. Fold the length of cloth over in the various ways shown at **A**, **B**, and **C**.

Textures for Weaving the Folder:
Heavy:
    Warp—16/3 or 20/4 set at 20 per in.
    Weft—Pattern: Perle 3
           Tabby: Like warp

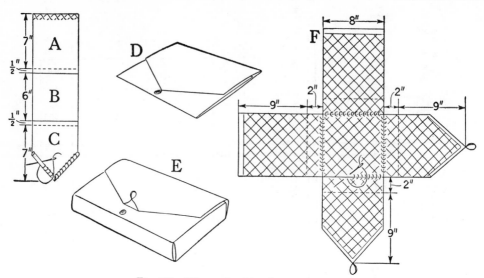

Fig. 153—Gifts made of handwoven runners.

Medium:

    Warp—24/3 or 20/2 set at 30 per in.

    Weft—Pattern: Crochet cotton or
Perle 5

    Tabby: Like warp

Straps for Tying: For straps to fasten around the folders, use strips of belt weaving measuring from 1 in. to 2 in. in width. These may be woven on a regular loom or made by using any of the fascinating belt-weave methods without looms: Egyptian Card Weaving, Inkle Loom Weaving, Braided Belt Weaving, etc.

Adjusting Straps: Two narrow straps or hand-woven bands may be used as shown at **A.** Use snaps or buttons to fasten the pointed ends. At **B** is shown a smart fastening made by inserting one wide band through ivory rings. At **C** is shown an easy tie made of a belt strip simply wrapped around the case and tied in a loop, with fringe hanging attractively in the front.

Bright pretty colors are in order for the belt designs; if you know the color scheme of your friend's china and linens, match them with the gift folder.

Gifts Made of Hand-Woven Runners

Hand-woven runners in solid Pattern Weave make adorable gift cases for use at home or when traveling. The firm pattern texture requires no lining, and smooth selvages do away with side hems.

Handkerchief Case: Just a single strip 7 in. wide and 21 in. in length will make a handkerchief case 6 in. × 7 in. Weave the strip, A, B, C in Fig. 153 in patterns of small repeats, like Twill, Herringbone, Diamond, Honeysuckle, or Summer and Winter. Divide the strip into three sections 7 in. long. Use the ½-in. space marked by dotted lines on each side of the center piece **B** for thickness in folding over the handkerchiefs. Finish the ends of the other two sections, **A** and **C**, as shown.

Cut the end of section **C** into a blunt point and roll it over into two meeting hems; then overcast them with soft Perle yarn. Roll the other end of section **A** into a hem as shown, and overcast it with yarn. A second row of stitches in the opposite direction is effective, as shown at the top of section **A.** Add a loop at the

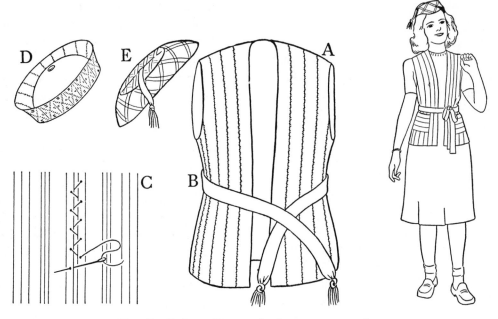

Fig. 154—Jacket and tam made of narrow woven strips.

end of section **C**. Fasten the finished case at **D** with a loop and a large button.

Case for Pajamas or Lingerie: A larger case **E**, 8 in. by 8 in., in which to pack pajamas or lingerie on week-end trips, is made of two hand-woven strips measuring 8 in. × 30 in., as at **F**. Fold each strip as follows: Make sections at both ends 9 in. long, allow 2 in. next to these for folding, and make the center or base 8 in. long. Finish each strip like the single strip at **A, B, C**. Lay the strips across each other at their centers, and attach their edges around the center square by overcasting, as shown. Fold the case together, folding from side to side at first, and then folding the ends of the vertical strip. Fasten with a button and a loop, or with snaps.

A Jacket and Tam Made of Narrow Woven Strips

The jacket and beret shown in Fig. 154 were made of narrow strips woven on a small loom. The jacket is useful over a thin summer dress or under a coat when motoring. Weave the strips in Plain Weave, using heavy colorful yarn or tufting cotton. Suitable belt weaves, which are also practical to use, are: Inkle Loom Weaving, Indian Belts, Braidweave, Hungarian Belts, and Egyptian Card Weaving. Narrow woven strips are interesting and convenient to work with, and are easily adjustable to an article of any shape or size.

Sewing the Strips Together: For the method of making up a jacket out of the narrow woven bands, see the plan at **A**. It is easy to sew together the strips, measuring 2 in. to 3 in. wide, using the Figure-of-Eight Stitch shown in Fig. 154 at **C**. First make up a little muslin pattern to fit yourself or a friend, adjust it carefully, and baste the two front pieces to the back. Measure off the required number of woven pieces to cover it. About four strips serve for each front piece, ten to twelve are needed for the back, and two or three shorter lengths go under each arm. Weave an additional strip for a tying belt, as at **B**. Attach the strips **C**. Discard the paper lining.

For the beret **D** the best plan is to buy a cheap cloth hat in the 5-and-10-cent store, and cover it with the strips. Get it larger than necessary, to make room for the thickness of the strips. A Scotch tam **E** is also effective.

Handy Bag

A very useful bag for holding magazines and pencils, paper, and notes may be made for the person confined to bed, to be slipped under the mattress beneath the pillow and hung within arm's reach. The upper part, to be inserted horizontally under the mattress, as shown in Fig. 155, is a stiff piece of cardboard covered with cloth. Below this hangs a pouch or bag to hold items of usefulness for the invalid. There are also two straps or tabs at the top of the bag part, planned to hold a flashlight or a fountain pen. The bag should be made of bright cheery cloth, and hand-woven material works up attractively.

How to Make the Bag: For the stiff horizontal section, cut a piece of cardboard **A**, 12 in. square. Cut a piece of material both to cover this and to form the bag. This piece should measure ½ in. wider than the cardboard, or 13 in. wide; and its length should be adequate to cover the cardboard and form the pouch, a length of 54 in. being needed in this case.

Hem one end on the wrong side, as at **B**. Turn this end of material back on itself, and sew the side edges together with running stitches ⅜ in. from the edges, as at **C**. Turn the sewed part over to the right side like a pillow, and slip the card-

board into the opening, as at **D**. Finish the edges of the bag part by turning the edges ove. and basting them down on the inside, as at **E**.

Lining the Bag: Make a lining **F**, measuring 13 in. wide and 30 in. long, out of cheaper material. Slip one end of the lining into the opening, on top of the cardboard. Hem down the rest of the lining as shown, attaching it to the edge of the basted length of material.

Make two tabs **G** out of heavy tape or the bag material sewed double or lined. These should measure ¾ in. wide and 6 in. long, when finished. Fold each one over double, and slip it into the pocket with the loops extending outside, as at **G**. Make them the right size for a flashlight or pen **J** or some other much-used implement. Now hem down the edge of the opening so as to conceal the cardboard, as at **H**. One may add various interesting parts, such as a pencil pouch that is quite separate and hangs down on the inside of the bag.

Inserting Side Extensions or Gussets: To provide some width for the bag that is suspended, insert gussets at the sides. These may be made in triangular form, as at **K**, and lined; or of oblong form, as at **L**, and shirred. In this case turn down the top edge into a hem for an elastic band, or make a heading, as at **M**, and run the tape through. Shir the bottom as tightly as possible. Line the material if desired. Insert the gusset into the material so that a hinge **N** 3 in. wide will be left free to hang over the roll of the mattress.

Hand-Woven Covering for the Bag: If using hand-woven material, simply weave this in the width desired and use the selvage as the outside edge without turning in any material; but fold the lining

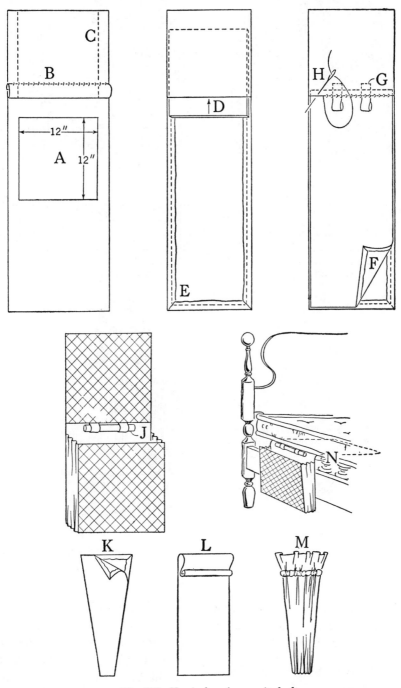

Fig. 155—Handy bag for use in bed.

H.4	X				X			
H.3		X				X		
H.2			X				X	
H.1				X				X

The Twill

H.4	X				O				X				O
H.3		X				O				X				O
H.2			X				O				X				O
H.1				X				O				X				O

The Shepherds' Check

Fig. 156—Jackets and suits woven in Twill Weave or Sheperds' Check.

under to meet this selvage. The lining may be omitted if the woven material is sufficiently heavy and firm in its weave.

Jackets and Suits Woven in Twill Weave or Shepherds' Check

At times it becomes the fashion to combine plaid and plain materials in wearing apparel. In Fig. 156 is shown a plaid jacket with a plain dress and belt. The jacket is effective when set off like a picture in a frame by the soft background color. This combined ensemble might be called a plaid and plain suit. Our hand weavers should not miss this opportunity to design a smart suit, weaving a plaid strip to be made up into a jacket. Several plans are as follows:

Plan 1. A Warm Sports Jacket of Coarse Mesh:

Design: We suggest a soft plaid in two or three colors, or a Twill, woven with a medium-weight spun wool, such as Saxony, Zephyr, or Germantown, 4-fold. For effective plaid designs, see Figs. 53, 61, 85, 86, 88, and 89.

Width of Material: For a jacket cut to a pattern, first buy a pattern and estimate the amount of cloth needed, planing for the sleeveless jacket shown in Fig. 156 at the left. This may be put together with very little cutting, by weaving strips in the desired width.

Warp Plan:
Width of warp: 14 in.
Threads per inch: 10 or 12
Total number of threads: 140 or 168

Threading Plan: Thread Hs. 1, 2, 3, 4 and repeat as in the Twill draft, changing colors at intervals if a plaid is desired.

Weaving Plan: For a mottled texture, use Hs. 2 and 4; 1 and 2; 1 and 3: 3 and 4; 2 and 4; 1 and 4; 1 and 3; and 2 and 3. Repeat all. The cloth may also be woven as a Twill, weaving Hs. 1 and 2, 2 and 3, 3 and 4, and 4 and 1, and using the same succession and proportions of colors in the weft as those planned for the warp. Other attractive textures are found in the suggestions given in Plans 2, 3, and 4.

Making Jacket: First weave the two front panels by making a strip 14 in. wide and 60 in. long and cutting it in half from selvage to selvage. Note that the material shrinks both ways, and the final strips will be 12 in. wide. Sew the panels together with heavy yarn and attractive joining stitches. For the back, take out warp threads until the width of the warp is 12 in., which will shrink to a width of 10 in. Weave another strip 60 in. long and cut it in half to make two back sections.

Sew the parts together as shown in the diagram in Fig. 156 at the right.

Plan 2. A Light-Weight Jacket of Fine Mesh:

Design: We suggest a plaid in three soft colors, woven as Tabby or Twill and using fine 2-ply wool for the warp and weft. See the sketch of the girl in Fig. 156. Plan your plaid on check paper in your most becoming shades. Make each check indicate a certain number of threads.

Width of Material: A 22-in. width cuts to advantage, and this same width may be used for neckties with very little waste. For a jacket with sleeves, you will need 3 yards of finished cloth and 1 pound of the fine 2-ply yarn divided among the various colors chosen.

Warp Plan:
Width of warp: 22 in.
Threads per inch: 20
Total number of threads: 440

Weave as a plaid, changing the weft colors like the warp.

Plan 3. A Simple Twill Cloth Jacket:

Use a good quality of wool which will be shown to the best advantage in a simple threading. Choose two colors or two shades of the same color, one for warp and one for weft.

Warp Plan:
Warp: 2-ply medium-weight yarn, set at 18 or 20 threads per inch
Weft: Same as warp but different color

Threading Plan: Thread as Twill or Herringbone.

Weaving Plan: Use one color only, but make the shade of the weft different from that of the warp. This brings out the Twill texture and gives life to the material. Weave Hs. 1 and 2, 2 and 3, 3 and 4, and 4 and 1; repeat all. Or, for Herringbone, weave Hs. 1 and 2, 2 and 3, 3 and 4, 4 and 1, 3 and 4, and 2 and 3; and repeat all.

One may also make this plain cloth into a simple plaid by using four threads of a dark color at intervals of 2 inches in the warp. Weave the weft with the same proportions and colors, or make the lighter background weft color slightly different from the warp to bring out the Twill texture.

Plan 4. Shepherds' Check Threading: For the Shepherds' Check Plaid shown in Fig. 156 at the center right, choose two colors, a light one (o) and a dark one (×). Thread four of each as shown, following the Twill succession.

Weaving Plan: Use the same two colors. Weave with the first color Hs. 1 and 2, 2 and 3, 3 and 4, and 4 and 1, once each. Weave with the second color Hs. 1 and 2, 2 and 3, 3 and 4, and 4 and 1, once each. Alternate sections of four rows of each color. For the fabric effect, see the jacket at the upper right in Fig. 156.

Appendix

Definitions of Terms Used in Weaving

Adjacent Blocks: Those arrangements of harness combinations in which the harness numbers of one block, such as Hs. 1, 2, 1, 2, have a note or harness number that is common to the block that follows it on the draft, such as Hs. 2, 3, 2, 3, where harness 2 is common to both blocks.

Animal Fibers: Fibers found in the animal kingdom, such as sheep's wool, camels' hair, angora wool, rabbits' hair, and silk.

Apron: A length of sturdy denim, duck, or heavy unbleached muslin attached to the cloth-roller at the front of the loom to which the warp threads are tied.

Asbestos Thread: Thread made by twisting together the fibers found in asbestos rock, a mineral substance.

As-Drawn-In or **As-Threaded:** Weaving a pattern on the diagonal according to the succession of blocks that occurs in the draft.

At Rest: The position of the harnesses when they are "neutral," i.e., when all harnesses are at the same level and no shed is being made.

Authentic Succession of Treadles: Procedure in which the pattern is woven as-threaded, or as-drawn-in, and the weaving progresses with each combination as it occurs from right to left on the draft.

Balanced Warp and Weft: The thread count of those hand-woven fabrics in which there are the same number of weft threads in an inch of woven material as there are warp threads set to the inch; sometimes called "fifty-fifty fabric."

Bars: See **Heddle Bars.**

Basket Weave: A woven texture resembling in-and-out wickerwork; is similar to Tabby in its threading and weaving, but must have a balanced warp and weft; instead of single threads, two or more warp threads are threaded side by side on the same harnesses and two or more weft threads interlace them.

Batten: See **Beater of the Loom.**

Beaming the Warp on the Roller: Winding the warp threads at a tension around the cylindrical warp-roller and holding them out to the same width on the roller as the width of the cloth one desires to make.

Beater of the Loom: Part of the loom structure which is moved back and forth to pack the weft rows taut; composed of two vertical side pieces and horizontal end pieces for holding the reed, the whole device working back and forth in an arc from its pivot at the base or top of the loom; also called **Batten.**

Binder: The Tabby weft when this is used to bind in a Pattern row or to follow a row of Laid-in or Design Weaving.

Block: A group of harnesses written as a unit on a draft and woven as a unit in the cloth, such as Hs. 1, 2, 1, 2, or Hs. 4, 1, 4, 1, 4, 1, 4.

Board Loom: A simple wooden frame or contrivance made out of a flat board, on which warp may be stretched taut to provide for weaving.

Bobbin: A small spool wound with thread and inserted into a shuttle for use as weft; also called a **Cop** or **Quill.**

Bobbin-Winder: A device consisting of a wheel that turns a metal rod on which the bobbins or cops used to hold the weft thread are placed to be wound.

Borders (in Weaving): Those sections of the draft or woven fabric planned to frame or set off the main portion or center of the pattern; may be vertical, running lengthwise of the fabric, or horizontal, woven across the warp from selvage to selvage.

Braid-Weave Rug Weaving: That form of weaving in which the weaver twines pairs of weft yarns around warp threads stretched on a board loom or frame.

Breast-Beam: The smooth wooden or metal bar at the front of the loom above the cloth-roller and parallel to the reed, the harnesses, and the back-beam, and over which the finished cloth passes on its way to the cloth-roller; also called **Front-Beam.**

Broken Twill: That method of weaving Twill in which the regular succession of harnesses woven as-drawn-in is interrupted and reversed at a certain point, as when one weaves Hs. 1 and 2, Hs. 2 and 3, Hs. 4 and 1, and Hs. 3 and 4; instead of Hs. 1 and 2, Hs. 2 and 3, Hs. 3 and 4, and Hs. 4 and 1.

Bronson Weave (Four-Harness): An open-work weave in which every second note of the draft is on harness 1, and alternate notes are distributed among harnesses 2, 3, and 4.

Bronson Weave (Lace): A weave in which there are two blocks, namely, Hs. 1 and 3 and Hs. 1 and 4, and the Tabby on Hs. 1 and 2 occurs either as a tie-down only after each block or as a section of border around the lace texture.

Bronson Weave (Spot): A weave in which the Tabby on Hs. 1 and 2 is extended to make a full third block in addition to the other two lace blocks, while little spots of lace made on Hs. 1 and 3 and on Hs. 1 and 4 occur between units of Tabby on Hs. 1 and 2.

Burlap: A coarse-textured cloth woven from the fibers of the jute plant.

Canvas Weave or **Monk's Cloth:** A weave resembling commercial monk's cloth in its texture; similar to the Reverse Twill in its threading, but at each reverse point, H. 1 or H. 4, several threads on the same harness are used instead of just a single thread, as Hs. 1, 1, 2, 3, 4, 4, 3, 2, etc.

Carding: The process of untangling and straightening out fibers preparatory to spinning; consists in running the fibers through two carding combs having wire teeth, and of making them into a smooth fluffy layer or roll easy to spin.

Castle: The upright supports of the harnesses at the center of the loom.

Centering the Warp in the Reed: Finding the planned width of the warp and spacing it at the center of the reed so that there is the same amount of empty space at both the right and left sides.

Chain Method of Warping: Method in which the warp threads are wound one by one or in small groups on a warping frame or revolving cylinder equipped with pegs on which to secure their "cross," being chained off by hand preparatory to beaming and threading.

Chaining off the Warp: The process of removing the groups of wound warp threads with their cross from the warping frame, and making of them a chain, similar to a crocheted chain, to keep them from tangling.

Checkerboard Overshot Weave: A weave made from a pattern threading having small equal blocks on opposites.

Cloth: A textile surface made of many threads interlaced or assembled in various ways.

Cloth-Roller: The smooth roller of wood placed beneath the breast-beam at the front of the loom, and around which the finished cloth rolls; corresponds to the warp-roller at the back of the loom.

Cloth, Woven: Cloth consisting of two sets of threads, called the warp and weft threads, that cross or interlace each other at right angles.

Colonial Overshot Pattern Weaving: That type of weaving in which the warp threads are threaded through the harnesses in groups, according to a set pattern plan, so that when the various sheds are made the weft threads show in overshots or skips across the openings made as the groups of warp threads are raised or lowered.

Comb: A name used for the raddle or reed through which the warp threads are evenly distributed for warping.

Cop: See **Bobbin.**

Cord-Heddles: Loops of cord attached to the heddle-rods of a primitive loom, to provide openings for threading the warp threads through for the purpose of making a shed when weaving.

Cotton Thread: Thread made by spinning or twisting together the fibers found in the boll or seed of the cotton plant.

Count of a Yarn: The number of skeins or hanks which a pound of the yarn makes when it is drawn out to a certain size.

Counterbalanced Loom: A loom in which the sets of harnesses are tied in such a way that, when the weaver presses on certain treadles, the harnesses attached to these treadles are lowered while all the others are raised.

Creel: A frame equipped with pegs to hold spools of warp thread, from which the threads are wound off on the sectional warp-roller.

Denier: Unit of measure for silk, designating the weight in drams of 1,000 yards of silk.

Dent: Any one of the vertical openings in the loom reed; reeds are named according to the number of dents per inch they carry, such as 16-dent reeds and 24-dent reeds.

Design: A term applied to any changes in Plain Weave brought about by variations in the character or color of the threads used; or by the laying-in of extra threads between the rows of Tabby Weave; or by the manipulation of the Tabby threads themselves to form lace or texture effects.

Designing Drafts: Writing one's own pattern drafts according to certain rules, so as to produce any desired pattern effect with its background of Tabby, or texture effects of one's own creation in which only a single weft is used.

Diagonal: A term referring to the diagonal trend of the blocks resulting on the woven surface when one weaves as-drawn-in.

Diagonal Trend of the Blocks: The diagonal line produced by successive blocks across the center of the woven pattern by the weaving of the blocks as-drawn-in. See **As-Drawn-In.**

Diamond Patterns: Those patterns formed by enlarging the simple succession of harness steps in the various Reverse Twills or Herringbones to form larger blocks; and by weaving them as-drawn-in.

Dornick Weave: A threading resembling the Two-Twill Herringbone, but with a short interruption or break in its draft caused by omission of the seventh and fourteenth threads, weaving Hs. 1, 2, 3, 4, 1, 2, (3 omitted), followed by Hs. 4, 3, 2, 1, 4, 3, (2 omitted), instead of Hs. 1, 2, 3, 4, 1, 2, 3, 4, 3, 2, 1, 4, 3, 2, and repeat.

Doups: The loops comprising the upper and lower parts of a cord-heddle.

Draft: A notation on check paper informing the weaver through what harnesses to thread the warp threads, the harness numbers planned for threading occurring in the desired order on the draft as horizontal rows of checks designated as the harness rows.

Drawing-In, or **Threading the Warp Through the Reed:** Drawing each warp thread in succession through the eyes of a heddle, or the dents of the reed.

Dressing the Loom: The processes of warping, beaming, and threading the loom.

"Dukagang," or **Scandinavian Laid-in:** A type of Laid-in Weaving in which the design threads are laid in through picked up groups of warp threads, with tie-downs occurring at planned intervals.

End: Another name for warp thread.

Entering: Same as **Drawing-In.**

Fell of the Cloth: The horizontal line between the finished cloth and the unwoven warp or, in other words, the last row of weaving; if the beater is true, the fell will be parallel to the front-beam.

Fibers (Natural): Small hair-like bits of substance from the animal kingdom, vegetable kingdom, or mineral kingdom which are twisted together to make thread.

Fibers (Synthetic): Those made by Man from wood pulp or cellulose by squeezing such substances through fine tubes.

Finger-Weaving: A term sometimes applied to Laid-in Weaving where the design is picked up by the fingers; also applied to Braid-Weave belt making.

Finished Cloth: Cloth woven by crossing the warp with the weft, and moved over the breast-beam at the front of the loom and wound around the cloth-roller.

Finished Material, Removal of, from the Loom: Ways in which finished work may be cut off the loom to make room for future weaving.

Flax: The fiber found in the stem of the flax plant and used for spinning into linen thread.

Foundation Threads: See **Warp Threads.**

Four-Harness Patterns: Those which are threaded on the four harnesses of a loom.

Fringe: Part of a piece of weaving consisting of the warp ends of the piece, often tied in even knots, loops or braids; and additional threads sometimes being added to the piece to make a heavier or more colorful fringe.

Front-Beam of the Loom. See **Breast-Beam.**

Gingham Weave: See **Plain Weave,** or **Tabby.**

Glass Thread: Thread made by pulling out into a long tensile length the transparent fluid made by melting sand, two or more strands of fine glass thread sometimes being spun together to make a heavier weaving thread.

Goose-Eye Pattern: That made by weaving a Reverse-Twill or Herringbone Pattern first twill-fashion, as Hs. 1 and 2, 2 and 3, 3 and 4, and 4 and 1; and then its reverse, i.e., Hs. 3 and 4, and 2 and 3; and repeat all.

Half-Tones: Those small areas found in a woven fabric on either side of the blocks, where the pattern thread passes over only one warp thread at a time, thus showing only slightly and being modified by the color of the warp and Tabby.

Hank: A unit of measure (840 yards of thread for cotton and 300 yards for linen).

Harnesses: The wooden or metal frames holding the heddles through which the warp threads are threaded, and being hung at the center of the loom about midway between the front-beam and back-beam.

Harness Apparatus: The harnesses at the center of the loom and their attachments, such as the rollers, harness ropes, heddle-bars, heddles, lams, treadles, and tie-ups.

Harness Combinations: The treadling of certain harnesses together in pairs or groups of three, such as Hs. 1 and 3, Hs. 2 and 4, Hs. 1 and 2, or Hs. 1, 2, and 3, together.

Heddles: Cord or wire loops attached to bars called heddle-bars in the harness frames, their purpose being to provide openings for threading through the warp threads so that the latter may be lifted to make the shed for weaving.

Heddle-Bars or **Heddle-Rods:** Flat metal or wooden rods set in the harnesses and over which the open ends of the heddles are placed to hold them erect in the harnesses.

Heddle-Frame: A steel or wood device consisting of alternate slots and holes through which the warp is threaded so that when the frame is lowered and raised the cross of alternate sheds in the warp threads is obtained; also called **Slot-and-Hole Heddle.**

Heddle-Ropes: Ropes or straps connecting the harnesses with pulleys, rollers, or jacks which in turn provide for the lowering or raising of the harnesses.

Hemp: A plant providing a coarse fiber used for twisting to make cord or rope.

Herringbone Pattern, or **Herringbone Weave:** The Twill threading with a reverse at any point in its draft, such as Hs. 1, 2, 3, (4), 3, 2, and repeat; or Hs. 1, 2, 3, 4, (1), 4, 3, 2, and repeat; or Hs. 1, 2, 3, 4, 1, 2, 3, (4), 3, 2, 1, 4, 3, 2, and repeat.

Honeycomb Technique: A way of weaving Overshot Patterns, in which the Pattern sections are woven with fine thread and the Tabby is woven with coarse thread which surrounds the depressed pattern blocks in curving lines, only one harness of each pattern combination being used at a time.

Honeysuckle Pattern: A popular pattern combining an oval-shaped figure and a cross, being threaded as Hs. 1, 2, 1, 2, 3, 2, 3, 4, 1, 2, 3, 2, 1, 4, 3, 2, 3, 2, 1, 2, 1, 4, 1, 4, 1, 4, and repeat.

Horizontal Borders: Those running crosswise of the material, being woven across the warp from selvage to selvage.

Huck Weave: A development of the Reverse Twill woven in such a way as to make small nubs in the weft on one side of the cloth and raised warps for a short space on the other side.

In-and-Out Weave: Another name for **Simple Weave, Plain Weave,** or **Tabby Weave;** also applied to Simple Weaving in Basketry.

Indian Loom: A type of loom in which the warp threads are stretched between opposite poles and the shed is made by a shed-stick and by the lifting of bars attached by loops to alternate threads.

Inserting an Additional Warp Thread: The manner of adding a colored or texture thread to the warp either in place of a regular warp thread or alongside of it through its same heddle and dent in the reed.

Jack Loom: A loom in which the harnesses are operated by jacks which lift them up when the treadles are manipulated to make a shed.

Jeans Twill: A traditional Southern weave on a Three-Harness Twill threading, consisting of two alternating textures, as follows: first, a section woven as the Two-and-One Twill, or Hs. 1 and 2, 2 and 3, and 3 and 1; then, a section woven as the One-and-Two Twill, or H. 1 alone, H. 2 above, and H. 3 alone.

Jute: A fiber found in the stem of the jute plant and twisted into a tough thread for the weaving of burlap and for use as tying twine.

Kapok: A soft silky fiber found in the seed-pods of the ceiba tree and used for stuffing pillows.

Knots (Used in Weaving): The Weaver's Knot, the Square Knot, the Snitch Knot, and the Slip Knot.

Laid-in Weaving: That type of hand-woven fabric in which a design is laid-in through the warp threads in addition to the regular Tabby rows, which act as its background, the design threads extending as far as desired to stand out against the background by being laid-in through the regular Tabby shed, through a Pattern shed, or through a shed counted out by a stick with any series of warp threads desired.

Lam: An intermediary bar or lever hung midway between treadles and harnesses and attached to both, the use of lams enabling the weaver to bring down several harnesses at a time with one foot.

Laying-in: Adding an additional design thread in between the rows of Plain Weave.

Lease of the Warp Threads: The passing of the warp threads under and over two bars in alternation when warping, thus providing a consecutive crossing of the warp threads to keep the threads in their proper order, to keep them from tangling, and to give the weaver the cross for threading which is later preserved in the two Tabby sheds; also called the **Cross** or **Portee Cross.**

Lease-Rods: Two bars used to preserve the lease or cross when warping, so that each thread may be taken in its proper order when threading.

Levers: Bars controlling the raising and lowering of the harnesses by hand or foot.

Linen Thread: Thread made by twisting together the fibers of the flax plant by the process of spinning.

Log-Cabin Weave: A two-harness weave with a fabric design of alternating blocks or columns resulting from threading two colors alternately and changing their harnesses between blocks.

Loom: The framework across which threads are stretched in parallel order and at a tension for the weaving of cloth.

Main Pattern Texture: That texture created by the Pattern weft thread as it is woven through spaces made by the pattern sheds.

Mending Broken Warp Ends: Repairing breaks in one's warp when weaving; or avoiding knots in the weaving when warp ends have been knotted together.

Mineral Threads: Threads spun from mineral fibers, such as asbestos and glass.

Miniature Patterns: The condensed drafts of larger Overshot Patterns.

Monk's Belt Pattern: A popular four-harness pattern written on opposite blocks, preserved for us by European weavers of the Middle Ages.

M's and O's Weave: A traditional Colonial Weave comprised of two Tabby systems which alternate, one system being written on Hs. 1 and 3 and Hs. 2 and 4, and the other on Hs. 1 and 2 and Hs. 3 and 4.

Navajo Weaving: The weft-surface weavings of the Navajo Indians, which were produced by a method somewhat similar to Tapestry Weaving.

On Opposites: Either threading or weaving on opposite pattern blocks.

One-and-Three Twill: That manner of weaving the Twill resulting from treadling one harness at a time against the remaining three, i.e., H. 1 alone, H. 2 alone, H. 3 alone, H. 4 alone.

Overshot Pattern Weaving: That type in which the warp is threaded so as to form set pattern groupings when the various harness combinations are made, the weft being said to make "Overshots" of pattern as it passes between the spaces made by the respective shed openings.

Pairing: The process of interlacing pairs of threads or flexible fibers around firm warps or rigid fibers to form a basket-like texture.

Patch Patterns: That family of weaves in which the units are written on opposite blocks.

Pattern Shed: That shed made when the harnesses lift up the warp threads in definite groups because of their threading to a set pattern.

Pattern Weaving: That type of weaving in which the loom is so threaded that the harness combinations make regular repeats of a set pattern all across the warp, thus developing a woven fabric of repeated design.

Pattern Weft: The term applied to weft thread that is used as a filler through the pattern sheds in contrast to the Tabby weft used in the Plain Weave sheds.

Piecing: Starting a new thread where an old one has ended; when piecing weft, the new and old ends usually being overlapped or spliced instead of being tied, although the square knot may be used to connect weft ends temporarily; in the warp, the pieced threads being joined with a weaver's knot.

Pina Cloth: A fine transparent fabric made by weaving together the fine strands of thread made from Pineapple fiber.

Plaid, True: A woven plaid design in which the same succession and same proportion of colors are carried out in the weft as occur in the warp.

Plain Weaving: A method in which cloth is formed by the interlacing of two sets of threads placed at right angles, and in which the threads pass under and over one another in simple alternation.

Ply of Yarn: Its spinning construction, being called "singles" if it has one strand; 2-ply if it has two strands; 3-ply if it has three strands, etc.

Quill: See **Bobbin.**

Rag Rugs: Those in which the weft or weaving yarn consists of rags cut into strips.

Rain-Drops Weave: A simple development of the Reverse Twill or Herringbone, being woven so as to make small nubby spots at intervals; threaded Hs. 1, 2, 1, 4, 3, 4.

Ramie: A plant having strong fibers which are spun into thread called Ramie or Chinese Linen.

Rayon Thread: Thread made by squeezing a soft pulp through fine tubes, the pulp, which may be wood pulp, cellulose, or combinations of soft plant substances, hardening into a silk-like thread when dry.

Reed: A steel or wood device having separate openings or dents spaced at even distances, through which the successive warp threads are threaded to keep them parallel and properly spaced, being placed in the beater in many looms and being used also to pack the weft rows taut.

Rising Shed: The type of shed (found on a jack loom) in which the harnesses when at rest lie at their lowest level at the base of the reed or against the shuttle-race, the shed being made by raising some of them above the others.

Roller, Cloth: Roller at the lower front of the loom, on which extra yards of finished cloth are stored.

Roller, Warp: Roller at the lower rear of the loom, on which extra yards of unwoven warp are stored.

Rug Shuttle: A large shuttle used to hold heavy weft for the weaving of rugs, bath mats, etc., usually consisting of two flat stick-shuttles joined together by wooden supports at their ends which provide width between the shuttles for holding the bulky weft and around which the weft is wound.

Rhythm, Weaving to: Throwing and catching the shuttle with a rhythmic motion, the same succession of steps being repeated at every throw.

Sectional Method of Warping: That process in which the warp threads come directly from separate spools arranged on a rack or creel on which their cross is obtained and from which they are wound directly around consecutive sections on the warp-roller of the loom.

Selvage of Cloth: The edge formed when weaving, at the right or left side of the cloth, by the loops of the weft as it passes back and forth and around the outside warp threads.

Set, Sett, or **Setting of the Warp:** The number of warp threads per inch in the reed to obtain a certain texture.

Setting up the Loom: The processes preparatory to weaving, which consist of measuring off the warp thread, beaming it, threading it, sleying it through the reed, and tying it down.

Shed: The opening made between warp threads to provide for the passing through of the weft thread in the weaving of cloth, the different sheds being made possible by the lifting or lowering of certain warp threads above or below others by means of loops or heddles placed on bars or between harnesses.

Shed, Rising: A shed in which the harnesses are raised to make the opening for the weft; a characteristic of jack looms.

Shed, Sinking: A shed (found on a counterbalanced loom) in which the harnesses are lowered to make the opening for the weft.

Shed-Stick: A thin, wide, flat stick with smooth, pointed ends planned to aid the weaver in finding and keeping the shed opening.

Shot: Another name for a row of weft.

Shuttle: The stick or the boat-like container which holds the thread when weaving.

Shuttle-Race: A smooth narrow shelf or ledge placed at the front of the beater and at the base of the reed, to act as a support for the shuttle as it passes rapidly from selvage to selvage and to prevent it from slipping through the warp threads; not an essential part of the loom, but convenient.

Shepherds' Check Pattern: A variation of the Twill with both warp and weft having the same succession of an even number of alternating thread colors.

Silk: A fiber found already made by nature in the twisted silk filament which the silkworm spins and emits from its mouth by means of the spinneret, a tiny device like a corkscrew, on its lower lip.

Simple In-and-Out Weave: See **Tabby Weave.**

Simple Plain Weave: See **Plain Weaving.**

Simple Weave: See **Tabby Weave.**

Singles Yarn: Any yarn that consists of a single continuous length of fibers spun together once only, as distinguished from the term **ply yarn,** which designates several strands of singles plied together.

Sinking Shed: See **Shed.**

Size of a Yarn: The thickness of a strand of thread; also the number of hanks of it necessary to make a pound.

Sley: To thread the warp threads through the reed; also another name for the reed.

Slip Knot: The knot used when tying groups of threads temporarily, being readily untied.

Snitch Knot: The knot used to tie the treadles either to the lams or directly to the harnesses when tying up the loom for weaving the treadle combinations.

Spinning: The process of twisting fibers together to make continuous thread.

Splicing: Piecing thread ends together.

Square Knot: The knot used to tie threads together when it is desired to have a temporary knot, because it may be readily undone; used to tie weft ends together temporarily, but never for piecing warps.

Squaring a Block: Weaving the number of times that will make the height of a block equal to its width when woven.

Star-and-Rose Fashion of Weaving: Weaving a small cross or a reverse unit of the draft as drawn in, thus producing a Star with pattern blocks showing at the corners and diagonally across the center; or weaving this same pattern unit of the draft with Tabby at those places where Pattern occurs in the Star, and with Pattern at those places where Tabby occurs in the Star, thus producing a Rose.

Stick-Shuttle: A thin flat stick with grooves or openings at its ends around which the weft thread is wound lengthwise.

Straight Laid-in Weaving: That type of Laid-in Weaving in which the design threads are laid in through the regular Tabby shed (**i.e.,** under and over single warp threads) and the Tabby or binder follows through the same shed; also called **American Laid-in.**

Stretching the Warp: Measuring the warp threads to the desired number of yards on the warping frame; also called **Measuring off the Warp.**

Stringing the Loom Frame: Stretching thread on a board loom or frame, preparatory to weaving cloth across the stretched threads.

Striped Warp: Weaving that has changes of color or texture occurring among the warp threads and appearing as vertical stripes in the finished fabric.

Striped Weft: Weaving in which the weaver changes thread colors or textures in the weft, making a fabric of horizontal stripes.

Summer and Winter Technique: A special technique which results in a closely knit weave with the pattern threads bound down by every fourth warp thread, every second note of the draft alternating on Hs. 1 and 2 and the notes in between occurring on Hs. 3 and 4, as Hs. (1), 3, (2), 3 for the block on H. 3 and Hs. (1), 4, (2), 4 for the block on H. 4.

Swift: A device to hold skeins of yarn when winding; it usually rotates.

Synthetic Thread: Thread made by squeezing the pulp of cellulose obtained from processed plant or wood fibers through tubes to make a long tensile length.

Tabby: The term applied to Plain Weave in which the warp and weft threads interlace each other at right angles and the weaving progresses under and over single threads or groups of threads handled as single threads.

Tabby Texture: Plain Weave made wherever the Tabby thread or binder interlaces the warp threads by passing under and over single threads in succession, as distinguished from Overshot Pattern Weaving, in which the Tabby rows occur between the sec-

tions of Pattern texture and act only as a background to them.

Tabby Weft: That weft which makes Plain Weave as it passes through a shed consisting of alternate threads raised and lowered.

Take-up of Warp: The lessening of the length of the warp threads because of their curving trend under and over the weft rows as they are beat tight to form the cloth.

Tapestry Technique: That type of weaving in which designs are interwoven into the fabric as a very part of its texture, the design threads of one part interlocking with those of the adjacent part which carry on the row of weaving in progress at the time, in contrast to Laid-in Weaving in which additional design threads are superimposed on a background texture of Tabby.

Tasseled Fringe: A fringe in which additional threads are added to the warp ends or loops already at the end of a piece and are finished in the form of tassels.

Temple: An adjustable bar-like device attached to the cloth last finished between its selvages, to keep the edges of the weaving from drawing in.

Texture of a Woven Piece: The appearance and feel of its fabric surface.

Thread: A long tensile length of many fibers twisted together.

Thread in Common: The thread shared by two adjacent blocks and occurring as the last note of one block and the first note of the next block, harness 2 being the thread in common between block 1 and 2 and block 2 and 3 in the succession Hs. 1, 2, 1, (2), 3, 2, 3.

Threading Draft: A threading plan written on check paper and giving the succession of harnesses necessary to thread a certain pattern.

Threading-Hook: A steel or wooden device with a hook at one end, by the use of which the warp threads are easily pulled through the heddle openings and reed.

Threading Plan, Making a: Planning out the width of the warp and the desired number of repeats for the pattern units of the draft, with provision for selvages, borders, and center, or any desired balance for the woven pattern.

Threading the Warp Through the Harnesses: Threading each warp thread in succession, as it comes from the cross on the lease-rods, through the heddle-eyes of the harnesses in the order designated by the pattern draft.

Three-Harness Twill: A Twill weave written on three harnesses in the order Hs. 1, 2, 3, and repeat or in the order Hs. 3, 2, 1, and repeat.

Thrift Materials: Materials which, instead of being discarded, are cut into narrow strips to be woven through a warp.

Throw-Shuttle: A boat-shaped device containing a bobbin, quill, or cop for holding thread, the bobbin being placed on a steel pin or wire inserted in the shuttle opening.

Thrums: Waste ends of warp cut from the loom.

Tie-up of the Loom for Treadling: The system or planned way in which the harnesses are tied to the treadles through the intermediary use of the lams, in order that, by manipulating a single treadle, several harnesses may be raised or lowered at a time to make the shed opening.

Treadle: A lever that is raised or lowered by the hand or foot to cause the harnesses to rise or sink for making the shed opening.

True Plaid: A plaid in which the same succession and proportion of colors and design are carried out in the weft as are planned in the warp.

Twill Family of Weaves: All weaves developed from the simple Twill succession, as Hs. 1, 2, 3, 4 or their reverse, as Hs. 1, 2, 3, 4, 3, 2.

Twill-Fashion Weaving: Weaving the harness combinations according to the succession of harnesses given in the simple Twill, i.e., Hs. 1 and 2; 2 and 3; 3 and 4; 4 and 1.

Twill on Opposites: That method of weaving the Twill in which each woven harness group is followed by all the other harnesses, Hs. 1 and 2 being followed by Hs. 3 and 4; Hs. 1, 2, and 3 woven together being followed by H. 4; Hs. 4 and 1 being followed by Hs. 2 and 3; and H. 2 alone being followed by Hs. 1 and 3, and 4; etc.

Twill, One-and-Three: That method of weaving the Twill in which one weaves each harness alone in consecutive order, as H. 1, H. 2, H. 3, and H. 4, the other three harnesses rising as each harness is lowered.

Twill, Three-and-One: That method of weaving Twill in which one lowers or raises three harnesses at a time in consecutive order, as Hs. 1, 2, and 3 together; Hs. 2, 3, and 4; Hs. 3, 4, and 1; and Hs. 4, 1, and 2.

Twill, Two-and-Two: That method of weaving the Twill in which one lowers or raises two harnesses at a time in consecutive order, i.e., Hs. 1 and 2, 2 and 3, 3 and 4, and 4 and 1.

Twill Threading Used for Borders: The repeat of the Twill threading to form borders for Pattern threadings.

Twill Weave: A consecutive threading of the harnesses and their weaving in the same order, such as Hs. 1, 2, 3, 4 or Hs. 4, 3, 2, 1, the resulting texture being of diagonal pattern lines acoss the fabric; or other threadings covering all four harnesses, such as Hs. 1, 3, 2, 4 or Hs. 1, 4, 2, 3, woven as-drawn-in.

Twist: A term referring to the number of turns per inch spun into a strand of ply-yarn.

Two-Harness Loom: A loom frame having two bars with their cord-heddles or two harnesses which provide for two alternating Tabby or Plain-Weave sheds.

Tying Down the Warp to the Warp-Roller: Pulling the warp threads taut and tying them in groups to a rod or tapes attached to the warp-roller, this tying sometimes being done before the threading and sometimes afterward.

Tying Down to Front- or Cloth-Roller: Tying down groups of warp threads to a rod or tapes attached to the cloth-roller at the front of the loom, thus making it possible to hold the warp taut and to wind the finished cloth up when weaving.

Unit of Measure for Cottons: A hank consisting of 840 yards of cotton thread.

Unit of Measure for Linens: A hank consisting of 300 yards of linen thread.

Unit of Measure for Silk: The "denier," which is the weight in drams of 1,000 yards of silk.

Units of Measure for Wools: Formerly, a skein consisting of 256 yards; today, 200-yard, 300-yard, and 400-yard skeins, or 1-ounce, 2-ounce, and 4-ounce skeins or balls.

Unit of Plain Weave: The smallest complete unit of the weave possible to make, **i.e.,** a small section of two warp threads covered by two wefts as they pass under and over the warp threads alternately.

Vertical Borders: Borders running lengthwise of the material, usually threaded into the warp at the selvages and appearing as vertical pattern motifs at the sides of the woven cloth.

Waffle Weave: A threading derived from the Herringbone or simple Reverse Twill, with the reverse points enlarged, the effect when woven being a texture of square ridges framing small depressed Tabby sections, quite similar to the contour of a waffle.

Warp: The name given to the series of threads stretched lengthwise of the loom.

Warp-Face Cloth: That type of hand-woven fabric in which the warp only shows, the warp threads being set so closely together that the weft is entirely covered by them; also called **Warp-Surface Cloth** or **Weft-Rep.**

Warp Plan: A list of the essential factors in one's plan for weaving, with answers to such questions as length of warp, kind of warp used, number of threads per inch, total number of warp threads, and width planned for the warp on the loom.

Warp-Roller: The cylindrical device at the rear of the loom around which the warp threads are wrapped taut for future storage.

Warp-Sticks: Smooth narrow sticks inserted between successive rounds of warp to keep it smooth on the warp-roller.

Warp Threads: The foundation threads stretched taut on a loom and interlaced by the weft threads to make cloth.

Warping a Loom: Stretching the threads for the warp to a desired length, beaming them, threading them, sleying them through the reed, and tying them down; sometimes called **Dressing the Loom.**

Warping Board: A square framework or a cylindrical drum of wood with pegs arranged in such positions that a definite number of yards may be measured off by their use when warping the warp threads.

Warping Paddle: A device which enables one to warp groups of warp threads instead of single threads by the chain method, and which keeps the separate threads of each group in consecutive order by establishing a cross for each section that is measured off.

Warping Several Threads Together: Winding groups of from four to ten threads together on the warping frame, instead of single threads only, the purpose being to save time when warping; the warping paddle is most useful in this process.

Wattling: The ancient process of interlacing rigid sticks by the twisting of pairs of softer fibers around them; known today as **Pairing.**

Weaver's Knot: The knot used for the piecing of warp threads; known as the **Bowline on the Bight** when used by sailors.

Weaving: The interlacing of two sets of threads at right angles to each other in various ways to form a fabric or cloth.

Weaving as Drawn in: See **As Drawn In.**

Weaving on Opposites: Weaving two opposite sets of harnesses in alternation, such as Hs. 1 and 2 followed by Hs. 3 and 4; or Hs. 2 and 3 followed by Hs. 4 and 1; or H. 3 followed by Hs. 1, 2, and 4 together.

Weaving Twill-Fashion: See **Twill-Fashion Weaving.**

Weaving Plan: A written chart of the succession of harnesses desired to develop a certain woven pattern.

Weft: The name given to the weaving thread used crosswise of the warp through the sheds made by the harnesses; also called the **Filler** or **Woof.**

Weft-Face Cloth: That type of hand-woven fabric in which only the weft shows, the warp threads being set so far apart that the weft packs down between them and completely covers the warp; also called **Weft-Surface Cloth** or **Warp-Rep.**

Weft Row: One passage of the thread between the warp threads from selvage to selvage; also called a **Row of Weft, a Pick,** or a **Shot.**

Weft Threads: The threads that are laid through the warp threads in various ways to produce woven cloth; also called **Filler Threads, Woof Threads,** or **Weaving Threads.**

Winder, Bobbin: A device for holding bobbins, cops, or quills for the purpose of filling them with weft thread by the process of winding.

Wool: The fiber that comes from various hairy and woolly animals, found as small, kinky, barbed hairs which are readily spun into thread because of their clinging qualities.

Wrap-Around Loom: A frame or a board around which thread is wrapped to provide warp for weaving, generally having some arrangement for keeping the warp threads spread evenly apart and parallel.

Writing Drafts: Planning on check paper the succession of harnesses necessary to make a certain fabric pattern.

Yardage: The term applied to the number of yards in a pound of thread or to the length of a warp or finished cloth.

Yarn: The term given to material spun and prepared for use as thread in weaving, referring most often to wool but also being used today in connection with cotton, linen, or silk, and in fact any kind of thread.

Bibliography

TEXTBOOKS FOR HOME, SCHOOL, OR COMMERCIAL WEAVERS

Atwater, Mary, *Shuttlecraft Book of American Handweaving*. Origins, development, decline, and modern revival of our national art of handweaving. Includes 132 illustrations for North and South American weaves.

Atwater, Mary, *The Recipe Book of Patterns for Handweavers*. Directions for weaving 129 patterns for clothing and upholstery, coverlets, rugs, draperies, etc. Profusely illustrated.

Beriau, Oscar, *Home Weaving*. A comprehensive study of equipment and accessories and the principles of weaving. Excellent illustrations of fabrics.

Black, Mary E., *New Key to Weaving*. Complete directions for handweaving, with more than 600 original drawings and photographs on 571 pages. Covers basic methods and unusual weaves such as Gobelin and Swedish tapestries.

Blum, Grace D., *Functional Overshot*. A basic source for modern fabric design with 32 handwoven swatches and a lucid text.

Cyrus, Ulla, *Manual of Swedish Handweaving*. A text on general weaving methods and practical skills. Illustrated.

Davison, M.P., *A Handweaver's Pattern Book*. A modern handbook of four-harness patterns for amateur and professional weavers. Contains 345 threading directions and over 1200 weaving variations.

Davison, M.P., ed., *A Handweaver's Source Book*. A selection of 224 patterns from the Laura M. Allen Collection. Beautifully printed on 240 pages.

Douglas, Harriet C., *Handweaver's Instruction Manual*. Basic information on techniques and drafts. Clear illustrations and explanations of looms, yarns, tie-up, and warping.

Frey, Berta, *Designing and Drafting for Handweavers*. An important guide covering the major points of drawing down drafts. Classifies fabrics according to their structure.

Gallinger, Osma and Del Deo, Josephine, *Rugweaving for Everyone*. Clear directions for 38 techniques for rugs, pillows, bathmats, upholstery, runners, etc. Step-by-step directions; rug designing both traditional and modern; information on rug borders and finishes. Over 130 illustrations, 294 pages.

Greer, Gertrude, *Adventures in Weaving*. Techniques for 2- to 24-harness looms; 428 pages, 347 illustrations, 300 patterns. Beautiful color plates.

Hooper, Luther, *Hand-Loom Weaving, Plain and Ornamental*. A truly great classic of weaving literature, with detailed descriptions of loom processes and unusual techniques and equipment.

Kirby, Mary, *Designing on the Loom*. A book for the advanced weaver, with 100 photographs of woven fabrics, plus drafts and analyses, color and weave effects, loom techniques for two warp beams, weaves for 16-harness looms.

Oelsner, G.H., *Handbook of Weaves*. Contains 402 plates with 1875 working diagrams. Covers textile design from plain weave to complicated, fancy weaves.

Overman, R. and Smith, L., *Contemporary Handweaving*. A beautiful book emphasizing design. Good for beginners, weaving teachers, and schools.

Selander, Malin, *Weaving Patterns*. An excellent book of 180 weaving patterns and treadling drafts, with 133 of them woven in full color.

Thorpe, Heather G., *Handweaver's Workbook*. A manual giving descriptions of the loom and its parts, directions for weaving processes, and valuable hints.

Tidball, Harriet, *The Handloom Weaves*. An analysis of the 52 most important harness-controlled weaves, with illustrations, drafts, tie-ups, treadling orders, and selvage threadings. Contains 66 photographs of textiles.

Zielinski, S.A., *Encyclopedia of Handweaving*. Information explaining weaving terminology. Photographs of patterns, textures, looms and parts.

BOOKS ON SMALL WEAVING APPLIANCES

Allen, Edith, *Weaving You Can Do*. A simple beginner's book giving the basic weaves for two- and four-harness looms.

Atwater, Mary, *Byways in Hand-weaving*. Complete coverage of the belt weaves of North and South America. Illustrated; eight color pages.

Atwater, Mary (Tod, Osma Gallinger, ed.), *Inkle Loom Weaving*. A booklet giving full details of the methods of setting up and weaving on an Inkle loom, with suggested patterns.

Blumeneau, Lili, *The Art and Craft of Handweaving*. A beginner's book giving the basic knowledge of looms, fibers, weaves, and designs.

Brown, H.J., *Handweaving for Pleasure and Profit*. A good book on two-harness weaving for those who must work without the aid of a teacher.

Clifford, Lois, *Egyptian Card Weaving*. Excellent new methods of warping and obtaining designs.

Gallinger, Osma, *Belts and How to Weave Them*. Clear diagrams and directions for braided belts, Guianan, Hungarian, Peruvian, Mexican, and American Indian belt weaves in reverse-warp technique.

Gallinger, Osma, *How to Make an Inkle Loom*. A folio giving diagrams, description, and method for making an Inkle loom at home.

Groff, Russell E., *Card Weaving or Tablet Weaving*. Describes the making of warps, setting up cards, and weaving narrow bands. Excellent photos, 53 patterns.

Simpson and Weir, *The Weaver's Craft*. Discusses simple equipment for weaving and spinning. Describes the making of hand-woven articles on table and floor looms.

Trotzig and Axelsson, eds., "Band," *Narrow Band Weavings*. Beautiful color plates of inkle bands, braids, belts, ribbons, and tapes; free Swedish-English glossary.

Van Cleve, Kate, *Hand Loom Weaving for Amateurs*. A book for beginners on the use of two-harness table looms.

SPECIALIZED WEAVING TOPICS AND RELATED BOOKS

Aarnio, Rauha, *Beauty on the Loom (Kaunista Kangaspuissa)*. A collection of contemporary home furnishing fabrics; 60 handsome designs, 150 photographs.

Bain, Robert, *The Clans and Tartans of Scotland*. Designs and histories of the Scottish tartans with 130 superb color illustrations.

Black, Mary E., *The Sett and Weaving of Tartans*. A study of tartan designs with 47 pages of concise weaving instructions, plus 14 color plates.

Bronson, J. and R., *Domestic Manufacturers' Assistant and Family Directory in the Arts of Weaving and Dyeing*. Reprint of the first weaving book in the United States. Directions for the Bronson Weave.

Brooks, M., *Thread Techniques*. Ten folders for two-harness looms, with directions for encircling bands, Bratten Lace Weave, Brooks Bouquet, etc.

Frey, Berta, *Seven Projects in Rosepath*. Designs possible with the Rosepath threading; warp yarn variation; color and texture changes; lace weaves; interwoven Rosepath; double width; bound weaving.

Hickman, Elmer, *Fabrics for the Home*. A folio containing samples of 26 outstanding fabrics for home use.

Hoffman, Henry A., *Weaving on Paper or Draw-Down Made Easy*. A quick, easy, and accurate method for trying out a draft before putting it on a loom.

Ingers and Fischer, *Flemish Tapestry*. A beautifully illustrated book on tapestry weaving. Working sheets for 17 tapestries.

Jornung, J., *Weaving Patterns for Laid-in (Vaevemonstre)*. A portfolio of 150 laid-in designs shown on 20 plates.

Lemos, Pedro J., *Guatemala Arts and Crafts*. Well illustrated with 41 pages showing Indian handweavers, their looms, equipment, and costumes; also basket making.

Lorenz, Dorothy S., *Finnish Lace*. A concise 16-page pamphlet on Finnish Leno.

Millen, Roger, *Weave Your Own Tweeds*. A treatment of the weaving of true tweeds. Instructions for making a four-harness loom.

Rugs in Rolakan, Flossa and Rosepath, (Monsterblad, Vol. 1). Portfolio of eight color plates with 14 examples of Swedish rugs and mats. In English.

Upholstery Materials, Slip Covers, Drapery, Bedspreads, (Monsterblad, Vol. 3). Full-color plates with 35 examples of handweavings; also 21 texture and pattern weavings in black and white.

Linen Weavings, (Monsterblad, Vol. 10). Fifteen plates showing 105 linen textiles with draft, tie-up, and weaving directions.

Patterns for Wool Weaving, (Monsterblad, Vol. 11). Eight color plates for clothing, scarves, and blankets. Excellent stripe, plaid, and color ideas.

Neher, Evelyn, *Four-harness Huck*. A popular book illustrating the application of huck to many purposes.

Pritchard, M.E., *A Short Dictionary of Weaving*. Includes spinning, dyeing, and textile terms and their definitions.

Ringler, Aina, *Finnish-English Weaving Glossary*. Pamphlet containing 450 Finnish weaving terms and their definitions.

Saunders, Virginia, *Reweave It Yourself*. A simple, clear explanation of the processes of inweaving, French reweaving, stoting, repair, etc. Analysis of Basket Weave, Serge, Herringbone, Worsted, Camel's Hair, and others.

Snyder, Mary E., *Lace and Lacey Weaves*. Illustrated book of 47 lace projects: Bronson and Swedish lace, Barleycorn, Diaper, Canvas weave and pick-up laces.

Tidball, Harriet, *The Double Weave, Plain and Patterned.* A study of the Double Weave, pick-up methods, texture variations, double width and tubular cloth, quilted fabrics, pleats and tucks.

Tod, Osma Gallinger, *Hints for the Handweaver.* One hundred useful suggestions on the mechanics of weaving, with illustrated answers to such problems as mending broken warps, threading drafts for better selvages, loom adjustments, warping methods to choose from, weaving finishes, methods of tying down, etc.

Tod, Osma Gallinger, *Weaving Booklets.* Folios for special techniques: Rug Methods; Flossa Rugs; Navajo rugs; etc. Lace-Weave Techniques; Leno, Spanish Openwork, Danish Medallion, French Buratto, Mexican Lace, Lace with Doupes, Brooks Bouquet, Texture Lace and Lace Designs. Laid-in Methods: Scandinavian, Italian, Russian, Mexican, and American techniques. Raising Flax and Weaving Linens. Weaving Poems.

Young, Helen D. *Heritage Linens with Modern Ideas.* Drafts and directions for weaving some of the finest traditional linens available.

SPINNING AND WEAVING FIBERS

Crowfoot, Grace M., *Methods of Handspinning in Egypt and the Sudan.*

Davenport, Elsie, *Your Handspinning.* Instructions for dyeing yarns.

Holding, M., *Notes on Spinning and Dyeing Wool.* Recipes; key to colors.

Tod, Osma, *History and Methods of Spinning.* Spinning wheels; vegetable dying.

NARRATIVE BOOKS ON WEAVING
AND BOOKS OF HISTORICAL BACKGROUND

Baity, Elizabeth, *Man Is a Weaver.* Traces the origins of weaving in all countries and provides well correlated information. Delightfully told and illustrated.

d'Harcourt, Raoul, *Textiles of Ancient Peru and Their Techniques.* Well illustrated book describing varied techniques of pre-Columbian weaving embroidery, etc. A wealth of information on different warp-and-weft handling.

Reichard, Gladys, *Navajo Shepherd and Weaver* and *The Spider Woman.* Navajo Indian methods for making blankets and rugs. Available only in libraries.

Rodier, *The Romance of French Weaving.* A fascinating history of the development of

weaving on the European continent, with stories of the origins of certain types of textiles. Beautifully illustrated. Available only in libraries.

Roth, H. Ling, *Studies in Primitive Looms.* Descriptions of the primitive looms of Africa, Indonesia, the Solomon Islands, etc.; evolution of the shuttle.

Tattersall, C.E., *Notes on Ancient Carpet Knotting and Weaving.* Information on the hand-knotted carpets of Persia, Turkey, and other Eastern countries.

Tod, Osma Gallinger, *Stories of the Weaves We Use.* A booklet giving a description and history of many fascinating hand weaves.

Index

A CATALOGUE OF SELECTED DOVER BOOKS
IN ALL FIELDS OF INTEREST

A CATALOGUE OF SELECTED DOVER BOOKS
IN ALL FIELDS OF INTEREST

LEATHER TOOLING AND CARVING, Chris H. Groneman. One of few books concentrating on tooling and carving, with complete instructions and grid designs for 39 projects ranging from bookmarks to bags. 148 illustrations. 111pp. 7⅞ x 10.
23061-9 Pa. $2.50

THE CODEX NUTTALL, A PICTURE MANUSCRIPT FROM ANCIENT MEXICO, as first edited by Zelia Nuttall. Only inexpensive edition, in full color, of a pre-Columbian Mexican (Mixtec) book. 88 color plates show kings, gods, heroes, temples, sacrifices. New explanatory, historical introduction by Arthur G. Miller. 96pp. 11⅜ x 8½.
23168-2 Pa. $7.50

AMERICAN PRIMITIVE PAINTING, Jean Lipman. Classic collection of an enduring American tradition. 109 plates, 8 in full color—portraits, landscapes, Biblical and historical scenes, etc., showing family groups, farm life, and so on. 80pp. of lucid text. 8⅜ x 11¼.
22815-0 Pa. $4.00

WILL BRADLEY: HIS GRAPHIC ART, edited by Clarence P. Hornung. Striking collection of work by foremost practitioner of Art Nouveau in America: posters, cover designs, sample pages, advertisements, other illustrations. 97 plates, including 8 in full color and 19 in two colors. 97pp. 9⅜ x 12¼.
20701-3 Pa. $4.00
22120-2 Clothbd. $10.00

THE UNDERGROUND SKETCHBOOK OF JAN FAUST, Jan Faust. 101 bitter, horrifying, black-humorous, penetrating sketches on sex, war, greed, various liberations, etc. Sometimes sexual, but not pornographic. Not for prudish. 101pp. 6½ x 9¼.
22740-5 Pa. $1.50

THE GIBSON GIRL AND HER AMERICA, Charles Dana Gibson. 155 finest drawings of effervescent world of 1900-1910: the Gibson Girl and her loves, amusements, adventures, Mr. Pipp, etc. Selected by E. Gillon; introduction by Henry Pitz. 144pp. 8¼ x 11⅜.
21986-0 Pa. $3.50

STAINED GLASS CRAFT, J.A.F. Divine, G. Blachford. One of the very few books that tell the beginner exactly what he needs to know: planning cuts, making shapes, avoiding design weaknesses, fitting glass, etc. 93 illustrations. 115pp.
22812-6 Pa. $1.50

HOW TO SOLVE CHESS PROBLEMS, Kenneth S. Howard. Practical suggestions on problem solving for very beginners. 58 two-move problems, 46 3-movers, 8 4-movers for practice, plus hints. 171pp. 20748-X Pa. $2.00

A GUIDE TO FAIRY CHESS, Anthony Dickins. 3-D chess, 4-D chess, chess on a cylindrical board, reflecting pieces that bounce off edges, cooperative chess, retrograde chess, maximummers, much more. Most based on work of great Dawson. Full handbook, 100 problems. 66pp. 7⅞ x 10¾. 22687-5 Pa. $2.00

WIN AT BACKGAMMON, Millard Hopper. Best opening moves, running game, blocking game, back game, tables of odds, etc. Hopper makes the game clear enough for anyone to play, and win. 43 diagrams. 111pp. 22894-0 Pa. $1.50

BIDDING A BRIDGE HAND, Terence Reese. Master player "thinks out loud" the binding of 75 hands that defy point count systems. Organized by bidding problem—no-fit situations, overbidding, underbidding, cueing your defense, etc. 254pp. EBE 22830-4 Pa. $2.50

THE PRECISION BIDDING SYSTEM IN BRIDGE, C.C. Wei, edited by Alan Truscott. Inventor of precision bidding presents average hands and hands from actual play, including games from 1969 Bermuda Bowl where system emerged. 114 exercises. 116pp. 21171-1 Pa. $1.75

LEARN MAGIC, Henry Hay. 20 simple, easy-to-follow lessons on magic for the new magician: illusions, card tricks, silks, sleights of hand, coin manipulations, escapes, and more —all with a minimum amount of equipment. Final chapter explains the great stage illusions. 92 illustrations. 285pp. 21238-6 Pa. $2.95

THE NEW MAGICIAN'S MANUAL, Walter B. Gibson. Step-by-step instructions and clear illustrations guide the novice in mastering 36 tricks; much equipment supplied on 16 pages of cut-out materials. 36 additional tricks. 64 illustrations. 159pp. 6⅝ x 10. 23113-5 Pa. $3.00

PROFESSIONAL MAGIC FOR AMATEURS, Walter B. Gibson. 50 easy, effective tricks used by professionals —cards, string, tumblers, handkerchiefs, mental magic, etc. 63 illustrations. 223pp. 23012-0 Pa. $2.50

CARD MANIPULATIONS, Jean Hugard. Very rich collection of manipulations; has taught thousands of fine magicians tricks that are really workable, eye-catching. Easily followed, serious work. Over 200 illustrations. 163pp. 20539-8 Pa. $2.00

ABBOTT'S ENCYCLOPEDIA OF ROPE TRICKS FOR MAGICIANS, Stewart James. Complete reference book for amateur and professional magicians containing more than 150 tricks involving knots, penetrations, cut and restored rope, etc. 510 illustrations. Reprint of 3rd edition. 400pp. 23206-9 Pa. $3.50

THE SECRETS OF HOUDINI, J.C. Cannell. Classic study of Houdini's incredible magic, exposing closely-kept professional secrets and revealing, in general terms, the whole art of stage magic. 67 illustrations. 279pp. 22913-0 Pa. $2.50

THE MAGIC MOVING PICTURE BOOK, Bliss, Sands & Co. The pictures in this book move! Volcanoes erupt, a house burns, a serpentine dancer wiggles her way through a number. By using a specially ruled acetate screen provided, you can obtain these and 15 other startling effects. Originally "The Motograph Moving Picture Book." 32pp. 8¼ x 11. 23224-7 Pa. $1.75

STRING FIGURES AND HOW TO MAKE THEM, Caroline F. Jayne. Fullest, clearest instructions on string figures from around world: Eskimo, Navajo, Lapp, Europe, more. Cats cradle, moving spear, lightning, stars. Introduction by A.C. Haddon. 950 illustrations. 407pp. 20152-X Pa. $3.00

PAPER FOLDING FOR BEGINNERS, William D. Murray and Francis J. Rigney. Clearest book on market for making origami sail boats, roosters, frogs that move legs, cups, bonbon boxes. 40 projects. More than 275 illustrations. Photographs. 94pp. 20713-7 Pa. $1.25

INDIAN SIGN LANGUAGE, William Tomkins. Over 525 signs developed by Sioux, Blackfoot, Cheyenne, Arapahoe and other tribes. Written instructions and diagrams: how to make words, construct sentences. Also 290 pictographs of Sioux and Ojibway tribes. 111pp. 6⅛ x 9¼. 22029-X Pa. $1.50

BOOMERANGS: HOW TO MAKE AND THROW THEM, Bernard S. Mason. Easy to make and throw, dozens of designs: cross-stick, pinwheel, boomabird, tumblestick, Australian curved stick boomerang. Complete throwing instructions. All safe. 99pp. 23028-7 Pa. $1.50

25 KITES THAT FLY, Leslie Hunt. Full, easy to follow instructions for kites made from inexpensive materials. Many novelties. Reeling, raising, designing your own. 70 illustrations. 110pp. 22550-X Pa. $1.25

TRICKS AND GAMES ON THE POOL TABLE, Fred Herrmann. 79 tricks and games, some solitaires, some for 2 or more players, some competitive; mystifying shots and throws, unusual carom, tricks involving cork, coins, a hat, more. 77 figures. 95pp. 21814-7 Pa. $1.25

WOODCRAFT AND CAMPING, Bernard S. Mason. How to make a quick emergency shelter, select woods that will burn immediately, make do with limited supplies, etc. Also making many things out of wood, rawhide, bark, at camp. Formerly titled Woodcraft. 295 illustrations. 580pp. 21951-8 Pa. $4.00

AN INTRODUCTION TO CHESS MOVES AND TACTICS SIMPLY EXPLAINED, Leonard Barden. Informal intermediate introduction: reasons for moves, tactics, openings, traps, positional play, endgame. Isolates patterns. 102pp. USO 21210-6 Pa. $1.35

LASKER'S MANUAL OF CHESS, Dr. Emanuel Lasker. Great world champion offers very thorough coverage of all aspects of chess. Combinations, position play, openings, endgame, aesthetics of chess, philosophy of struggle, much more. Filled with analyzed games. 390pp. 20640-8 Pa. $3.50